# READING WITH EARTH

T&T Clark Explorations in Theology, Gender and Ecology

Series editors
Hilda P. Koster: University of St Michael's College, Toronto, Canada
Arnfríður Guðmundsdóttir: University of Iceland, Reykjavík, Iceland

READING WITH EARTH

Contributions of the New Materialism to an Ecological Feminist Hermeneutics

Anne Elvey

LONDON • NEW YORK • OXFORD • NEW DELHI • SYDNEY

T&T CLARK
Bloomsbury Publishing Plc
50 Bedford Square, London, WC1B 3DP, UK
1385 Broadway, New York, NY 10018, USA
29 Earlsfort Terrace, Dublin 2, Ireland

BLOOMSBURY, T&T CLARK and the T&T Clark logo
are trademarks of Bloomsbury Publishing Plc

First published in Great Britain 2023
Paperback edition published 2024

Copyright © Anne Elvey, 2023

Anne Elvey has asserted her right under the Copyright,
Designs and Patents Act, 1988, to be identified as Author of this work.

For legal purposes the Acknowledgements on pp. xii–xv constitute an
extension of this copyright page.

Cover design: Terry Woodley
Cover image: *Lake edge* by Sophie Finlay

All rights reserved. No part of this publication may be reproduced or transmitted
in any form or by any means, electronic or mechanical, including photocopying,
recording, or any information storage or retrieval system, without prior
permission in writing from the publishers.

Bloomsbury Publishing Plc does not have any control over, or responsibility for, any
third-party websites referred to or in this book. All internet addresses given in this book
were correct at the time of going to press. The author and publisher regret
any inconvenience caused if addresses have changed or sites have ceased
to exist, but can accept no responsibility for any such changes.

Unless otherwise noted, Scripture quotations are from New Revised Standard Version
Bible, copyright © 1989 National Council of the Churches of Christ in the United States of
America. Used by permission. All rights reserved worldwide.

A catalogue record for this book is available from the British Library.

Library of Congress Cataloging-in-Publication Data
Names: Elvey, Anne F., author.
Title: Reading with Earth : contributions of the new materialism to an
ecological feminist hermeneutics / Anne Elvey.
Description: London ; New York : T&tT Clark, 2022. |
Series: T&T Clark explorations in theology, gender and ecology |
Includes bibliographical references and index. |
Identifiers: LCCN 2022012243 (print) | LCCN 2022012244 (ebook) |
ISBN 9780567695116 (hb) | ISBN 9780567695123 (epdf) |
ISBN 9780567695147 (epub)
Subjects: LCSH: Ecofeminism–Religious aspects–Christianity. |
Materialism–Religious aspects–Christianity. | Human ecology in the Bible. |
Ecotheology. | Bible. Luke--Feminist criticism.
Classification: LCC BT695.5 .E5765 2022 (print) |
LCC BT695.5 (ebook) | DDC 261.8/8--dc23/eng/20220615
LC record available at https://lccn.loc.gov/2022012243
LC ebook record available at https://lccn.loc.gov/2022012244

ISBN: HB: 978-0-5676-9511-6
PB: 978-0-5677-0832-8
ePDF: 978-0-5676-9512-3
eBook: 978-0-5676-9514-7

Series: T&T Clark Explorations in Theology, Gender and Ecology

Typeset by Integra Software Services Pvt. Ltd.

To find out more about our authors and books visit www.bloomsbury.com
and sign up for our newsletters.

for Kate Rigby
friend, mentor and honoured teacher of Earth kinship and care

CONTENTS

List of illustrations	xi
Acknowledgements	xii
Abbreviations	xvi

Chapter 1
INTRODUCTION: FEMINISMS, MATERIALISMS AND BRAIDED
READING WITH EARTH 1
   A hermeneutic focus 3
      Reading with Earth 6
   Ecological feminism, the material given and the matter of the text . . . 10
      The material given 12
      The matter of the text 13
      Situational materialities 15
         The white woman 17
   Ecological feminist hermeneutic weavings 18
      An outline 20

Section 1
THE MATERIALITY OF BREATH

Chapter 2
BREATH AND EARTH VOICE: EXPLORING AN ECOLOGICAL
HERMENEUTICS OF RETRIEVAL 25
   An ecological hermeneutics of retrieval and the principle of voice . . . 28
   The Magnificat 33
      An Earth voice in the Magnificat 34
         Earth speaks through the materiality of the text 34
         Earth speaks to and through the body, the human senses
         and the breath 38
         Earth, poverty and riches 40
         Earth and the promise to the ancestors 42
   Conclusion 43

Chapter 3
RETRIEVING AN EARTH VOICE: READING MATERIALLY
'AS IF IT'S HOLY' 45
   A material sacred 45
   An Earth voice? 50

The matter of voice	54
The text as a material thing	56
'Parchment' (Boisseau)	56
'O Taste and See' (Levertov)	57
'To Live in the Mercy of God' (Levertov)	58
Reading 'as if it is holy'	59
Conclusion	61

Chapter 4
STRAINED BREATH AND OPEN TEXT: EXPLORING THE MATERIALITY OF BREATH IN RELATION TO LUKE 4.16-30

	63
The materiality of air and breath	64
Ecologies of breath and corporealities of resistance	66
Breath as intertext	70
Some matters of biblical breath	71
A performative reading of Luke 4.16-30	74
Conclusion	79

Section 2
SITUATING ECOLOGICAL MATERIALISM

Chapter 5
REFRAMING FEMINIST APPROACHES ECOLOGICALLY: MATTER, FREEDOM AND THE FUTURE

	83
Matter, materialities and materialisms	86
A materialist frame and matter-spirit dualism	88
Material agency	90
A materialist freedom	93
Summary	95
Freedom and a future unlike the present	95
The materiality of who we are	97
Conclusion	100

Chapter 6
CLIMATE CHANGE AS MATERIAL SITUATION: INTERPRETING THE PRESENT PERIOD (ΚΑΙΡΟΣ) ALONGSIDE LUKE 12.54-56

	103
The Anthropocene and a deep future	104
Hermeneutic questions	107
Interpreting the time: Climate in Luke	109
Narrative context and judgement	110
Time, season, period (Καιρός)	111
To interpret (Δοκιμάζω)	113
Re-framing climate change	115
Conclusion	117

Chapter 7
RETHINKING NEIGHBOUR LOVE: POLITICAL THEOLOGY, SOVEREIGNTY
AND AN ECOLOGICAL MATERIALIST READING OF LUKE 10.25-37   121
   Political theology, ecological ethics and ecological feminist
   hermeneutics   122
      A conversation   124
      An ecological materialism   124
   Lukan sovereignties   126
   The parable of the Good Samaritan   129
   Towards an ecological materialist conversation   135
   Conclusion   138

Section 3
SHARED VULNERABILITIES

Chapter 8
AN ECOLOGICAL FEMINIST APPROACH TO CROSS SPECIES
RELATEDNESS: COMPASSION AND LUKE 10.30-37   141
   Roadsides   142
   Relatedness   143
   Compassion   144
   A Lukan Story of the Road: Luke 10.30-37   147
   A fleshy space of solidarity   149
   Entanglements and ecological conversion   150
      Entangled life and kin   151
      Ecological conversion   152
   Conclusion   153

Chapter 9
MOUNTAINTOP REMOVAL MINING (MTR) AND ISAIAH 40.4
(AND LUKE 3.5): RESISTING THE VIOLENCE OF HOMOGENIZATION   155
   Mountaintop Removal Mining (MTR)   156
   An ecological feminist analysis of homogenization   160
   Homogenization, MTR and Isaiah 40.4   162
      The Bible and MTR   164
      MTR and Isaiah 40.4   165
   The force of metaphor in Isaiah 40.4   169
      A lively, responsive Earth and cosmos   173
   Conclusion   175

Chapter 10
THE GREAT BARRIER REEF AND READING TOWARDS ACTIVISM:
TRANSFIGURATIONS AND DISFIGURATIONS   179
   Towards an ecological feminist aesthetics   182

Wonder and grief	182
Colour and a material ecstatics	184
Beauty and alterity	185
Ecological feminist hermeneutic weavings	186
The Lukan Transfiguration (Luke 9.28-36) and The Great Barrier Reef	187
The Great Barrier Reef	190
The call of the visible	192
Transfigurations and disfigurations	193
The face of the Reef	196
Vibrant materiality: Reef and mountain	197
Sacred/Divine listening	197
Conclusion	198

Chapter 11
CONCLUDING REFLECTION ... 199
    Exhortation, encouragement and consolation ... 200

Bibliography ... 203
Index of references ... 232
Index of names ... 235
Index of subjects ... 237

ILLUSTRATIONS

1. 'Breath no. 9305 caught at The Lock-Up in Newcastle, New South Wales, Australia, on 18th March 2018 at 11:54 AM' © Andrew Styan 2018. Reproduced by permission of Andrew Styan — 26
2. Magnificat — 36
3. John Reid, *Performance for 25 Passing Vehicles. Australia. Newell Highway, 23 July 1989*. 1989, 48.0 × 134.0 cm. Silver gelation photographic print © John Reid. Reproduced by permission of the artist — 145

ACKNOWLEDGEMENTS

This book took shape on the lands of the Kulin Nation, on unceded Bunurong (Boon Wurrung) Country where I live and work in Seaford, Victoria, a bayside suburb of Melbourne, Australia, and on Wurundjeri (Woi Wurrung) Country. I acknowledge the lands, waters and skies of Bunurong and Wurundjeri Country and pay my respects to elders, past and present, recognizing their ongoing connection to and care for Country. I honour Earth and all those more-than-human Earthkind who have contributed to my thinking and capacity to give time to writing. I honour the stories of places referenced in this book, especially the roadsides throughout this continent, the Appalachian Mountains in the United States and The Great Barrier Reef. In this period of ecological grief and wonder, I appreciate the active call of habitats and co-inhabitants near and far to listen, listen again and act.

In writing this book, I have drawn on work undertaken largely over the past eight years, but with tendrils reaching back to my doctoral work completed in 1999, and in one instance my MTheol work completed in 1994. The seeding and growth of the work, still so very young in relation to forests, mountains and oceans, carry a debt to many friends, colleagues and mentors – scholars in the environmental humanities, poets, biblical scholars and ecotheologians – who taught me, engaged with my work, challenged and supported me in a variety of ways, so I mention, Mark Brett, Brendan Byrne, Alan Cadwallader, Michelle Cahill, Anne M Carson, Jennifer Compton, Garry Deverell, Elizabeth Dowling, Heather Eaton, Susan Fealy, Anne Gleeson, Deborah Guess, Norm Habel, Veronica Lawson, Jeanine Leane, Rose Lucas, Kath McPhillips, Alex Skovron, Mark Tredinnick, Robyn Whitaker, The Bible and Critical Theory Seminar, Fellowship for Biblical Studies, Australian Catholic Biblical Association and Association for the Study of Literature, Culture and Environment-ANZ. In particular, my warm appreciation for sustaining connection and friendship to: Peter Boyle, Ruth Harrison, Freya Mathews, the late Deborah Bird Rose, Kate Rigby, to whom this book is dedicated; Anne Ryan for sharing creative becoming in the 1990s at The Grove; and for more than I can say: Elaine Wainwright.

Thank you to the following artists for permission to reproduce their work:

Andrew Styan for: 'Breath no. 9305 caught at The Lock-Up in Newcastle, New South Wales, Australia, on 18th March 2018 at 11:54 AM', © Andrew Styan 2018. Reproduced by permission of Andrew Styan.

John Reid for: *Performance for 25 Passing Vehicles. Australia. Newell Highway, 23 July 1989*, 1989, 48.0 × 134.0 cm, Silver gelation photographic print, © John Reid. Reproduced by permission of the artist.

Thank you to poets and their publishers for permission to reproduce lines from:

'Parchment' from *Trembling Air*. Copyright © 2003 by Michelle Boisseau. Reprinted with the permission of The Permissions Company, LLC on behalf of the University of Arkansas Press, www.uapress.com.

'O Taste and See' by Denise Levertov, from POEMS 1960-1967, copyright ©1964 by Denise Levertov. Reprinted by permission of New Directions Publishing Corp. and Bloodaxe Books.

'To Live in the Mercy of God' by Denise Levertov, from SANDS OF THE WELL, copyright ©1996 by Denise Levertov. Reprinted by permission of New Directions Publishing Corp.

Jennifer Harrison, for 'Book Sculptor', *Salt Lick Quarterly* (Autumn 2003), p. 9. Quoted with permission of the author and a later version, 'Book Sculptor', in *Colombine: New and Selected Poems* (North Fitzroy: Black Pepper, 2010), p. 223. Quoted with permission of the author and publisher.

'A Sort of a Song' by William Carlos Williams, from THE COLLECTED POEMS: VOLUME II, 1939-1962, copyright ©1944 by William Carlos Williams. Reprinted by permission of New Directions Publishing Corp. and Carcanet Press.

Kristin Hannaford, 'Coral not Coal', in *hope for whole: poets speak up to Adani* (ed. Anne Elvey; eBook; Seaford, Vic.: Rosslyn Avenue Productions, 2018), p. 39. Reproduced by permission of the author.

Caitlin Maling, 'Recommendations for a Western Australian Coastal Pastoral', in *hope for whole*, (ed. Anne Elvey; eBook; Seaford, Vic.: Rosslyn Avenue Productions, 2018), pp. 102–3; previously published in *Cordite* 54: No Theme V (May 2016). Reproduced by permission of the author.

A number of chapters in this book revise and build on work I published previously. I am grateful to the editors and publishers of these works and acknowledge their prior publication:

Anne Elvey, 'A Hermeneutics of Retrieval: Breath and Earth Voice in Luke's Magnificat – Does Earth Care for the Poor?', *AusBR* 63 (2015), pp. 68–84. (Chapter 2).

Anne Elvey, 'Retrieving an Earth Voice: Ecological Hermeneutics, the Matter of the Text and Reading "as if it's holy" (Jennifer Harrison, "Book Sculptor")', *AeJT* 22, no. 2 (August 2015), pp. 81–94. (Chapter 3).

Anne Elvey, 'Strained Breath and Open Text: Exploring the Materiality of Breath in Relation to Reading Luke 4.16-30', *BCT* 16, nos 1-2 (2020), pp. 1-14. (Chapter 4).

Anne Elvey, 'Matter, Freedom and the Future: Re-framing Feminist Theologies through an Ecological Materialist Lens', *Feminist Theology* 23, no. 2 (2015), pp. 186-204. First published by SAGE. (Chapter 5).

Anne Elvey, 'Interpreting the Time: Climate Change and the Climate in/of the Gospel of Luke', in *Climate Change – Cultural Change: Religious Responses and Responsibilities* (ed. Anne Elvey and David Gormley O'Brien; Preston, Vic.: Mosaic Press, 2013), pp. 78-91. (Chapter 6).

Anne Elvey, 'Rethinking Neighbour Love: A Conversation between Political Theology and Ecological Ethics', in *'Where the Wild Ox Roams': Biblical Essays in Honour of Norman C. Habel* (ed. Alan H. Cadwallader and Peter L. Trudinger; HBM, 59; Sheffield: Sheffield Phoenix, 2013), pp. 58-75. Reused with permission of the publisher. (Chapter 7).

Anne Elvey, 'Roadsides: Toward an Ecological Feminist Theology of Cross-Species Compassion', in *Contemporary Feminist Theologies: Power, Authority, Love* (ed. Kerrie Handasyde, Cathryn McKinney and Rebekah Pryor; London: Routledge, 2021), pp. 133-44. Copyright © Anne Elvey 2021. Reproduced by permission of Taylor & Francis Group. (Chapter 8).

Anne Elvey, 'Homogenizing Violence, Isa 40:4 (and Luke 3:5) and MTR (Mountaintop Removal Mining)', *Worldviews* 19, no. 3 (2015), pp. 226-44. (Chapter 9).

Short excerpts from the following articles and essays also appear in the book: Anne Elvey 'Climate Embodied: Exploring a Poetics of Strained Breath', *Axon* 10, no. 1 (May 2020); Anne Elvey, 'Reimagining Decolonising Praxis for a Just and Ecologically Sustainable Peace in an Australian Context', in *Towards a Just and Ecologically Sustainable Peace: Navigating the Great Transition* (ed. Joseph Camilleri and Deborah Guess; Singapore: Palgrave Macmillan, 2020), pp. 275-95 (285-6, 288); Anne Elvey, 'Can There Be a Forgiveness That Makes a Difference Ecologically? An Eco-materialist Account of Forgiveness as Freedom (ἄφεσις) in the Gospel of Luke', *Pacifica* 22, no. 2 (2009), pp. 148-70 (153-4).

University of Divinity supported the preparation of this book with a Small Research Grant, as well as a conference travel grant that enabled me to attend the Society of Biblical Literature Annual Meeting in San Diego in November 2019, where I gave papers that form the basis of Chapters 4 and 10. I thank Scott Kirkland in his role as Research Coordinator at Trinity College Theological School, University of Divinity, where I am an Honorary Research Associate. Monash University where I am an Adjunct Research Fellow supported the research for this book through the provision of excellent library resources, especially online resources which were a great help during Covid-19 lockdowns in 2020 and 2021.

Special thanks to my research assistant Kerrie Handasyde for her excellent help to update research on Mountaintop Removal Mining, The Great Barrier Reef, and for initial editing and preparation of the bibliography. Appreciation, too, to Alda Balthrop-Lewis and Kylie Crabbe for reading sections of the manuscript and providing very helpful feedback on the writing and the biblical interpretation, respectively. Many thanks to Sinead O'Connor of Bloomsbury T&T Clark for her cheerful assistance over email and her understanding of delays due to the current pandemic and its challenges. Deep appreciation to series editors Arnfríður Guðmundsdóttir and Hilda Koster for their interest in and support of this work, and to two anonymous reviewers for their very helpful recommendations. Thank you to Dharanivel Baskar and the team at Integra for careful production of the book. Special thanks to artist and poet Sophie Finlay for the cover image *Lake Edge*.

Finally, my thanks to my neighbour poet Anne M. Carson for her support and friendship over the past few years, together with Rose Lucas, especially during the pandemic. To my family, for their companionship, support of this work, ecological commitments and love, I offer deep thanks and respect to my partner, Greg Price; sons Matthew and Andrew Elvey Price; my brothers and their families, Frank and Annette, Paul and Marie, Monica and Phil; and my mother, Honora Elvey, whose resilience, generosity and lifelong learning inspire me and many others. To the many places that sustained our ancestors and nourish us, I offer thanks.

ABBREVIATIONS

AAR	American Academy of Religion
AB	Anchor Bible
ABC	Australian Broadcasting Corporation
ACR	*The Australasian Catholic Record*
AeJT	*Australian e-Journal of Theology*
AMCS	Australian Marine Conservation Society
ATF	Australian Theological Forum
AusBR	*Australian Biblical Review*
BAGD	Walter Bauer, *A Greek–English Lexicon of the New Testament and Other Early Christian Literature* (trans., rev. and augmented William F. Arndt, F. Wilbur Gingrich and Frederick W. Danker; Chicago: University of Chicago Press, 1979).
BCT	*The Bible & Critical Theory*
BDB	Francis Brown, S. R. Driver and Charles A. Briggs (eds.), *A Hebrew and English Lexicon of the Old Testament: With an Appendix Containing the Biblical Aramaic* (based on the Lexicon of William Genesius; trans. Edward Robinson; Oxford: Clarendon Press, 1951).
BibInt	*Biblical Interpretation: A Journal of Contemporary Approaches*
BMW	Bible in the Modern World
BSac	*Bibliotheca Sacra*
BZNW	Beihefte zur Zeitschrift für die neutestamentliche Wissenschaft
CFTM	Christians for the Mountains
Colloquium	*Colloquium: The Australian and New Zealand Theological Review*
CurBR	*Currents in Biblical Research*
CurTM	*Currents in Theology and Mission*
Dialog	*Dialog: A Journal of Theology*
Ecocene	*Ecocene: Cappadocia Journal of Environmental Humanities*
FCNTECW	Feminist Companion to the New Testament and Early Christian Writings
GBRMPA	Great Barrier Reef Marine Park Authority
Green Letters	*Green Letters: Studies in Ecocriticism*
GS	Vatican II, *Gaudium et Spes* (7 December 1965), in *Vatican Council II: The Conciliar and Post Conciliar Documents* (ed. Austin Flannery, O.P.; Collegeville: Liturgical Press, 1975).
HBM	Hebrew Bible Monographs
IBC	Interpretation: A Bible Commentary for Teaching and Preaching
ICC	International Critical Commentary
Int	*Interpretation: A Journal of Bible and Theology*
IPCC	Intergovernmental Panel on Climate Change
IWDA	International Women's Development Agency
JAAR	*Journal of the American Academy of Religion*

JBL	*Journal of Biblical Literature*
JFSR	*Journal of Feminist Studies in Religion*
JJS	*Journal of Jewish Studies*
JSNT	*Journal for the Study of the New Testament*
JSNTSup	Journal for the Study of the New Testament Supplement Series
JSOT	*Journal for the Study of the Old Testament*
JSP	*Journal for the Study of the Pseudepigrapha*
L.A.B.	Pseudo-Philo's *Biblical Antiquities* (*Liber Antiquitatum Biblicarum*)
LS	Pope Francis, *Encyclical Letter Laudato Si' of the Holy Father Francis on Care for Our Common Home* (Australian edn; Strathfield, NSW: St Pauls, 2015).
NICNT	The New International Commentary on the New Testament
NIGTC	The New International Greek Testament Commentary
NovT	*Novum Testamentum*
NTS	New Testament Studies
NRSV	New Revised Standard Version
OED	Oxford English Dictionary
PAN	*PAN: Philosophy, Activism, Nature*
Plumwood Mountain	*Plumwood Mountain: An Australian Journal of Ecopoetry and Ecopoetics*
RevExp	*Review and Expositor*
SBL	Society of Biblical Literature
Sea Changes	*Sea Changes: Journal of Women Scholars of Religion and Theology*
SemeiaSt	Semeia Studies
SP	Sacra Pagina
ST	*Studia Theologica*
SUNY	State University of New York
TBT	*The Bible Today*
TS	*Theological Studies*
UBEE	Uses of the Bible in Environmental Ethics Project at the University of Exeter
UNESCO	United Nations Educational, Scientific and Cultural Organization
WGRWSup	Writings from the Greco-Roman World Supplement Series
Worldviews	*Worldviews: Global Religions, Culture, and Ecology*
WUNT	Wissenschaftliche Untersuchungen zum Neuen Testament

Chapter 1

INTRODUCTION: FEMINISMS, MATERIALISMS AND BRAIDED READING WITH EARTH

To read with Earth is to be braided with matter, history and word, entangled with intersecting ecological and social traumas that make a moral claim on me. Being reader, writer and sometime activist in Australia, I am enmeshed in contemporary relations of inhabitation, as settler descendant and visitor.[1] The eco-social histories I inherit are not past but remain a potent challenge informing my ecological feminist thinking and action in the present and for the future.[2] By way of example, I begin with an anecdote.

In Spring 2018 I spent a week in a cabin by the Avon River at Stratford on Brayakoolong Country, in Gippsland, Victoria. The Brayakoolong people are part of the Gunaikurnai nation. As I walked around the modest country town, I was struck by two stories in conflict with each other. The town and the river are named colonially after a place associated with an English bard whose writings, for some, form a canon to rival the biblical ones with which this book engages. The Gippsland town of Stratford once had a Shakespeare pub (hotel), remembered now with a monument. There were other monuments I noted more intensely in my daily walks. An information board in Stratford's Memorial Park welcomes visitors to Brayakoolong Country with a narrative of massacres of Gunaikurnai people at the hands of Angus McMillan and several others, during the contact wars in the mid-nineteenth century. Such massacres usually occurred in retaliation for the killing of very small numbers of livestock for food, on land being taken over by European agriculture that displaced local sources of sustenance.

Stratford has a street named McMillan and at the three-way intersection of this street with Merrick and Blackburn Streets stands a cairn with the inscription:

---

1. In this book, I have made a choice mostly to use the first person singular pronoun rather than plural for two reasons: (1) the use of first person plural can suggest an inclusivity that may be counter to readers' experience; (2) in the context of reading with Earth, 'I' can be taken not (or not only) as an expression of ego, but of self as already self-in-relation with and constituted by more-than-human others.

2. These eco-social histories might also challenge the way categories of past, present and future should be understood, but for now I use the conventional terminology.

> TO COMMEMORATE THE
> CROSSING OF THIS RIVER BY
> ANGUS MCMILLAN
> EXPLORER OF GIPPSLAND.
> 21.1.1840.

Nearby, overlooking the river is a 'Garden for Humanity' which has installations of Indigenous message sticks, tiles of peace – some of which incorporate ancient European goddess imagery – and seats for meditation. While on writing retreat in this place, I read part of the Final Report of the Australian Royal Commission into Institutional Responses to Child Sexual Abuse, namely Volume 16 Book 2 (the section on the Catholic Church). As birds sang from the scrub, I also read an information board that described the work of local school children who helped bring a waterway back from desolation. In Stratford there stood majestic river red gums older than colonization. I learnt, too, that the standing remains of dead trees held nesting hollows. On the cliff outside my cabin, water dragons visited.

On other trips into Gippsland, in towns such as Yarram, I have encountered further monuments to Angus McMillan and his 'exploration'. When the Black Lives Matter movement gained global force in the wake of the death of George Floyd on 25 May 2020, First Nations people and their allies in Australia stood in solidarity with the global Black Lives Matter movement, at the same time highlighting racist violence in this nation, especially Aboriginal Deaths in Custody. Soon afterward, as part of the same movement, monuments to perpetrators and beneficiaries of colonial invasion, slavery and racist violence were put in the spotlight around the world. Signs acknowledging McMillan's violent legacy appeared on cairns in Stratford and Rosedale, referencing Black Deaths in Custody and Black Lives Matter, and the dying words of Eric Garner, George Floyd and David Dungay: 'I can't breathe'. In Gippsland, Wellington Shire Council voted on removing the monuments to Angus McMillan.[3] Gunaikurnai elders commented that removing these cairns would not remove the history, but it would be a step towards allowing the trauma passed down through generations to heal; the Council decided to keep the monuments.[4]

I start with this narrative of intersections of colonial violence, First Nations' agency and resistance, Catholic Church criminal failures to protect children, and

---

3. Kellie Lazzaro, 'Angus McMillan Monument Removal Considered by Council over His Links to Indigenous Murders', ABC Gippsland (16 June 2020), available online: https://www.abc.net.au/news/2020-06-16/victorian-council-to-vote-on-removal-of-angus-mcmillan-monuments/12355930 (accessed 21 July 2020).

4. Jedda Costa, 'Wellington Shire Council Votes to Keep Angus McMillan Monuments, Despite Explorer's Link to Murders', ABC Gippsland (17 June 2020), available online: https://www.abc.net.au/news/2020-06-17/wellington-council-votes-down-mcmillan-cairn-removal/12361546 (accessed 21 July 2020).

community labour for ecological wholeness and peace, in order to signal the complex material context in which I am writing towards an ecological feminist hermeneutics in Australia. This 'modern' nation is in reality many First Nations, whose lands (known as Country) have never been ceded.[5] Environmental actions from Governments, limited as such actions are, too rarely involve First Nations in meaningful ways. During, and in the aftermath of, the 2019–20 Spring-Summer bushfires, wider community interest in First Nations fire management practices grew from self-interest.[6] Both the fires and the Covid-19 virus have shown at a visceral level the material agency of more than humans and their intersections with political, economic, social and corporeal materialities.[7] This multi-faceted situation of intersecting materialities will inform the conversations in this book between ecological feminist hermeneutics and the new materialism.

A hermeneutic focus

Specifically, my hermeneutic focus is biblical interpretation in this material context where ecological and social justice intersect with the legacies of colonization and biblical religion. While the Bible is a collection of texts in multiple genres from earlier times, cultures and places, biblical literature remains part of a twenty-first-century material situation. This situation is marked by ecological destruction – including climate change, pollution, biodiversity and habitat losses, extinction and food insecurity – and the ongoing situation of colonial invasion in settler states like Australia, racism, gender violence, modern slavery, forced migration, and

---

5. In Aboriginal English, used without the article, 'Country' signifies the lands, waters and skies, of a particular Aboriginal language group, e.g. Boon Wurrung Country, Woi Wurrung Country, Nyoongar Country, Arrernte Country, and evokes the relations of kinship and law that co-constitute Indigenous people and land. See Garry Worete Deverell, *Gondwana Theology: A Trawloolway Man Reflects on Christian Faith* (Reservoir, Vic.: Morning Star Publishing, 2018), p. 14; Deborah Bird Rose, *Nourishing Terrains: Australian Aboriginal Views of Landscape and Wilderness* (Canberra: Australian Heritage Commission, 1996), p. 6. In this book, where possible I refer to a specific Country and language group; otherwise, I use First Nations or Indigenous, the latter usually where this is the preferred terminology in a text I am referencing. I recognize that among First Nations, in what is called colonially Australia, preferences differ in relation to naming.

6. On Indigenous fire management, see Victor Steffensen, *Fire Country: How Indigenous Fire Management Could Help Save Australia* (Richmond, Vic.: Hardie Grant Travel, 2020).

7. I use the term 'more than human' to refer to both human and other-than-human constituents of Earth and cosmos. The term is intended to resist the kind of dualism set up by pairs such as human and non-human. 'More than human' includes humankind among many other beings (rocks, trees, mammals, mountains and stars) that are part of the multiplicity of Earth and cosmos. Humans do not exist outside of this more-than-human world. See David Abram, *The Spell of the Sensuous* (New York: Vintage Books, 1997), p. 22.

the grief and resistances accompanying these. For some the Bible has authority to speak into these situations. This is not my starting point.

My position is this: as a collection of texts received as sacred and imposed colonially by British and other European nations, the Bible haunts western and many western-influenced cultures even where those societies are, like Australia, avowedly secular. By haunting, I want to suggest both the capacity for damage to vulnerable (more-than-human) communities and the potential for disturbance of a destructive capitalist consumer status quo.

At one level, I engage with biblical literature because biblical scholarship is a focus of my academic training. At another level, and because of this training, I am embedded in the histories of interpretation of biblical texts, including the uses of the Bible for violence against women and Earth, as well as for more-than-human flourishing. The texts that make up the Bible are already potent interpretations of human experience and human understandings of being social creatures in a more-than-human world where matter and spirit are deeply interrelated.[8] Over two millennia of interpretation and use of the Bible by religious leaders, Jewish and Christian believers, politicians, activists for social change, poets and artists, underscore my choice to read biblical literature in a context of ecological feminist concern for Earth flourishing.

Reading is the focus of my book. How do I read in a way that opens to the cry of Earth in this moment? How do I read *with* Earth as habitat, agent, judge?

The book offers a series of readings that situate selected biblical texts in wider ecological contexts. These readings are not straightforward. They are braided conversations between contemporary contexts, close readings of biblical texts with an ear to the original languages, material situations in and behind the texts, and the literary character of the texts.[9] They are creative conversations which take contemporary poetry and poetics as partners in reading. These interpretive braidings take seriously the materiality of the biblical text as part of the dynamic materiality of Earth.

My readings also affirm the role of voice, and the voices of Earth and its many constituents, especially those that are supposedly mute from the perspective of human languages. As I will argue, attentiveness to such voices is a key component of an ecological feminist hermeneutics. Importantly, when reading with Earth, more-than-human voices may summon the interpreter like a cry, perceived through senses other than hearing. Through sight, a cry may present as a visible voice, for example, in the material situation of perceptible damage to violated animal (including human) bodies and ecological systems. I will suggest in Chapter 7 that the assaulted person on the side of the road in the Lukan parable of the Good Samaritan and in Chapter 10 that coral bleaching in the Great Barrier Reef under

---

8. In later chapters, I will discuss how matter and spirit can be understood ecologically.

9. For readers unfamiliar with biblical Hebrew and Greek, I have in large part put an English approximation first and the Hebrew or Greek in brackets, except where I am discussing particular Hebrew or Greek words or phrases in detail.

the stress of climate change are visible voices. Reading with Earth requires that the interpreter develop a critical and attentive attunement to the cry of such voices as they present themselves to the engaged reader through the senses.

In this book, I aim to shape a non-rigid framework for braided readings of selected biblical texts, mostly from the Gospel of Luke, in a twenty-first-century situation of ecological damage, at the intersection of social and ecological justice, climate change, animal ethics and resistance to extractivism. Specific situations to which my readings harken, as to a cry, include human poverty, road kill, mountaintop removal mining, and the impacts of climate change on weather and on ecosystems such as the Great Barrier Reef. I stage conversations sometimes with biblical texts that have resonance with the contemporary material situation, for example, climate change and the talk about the weather in Luke 12, and sometimes where the text seems on the surface not to speak of other-than-human interests at all, for example, the Lukan Magnificat. The approach I take is informed by ecological feminism, the new materialism and ecocritical poetics.

An ecological feminist analysis of the interrelationship of ecological destruction and kyriarchal oppression which is underscored by patriarchal violence towards women forms a starting point for an ecological feminist hermeneutics.[10] This ecological feminist perspective is strengthened by a new materialist focus on more-than-human interests and agency. New materialism informed by ecological feminism, in turn, becomes an ecological materialism. My intention is to use a process of braiding or interweaving to unsettle the anthropocentrism of reading, in part by destabilizing the individual subjectivity of the reader both through emphasis on the co-agency of more than humans and through the inclusion of creative reading practices informed by poetry and eco-poetics. While, as I discuss below, my work is informed by ecological hermeneutics, there exist few specifically ecological feminist readings of biblical texts and fewer that marry these with the new materialism or ecological poetics.[11] My book, I hope, contributes a

---

10. The notion of 'kyriarchal' oppression comes from Elisabeth Schüssler Fiorenza, *But She Said: Feminist Practices of Biblical Interpretation* (Boston: Beacon, 1992), pp. 8, 123; see further, idem, *Congress of Wo/men: Religion, Gender, and Kyriarchal Power* (Cambridge, MA: Feminist Studies in Religion Books, 2016).

11. Elaine Wainwright develops a multidimensional approach to biblical interpretation and theology, incorporating feminist, post-colonial, ecological and new materialist perspectives. She shapes an ecological hermeneutics with a focus on habitat, in dialogue with Lorraine Code's 'ecological thinking'. See Elaine M. Wainwright, *Women Healing/Healing Women: The Genderization of Healing in Early Christianity* (London: Equinox, 2006); idem, 'Images, Words, Stories: Exploring Their Transformative Power in Reading Biblical Texts Ecologically', *BibInt* 20 (2012), pp. 280–304; idem, *Habitat, Human, and Holy: An Eco-Rhetorical Reading of the Gospel of Matthew* (Earth Bible Commentary, 6; Sheffield: Sheffield Phoenix, 2016); Lorraine L. Code, *Ecological Thinking: The Politics of Epistemic Location* (New York: Oxford University Press, 2006). See further, Anne Elvey, 'Feminist

fresh work of creative biblical study within the evolving field of the environmental humanities, in a series dedicated to scholarship at the intersection of ecology, gender and theology.

Therefore, this book is not simply a series of readings of biblical texts, nor is it addressed to biblical scholars alone. I include sections exploring voice, feminist theory, the new materialism and the Anthropocene. I undertake biblical readings in the wider context of my ongoing reflection towards ecological feminist theologies and poetics, where my reading and writing are responsive to material situation. In this material situation, biblical religion is entangled both with settler colonialism and with Earth itself. I recognize that the ecological feminist and the new materialist bases of my approach must be evaluated, too, insofar as they maintain colonial norms. This ongoing critique is part of my braided reading practice. The potential for interpretive response emerging from this mesh/mess is for me a 'Reading with Earth'.

Reading with Earth

I have called this book *Reading with Earth* because I receive this planet as the underlying and embracing context for the ecological trauma of our time in all its tragedy and complexity. I build on two major ecological hermeneutic projects, the Earth Bible Project, the Uses of the Bible in Environmental Ethics Project and their subsequent combined Ecological Hermeneutics focus, as well as my earlier work on the material given. The Earth Bible project originated in Adelaide under the chief editorship of Norman Habel and was the first major project to develop

---

Ecologies in Religious Interpretation: Australian Influences', in *Feminist Ecologies: Changing Environments in the* Anthropocene (ed. Lara Stevens, Peta Tait and Denise Varney; Cham, Switzerland: Palgrave Macmillan, 2018), pp. 209–29; idem, 'Ecological Feminist Hermeneutics', in *The Oxford Handbook for Bible and Ecology* (ed. Hilary Marlow and Mark Harris; Oxford: Oxford University Press, 2022), pp. 35–48; idem, 'A Multidimensional Approach in Feminist Ecological Biblical Studies', in *The Oxford Handbook of Feminist Approaches to the Hebrew Bible* (ed. Susanne Scholz; Oxford: Oxford University Press, 2021), pp. 555–73, where I hold that 'despite individual essays and occasional books that advance ecological approaches that are informed by feminist, womanist, liberation, or *bosadi* thinking, a strongly focused ecological feminist hermeneutics has not been developed in Hebrew Bible studies'. A similar situation holds in Second Testament and related studies, but see, in addition to Wainwright's work, Catherine Keller, *Apocalypse Now and Then: A Feminist Guide to the End of the World* (Boston: Beacon, 1996); Anne Elvey, *An Ecological Feminist Reading of the Gospel of Luke: A Gestational Paradigm* (Studies in Women and Religion, 45; Lewiston, NY: Edwin Mellen, 2005).

an ecological approach to biblical interpretation.[12] As Habel argues, the Bible cannot be taken as wholly unproblematic either as a conversation partner or as a normative text from which to engage with contemporary ecological concerns.[13] The Earth Bible Team developed six ecojustice principles for reading biblical texts.[14] These are principles of interconnectedness, intrinsic worth, voice, purpose, mutual custodianship and resistance, principles which ascribe these characteristics to Earth and its constituents, including humans.[15] The team developed these principles in conversation with ecologists, feminist theorists and First Nations, and focused on both the intersection between ecological destruction and social injustice and the extension of the notion of social justice to other-than-human contexts, that is, to the context of justice for Earth.[16] Interpreters in the Earth Bible

---

12. See Norman C. Habel (ed.), *Readings from the Perspective of Earth* (Earth Bible, 1; Sheffield: Sheffield Academic, 2000); Norman C. Habel and Shirley Wurst (eds), *The Earth Story in Genesis* (Earth Bible, 2; Sheffield: Sheffield Academic, 2000); Norman C. Habel and Shirley Wurst (eds), *The Earth Story in Wisdom Traditions* (Earth Bible, 3; Sheffield: Sheffield Academic, 2001); Norman C. Habel (ed.), *The Earth Story in the Psalms and the Prophets* (Earth Bible, 4; Sheffield: Sheffield Academic, 2001); Vicky Balabanski and Norman C. Habel (eds), *The Earth Story in the New Testament* (Earth Bible, 5; London: Sheffield Academic, 2002). Earlier work investigating the Bible and ecology includes: James Barr, 'Man and Nature: The Ecological Controversy and the Old Testament', in *Ecology and Religion in History* (ed. David Spring and Eileen Spring; New York: Harper and Row, 1974), pp. 48–75; Susan Power Bratton, 'Christian Ecotheology in the Old Testament', *Environmental Ethics* 6 (1984), pp. 195–209; Brendan Byrne, *Inheriting the Earth: The Pauline Basis of a Spirituality for our Time* (Homebush, NSW: St Paul Publications, 1990); Richard H. Hiers, 'Ecology, Biblical Theology, and Methodology: Biblical Perspectives on the Environment', *Zygon* 19, no. 1 (1984), pp. 43–59; Keller, *Apocalypse Now and Then*; David Rhoads, 'Reading the New Testament in the Environmental Age', *CurTM* 24, no. 3 (1997), pp. 259–66; M.-E. Rosenblatt, 'Ecology and the Gospels', *TBT* 33, no. 1 (1995), pp. 28–32; Rosemary Radford Ruether, 'The Biblical Vision of the Ecological Crisis', in *Readings in Ecology and Feminist Theology* (ed. Mary Heather MacKinnon and Moni McIntyre; Kansas City: Sheed and Ward, 1995), pp. 75–81; Ronald A. Simkins, *Creator and Creation: Nature in the Worldview of Ancient Israel* (Peabody, MA: Hendricksons, 1994); Sun Ai Lee-Park, 'The Forbidden Tree and the Year of the Lord', in *Women Healing Earth: Third World Women on Ecology, Feminism, and Religion* (ed. Rosemary Radford Ruether; Maryknoll: Orbis Books, 1996), pp. 107–16; Gene Tucker, 'Rain on a Land Where No One Lives: The Hebrew Bible on the Environment', *JBL* 116 (1997), pp. 3–17; Elaine M. Wainwright, 'A Metaphorical Walk through Scripture in an Ecological Age', *Pacifica* 4, no. 3 (1991), pp. 273–94.

13. Norman Habel, *An Inconvenient Text: Is a Green Reading of the Bible Possible?* (Hindmarsh, SA: ATF Press, 2009).

14. Habel (ed.), *Readings from the Perspective of Earth*, p. 24.

15. Habel (ed.), *Readings from the Perspective of Earth*, p. 24.

16. Norman Habel, 'Introducing the Earth Bible', in *Readings from the Perspective of Earth* (ed. Normal C. Habel; Earth Bible, 1; Sheffield: Sheffield Academic, 2000), pp. 25–37.

series were asked to bring one or more of these ecojustice principles to bear on the texts they read.

Through the Society of Biblical Literature Ecological Hermeneutics consultation, Habel and his collaborators developed three ecological hermeneutics as a further point of reference for the engagement between biblical studies and contemporary ecological concern. Like the ecojustice principles, ecological hermeneutics of suspicion (especially of anthropocentrism in texts, readings and readers); identification (with a wider Earth community of which human readers are part and with Earth others as agents within the text); and retrieval (of an Earth perspective and voice in the text), focus on Earth as primary in the conversation.[17] This is somewhat in the mode of the liberationist 'preferential option for the poor', where Earth, through human action, has become 'the poor'.

A second major project in this area takes a different approach. The Uses of the Bible in Environmental Ethics (UBEE) Project at the University of Exeter, under the leadership of David Horrell, developed biblically based doctrinal and ethical lenses for an ecological hermeneutics.[18] Criticizing on the one hand a 'recovery' position, that seeks to reclaim the Bible as a book with 'a clearly "green" message', and on the other hand what they read as an unsympathetic approach of the Earth Bible to the biblical texts, the UBEE team sought middle ground.[19] Their work offers 'an attempt to construct an ecological theology which, while innovative, is nonetheless coherent (and in dialogue) with a scripturally shaped Christian orthodoxy... sufficiently faithful to the tradition to be authentically Christian yet sufficiently creative to reshape a tradition that has by and large been preoccupied with issues of human behaviour and salvation.'[20] This last point is key for all ecological readings of biblical texts. Considerations of human behaviour are critical for a response to climate change, for example, but the focus needs to expand. Ecological hermeneutics should situate human behaviour in a wider context where humans are interconnected and interdependent with a broader constituency of Earth beings, with whom they might co-exist and share something like agency. The Earth Bible project puts the focus on this Earth context as the prevailing

---

17. Norman C. Habel, 'Introducing Ecological Hermeneutics', in *Exploring Ecological Hermeneutics* (ed. Norman C. Habel and Peter L. Trudinger; SBL Symposium Series, 46; Atlanta, GA: SBL, 2008), pp. 1–8 (3–8).

18. David G. Horrell, Cherryl Hunt, and Christopher Southgate, 'Appeals to the Bible in Ecotheology and Environmental Ethics: A Typology of Hermeneutical Stances', *Studies in Christian Ethics* 21, no. 2 (2008), pp. 219–38; David G. Horrell, Cherryl Hunt, Christopher Southgate and Francesca Stavrakopoulou (eds), *Ecological Hermeneutics: Biblical, Historical and Theological Perspectives* (London: T&T Clark, 2010).

19. David G. Horrell, 'Introduction', in *Ecological Hermeneutics: Biblical, Historical and Theological Perspectives* (ed. David G. Horrell, Cherryl Hunt, Christopher Southgate and Francesca Stavrakopoulou; London: T&T Clark, 2010), pp. 1–12 (8).

20. Horrell, 'Introduction', pp. 8–9.

hermeneutic key; the UBEE project seeks to uncover biblical hermeneutic keys that are resonant with, and can be applied to, this Earth context.

As I discuss further below, the Bible itself is a material artefact and agent of colonization and in concert with ecological hermeneutics of suspicion, identification and retrieval elsewhere I have applied hermeneutics of restraint, intertextual engagement and creative witness.[21] Several related approaches have appeared over the last thirty or so years; these bring together liberation theological and ecological perspectives, ecological and feminist perspectives, postcolonial and ecological perspectives, multidimensional hermeneutics and ecological materialist approaches.[22] Scholars working in these modes combine ecological concerns such as climate change and ecological principles such as interconnectedness and interdependence with feminist foci such as embodiment; postcolonial critiques of empire; liberationist understandings of social justice; and the new materialist foregrounding of matter to develop ways of reading biblical texts from and for a contemporary context. My personal leaning is towards a decolonizing ethic in a situation where colonial invasion is not past, and the intersections of ecological damage and dispossession of First Nations should be central in a context of environmental activism that recognizes Indigenous sovereignty and respects, without appropriating, Indigenous knowledges.[23]

For this decolonizing intent, ecological feminism is both helpful and limited. Nonetheless, feminisms and ecological feminisms offer a number of challenges and resources for engaging in ethically accountable theology and biblical studies[24]:

1. not accepting without question received worldviews;
2. reconstructing not only Christian origins but my origins and orientations as a human being who is part of a more-than-human world;
3. recognizing my embodiment and so understanding human continuity with other mammals and more broadly with other things;

---

21. Anne Elvey, *The Matter of the Text: Material Engagements between Luke and the Five Senses* (BMW, 37; Sheffield: Sheffield Phoenix, 2011), pp. 70-7; idem, *Reading the Magnificat in Australia: Unsettling Engagements* (Sheffield: Sheffield Phoenix, 2020), p. 20.

22. See e.g., Ivone Gebara, *Longing for Running Water: Ecofeminism and Liberation* (Minneapolis: Fortress, 1999); Jea Sophia Oh, *A Postcolonial Theology of Life: Planetarity East and West* (Upland, CA: Sopher Press, 2011); Wainwright, *Women Healing*, esp. pp. 7-23; Elvey, *Ecological Feminist Reading*; idem, *Matter of the Text*.

23. See Tony Birch, '"We've Seen the End of the World and We Don't Accept It": Protection of Indigenous Country and Climate Justice', in *Places of Privilege: Interdisciplinary Perspectives on Identities, Change and Resistance* (ed. Nicole Oke, Christopher Sonn and Alison Baker; Leiden: Brill, 2018), pp. 139-52.

24. Heather Eaton, 'Ecofeminist Contributions to an Ecojustice Hermeneutics', in *Readings from the Perspective of Earth* (ed. Normal C. Habel; Earth Bible, 1; Sheffield: Sheffield Academic, 2000), pp. 54-71.

4. understanding that my being embodied is complex and diverse, and encompasses a range of human experiences of relationality, sexuality and language, that cannot be easily categorized;
5. putting at the heart of my work the knowledge that my work is dependent on prior and ongoing injustices, such as invasion and colonization, and the privileges that I have accrued as a result;
6. opening spaces where I can stand with what I cannot know – the space of the other, the space between self and other – and which I can inhabit in hospitality and hope.[25]

Feminisms open spaces for critiquing received understandings of the world. Where feminist categories of sex and gender have been a vital analytical key, feminisms especially in an ecological feminist mode prompt broader analyses of what it is to be human. The consideration of what it is to be sexually embodied human beings who are different in ways that queer theory invites me to see as more than male or female extends to considerations of what it is to be a human being in a more-than-human framework. The capacity to think beyond normative assumptions about sex, gender and sexuality can inform my ability to think beyond normative assumptions about being human. The new materialism, or the material turn, is helpful here, inviting me to take as foundational the materiality I share with all other things in the cosmos. This conceptual tool, I suggest, can support an ecological feminist rethinking of what it is to be human.

Ecological feminism, the material given and the matter of the text[26]

Ecological feminist hermeneutics and theology have developed from the multiple forms of ecological feminism that emerged by the 1970s in two key modes: cultural or spiritual and social or socialist.[27] Both modes recognize a critical relationship between women and the wider Earth community. Cultural ecological feminisms

---

25. See further, Anne Elvey, 'Matter, Freedom and the Future: Re-framing Feminist Theologies through an Ecological Materialist Lens', *Feminist Theology* 23, no. 2 (2015), pp. 186–204 (187–9).

26. The following three paragraphs are excerpted, with slight revisions, from Anne Elvey, 'Roadsides: Toward an Ecological Feminist Theology of Cross-species Compassion', in *Contemporary Feminist Theologies: Power, Authority, Love* (ed. Kerrie Handasyde, Cathryn McKinney and Rebekah Pryor; London: Routledge, 2021), pp. 133–44 (134–5).

27. See Kate Rigby, 'Women and Nature Revisited: Ecofeminist Reconfigurations of an Old Association', in *Feminist Ecologies* (ed. Lara Stevens, Peta Tait and Denise Varney; Cham, Switzerland: Palgrave Macmillan, 2018), pp. 57–81 (64–5). For a genealogy of ecofeminist thinking, see Niamh Moore, 'Eco/feminist Genealogies: Renewing Promises and New Possibilities', in *Contemporary Perspectives on Ecofeminism* (ed. Mary Phillips and Nick Rumens; Routledge Explorations in Environmental Studies; Milton Park, Abingdon: Routledge, 2016), pp. 19–37.

affirm and celebrate an affinity between Earth and women, for example, in Goddess spiritualities; there is a danger, however, that this form of feminism perpetuates a patriarchal identification of women and nature, which has devalued both.[28] Social ecological feminisms identify the economic, political, cultural and social factors linking destruction of Earth with oppression of women. Both streams of ecological feminism understand that this shared trauma is a symptom of a patriarchal (dis)order, or more precisely what Elisabeth Schüssler Fiorenza describes as 'kyriarchy'.[29] Environmental activism by women's grassroots collectives was also a central feature of early ecological feminisms.[30] People of colour were and are critical of ecological feminism, however, for its white bias and many favour an environmental justice approach, which includes a comprehensive interweaving of social justice, ecological wholeness and anti-racism, together grounded in recognition of First Nations' sovereignty.[31]

Contemporary ecological feminist hermeneutics are multidimensional in acknowledgement that gender, race, class, location and species are intersecting factors in the exercise and experience of oppression and power.[32] Situation or location is critical. The 'ecological thinking' in which a contemporary ecological feminist hermeneutics is situated offers a focus on habitat, as 'epistemic location'.[33] Knowing is situated in habitats, which are physical places of more-than-human sociality. In a habitat, human agencies meet the agencies of other kind. A challenge of ecological thinking is for human 'co-habitat-ion', that is, for humans to inhabit shared places of being and agency in ways that are counter-hegemonic.[34]

---

28. In relation to criticisms of ecofeminism as essentialist, Greta Gaard traces the interlinked history of the development of ecofeminism in its several forms and its elision from feminist theory, arguing for its ongoing relevance. Greta Gaard, 'Rejecting Essentialism and Re-Placing Species in a Material Feminist Environmentalism', *Feminist Formations* 23, no. 2 (Summer 2011), pp. 26–53. See also, Emma Foster, 'Ecofeminism Revisited: Critical Insights on Contemporary Environmental Governance', *Feminist Theory* 22, no. 2 (2021), pp. 190–205. While Foster's appraisal of ecofeminisms is, on my reading, not as nuanced as Gaard's, she argues that ecofeminist insights and analyses offer useful 'counters to rationalism and technocentrism' (203).

29. Schüssler Fiorenza, *But She Said*, pp. 8, 123.

30. Mary Mellor, *Feminism and Ecology* (Cambridge: Polity, 1997), pp. 17–25.

31. See, e.g., Dorceta E. Taylor, 'Women of Color, Environmental Justice, and Ecofeminism', in *Ecofeminism: Women, Culture, Nature* (ed. Karen J. Warren; Bloomington: Indiana University Press, 1997), pp. 38–81. See also, Jeanine Leane, 'Voicing the Unsettled Space: Rewriting the Colonial Mythscape', paper given at Unsettling Ecological Poetics Conference, University of Sydney, Thursday, 24 October 2019.

32. Wainwright, *Habitat, Human, and Holy*, pp. 18–21, 49.

33. Code, *Ecological Thinking*, pp. 25, 37; Wainwright, *Habitat, Human, and Holy*, pp. 21–5.

34. Donna Haraway, 'Otherworldly Conversations; Terran Topics; Local Terms', *Science as Culture* 3, no. 1 (1992), pp. 64–98 (70); Wainwright, 'Images, Words, Stories', p. 293.

The material given

One ecological feminist focus for such counter-hegemonic thinking, both philosophically and theologically, is 'the material given'.[35] The concept of the material given contains the idea that matter is a given of existence. In a human frame, the notion of the material given pertains in a particular way to those things necessary for human (and other mammalian) life and affirms that such givens have characteristic features for which I borrow the terms 'prepropriation' and 'aneconomic' from Gayatri Spivak and Jacques Derrida respectively.[36] Gayatri Spivak describes the body in pregnancy as 'prepropriative'; it is the 'wholly other', resistant to the patriarchal economy where woman is construed as the 'man-consolidating other'.[37] That pregnant bodies, for example, are 'prepropriative' means they exist in their own right inter-relationally, prior to being construed (falsely) as property. In a related vein, Jacques Derrida deconstructs the notion of gift and its return by way of the notion of the 'aneconomic'; properly the 'gift' is outside of and resists economies of exchange.[38] My contention is that 'the material given' by definition is gift-like in these senses, resisting economies of possession, consumption and exchange.

To explain further: bodies, pregnant mammalian bodies in particular, and Earth are necessities for life in ways that are not bound by economic accounting.[39] Capitalist economies may put a price on the bodies of other animals; bodies of women and children become economic 'goods' in human trafficking; land is bought and sold for profit; minerals are extracted from Indigenous Country. Nonetheless, at the same time, in the pregnant body, a non-dualistic relationship exists between self and other, mediated by flesh. The one and the other are neither one nor two (or more in the case of twins and so on). They embody a logic of interconnection that is oriented towards sustenance and life, even when tragically this is not the outcome. The pregnant body is a paradigm of 'the material given'.[40] The material given, of which bodies, pregnant bodies and Earth are privileged exemplars, is a gift-life necessity for mammalian life.[41] As aneconomic and prepropriative, the material given embodies, or I could say en-matters, a logic of being that precedes

---

35. I develop the concept of 'the material given' more fully in earlier work, drawing on Gayatri Spivak's notion of 'prepropriation', Jacques Derrida's concept of the gift as 'aneconomic' and Jean-Luc Marion on givenness. Elvey, *Ecological Feminist Reading*, pp. 98–102.

36. Elvey, *Ecological Feminist Reading*, p. 98; Gayatri Chakravorty Spivak, *Outside in the Teaching Machine* (London: Routledge, 1993), pp. 141–71 (148); Jacques Derrida, *Given Time: 1. Counterfeit Money* (trans. Peggy Kamuf; Chicago: University of Chicago Press, 1992), p. 7.

37. Spivak, *Outside in the Teaching Machine*, p. 148.

38. Derrida, *Given Time*, p. 7.

39. Elvey, *Ecological Feminist Reading*, pp. 98–102.

40. Elvey, *Ecological Feminist Reading*, p. 101.

41. Elvey, *Ecological Feminist Reading*, p. 98.

and unsettles a logic of capitalist exchange. The material given enacts 'holding labour' which is both life-giving and often devalued; 'holding labour' is the kind of corporeal, material work that occurs in reproduction, domestic labour, childcare and subsistence agriculture; it is the work of a habitat – of Country – that sustains and is maintained by multiple beings.[42] In this sense, the material given, as already a complex of coagents and inter-agencies, is not static.[43] Material givenness itself needs to be understood as dynamic. It both is and provides what Teresa Brennan describes as 'an interactive energetic economy'.[44]

The mutual agencies that together enact the holding labour of the material given, however, are strained. Through material entanglements, bodies, pregnant bodies and Earth, habitats and Country – including sea Country and sky Country – bear the eco-social trauma of extinctions, climate change, pollution, deforestation and biodiversity loss, social oppression, genocide, racism, human trafficking, homelessness and hunger, disease and war.[45] In an ecological feminist frame, these stressed enmeshments of, and in, the material given, its relation to the maternal and the semiotic, have both the potential for increased injury and a transformative holding of 'new possibilities for collective life', which 'an ethics of entanglement' requires.[46] In an eco-sociality, matter – in its vibrancy and complex interrelatedness – matters.

The matter of the text

Biblical texts themselves bear numerous relations to matter. In *The Matter of the Text*, I argue for considering the materiality of the text as a participating partner in biblical studies; such considerations call into question both the stability of any text across multiple media and the purity of interpretations that presume such stability.[47] Biblical studies has a tendency to treat a text such as the Gospel of Luke, if not exactly as singular – given its several versions in koine Greek and

---

42. Ariel Salleh, *Ecofeminism as Politics: Nature, Marx and the Postmodern* (London: Zed Books, 1997), pp. 143, 153, 190.

43. Cf. Karen Barad, 'What Flashes Up: Theological-Political-Scientific Fragments', in *Entangled Worlds: Religion, Science, and New Materialism* (ed. Catherine Keller and Mary-Jane Rubenstein; New York: Fordham University Press, 2017), pp. 21–88 (38).

44. Teresa Brennan, *Exhausting Modernity: Grounds for a New Economy* (London: Routledge, 2000), p. 41.

45. See, e.g., the account of such material entanglements in Hilda P. Koster, 'Trafficked Lands: Sexual Violence, Oil, and Structural Evil in the Dakotas', in *Planetary Solidarity: Global Women's Voices on Christian Doctrine and Climate Justice* (ed. Grace Ji-Sun Kim and Hilda P. Koster; Minneapolis: Ausburg Fortress, 2017), pp. 155–75.

46. Eric L. Santner, *On Creaturely Life: Rilke, Benjamin, Sebald* (Chicago: The University of Chicago Press, 2006), pp. 58, 133; see also Barad, 'What Flashes Up', pp. 38, 49.

47. Elvey, *Matter of the Text*.

its translations into many languages – then as transferable across multiple media (codices, papyri, printed books, screenshots and so on). Yet, each instance of a given text is materially different, even when they are two instances of the same print run of the NRSV for example. The paper pulp from trees in one book is materially different from that in another book. Technologies of print and electronic publication, as well as the relation of industries of publication to the extraction of so-called 'natural resources' and the marketing of books, co-constitute the materiality of the Bible.[48] The culture, politics, economics and ecological impacts of consumer capital are materially present in the matter of a biblical text. As a religious phenomenon, the Bible is itself entangled with its social, cultural and ecological contexts, its many habitats, past and present, and is produced through multiple agencies and types of agency.[49]

The matter of a text can be approached by way of attentiveness to a material intertextuality, which includes the 'inter-con/textuality' of which Elaine Wainwright writes.[50] I understand intertextuality not only as a practice of citation and allusion, but building on Julia Kristeva it is also the complex relation of textuality to the semiotic space of the maternal and the material.[51] Attention to this material intertextuality can function to call forth the repressed voices of Earth in the multiplicities of existence and agency across place, space and time. Through its expression in bodies, pregnant bodies and Earth, the material given has a relation to the senses and the breath, to habitat as epistemic location, and these in turn are spaces of corporeal relation to the materiality of texts for an ecological feminist reader.

Neither the material given nor the matter of a text is static; rather from a new materialist perspective, matter itself has agency in the sense that, as Jane Bennett argues, matter is 'vibrant', and everyday human actions occur as complex interactions with other-than-human things.[52] For example, climate change is a product of both human action (so anthropogenic) and the properties for example of

---

48. Elvey, *Matter of the Text*, pp. 28–43.

49. See, Catherine Keller and Mary-Jane Rubenstein, 'Introduction: Tangled Matters', in *Entangled Worlds: Religion, Science, and New Materialism* (ed. Catherine Keller and Mary-Jane Rubenstein; New York: Fordham University Press, 2017), pp. 1–18 (12); Manuel A. Vásquez, 'Vascularizing the Study of Religion: Multi-Agent Figurations and Cosmopolitics', in *Entangled Worlds: Religion, Science, and New Materialism* (ed. Catherine Keller and Mary-Jane Rubenstein; New York: Fordham University Press, 2017), pp. 228–47 (228).

50. Wainwright, *Habitat, Human, and Holy*, p. 24.

51. Julia Kristeva, *Revolution in Poetic Language* (trans. Margaret Waller; New York: Columbia University Press, 1984), pp. 43–51, 57–71; Elvey, *Matter of the Text*, pp. 28–43.

52. Jane Bennett, *Vibrant Matter: A Political Ecology of Things* (Durham, NC: Duke University Press, 2010); see also, Lambros Malafouris, 'At the Potter's Wheel: An Argument for Material Agency', in *Material Agency: Toward a Non-Anthropocentric Approach* (ed. Carl Knappett and Lambros Malafouris; New York: Springer, 2008), pp. 19–36.

fossil fuels, atmosphere, seas, glaciers.[53] The material properties, interrelationships and agencies of a multiplicity of things – including fossil fuels, human beings and their habitual behaviours – acting together produce the contemporary situation of climate change.

In relation to the Bible, in the ongoing context of colonial invasion with which I began this chapter, a crucial aspect of the materiality of biblical texts is the reality that the Bible arrived in the continent where I live as a material artefact of colonization, with complex, ambiguous relations both to the violence of that project and to the existing spiritual, cultural, religious practices of First Nations.[54] The material things that we call Bibles, those who brought them and those who read them, have been, and in some cases continue to be, co-agents of colonization. So, the Bible is part of the situational materiality of colonization.

Situational materialities

Matter assembles in situational materialities. Not only is matter a constitutive 'stuff' that offers a basis for thinking connection or relation across genres of organic-inorganic, plant-fungal-animal (including human), terran and extra-terran, the atomic and the cosmic, solid-liquid-gas and viral, but also matter is properly unknowable at a quantum level; it is a kind of energetic, slippery alterity constituting things in specific situations. For humans, corporeal enmeshments with social and ecological systems mark these situational materialities, where exercises of power and constructions of 'the human' serve as pretexts for both violence and protection from violence.

Violence is both material and linguistic, where the linguistic is understood as shaping and shaped by matter and the situational materialities in which language, discourse, texts and their usages are entangled. In this context, the question of matter and the dualisms in which a trajectory of western thinking has opposed matter to spirit has a particular focus in the hyper-separation of animals and humans, with its strategic elision of some privileged human beings from the category 'animal'.[55]

---

53. Deborah Guess, 'Oil beyond War and Peace: Rethinking the Meaning of Matter', in *Ecological Aspects of War: Religious and Theological Perspectives* (ed. Anne Elvey, Deborah Guess and Keith Dyer, *A Forum for Theology in the World* 3, no. 2; Adelaide: ATF Theology, 2016), pp. 73–93.

54. See, e.g., Anne Pattel-Gray, *The Great White Flood: Racism in Australia: Critically Appraised from an Aboriginal Historico-Theological Viewpoint* (American Academy of Religion Cultural Criticism Series, 2; Atlanta: Scholars Press, 1998), pp. 127, 158–9; idem, 'Dreaming: An Aboriginal Interpretation of the Bible', in *Text and Experience: Toward a Cultural Exegesis of the Bible* (ed. Daniel L. Smith-Christopher; Sheffield: Sheffield Academic, 1995), pp. 247–59; Graham Paulson and Mark Brett, 'Five Smooth Stones: Reading the Bible through Aboriginal Eyes', *Colloquium* 45, no. 2 (November 2013), pp. 199–214; Elvey, *Matter of the Text*, pp. 70–81.

55. The term 'hyper-separation' comes from Val Plumwood, *Environmental Culture: The Ecological Crisis of Reason* (Environmental Philosophies; London: Routledge, 2002), p. 101.

Zakiyyah Iman Jackson's work is helpful in understanding the racial construction of the category 'human'; she argues that during the 'Enlightenment', 'discourses on "the animal" and "the black"' were conjoined and now reinforce each other 'in the traveling racializations of the globalizing West'.[56] Such racializations violently impact not only people of African descent, but also First Nations in colonized settings such as the Americas and Australia. The complex overlay of racism and speciesism has implications, Jackson contends, not only for resisting the problematic of 'animalizing discourse that is directed primarily at people of African descent', but also for countering the 'abject abstraction of "the animal" more generally'.[57] This entangled experience of abjection calls into question the humanist project of defining 'the human' inclusively. For Jackson, 'the animalizations of humans and animals have contiguous and intersecting histories'.[58] The lived experience of racism highlights a particular embodied relation to the material world, from which a countering of anthropocentrism must interrogate the very notion of 'the human' which ecocritics, for example, have sought to decentre. As Jackson suggests in relation to animal advocacy, when ecocritics seek to decentre 'the human', without a critical race perspective, problematic uses of the category 'human' can remain intact.[59]

Through readings of literature by women of African descent, for example Octavia Butler and Audre Lorde, Jackson focuses on the embodied experience of Black women, and the nexus of material agencies entangled with this lived experience that crosses differences of class and education.[60] She contrasts a humanist abjection, objectification and plasticization of Black women's bodies, with the experience of 'matter-mater' entangled in/as a nexus of agencies: cultural, psychological, biological and environmental.[61] Black women in this context 'somatize' politics and its material insurgencies.[62]

Jackson's focus on the situational materialities of embodied experience – where 'matter-mater' is entangled – speaks to the concept of the material given and its relation to the maternal and the semiotic. Her work challenges me to recast the 'material given' as already unsettled by difference or *différance* through the way

---

56. Zakiyyah Iman Jackson, *Becoming Human: Matter and Meaning in an Antiblack World* (New York: New York University Press, 2020), p. 14.

57. Jackson, *Becoming Human*, p. 15.

58. Jackson, *Becoming Human*, p. 23.

59. Jackson, *Becoming Human*, p. 15; see also Rosi Braidotti, '"We" May Be in This Together, but We Are Not All Human and We Are Not One and the Same', *Ecocene* 1, no. 2 (June 2020), pp. 24–31 (28); Carol Wayne White, 'Stubborn Materiality: African American Religious Naturalism and Becoming Our Humanity', in *Entangled Worlds: Religion, Science, and New Materialism* (ed. Catherine Keller and Mary-Jane Rubenstein; New York: Fordham University Press, 2017), pp. 251–73 (252–3).

60. Jackson, *Becoming Human*, p. 23.

61. Jackson, *Becoming Human*, pp. 42–3, 164, 191.

62. Jackson, *Becoming Human*, p. 43.

racialization and animalization function in the (de)valuation of the maternal and the material. Conversely, Jackson's affirmation of a Black 'matter-mater' is an important focus for any discussion of material givenness that presumes a universality to categories of the maternal and the material. Such universalizing tendencies in white feminist discourse need to be unsettled in multiple ways.

The white woman Before Aileen Moreton-Robinson wrote of talking up to white women in the space of dialogue with secular feminists, Anne Pattel-Gray was speaking up to the churches in Australia and reminding Australian feminist theologians and religious scholars that we are 'not yet Tiddas (sisters)', that colonial women in Australia have a long history of oppressing their Aboriginal and Torres Strait Islander 'sisters' and benefiting from their oppression.[63] The histories of colonization are present, that is current, not only in intergenerational trauma and resistances but also in the ongoing fact of invasion in a place such as Australia, as well as globally in human trafficking and harsh border protection measures against asylum seekers here and in many other modern nations.

The kind of destructive logic that enables colonial praxis is, Val Plumwood argues, built on a system of mastery and enslavement that informs spirit-matter, man-woman, culture-nature, mind-body, human-animal, sacred-profane and related dualisms.[64] Plumwood's critique comes from a colonial inside as one trained in a western philosophical tradition, however marginal her insider position was as a white woman of her generation. The colonizing logic which she analyses critically from an ecological feminist perspective is already well-known to First Nations scholars as lived experience, written in the body and on the land, where Indigenous women affirm both the agency of other animals and important links between ecological labour and the maternal.[65] While this lived experience has resonances with the way white feminists experience and resist the colonizing logic of patriarchy in their own embodied material situations, it is substantially different.

---

63. Aileen Moreton-Robinson, *Talkin' Up to the White Woman: Indigenous Women and Feminism* (St Lucia, Qld: University of Queensland Press, 2000); Anne Pattel-Gray, 'Not Yet Tiddas: An Aboriginal Womanist Critique of Australian Church Feminism', in *Freedom and Entrapment: Women Thinking Theology* (ed. Maryanne Confoy, Dorothy A. Lee and Joan Nowotny; North Blackburn: Collins Dove, 1995), pp. 165-92; idem, *The Great White Flood*; see also, Lee Miena Skye, *Kerygmatics of the New Millennium: A Study of Australian Aboriginal Women's Christology* (Delhi: ISPCK, 2007).

64. Val Plumwood, *Feminism and the Mastery of Nature* (Feminism for Today; London: Routledge, 1993), pp. 41-68.

65. See Leane, 'Voicing'. Also, private email communication with Jeanine Leane. Cf. Greta Gaard, 'Toward an Ecofeminist Aesthetic of Reconnection', in *Ecocritical Aesthetics: Language, Beauty, and the Environment* (ed. Peter Quigley and Scott Slovic; Bloomington: Indiana University Press, 2018), pp. 97-113 (99-100).

Moreover, in Australia from a First Nations perspective, white settler women have been the face of colonial violence, especially to Indigenous children taken into state or church care, and to Indigenous girls and women enlisted as unpaid domestic labourers in white settler households.[66] An issue for this book is not whether all white women are racist, but that systemically white feminists are situated in the 'between' as beneficiaries of racist use and policing of Black bodies even while they are bound by problematic patriarchal (internalized) constructions of themselves as in need of protection. The two branches of this 'between' are uneven on the whole, as the first is directly life-threatening while the latter is usually less so.

I raise these questions of race and whiteness, which is often constructed as racially unmarked, because they are important aspects that speak into and unsettle the grounds of an ecological feminist hermeneutics, precisely at the point of our situated materialities. So, as Wainwright argues, hermeneutics which focuses on the intersecting relations between women and Earth as subject to patriarchal, anthropocentrically mediated violence needs to be 'multidimensional'.[67] I am using Wainwright's term multidimensional rather than intersectional, though they are similar. Intersectionality must not be understood simply as adding one more category of analysis of oppression and power to a list, but should be a means of recognizing and examining the way such intersections operate together 'historically and culturally' not only to complicate any one node of experience but also to support or resist existing power relations.[68] From a materialist perspective, all interactions involve intersections of more-than-human entangled worlds.[69] A multidimensional approach foregrounds attention both to the complex intersections of lived experience marked by race, class, gender, sexuality, species and location, and to the many dimensional materialities and exercises of power that constitute lived experience. As a white reader such an approach entails for me a challenge to be unsettled in relation to my position in, and interpretation of, both contemporary contexts of ecological trauma and the ancient biblical texts in the multidimensional situations which they portray, from which they emerge and in which they have been read.

Ecological feminist hermeneutic weavings

Earlier in this chapter, I affirmed the importance of voice for an ecological feminist hermeneutics, and introduced the notion of braided reading. Supporting this understanding is an ecological feminist understanding of relatedness. The self

---

66. See Pattel-Gray, 'Not Yet Tiddas'; Moreton-Robinson, *Talkin' up*. See also on white fragility, Robin Diangelo, *White Fragility: Why It's So Hard for White People to Talk about Racism* (Boston: Beacon, 2018); and for a First Nations critique of Diangelo, see Alison Whittaker, 'So White. So What', *Meanjin* 79, no. 1 (Autumn 2020), pp. 50–61.

67. Wainwright, *Habitat, Human and Holy*, pp. 21, 37.

68. Jackson, *Becoming Human*, pp. 5, 10.

69. White, 'Stubborn Materiality', p. 266; Vásquez, 'Vascularizing', pp. 228–9.

is relational, as scholars such as Ivone Gebara and Greta Gaard maintain.[70] In Chapter 8, I will draw on Gebara's understanding of relatedness, and its intersections with ecological conceptions of interconnectedness, interdependence, enmeshment and entanglement. Relatedness is situated in the body; through the corporeality of the senses and the sensual, we open ourselves to the alterity of the material. Kate Rigby writes of consciously choosing the body, of cultivating attention to the body in the here and now.[71] In accepting the messiness and limits of the corporeal, we face our own mortality, and that of more-than-human others, especially those we hold dearest.[72] The relationality of the corporeal means our situation in the social is ecological. As I will note in Chapter 9, in any place more-than-human co-inhabitants (including ourselves), their (and our) habits and habitats are entangled. Stacy Alaimo uses the term 'trans-corporeality' to describe 'the time-space where human corporeality, in all its material fleshiness, is inseparable from "nature" or "environment"'.[73] This inseparability renders embodied creatures such as ourselves susceptible to things and the 'atmospheres they generate', recognizing in them a shared existence.[74] We are already porous to the other and, as I will argue in Chapter 10, the other addresses me with a moral force that engages me in a deeper openness to its 'saying' (or voice).

For this porosity to more-than-human others and the deeper openness they elicit to extend beyond 'the personal experience of atmosphere to the level of a transformative social praxis', poets, for example, work not only to depict but to produce atmosphere in a way that might shift the perception of the reader or hearer.[75] For the ecological feminist hermeneutic weavings I am moving towards in this book, I suggest that reading itself might also function like poetry to depict, analyse and produce atmosphere, specifically through intertextual or cross-conversational readings that build on connections. In Chapter 4, for example, I read contemporary material context and ancient text, with a focus on breath, climate and material text; in Chapter 10, I move between the situation of the Great Barrier Reef, the Lukan Transfiguration account and poetry relating to the Reef, with a focus on sight and the perception of beauty, to evoke a hermeneutics of encounter.

Practised with an ear to the customs of historical and literary criticism of the text, and in conversation with social, scientific and poetic articulations of situated materialities, an ecological feminist reading is a weaving. With a focus on the Great

---

70. Gebara, *Longing for Running Water*, pp. 84–5, 90, 103–5; Gaard, 'Toward an Ecofeminist Aesthetic of Reconnection', pp. 98–9.

71. Kate Rigby, *Reclaiming Romanticism: Towards an Ecopoetics of Decolonization* (Environmental Culture Series; London: Bloomsbury, 2020), pp. 61–2.

72. On accepting our limits and mortality, see Rigby, *Reclaiming Romanticism*, p. 61.

73. Stacy Alaimo, 'Trans-corporeal Feminism and the Ethical Space of Nature', in *Material Feminisms* (ed. Stacy Alaimo and Susan Hekman; Bloomington: Indiana University Press, 2008), pp. 237–64 (238).

74. Rigby, *Reclaiming Romanticism*, p. 63.

75. Rigby, *Reclaiming Romanticism*, p. 65.

Barrier Reef, Sarah Hamylton, Leah Gibbs, Kim Williams and Lucas Ihlein explore the possibilities of plaited scholarship in relation to climate crisis.[76] They argue for interdisciplinary approaches that 'enliven and challenge' readers, empowering response, through a plaiting of narratives that brings together 'affective and cognitive' learning, opening up perception not only through similarities and connections but through the tensions that arise in the disjunctions or gaps.[77] The readings in this book take a plaited or braided approach to weave somewhat eclectically a fabric of conversation between ancient text, contemporary ecological situations and possibilities for responsiveness to the moral force of more than humans.

An outline

This book builds on two important responses to twentieth- and twenty-first-century situations of ecological trauma, especially the complex context of climate change: first, ecological feminism; second, ecological hermeneutics in the Earth Bible tradition. In the book, these two responses are refracted through the lens of the new materialism to engage in a re-envisioned ecological feminist hermeneutics. Essential for a contemporary ecological feminist hermeneutics is an ethic of decolonization. In the colonized and globalized spaces of the twenty-first century, power is distributed in multiple rather than singular or dualistic modes. Race, class and species are among the categories of analysis entangled with gender in contemporary ecological feminisms. The material turn (also called the new materialism) offers a strong basis for describing and deepening a multidimensional ecological feminist hermeneutics. Attentiveness to matter situates human bodies and textuality in their more-than-human contexts, where senses and breath, for example, act as mediators of more-than-human material relations and knowing. Breath is a key concept for a new materialist evaluation of, for example, the Earth Bible ecojustice principle of voice and the related ecological hermeneutics of retrieval. By way of readings of selected biblical texts, this book suggests that an ecological feminist aesthetics, bringing contemporary context and biblical text into conversation, including engagement with poetry, is helpful for the future of a decolonizing ecological feminist hermeneutics and ethics. Such an approach is both informed by and speaks back to the new materialism in ecological criticism.

Section 1 considers more-than-human breath and voice as keys for engaging with the materiality of both Earth and text. Chapter 2 focuses on the materiality of breath as a key for understanding the concept of an Earth voice, and applies this to a reading of Lk. 1.46-55 (the Magnificat), as a song of protest in a woman's voice, attentive to breath ($\pi\nu\varepsilon\tilde{\upsilon}\mu\alpha$). Chapter 3 moves from a focus on Earth voice to the

---

76. Sarah Hamylton, Leah Gibbs, Kim Williams and Lucas Ihlein, 'Can Interdisciplinary Insights Encourage Meaningful Response to the Climate Crisis? Narratives from the Great Barrier Reef, Australia', *GeoHumanities* 6, no. 2 (2020), pp. 394–412, available online: https://doi.org/10.1080/2373566X.2020.1819167.

77. Hamylton et al., 'Meaningful Response', pp. 406–9.

hermeneutic mode of 'retrieving' an Earth voice. With reference to modern and contemporary women's poetry I argue for a quality of attentiveness to material text and ecological context in this mode. Chapter 4 examines the materiality of breath as a way of engaging with the materiality of a text against a contemporary background where air and atmosphere are often strained. I offer a performative reading of Lk. 4.16-30 from the perspective of the interlinked materialities of breath, text and women's lives, arguing for a multi-layered approach to reading that attends to the markers of breath in the reader, the ways the text affects both readers' and characters' breath, and the way the text might speak into the strained breath of a climate change and pollution-affected Earth.

Section 2 explores ways the material turn might further inform ecological feminist hermeneutics. In Chapter 5 I argue that in reframing feminist approaches towards ecological feminist ones through a new materialist lens, the category of freedom is significant. This is a transformative 'freedom for' a future towards which I am responsible and for which I may yet hope. In Chapter 6, I suggest hermeneutic questions raised by future obligations occasioned by climate change as a sign of the time. This chapter offers a reading of Lk. 12.54-56 in relation to meteorological, social and theological signs, from an ecological materialist perspective, and asks how the present period (καιρός) in Lk. 12.56 might speak to the contemporary situation of climate change. Chapter 7 develops the notion of 'freedom for' through readings attentive to kyriarchal anthropocentric power and its unsettlings by ecologically inflected understandings of neighbour love. I consider some inter-implications of the notions of sovereignty and neighbour love in relation to Lk. 10.25-37. I ask if Earth's life-sustaining capacity can be understood as both a kind of neighbour love and a kind of sovereignty each of which is disturbed materially by human co-engagement with fossil fuels affecting climate.

Section 3 practises ecological feminist materialist readings in the contexts of contemporary shared vulnerability, ecological trauma and resistance. In Chapter 8, the material givenness of relatedness forms a context for considering compassion as a cross-species practice. Introduced in the previous chapter, a Lukan road text, Lk. 10.30-37 (the parable of the Good Samaritan), suggests a formulation of compassion across species, where compassion is exercised as a complex of more-than-human agencies. The road becomes a risky habitat, a way of shared vulnerability, a fleshy space of solidarity and resistance. Assent to shared vulnerability is a basis for ecological conversion. Chapter 9 analyses uses of biblical texts in fossil fuel extraction, in particular the practice of Mountaintop Removal Mining and uses of Isa. 40.4 (and Lk. 3.5) by both proponents and opponents of this practice. I ask if the liveliness underlying the mountains and hills of the Isaian metaphor can prompt a renewed focus on, and solidarity with, the Appalachian Mountains and their communities. Chapter 10 approaches the Great Barrier Reef as living, active material context, with particular reference to events of bleaching, both in relation to their impact on the ecology of the reef and on human observers, especially scientists, poets and activists. The destructive transfiguration (disfiguration) of the reef, through bleaching, suggests a point of conversation with the Lukan Transfiguration account. The Lukan reference to Jesus' departure (ἔξοδος) in Jerusalem (Lk. 9.31) is understood as a moment of deep compassion in response to the suffering ahead, that is transformative, a sending out to complex, responsive and difficult, sometimes silence-inducing, action, which has resonances for activism now.

Through engagements with contemporary contexts and conversations with ancient texts, I propose critical creative readings undertaken in the midst of ecological trauma as enabling socio-political reflection and action. I undertake these braided readings as a mode of ecological feminist hermeneutics informed by the material turn, where matter and the maternal, the corporeal and the semiotic, are entangled in situational materialities that from a white settler reading position need to be regularly and resolutely unsettled and risked. Knowing my part as a reader entangled materially through ecological interconnections and socio-cultural relations that are more-than-human will, I hope, provoke readings open to the sacred breath of other kind, readings that in the face of ecological damage and social oppression are oriented towards otherwise possibilities for collective life.[78]

---

78. The concept 'otherwise possibilities for collective life' brings together two ideas discussed in this book, namely 'otherwise possibilities' and 'new possibilities for collective life', respectively, from Ashon T. Crawley, *Blackpentecostal Breath: The Aesthetics of Possibility* (New York: Fordham University Press, 2017), pp. 2, 85, and Santner, *On Creaturely Life*, pp. 58, 133.

Section 1

THE MATERIALITY OF BREATH

Chapter 2

BREATH AND EARTH VOICE: EXPLORING AN ECOLOGICAL HERMENEUTICS OF RETRIEVAL

Breath, creaturely breath which is not only human, is a phenomenon that connects humans with the wider Earth community. Below is a picture of a breath.[1] It is breath no. 9305 caught at The Lock-Up in Newcastle, New South Wales, on 18 March 2018 at 11.54 am. This imaging of breath is part of a project by installation artist Andrew Styan whose 'Catch Your Breath reflects on the intimacy of breathing and the idea of a collective breath'.[2] In his project: 'Breath is captured as a digital image using high-speed flash photography and a glass tank of water with participants contributing their breath as a bubble blown in the water.'[3] In this collaborative process, the artist captures visually the materiality of breath and breathing.

As Styan notes in his commentary, 'The air in every breath we take is shared with all other living things: past, present and future, and through the cycles of life and death, with the planet itself. And yet this process is completely invisible. In *Catch Your Breath* high-speed photography catches the act of breathing and makes it visible.'[4] In his delightful book, *Air: The Restless Shaper of the World*, William Bryant Logan comments that more than humans on a reserve near his upstate New York home 'breathe better than ten million gallons of air in a single day'.[5] Earth's atmosphere itself 'is regulated by the living'; from 'air and water, all the living are derived through the medium of breath'.[6] Breathing, he writes, 'is the body's constant

---

1. This chapter is based in large part on, and revises, my article, Anne Elvey, 'A Hermeneutics of Retrieval: Breath and Earth Voice in Luke's Magnificat – Does Earth Care for the Poor?', *AusBR* 63 (2015), pp. 68–84.

2. Andrew Styan, *Catch Your Breath*, available online: https://catch-your-breath.com/ (accessed 2 July 2019).

3. Styan, *Catch Your Breath*, available online: http://catch-your-breath.com/about/ (accessed 2 July 2019).

4. Styan, *Catch Your Breath*, available online: http://catch-your-breath.com/2018/03/18/catch-your-breath-9305-11-54-am/ (accessed 2 July 2019). On chilly days, however, breath does become visible.

5. William Bryant Logan, *Air: The Restless Shaper of the World* (eBook; New York: Norton, 2012), p. 320.

6. Logan, *Air*, p. 321.

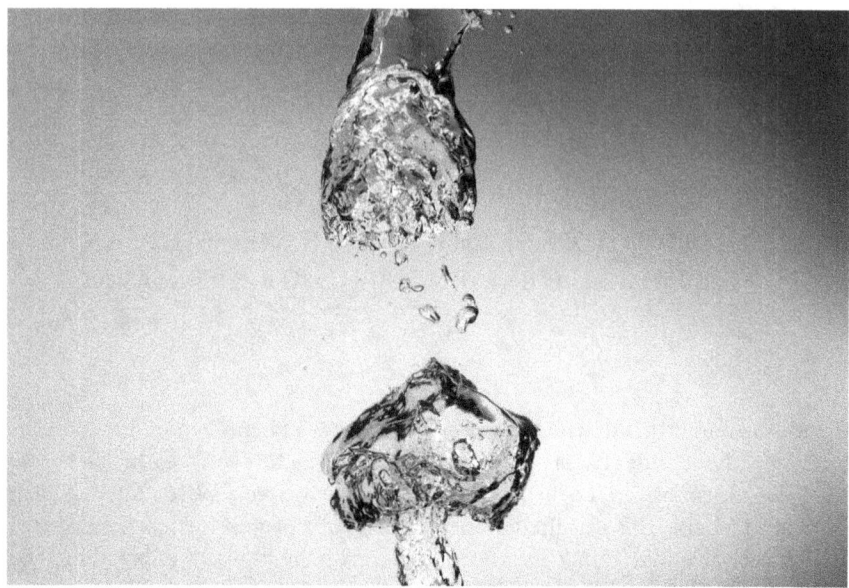

Figure 1 'Breath no. 9305 caught at The Lock-Up in Newcastle, New South Wales, Australia, on 18 March 2018 at 11:54 AM' © Andrew Styan 2018. Reproduced with permission of Andrew Styan.

ceremony as long as we live'.[7] In the act of breathing, I recall the materiality of air as a forgotten given of human being and thinking.[8]

Breath is an important part of language, of the space between words, inhabiting different sounds and cadences, making speech and singing possible.[9] The koine Greek word for 'breath' is πνεῦμα, often translated as 'spirit' in biblical texts but also meaning 'blowing', 'breathing' and '(life-)spirit', sometimes also 'wind'.[10] The Greek πνεῦμα takes me back to the Hebrew רוח, a concept which connects air, wind, breath and the sacred.[11] רוח is 'the air of both atmospheric winds and animal respiration'.[12] These biblical concepts – רוח and πνεῦμα – not only link 'breath' and

---

7. Logan, *Air*, p. 324.

8. Luce Irigaray, *The Forgetting of Air in Martin Heidegger* (trans. Mary Beth Mader; Austin, TX: University of Texas Press, 1999); I will discuss this further in Chapter 4.

9. See, e.g., David Abram's comments on the breathing spaces between the consonants of unpointed Hebrew; David Abram, *The Spell of the Sensuous* (New York: Vintage Books, 1997), p. 99.

10. BAGD, pp. 674–5.

11. Theodore Hiebert, 'Air, the First Sacred Thing: The Conception of רוח in the Hebrew Scriptures', in *Exploring Ecological Hermeneutics* (ed. Norman C. Habel and Peter Trudinger; Atlanta: Society of Biblical Literature, 2008), pp. 9–19.

12. Hiebert, 'Air', p. 13.

'spirit', but also signal the lively interconnectedness of breathing creatures with air and atmosphere, wind and climate.[13]

My own body, as well as weather and seas, is already responding to climate change, even though I do not quite know how. Through my breath and through my senses, as I touch, smell, taste, hear and see, I encounter a changing Earth. As a breathing, fleshy creature, I know and experience my interrelationship with Earth systems, even when I do not bring this knowledge to consciousness. In this chapter, I suggest that the material engagements of being a breathing creature among other creatures of Earth can form an entry point for engaging ecologically with biblical texts, such as Luke's gospel.

My focus here on creaturely breath prompts me to revisit an ecological hermeneutics of retrieval which attempts to recover and 'speak' an Earth voice in human words.[14] Concerning the process of retrieval, Norman Habel writes: 'As the interpreter exposes the various anthropocentric dimensions of the text – the ways in which the human agenda and bias are sustained either by the reader or the implied author – the text may reveal a number of surprises about the nonhuman characters in the story.'[15] Spaces in the text may open for the reader a recollection of the breathy voices of other kind and of Earth itself. But what of texts in which there are no other-than-human characters, where the text seems focused on human concerns without any apparent reference to other than humans, even as background?

The text on which I focus in this chapter is the Magnificat from Luke's infancy narrative. No creatures other than humans seem evident as characters or referents in the text. Nevertheless, with its reference to 'my breath' (τὸ πνεῦμα μου) in the second line, the song invites the reader to employ breath as an interpretive key. In the Magnificat, a woman's breath carries a song of reversal, a song of liberation,

---

13. Ecotheologians Denis Edwards and Celia Deane-Drummond recover the material relation implicit in the words πνεῦμα and רוח when they write of Spirit as the Breath of G-d. Denis Edwards, *Breath of Life: A Theology of the Creator Spirit* (Maryknoll: Orbis, 2004); Celia Deane-Drummond, *Eco-Theology* (London: Darton, Longman and Todd, 2008), pp. 130–45. See also, Mark I. Wallace, *Finding God in the Singing River: Christianity, Spirit, Nature* (Minneapolis: Fortress, 2005); Sigurd Bergmann, *Creation Set Free: The Spirit as Liberator of Nature* (trans. Douglas Stott; Grand Rapids: Eerdmans, 2005). In this chapter, I focus on creaturely breath, and will come in Chapter 4 to consider ways the breathing creature and the divine breath correlate – not only in creation (Gen. 2.7), but also in proclamation of liberation (Lk. 4.16-30).

14. On ecological hermeneutics of retrieval, see Norman C. Habel, 'Introducing Ecological Hermeneutics', in *Exploring Ecological Hermeneutics* (ed. Norman C. Habel and Peter L. Trudinger; Atlanta: Society of Biblical Literature, 2008), pp. 1–8 (7–8).

15. Habel, 'Introducing Ecological Hermeneutics', p. 5.

a song of life-affirming possibility in the face of oppression.[16] For Ashon T. Crawley, the words of Eric Garner 'I can't breathe' repeated multiple times as he was murdered by police in the United States form 'an ethical charge' to the living, in the face of the systemic violence that produced 'the moment of his assault and murder'.[17] Responding to a different situation of systemic violence, a woman – the Lukan Mary – breathes; she inhales and exhales into the air/atmosphere of Earth, giving voice to possibilities countering oppression. How does her voice intersect with an Earth voice when she sings the reversal of poor and rich? In exploring the potential retrieval of an Earth voice that is not obvious in the text, I bring to my reading of the Magnificat the question: how is Earth materially active with the divine in the liberation from oppression proclaimed by the Lukan Mary?

An ecological hermeneutics of retrieval and the principle of voice

To address this question, I consider first how I might listen to the Magnificat with an ear to an Earth voice.[18] The ecological hermeneutic of retrieval comes in a series of three: suspicion, identification and retrieval. A hermeneutics of suspicion concerns an alertness to the anthropocentrism of biblical texts and interpretations.[19] A hermeneutics of identification involves the 'task of empathy' and requires the reader to endeavour 'to come to terms with his or her deep ecological connections', and to acknowledge and take in 'the prior ecological reality of our kinship with Earth'.[20] My focus on breath as an interpretive key is

---

16. Barbara E. Reid, 'An Overture to the Gospel of Luke', *CurTM* 39, no. 6 (December 2012), pp. 428–34 (429). See also, idem, *Taking Up the Cross: New Testament Interpretations through Latina and Feminist Eyes* (Minneapolis: Fortress, 2007), pp. 102–6; Warren Carter, 'Singing in the Reign: Performing Luke's Songs and Negotiating the Roman Empire (Luke 1–2)', in *Luke-Acts and Empire: Essays in Honor of Robert L. Brawley* (ed. David Rhoads, David Esterline and Jae Won Lee; Princeton Theological Monograph Series, 151; Eugene, OR: Pickwick, 2011), pp. 23–43 (28, 30–41).

17. Ashon T. Crawley, *Blackpentecostal Breath: The Aesthetics of Possibility* (New York: Fordham University Press, 2017), pp. 1–2. I return to this work in Chapter 4.

18. The recovery of an Earth 'voice' or 'voices' in human words is itself problematic, as Gene Tucker and David Horrell show in different ways, but it is also akin to a feminist recovery of suppressed women's voices, as Elaine Wainwright argues. See, Earth Bible Team, 'Conversations with Gene Tucker and Other Writers', in *The Earth Story in Genesis* (ed. Norman C. Habel and Shirley Wurst; Earth Bible, 2; Sheffield: Sheffield Academic, 2000), pp. 21–33 (29–30); David G. Horrell, 'Ecological Hermeneutics: Reflections on Method and Prospects for the Future', *Colloquium* 46, no. 2 (November 2014), pp. 139–65 (156). Cf. Elaine M. Wainwright's response to Horrell, *Colloquium* 4, no. 2 (November 2014), pp. 166–9 and the earlier Earth Bible Team, 'The Voice of the Earth: More Than Metaphor?', in *The Earth Story in the Psalms and the Prophets* (ed. Norman C. Habel; Earth Bible, 4; Sheffield: Sheffield Academic, 2001), pp. 23–8. I explore the problems and possibilities of this concept of Earth voice more fully in Chapter 3.

19. Habel, 'Introducing Ecological Hermeneutics', p. 4.

20. Habel, 'Introducing Ecological Hermeneutics', p. 4.

one way of affirming this ecological connection and kinship. The hermeneutic of identification is a necessary step between suspicion and retrieval, one requiring of the interpreter an ecological conversion to the other, to Earth as other.[21]

It is important to note two things sometimes elided when ecological conversion and related transformations are called forth. First is the indebtedness of much ecological thinking to First Nations cultures and perspectives.[22] The Earth Bible Team acknowledges learning from, and collaboration with, the First Peoples of what is now called Australia.[23] Notably, for First Peoples Earth is not 'other'; rather land or in Australian Aboriginal English, 'Country', is people's material context and home. Country is a proper noun: 'People talk about country in the same way that they would talk about a person: they speak to country, sing to country, visit country, worry about country, feel sorry for country, and long for country. People say that country knows, hears, smells, takes notice, takes care, is sorry or happy.'[24] As Garry Deverell explains: Country 'represents, also, a place of sacred communion with our ancestors, a communion in which we might learn both who

---

21. Vicky Balabanski, 'The Step of "Identification" in Norman Habel's Ecological Hermeneutics: Hermeneutical Reflections on "Ecological Conversion"', in *Where the Wild Ox Roams: Biblical Essays in Honour of Norman C. Habel* (ed. Alan H. Cadwallader with Peter L. Trudinger; HBM, 59; Sheffield: Sheffield Phoenix, 2013), pp. 20-31.

22. Writing of the emerging field of 'peace ecology', e.g., Úrsula Oswald Spring, Hans Günter Brauch and Keith G. Tidball comment that the '*ecology* concept coined by Ernst Haeckel (1834-1919)' was 'developed by many scientists from different disciplines and world regions, based in part upon observations of indigenous cultures in the Americas, in China, India and the Middle East where knowledge on the use and dangers of plants and animals were crucial for human survival and cultural development'. Úrsula Oswald Spring, Hans Günter Brauch and Keith G. Tidball, 'Expanding Peace Ecology: Peace, Security, Sustainability, Equity, and Gender', in *Expanding Peace Ecology: Peace, Security, Sustainability, Equity and Gender. Perspectives of IPRA's Ecology and Peace Commission* (ed. Úrsula Oswald Spring, Hans Günter Brauch and Keith G. Tidball; Springer Briefs in Environment, Security, Development and Peace, Peace and Security Studies, 12; Cham, Switzerland: Springer, 2014), pp. 1-30 (6), emphasis in original.

23. Norman C. Habel, 'Introducing the Earth Bible', in *Readings from the Perspective of Earth* (ed. Norman C. Habel; Earth Bible, 1; Sheffield: Sheffield Academic, 2000), pp. 25-37 (26); Earth Bible Team, 'Guiding Ecojustice Principles', in *Readings from the Perspective of Earth* (ed. Norman C. Habel; Earth Bible, 1; Sheffield: Sheffield Academic, 2000), pp. 38-53 (52); so, too, Environmental Humanities scholars like Deborah Bird Rose, 'Country and the Gift', in *Humanities for the Environment: Integrating Knowledge, Forging New Constellations of Practice* (ed. Joni Adamson and Michael Davis; London: Routledge, 2017), pp. 33-44 (33).

24. Deborah Bird Rose, *Nourishing Terrains: Australian Aboriginal Views of Landscape and Wilderness* (Canberra: Australian Heritage Commission, 1996), p. 6; Garry Worete Deverell, *Gondwana Theology: A Trawloolway Man Reflects on Christian Faith* (Reservoir, Vic.: Morning Star Publishing, 2018), p. 14.

we are and what our unique vocation or responsibility in the world might be'.[25] Country is alive and active.

Second is this: the implied addressee of calls to ecological conversion is generally western, or western-influenced, since it is the colonizing regimes, including the slave trade, of European and North American industrialization and capitalism that historically prompted and exacerbated climate change, and related ecological traumas, including biodiversity loss, extinctions and pollution. A 'logic of colonization' is a mode of thinking and action modelled on the relation between master and enslaved; the unacknowledged dependence of the privileged on those they construct as other is entrenched in hyper-separate pairings, such as human/animal where the first 'term' is seen as superior and opposed to the second.[26] In this othering, those constructed as other tend to be cross-identified, so that 'nature' for example is feminized, and both women and Earth are subject to appropriative violence.

Against this colonizing context, the otherness of Earth is such that human beings, and human communities, interpreters and readers, are enmeshed and entangled with Earth. Identification with Earth is complex, entailing not so much an identification with an 'other' from which/whom humans stand separate but an identification that may prompt biblical readers to know themselves otherwise, to know themselves through a reorientation towards another frame of reference. In this frame, readers understand themselves as enmeshed, and sharing habitation, with many others, entangled in life-affirming and death-dealing ways through material agencies of sustenance, coexistence and power. Elaine Wainwright proposes that readers bring to the interpretation of biblical texts the concept of 'habitat' as locus of the entanglements that shape more-than-human co-being.[27] She writes that: 'Habitat is not just place in its materiality but place in which materiality is inextricably linked to sociality'.[28] Situating readers in the context of their more-than-human relationships becomes a basis for identification with other kind. As Vicky Balabanski argues, identification requires imagination, self-reflection, critique and, cautiously, a 'self-transcendence' where transcendence means going beyond 'the narrowly defined individualized self'; such identification requires an ability to draw connections.[29]

---

25. Deverell, *Gondwana Theology*, p. 11.

26. Val Plumwood, *Feminism and the Mastery of Nature* (Feminism for Today; London: Routledge, 1993), esp. pp. 41–68; idem, 'Decolonizing Relationships with Nature', in *Decolonizing Nature: Strategies for Conservation in a Post-colonial Era* (ed. William M. Adams and Martin Mulligan; London: Earthscan, 2003), pp. 51–78.

27. Elaine M. Wainwright, 'Images, Words, Stories: Exploring Their Transformative Power in Reading Biblical Texts Ecologically', *BibInt* 20 (2012), pp. 280–304 (292-3); idem, *Habitat, Human, and Holy: An Eco-Rhetorical Reading of the Gospel of Matthew* (Earth Bible Commentary, 6; Sheffield: Sheffield Phoenix, 2016).

28. Wainwright, *Habitat, Human, and Holy*, p. 21.

29. Balabanski, 'Step of "Identification"', pp. 22-3, 31.

A hermeneutic of retrieval builds on identification and ideally employs writing styles that invite from readers sympathetic and empathic identification with Earth others, or that shift the perception of the readers' anthropocentrism or their habitual identifications with human concerns.[30] Such writing needs to offer more than discursive language that tells the reader what to think but does not 'turn the breath' towards empathy; it needs to employ effective creative language in order to occasion a turn in human perception of ourselves in relation to Earth, and so to enable a more attentive and less destructive mode of human dwelling and acting in the Earth community.[31] Much as Elisabeth Schüssler Fiorenza argues in a feminist frame, the three hermeneutics (suspicion, identification and retrieval) are not simply applied consecutively but form a circle or web, so that suspicion is re-applied to our ecological identifications and retrievals, with an ear for example to where an ecological interpretation may be 'colonizing the referent', namely Earth or members of Earth community.[32]

A key part of the retrieval process is to discern 'Earth and members of Earth community as subjects with a voice'.[33] As Habel explains, 'In some contexts, their voices are evident but have been traditionally ignored by exegetes. In other contexts the voice of Earth and Earth community is not explicit, but nevertheless present and powerful.'[34] The question concerning whether 'Earth voice' is metaphor or more than metaphor points to an important question about the relationship between Earth and human language, and is a question of the materiality of language and texts themselves.[35] That metaphor is lively is in no small part due to the liveliness of that to which it refers.[36] That the retrieval of an Earth voice occurs in human speech acts and written texts can prompt readers to consider their materiality, their status as 'bits' of Earth, including atmosphere/air, albeit mediated by way of more-than-human labour.[37]

30. I experiment with creative writing in this vein, in Anne Elvey, *Reading the Magnificat in Australia: Unsettling Engagements* (Sheffield: Sheffield Phoenix, 2020).

31. The concept of turning the breath comes from the great post-Holocaust poet Paul Celan, 'The Meridian' (trans. Rosemarie Waldrop), in *Selections* (ed. and with an introduction by Pierre Joris; Berkeley: University of California Press, 2005), pp. 154–69 (162).

32. Elisabeth Schüssler Fiorenza, *But She Said: Feminist Practices of Biblical Interpretation* (Boston: Beacon, 1992), pp. 52–76; Jonathan Skinner, 'Thoughts on Things: Poetics of the Third Landscape', in *)((ECO(LANG)(UAGE(READER))): The Eco Language Reader* (ed. Brenda Iijima; New York: Portable Press at Yo-Yo Labs and Nightboat Books, 2010), pp. 9–51 (39).

33. Habel, 'Introducing Ecological Hermeneutics', p. 5.

34. Habel, 'Introducing Ecological Hermeneutics', p. 5.

35. Earth Bible Team, 'Voice of the Earth', pp. 23–8.

36. Paul Ricoeur, *The Rule of Metaphor: The Creation of Meaning in Language* (trans. Robert Czerny, Kathleen McLaughlin and John Costello, SJ; Routledge Classics; London: Routledge, 2003), p. 48.

37. See Anne Elvey, *The Matter of the Text: Material Engagements between Luke and the Five Senses* (BMW, 37; Sheffield: Sheffield Phoenix, 2011).

Furthermore, instances in the Bible when 'nonhuman figures' communicate 'in some way – mourning, praising, and singing', suggest that the principle of voice is in effect already a biblical principle.[38] Earth itself is responsive.[39] There is in play, especially in the Hebrew Bible, a biblical animism, that readers should not assume is outside the background of the Gospel narratives (and other Second Testament writings). An understanding of land, sea, sky and other animals as potential (and potent) respondents to each other, to humans and to the divine, is part of the Hebrew scriptural ethos inherited by first century CE biblical writers and their hearers (see, e.g., Lk. 19.40).[40] The ecojustice principle of voice, therefore, is not simply a metaphor enabling biblical interpreters to attend to an Earth community of which humans are part, as if Earth had a voice like a human subject. The principle of voice is also a biblical principle, evident in the psalms (e.g., Ps. 98.7-9), which can be read as expressing a biblical animism where Earth has subjecthood and agency.

The senses play a key role in mediating an Earth voice, because like other animals, through the senses humans are immersed in the materiality – of Earth and cosmos – that flows over our skin or hide, in and through our nostrils, mouths, ears, eyes, antennae and so on. As Heather Eaton writes: 'To experience the Earth as a "speaking" subject, a living entity, is to engage all of the senses.'[41] Moreover, not only the senses but also, more particularly, life-sustaining bodily processes, such as breathing and eating, mediate human interconnectedness with the Earth community of which we are part.

While all animals breathe while they live, it is perhaps the activity of eating (and drinking) that marks the relation of the animal to the question of a life sufficiently sustained or otherwise. Myriad human beings remain unable to feed themselves adequately, and the question of other animals forced into poverty through loss of food sources and habitat needs to be considered as part of the interpretive context for contemporary readers. The Magnificat specifically recalls

---

38. Habel, 'Introducing Ecological Hermeneutics', p. 5.

39. See, e.g., the discussion in Brian J. Walsh, Marianne B. Karsh, and Nik Ansell, 'Trees, Forestry, and the Responsiveness of Creation', in *This Sacred Earth: Religion, Nature, Environment* (ed. Roger S. Gottlieb; New York: Routledge, 1996), pp. 423-35.

40. See the discussion in Karen J. Wenell, *Jesus and Land: Sacred and Social Space in Second Temple Judaism* (London: T&T Clark, 2007), esp. pp. 1-2, 6-7. See also, Michael Trainor, *About Earth's Child: An Ecological Listening to the Gospel of Luke* (Earth Bible Commentary, 2; Sheffield: Sheffield Phoenix, 2012), pp. 10-11, where Trainor argues that 'Luke's inheritance of the Genesis accounts of creation… [is] reflected in his portrait of Jesus'.

41. Heather Eaton, 'Ecofeminist Contributions to an Ecojustice Hermeneutics', in *Readings from the Perspective of Earth* (ed. Norman C. Habel; Earth Bible, 1; Sheffield: Sheffield Academic, 2000), pp. 54-71 (66).

the hungry, and in the context of the wider Lukan narrative the song's references to power also remind the reader of related issues of land tenure and work under imperial rule.[42]

The Magnificat

Mary's song comes towards the close of the visitation episode (Lk. 1.39-56), where, rather than focusing on the supposed competition between two sons (yet *in utero*), as many commentators were once wont to do, the scene depicts two women who, it can be argued, mediate the divine to each other (with the breath/spirit as catalyst, and through the breath/voice of prophecy and blessing).[43] Moreover, this mediation can be seen as an inter-generational mentoring between women, a sign of female-empowered resilience in situations of oppression.[44] The song then becomes part of a pattern of call-response between two women, where pregnant bodies already mediate the kind of gift relation that occurs between Earth (through local habitats) and animals (including humans). While I am not arguing for speaking of Earth in maternal language, as Mother Earth, nonetheless Earth and the pregnant body have characteristics in common precisely in regard to their necessity for certain forms of life, a necessity that can be figured as a material givenness that is gift-like.[45]

Spoken into this context of the gift-like givenness of Earth life, the Magnificat echoes the songs of Miriam (Exod. 15.19-21) and Hannah (1 Sam. 2.1-10), in the tradition of women's songs of victory, liberation and thanksgiving. Mary is a prophet in the tradition of Miriam, Judith and Deborah, proclaiming 'God's victorious power in song and dance'.[46] 'These are not sweet lullabies', writes Barbara Reid; 'they are militant songs that exult in the saving power of God that

---

42. As I discuss more fully in Chapter 7, imperial sovereignty, systems of debt and master-slave relations need to be accounted for when studying ancient biblical texts. See, e.g., Richard A. Horsley, 'Jesus and Empire', in *In the Shadow of Empire: Reclaiming the Bible as a History of Faithful Resistance* (ed. Richard A. Horsley; Louisville: Westminster John Knox, 2008), pp. 75–96 (94–5); Sharon Ringe, *Luke* (Westminster Bible Companion; Louisville: Westminster John Knox, 1995), p. 183.

43. Anne Elvey, 'The Fertility of God: A Study of the Characterizations of Pseudo-Philo's Hannah and Luke's Mary' (unpublished TheolM Dissertation, Melbourne College of Divinity, Biblical Studies, 1994).

44. See, e.g., Stephanie Buckhanon Crowder, 'Another View of Community Mothering', in *Luke 1–9* (ed. Barbara E. Reid, OP, and Shelly Matthews; Wisdom Commentary; Collegeville: Liturgical Press, 2021), pp. 39–41. This collaborative feminist commentary by principal co-authors Barbara Reid and Shelly Matthews interpolates a selection of voices throughout in shaded text boxes.

45. Anne Elvey, *An Ecological Feminist Reading of the Gospel of Luke: A Gestational Paradigm* (Studies in Women and Religion, 45; Lewiston, NY: Edwin Mellen, 2005), pp. 98–102.

46. Reid, 'Overture', p. 429.

has brought defeat to those who had subjugated God's people. In the same vein, Mary's song declares the overthrow of Roman imperial ways and the triumph of God's reign.[47] Since at least the 1980s, the Magnificat has been received in Latin America, by liberation theologians and grassroots Christian communities as a 'rallying cry for political and social change'.[48] The Magnificat can be understood, along with the other songs of Luke's infancy narratives, as a protest song having the following dynamics: 'naming contexts of oppressive suffering', 'bestowing dignity', 'fostering hope for change' and 'securing communal solidarity'.[49] Mary's song names oppressive suffering in the references to humiliation and hunger, for example. Dignity appears in the use of voice to affirm divine favour and in appeals to ancestry. The proclamation of reversals and the recollection of divine promise foster hope for change. The song's recounting not only experiences of oppression but also shared ancestry and relation with the divine secures communal solidarity. With echoes of the exodus in her song, Luke's Mary, 'stands in direct line with Miriam and Hannah and sings of the same liberating and world-transforming God'.[50] But I am suspicious of a 'world-transforming God'; is Earth considered as agent, victim or otherwise in this transformation that is sung as liberating for humans?[51] Do human and wider Earth liberation coincide?

In the song of protest that Luke's Mary sings in a human woman's voice the reader can attend to an Earth voice in at least four ways:

1. through the materiality of the text;
2. through attention to the human body, especially the senses and the breath;
3. through attention to the sustaining capacity of Earth in relation to poverty and riches; and
4. through the implicit reference to the land in the promise to the ancestors.

An Earth voice in the Magnificat

Earth speaks through the materiality of the text The text itself is not simply words in koine Greek or in translation; rather the words of the song, its rhythms, the voice of the speaker or singers and the media in which the song comes to us across

---

47. Reid, 'Overture', p. 429. See also, idem, *Taking Up the Cross*, pp. 102–6.
48. Reid and Matthews, *Luke 1–9*, p. 43.
49. Warren Carter, 'Singing in the Reign: Performing Luke's Songs and Negotiating the Roman Empire (Luke 1–2)', in *Luke–Acts and Empire: Essays in Honor of Robert L. Brawley* (ed. David Rhoads, David Esterline, and Jae Won Lee; Princeton Theological Monograph Series, 151; Eugene, OR: Pickwick, 2011), pp. 23–43 (28, 30–41).
50. Gail O'Day, 'Singing Woman's Song: A Hermeneutic of Liberation', *CurTM* 12, no. 4 (August 1985), pp. 203–10 (205).
51. Norman Habel, *An Inconvenient Text: Is a Green Reading of the Bible Possible?* (Adelaide: ATF Press, 2009).

the centuries each have their own materiality, their Earthiness.[52] Bach's Magnificat in E flat major performed in Melbourne by the Brandenburg Orchestra and Choir on 22 February 2014 is one particular material instance (and interpretation) of this biblical song. The Greek version I can call up on screen in my Accordance software is another very different instance (with its links to a variety of metadata from commentaries and lexica). In the former, the breath of a cast of singers gives voice to the song, and the music interprets the lyrics in joyful, solemn and triumphal ways. In the latter, the breath is muted; the fan of the computer whirrs, but the breathing in the song itself appears in the spaces of white light between the black text on the screen, in the hyper-connections being made between primary and secondary texts, and in the breath of the producers and programmers of these texts and their electronic connections. Underlying these texts are the multiple intersecting relations of more-than human producers and sustainers of the texts as they appear in specific instances (e.g. the creatures and habitats that provide sustenance and shelter to the musicians and their audience to enable them to gather at the Melbourne Recital Centre on one Saturday night in February; or the plastics and metals, the transformed fossils and ores, that constitute this computer on which I can call up an electronic text).

To this extent, Mary's song, like every human text, speaks in more-than-human Earth voices. While it is important to affirm both the qualities of difference and continuity of humans and other than humans, it is necessary also to remember that humans, as Gen. 2.7 has it, are groundlings, Earth creatures, breathing members of an Earth community.[53] Human voices, born on the air and in the materiality of a text, are Earth voices, albeit partial, particular and limited.

Orality studies may be of assistance for reading the text with an ear to the rhythms of the breath that connect humans, their habitats and the atmosphere.[54] Richard Horsley suggests setting out the Greek text to show some of the movements

---

52. Here, for instance, the question of the original language of the song has a different resonance, since the human breath is marked differently in languages with vowels and those without. See, e.g., Stephen Farris, *The Hymns of Luke's Infancy Narratives* (JSNTSup, 9; Sheffield: JSOT Press, 1985), pp. 31–66. Moreover, the poetics itself may give evidence of its original language. Randall Buth argues that the shifts in tenses in the song are an aesthetic device employed in Hebrew poetry but not in Greek. This device has been carried over into the Greek song in the Lukan infancy narrative. Whether Buth is correct that there is an underlying Hebrew original, he offers evidence for Luke's use of this Semitic aesthetic device, from adoption and adaptation of a prior Hebrew song or songs, or from his familiarity with Semitic aesthetics as passed on in Greek translations or otherwise. See Randall Buth, 'Hebrew Poetic Tenses and the Magnificat', *JSNT* 21 (1984), pp. 67–83.

53. Plumwood, *Feminism*, p. 6.

54. See, e.g., Richard A. Horsley, Jonathan A. Draper, John Miles Foley and Werner H. Kelber, *Performing the Gospel: Orality, Memory, and Mark* (Minneapolis: Fortress, 2006).

	Μεγαλύνει	ἡ ψυχή μου	τὸν κύριον,
καὶ	ἠγαλλίασεν	τὸ πνεῦμά μου	ἐπὶ τῷ θεῷ τῷ σωτῆρί μου,

ὅτι ἐπέβλεψεν ἐπὶ τὴν ταπείνωσιν τῆς δούλης αὐτοῦ.
ἰδοὺ γὰρ ἀπὸ τοῦ νῦν μακαριοῦσίν με πᾶσαι αἱ γενεαί,

ὅτι ἐποίησέν μοι μεγάλα ὁ δυνατός.
καὶ ἅγιον τὸ ὄνομα αὐτοῦ,

καὶ τὸ ἔλεος αὐτοῦ
εἰς γενεὰς καὶ γενεὰς
τοῖς φοβουμένοις αὐτόν.

Ἐποίησεν κράτος ἐν βραχίονι αὐτοῦ,
διεσκόρπισεν ὑπερηφάνους διανοίᾳ καρδίας αὐτῶν.

καθεῖλεν δυνάστας ἀπὸ θρόνων
καὶ ὕψωσεν ταπεινούς,

πεινῶντας ἐνέπλεσεν ἀγαθῶν
καὶ πλουτοῦντας ἐξαπέστειλεν κενούς.

ἀντελάβετο Ἰσραὴλ παιδὸς αὐτοῦ,
μνησθῆναι ἐλέους,

καθὼς ἐλάλησεν πρὸς τοὺς πατέρας ἡμῶν,
τῷ Ἀβραὰμ
καὶ τῷ σπέρματι αὐτοῦ εἰς τὸν αἰῶνα.

Figure 2 Magnificat.

of the writing as it might have worked orally.[55] The above is my setting out of Lk. 1.46b-55.

The spaces are a visual way of representing the breath. Parallels, repetitions and echoes suggest interpretation. The trope of reversal is heightened by parallels that work as contrasts, for example, in lines 13 and 14, δυνάστας (the mighty/powerful)/ταπεινούς (the humble/humiliated) (1.52). In lines 4 and 5, the long vowels followed by σιν – ωσιν and οῦσίν, at the ends of ταπείνωσιν (humiliation) and μακαριοῦσίν ([they] will call happy/blessed) respectively – suggest an echo.[56]

55. Richard A. Horsley, 'Oral Communication, Oral Performance, and New Testament Interpretation', in *Method and Meaning: Essays on New Testament Interpretation in Honor of Harold W. Attridge* (ed. Andrew B. McGowan and Kent Harold Richards; Atlanta: SBL, 2011), pp. 125–55 (151).

56. These echoes occur even though ταπείνωσιν functions as a noun and μακαριοῦσίν as a verb.

The aural echo leads the auditor to hear these words together: humiliation and beatitude. Paralleling the two verbs ἐπέβλεψεν ([G-d] has looked) and μακαριοῦσίν ([they] will call happy/blessed) is another possibility (1.48). But Luke has brought together Hannah's proclamation of her humiliation in 1 Sam. 1.11 (LXX) and Leah's exclamation of good fortune in Gen. 30.13 (LXX).[57] The reversal of the fortunes of rich and poor, oppressor and oppressed, is anticipated in the singer's experience of beatitude in her humiliation. Hearing ταπείνωσιν echoing μακαριοῦσίν also recalls Elizabeth's makarism in relation to Mary in the visitation (Lk. 1.45). In the Magnificat, Mary's humiliation becomes fortunate, not because humiliation – 'social, political, or sexual' – is affirmed in itself, but through the affirmation that: the humiliations of violence, abuse and oppression do not define the survivor/s.[58]

Where Elizabeth spoke the beatitude in Lk. 1.45, all generations will speak it from now (1.48). Generations are repeated in the song, at 1.48 and 1.50 leading back at the end to previous generations, the ancestors, and present and future descendants of those ancestors into the ages (1.54-55).[59] The interplay between parent and child, ancestors and descendants, is expressed in verses 54 and 55 through this pattern:

Israel, G-d's servant/child
    our fathers/ancestors
    Abraham
his seed/descendants.

In relation to Israel, there is a crossing between the divine and the patriarchal ancestor Abraham. In an ecological framework I am tempted to read the generations of the people Israel as more-than-human generations, though I am not sure that

---

57. Farris, *Hymns of Luke's Infancy*, p. 25.

58. I accept that the Lukan Mary is the speaker of the song. Noting the reference to Hannah's song, recalling her barrenness, and in particular the humiliation of the speaker, ancient scribes and scholars have questioned whether Elizabeth perhaps was the intended speaker of the song, but the reference to humiliation accompanies the speaker's self-description as slave (δούλη, 1.48) echoing Mary's self-description in 1.38. Moreover, the Greek textual tradition supports the acceptance of Mary as speaker. See further, François Bovon, *Luke 1: A Commentary on the Gospel of Luke 1:1–9:50* (trans. Christine M. Thomas; Hermeneia, 63A; ed. Helmut Koester; Accordance electronic edn; Minneapolis: Fortress, 2002), p. 60. On translating ταπείνωσιν as 'humiliation', see Joseph A. Fitzmyer, *The Gospel According to Luke I-IX: Introduction, Translation, and Notes* (New York: Doubleday, 1981), p. 367. See further, Reid and Matthews, *Luke 1–9*, pp. 49–50; Jane Schaberg, *The Illegitimacy of Jesus: A Feminist Theological Interpretation of the Infancy Narratives* (New York: Crossroad, 1990), pp. 97–8.

59. The movement from past to future is already at play in Lk. 1.48 in the aorist 'already' of ἐπέβλεψεν and the 'to come' of the future μακαριοῦσίν.

the text can be pushed this far.⁶⁰ Although the generations in Mary's song seem to refer later to the ancestral line, described patriarchally, the reference in Lk. 1.48b to Leah's exclamation in Gen. 30.13 reminds the reader of women's proclamations of good fortune, but this recollection is at best ambiguous. On the one hand there is Elizabeth's proclamation in Lk. 1.45; on the other there is an unnamed woman's makarism in 11.27 which the Lukan Jesus apparently corrects in 11.28, potentially eliding the maternal.⁶¹ Nonetheless, the generations' proclamation of makarism need not be confined to the patriarchal lineage of Abraham (1.54-55) nor to human generations in isolation from the rest of creation. At the very least, the ecological reader can affirm the more-than-human interrelationships and interdependencies of these human generations, especially in considering the way the biblical language of generation evokes covenant and promise (1.55). One challenge today is to situate this generational imagination in relation not only to past humans, but to my planetary ancestors and kin, and to future generations, that are also more than human. Climate change makes me responsible for a deep future.⁶²

Earth speaks to and through the body, the human senses and the breath Human generations are linked to more-than-human generations through the sensing body embedded in its habitat. In his work on the five senses, Michel Serres describes a sixth or inner sense, necessary to the operation of the five 'external senses'.⁶³ Each of the senses (touch, taste, smell, sight, hearing) mediates an interchange of matter, light or sound waves, between the body and its habitat. The inner sense enfolds and interprets this interchange in the body, at the point where the personal subject and the subjecthood of Earth are in communion.⁶⁴ I want to suggest the Greek ψυχή (life, soul, psyche) conveys something like this inner sense, and represents in the text a potential point of connection between the voice of a woman and the voice of Earth. Rather than translating ψυχή as 'soul', the Greek word is better understood as 'life'.⁶⁵ Ψυχή, the eating, breathing life of the creature, is shaped by habitat; it can be enculturated in its place.

---

60. But see Kathleen P. Rushton's work on the ecological and cosmic scope of πάντα in the Johannine Prologue: 'The Cosmology of John 1:1-14 and Its Implications for Ethical Action in this Ecological Age', *Colloquium* 45, no. 2 (November 2013), pp. 137-53 (148-50).

61. Elvey, *Ecological Feminist Reading*, pp. 141-2, 153-4.

62. Richard W. Miller, 'Deep Responsibility for the Deep Future', *TS* 77, no. 2 (2016), pp. 436-65.

63. Michel Serres, *The Five Senses: A Philosophy of Mingled Bodies (I)* (trans. Margaret Sankey and Peter Cowley; London: Continuum, 2008 [Fre. 1985]), pp. 53-5.

64. Serres, *Five Senses*, p. 306.

65. Ulrich Luz, *Matthew 1-7: A Commentary on Matthew 1-7* (trans. James E. Crouch; Hermeneia, 61A; ed. Helmut Koester; Accordance electronic edn; Minneapolis: Fortress, 2007), p. 342.

Parallel with ψυχή in the song is the Greek word πνεῦμα. For Reid:

> Mary proclaims God's greatness with her whole being (v. 47). The Greek terms *psychē*, 'soul', and *pneuma*, 'spirit', are not different parts of the human, nor should they be understood as opposed to *sōma*, 'body', or *sarx*, 'flesh'. Rather, each term describes the whole human person as viewed from a particular perspective. Soul, *psychē*, refers to the whole living being, equivalent to the Hebrew *nepeš*. 'It expresses the vitality, consciousness, intelligence, and volition of a human being.' The meaning of *pneuma* is barely distinguishable from that of *psychē*. It suggests the aspect of the self that is particularly able to receive the Spirit. Both terms can be used simply as a substitute for the personal pronoun, 'I'. Mary, like Elizabeth, recognizes God in bodiliness, conception, and incarnation, not as removed to a purely spiritual plane. She proclaims this with her whole being.[66]

This emphasis on embodiment is important for an ecological reading, but I need also to recall that the word πνεῦμα, so often translated as 'spirit' in Second Testament writings means, as I noted earlier in this chapter, 'blowing', 'breathing', 'breath', '(life-)spirit', sometimes also 'wind',[67] and takes the reader back to the Hebrew concept רוח, that connects air, wind, breath and the sacred.[68] When the Lukan Mary sings, 'my breath exults/rejoices', the reader can hear the intake and exhalation of the breath, the living interplay of a human creature and the air/atmosphere. Considering air and atmosphere is a prompt to recollect that in many places today air is polluted and the atmosphere is warming in ways of dire concern for humans, and of violence also towards many other Earth kind.

The Lukan Mary feels the violence of others in her whole being (ψυχή) (2.35). Losing and saving life (ψυχή) is central to the Lukan project of liberation (6.9, 9.24, 17.33). In the parable of the rich fool, who stores up goods against the future, this concept of saving and losing life is performed. The man speaks to his life/soul (ψυχή) as if to a companion: 'And I will say to my soul (ψυχή), "soul (ψυχή), you have ample goods laid up for many years; relax, eat, drink, be merry"' (12.19). He is deluded: 'But G-d said to him, "You fool! This very night your life (ψυχή) is being demanded of you. And the things you have prepared, whose will they be?"' (12.20). In the logic of the parable, the rich fool is storing death when he attempts to secure life. This occurs in our own time when Earth is treated as resource, and matter as 'dead' matter, so that extracting and burning fossil fuels, manufacturing and discarding plastics, for example, occur as if these activities are exempt from Earth processes of life, death, life. Many of us find ourselves participants in a 'double death', where whole species, communities and cultures are extinguished or nearly so.[69]

---

66. Barbara E. Reid, *Choosing the Better Part? Women in the Gospel of Luke* (Collegeville: Liturgical Press, 1996), pp. 76–7.

67. BAGD, pp. 674–5.

68. Hiebert, 'Air'.

69. Deborah Bird Rose, 'Double Death', Love at the Edge of Extinction, available online: https://deborahbirdrose.com/144-2/ (accessed 3 July 2019).

The parable of storing up is followed by sayings attributed to Jesus: 'He said to his disciples, "Therefore I tell you, do not worry about your life (ψυχή), what you will eat, or about your body, what you will wear. For life (ψυχή) is more than food, and the body more than clothing"' (12.22-23). The Lukan Jesus continues 'Consider the ravens… Consider the lilies…'. At a first glance, these references to lilies and ravens seem friendly to an ecological ear, but they are ambiguous. The Semitic 'and how much more so' argument puts humans above these other creatures; at the same time all creatures, including humans, are described as recipients of divine care. Yet, 'do not be anxious' could be read as a licence to neglect ecological concern.

While the crowd is the audience for the parable of the rich fool, the disciples become the primary audience in 12.22 and following. They are probably not at this stage the rich fool who is storing up death, but perhaps they wish for the security of storehouses. Instead, they are challenged to receive as gift their embeddedness in the web of creation. In a contemporary situation this may be a challenge to recognize more deeply that my life/psyche is enmeshed or entangled with a wider creation, and to divest not simply from fossil fuel investments but from the kinds of behaviours that keep me storing up death. This is not once for all, because many of us live in a social order that pushes us towards and rewards us for our foolishness.

Earth, poverty and riches The interplay of life and breath in the Magnificat is not simply a 'nice' idea to mark our life-giving connectedness. This connectedness itself is an entanglement with the death-dealing that humans as a species have occasioned in Earth's atmosphere and our own habitats more generally. The song of the Lukan Mary is alert to the death-dealing that accompanies the Roman empire. Her breath is shaped around a refashioning of the destructiveness of empire even as it in some ways reinforces imperial values through the imagery of divine might and the portrayal of 'political victory', which at this stage of the Lukan narrative is 'nationalistic'.[70] Beneath the imagery of lord (κύριος) and enslaved woman (δούλη), the language of opposition – of humility and pride, plenty and want – and the appeal to power, might and thrones, is the real experience of oppression and poverty, hunger and servitude.[71] The freedom of which the biblical Miriam, Hannah and Mary each sing celebrates the hoped-for material restoration of the basic necessities that have been taken from the

---

70. J. Massyngbaerde Ford, *My Enemy Is My Guest: Jesus and Violence in Luke* (Maryknoll, NY: Orbis Books, 1984), p. 21; Christopher M. Hays, *Luke's Wealth Ethics: A Study in Their Coherence and Character* (WUNT 2, 275; Tübingen: Mohr Siebeck, 2010), p. 102.

71. Trainor outlines the likely social composition of Luke's audience and their respective stances to Earth, suggesting that Luke's audience is diverse as regards social and economic status, but excludes the ruling elite and the very lowest classes; Trainor, *About Earth's Child*, pp. 26–38.

poor.⁷² Nonetheless, the Magnificat not only resists 'Roman imperial order', but with other songs of Luke's infancy narrative Mary's song 'also reflect[s] aspects of that same order'.⁷³ As Warren Carter explains,

> Mary describes herself in 1.48 as a slave of God, thereby expressing her relationship to God in the language of one of the empire's most oppressive structures. While it can be argued that the language thereby contestively refuses allegiance to earthly masters and ascribes it to God, it nevertheless reinscribes the relationship with God in terms of the dominant imperial structure of master and slave. A similar dynamic exists in her language of 'savior'.⁷⁴

Similarly, I need to be wary of Luke's use of the term 'the proud' (1.51); what is meant, Carter argues, is 'the destruction of those who oppose their dominant power's will and agenda'.⁷⁵

In contrast, Reid argues that the reclamation of imperial language for G-d is a deliberate counter-ideology, the alternative reign (βασιλεία) of G-d.⁷⁶ The reversal

---

72. O'Day, 'Singing Woman's Song', p. 209. See also Raymond E. Brown, *The Birth of the Messiah: A Commentary on the Infancy Narratives of Matthew and Luke* (New York: Image Books, 1979), p. 363. Brown comments on 'the real poverty' and 'physical realities faced by early Christians'.

73. Carter, 'Singing in the Reign', p. 42; see also, Reid and Matthews, *Luke 1–9*, pp. 44–7.

74. Carter, 'Singing in the Reign', p. 42. Enslaved woman (δούλη, Lk. 1.38, 48), is a term taken over from both Jewish and Roman traditions with multiple resonances: practical and metaphorical; economic and religious. See, e.g., John Byron, *Slavery Metaphors in Early Judaism and Pauline Christianity* (Tübingen: Mohr Siebeck, 2003). The imperial kyriarchal language of lord/master (κύριος) and enslaved woman (δούλη) stands beside the Jewish tradition of the servant of Yhwh. See, e.g., Elizabeth V. Dowling, *Taking Away the Pound: Women, Theology and the Parable of the Pounds in the Gospel of Luke* (London: T&T Clark International, 2007), pp. 128–9; Brigitte Kahl, 'Reading Luke Against Luke: Non-Uniformity of Text, Hermeneutics of Conspiracy and the "Scriptural Principle"', in *A Feminist Companion to Luke* (ed. Amy-Jill Levine with Marianne Blickenstaff; FCNTECW, 3; London: Sheffield Academic, 2002), pp. 70–88 (80). See also the discussion in Amy-Jill Levine and Ben Witherington III, *The Gospel of Luke* (New Cambridge Bible Commentary; Cambridge: Cambridge University Press, 2018), p. 37; Elvey, *Reading the Magnificat*, pp. 93–5.

75. Carter, 'Singing in the Reign', p. 42. Carter notes that in Virgil's *Aeneid* (6.851-53) it is Rome's purpose to 'crush the proud'. In the Magnificat, this purpose is ascribed to G-d.

76. Barbara E. Reid, 'Women Prophets of God's Alternative Reign', in *Luke-Acts and Empire* (ed. David Rhoads, David Esterline, and Jae Won Lee; Princeton Theological Monograph Series, 151; Eugene, OR: Pickwick, 2011), pp. 44–59. See also Reid, 'Overture', pp. 429–30. On counter-imperial strategies of resistance in Luke, see also, Kahl, 'Reading Luke against Luke', and Virginia Burrus, 'The Gospel of Luke and the Acts of the Apostles', in *A Postcolonial Commentary on the New Testament Writings* (ed. Fernando F. Segovia and R. S. Sugitharajah; London: T&T Clark, 2009), pp. 133–55 (139–40).

of rich and poor, full and hungry – a theme not only in the Magnificat but in Luke's beatitudes and woes, Luke 16 and elsewhere – is part of this counter-ideology. The Lukan Mary 'subverts the system of enslaving subjected peoples by presenting herself as an empowered person who chooses to serve'.[77] The song, in its references to 'humiliation' (ταπείνωσιν) and the 'humbled/humiliated' (ταπεινούς) (1.48, 52), also 'voices the dream of having no more fear of sexual humiliation by occupying imperial forces'.[78]

In this breathy human singing of liberation for the poor and oppressed in the alternative reign (βασιλεία) of G-d, where is Earth? The material givenness of Earth; the life-sustaining capacities of soil, rain and sun; the more-than-human (including human) labour that makes possible the satiation of the hungry (including ravens); and the clothing of both lilies and disciples (12.24-28) must be retrieved for ecological readings.[79] The proclamation of an alternative reign (βασιλεία) requires this possibility: that Earth (and its climate) – however indifferently the soil might give itself to growing the seed, the rains and the sun to making ready the harvest – will give itself to the nourishment of the hungry. The imperial system of land debt, of lordship and absentee landlords, of peasants pushed into subsistence or beyond, also relies on the sustaining capacity of Earth, even where this is taken for profit.

What the song potentially proclaims, when read in the light of the Lukan Eucharistic feeding and last supper narratives, is a relationship to Earth where the capacity for Earth to sustain human life is received (not taken for profit) as gift.[80] In this grateful receptivity, oriented explicitly to G-d in the song is also the fissure: the imperial mode that links land and debt, that denies the gift, with all the potential for exploitation of Earth this might allow.

Earth and the promise to the ancestors The reference to what G-d spoke (ἐλάλησεν), that is, the promise to the ancestors (1.55), makes explicit that an alternative relation to land (and thus Earth) is at the heart of the Lukan vision for a rule that offers liberation for the hungry and enslaved. This reference recalls not only the promise of offspring (because of the context of the infancy narratives and the repetition of generations in 1.48, 50) but the promise of land. The promise to Abraham and to his seed (τῷ σπέρματι αὐτοῦ) is the promise of the land which invokes the biblical interrelationship between land, social justice, Torah/law and G-d. This relation to land, as I noted earlier, should not be read out of Second Testament texts because of silence; rather silence can

77. Reid, 'Women Prophets', p. 53. See also, Schaberg, *Illegitimacy of Jesus*, p. 100; Ringe, *Luke*, p. 34.

78. Reid, 'Women Prophets', p. 54.

79. Anne Elvey, 'Storing Up Death, Storing Up Life: An Earth Story in Luke 12:13-34', in *The Earth Story in the New Testament* (ed. Norman C. Habel and Vicky Balabanski; Earth Bible, 5; London: Sheffield Academic, 2002), pp. 95–107.

80. For an ecological reading of the feeding and last supper narratives, see, e.g., Elvey, *Matter of the Text*, pp. 175–7.

allow us to assume that the relation to land is inherent in such concepts as the twelve, and here in the Magnificat's reference to the ancestral promise.[81] Moreover, not only land but the story of creation lies within 'this narrative recall of the heritage of Israel's encounter with God's mercy'.[82] Mary's 'song of God's reign' is situated in Earth and cosmos; it is 'a mighty chorus [that] rises from the heart of humanity to fill the entire creation – the space-time of God's saving activity'.[83] By implication, the song promises more-than-human liberation; this is unsurprising since justice for humans and ecological flourishing are frequently enmeshed.

Conclusion

In this chapter, I have sketched a number of ways in which a text such as the Magnificat in the Gospel of Luke can be read with an ear to the voice of Earth, even where the text does not explicitly refer to other-than-human characters or interests. Through these sketches I have suggested that in the materiality of the text, the human voice of its speaker, the breath held in its language, the song's resistance to the death-dealing of empire, its reference to the biblical land promise (and the way that promise suggests a certain relationship to ecological justice) and the proclamation of good news for the poor (see also Lk. 4.18) can be heard together as conveying, albeit partially, an Earth voice.

In tension with this suggestion, I need also to hold the reality that Earth (and its climate) seems on some observation indifferent to the social, economic and power status of particular human groups, although not unaffected by these in terms of the damage such inequalities can occasion ecologically. As the encyclical of Pope Francis *Laudato Si'* insists, ecological destruction and human poverty are interrelated not only in their effects but in their root causes.[84] In terms of a contemporary ecological reading of the Lukan Magnificat, then, Earth occupies a complex position, as both potential sustainer of the hungry, coagent in their liberation and itself identifiable with 'the poor', while species become extinct, soils grow less fertile, seas warm, plastics form vast islands and pollution mars the atmosphere.

---

81. Wenell, *Jesus and Land*, pp. 104–38.
82. Trainor, *About Earth's Child*, p. 75.
83. C. S. Song, *Jesus and the Reign of God* (eBook; Minneapolis: Fortress, 1993), ch. 7.
84. Pope Francis, *Encyclical Letter Laudato Si' of the Holy Father Francis on Care for Our Common Home* (Australian edn; Strathfield, NSW: St Pauls, 2015). The United Nations Sustainable Development Goals address this nexus between ecological destruction and human poverty. See United Nations, Sustainable Development Knowledge Platform, available online: https://sustainabledevelopment.un.org/ (accessed 3 July 2019).

Attentiveness to an Earth voice, or better voices, in this context suggests less a creative 'writing' of these voices but a creative 'listening' through practices of interpretation attuned to a more-than-human Earth community.[85] Such is required for a hermeneutics of retrieval even where other-than-human characters or interests appear absent from the text. The next chapter explores the concept of an Earth voice further, and describes an orientation towards the holy as fundamental for a hermeneutics of retrieval that enacts a creative attunement towards Earth.

---

85. Trainor, *About Earth's Child*, esp. pp. 47–61.

Chapter 3

RETRIEVING AN EARTH VOICE: READING MATERIALLY 'AS IF IT'S HOLY'

If Earth has a voice, if Earth has a plenitude of more-than-human voices, how might I listen?[1] How as a reader might I retrieve an Earth voice from the texts I encounter? In this chapter, I address the question of the ecological hermeneutic of retrieval in relation to a concept of a material sacred, grounded in a sense of attunement to an Earth voice. I move from a focus on Earth voice to the hermeneutic mode of 'retrieving' an Earth voice. Late modern poetry and poetics offer me entry points for exploration of the disposition necessary for the exercise of a hermeneutic of retrieval. The relation between poetry and the human voice of the poet forms a basis for exploring the question of access to an Earth voice mediated through practices of writing and reading. Through readings of poems by Michelle Boisseau, Denise Levertov, Jennifer Harrison and William Carlos Williams, I argue for ecological hermeneutics of 'holy' attentiveness to material text and ecological context in a situation of colonial unsettlement.

A material sacred

In 1996 Routledge published a collection of writings under the title *This Sacred Earth* edited by Roger S. Gottlieb.[2] The subtitle of the 673 page collection, which included such staples as Lynn White's 1967 essay 'The Historical Roots of Our Ecological Crisis' and an excerpt from Annie Dillard's *Teaching a Stone to Talk*, was *Religion, Nature, Environment*.[3] A 2009 collection of Thomas Berry's writings

---

1. This chapter revises and builds on Anne Elvey, 'Retrieving an Earth Voice: Ecological Hermeneutics, the Matter of the Text and Reading "as if it's holy" (Jennifer Harrison, "Book Sculptor")', *AeJT* 22, no. 2 (August 2015), pp. 81–94.

2. Roger S. Gottlieb (ed.), *This Sacred Earth: Religion, Nature, Environment* (New York: Routledge, 1996).

3. Lynn White, 'The Historical Roots of Our Ecological Crisis' [1967], in *This Sacred Earth: Religion, Nature, Environment* (ed. Roger S. Gottlieb; New York: Routledge, 1996), pp. 184–93; Annie Dillard, 'Teaching a Stone to Talk', in *This Sacred Earth: Religion, Nature, Environment* (ed. Roger S. Gottlieb; New York: Routledge, 1996), pp. 32–6.

appeared under the title *The Sacred Universe* with a subtitle *Earth, Spirituality, and Religion in the Twenty-First Century*.[4] Published in 2012, Norman Habel's *Rainbow of Mysteries* carries the subtitle *Meeting the Sacred in Nature*.[5] These ecologically focused evocations of 'the sacred' are in debt to First Nations epistemologies and praxis expressed both in a spiritual orientation to land, sea and sky and concepts such as 'sacred sites'.[6] For Trawloolway theologian Garry Deverell, spirituality is 'an entirely ordinary, irreducibly earthy, way of life'; from his Indigenous Christian perspective, this way of life is 'informed and enabled by the Spirit of God'.[7] For First Nations in what is called colonially Australia, the land itself is a 'sacred text'.[8] In contexts of colonial invasion, many Indigenous peoples have been sundered from their sacred texts. The concept of 'sacred sites' is often at the crux of capitalist valuations of land as resource, especially for mining, with the accompanying ecological destruction of sacred places.[9]

Ecological concepts of a sacred Earth and a material sacred are also in debt to biblical, classical Greek, Latin and many other, including English, understandings

---

4. Thomas Berry, *The Sacred Universe: Earth, Spirituality, and Religion in the Twenty-First Century* (ed. Mary Evelyn Tucker; New York: Columbia University Press, 2009).

5. Norman Habel, *Rainbow of Mysteries: Meeting the Sacred in Nature* (eBook; Kelowna, BC: CopperHouse, 2012).

6. See, e.g., Leena Heinämäki and Thora Martina Herrmann (eds), *Experiencing and Protecting Sacred Natural Sites of Sámi and Other Indigenous Peoples: The Sacred Arctic* (1st edn; Springer Polar Sciences; Cham, Switzerland: Springer Nature, 2017); Natasha Bakht and Lynda Collins, '"The Earth Is Our Mother": Freedom of Religion and the Preservation of Indigenous Sacred Sites in Canada', *McGill Law Journal* 62, no. 3 (2017), pp. 777–812; Francesca Gottardi, 'Sacred Sites Protection and Indigenous Women's Activism: Empowering Grassroots Social Movements to Influence Public Policy. A Look into the "Women of Standing Rock" and "Idle No More" Indigenous Movements', *Religions* 11, no. 380 (2020), pp. 1–13; Aliza Taubman, 'Protecting Aboriginal Sacred Sites: The Aftermath of the Hindmarsh Island Dispute', *Environmental and Planning Law Journal* 19, no. 2 (2002), pp. 140–58; Thomas Wooden, 'The "1954 Hague Convention": Aboriginal and Torres Strait Islander Sacred Sites as Cultural Property', *Australian Year Book of International Law* 34 (2017), pp. 127–48.

7. Garry Worete Deverell, *Gondwana Theology: A Trawloolway Man Reflects on Christian Faith* (Reservoir, Vic.: Morning Star Publishing, 2018), p. 9.

8. Deverell, *Gondwana Theology*, p. 11.

9. Deverell, *Gondwana Theology*, p. 22; Lorena Allam and Calla Wahlquist, 'More Than 100 Aboriginal Sacred Sites – Some Dating before the Ice Age – Could Be Destroyed by Mining Companies', *The Guardian* (28 August 2020), available online: https://www.theguardian.com/australia-news/2020/aug/28/more-than-100-aboriginal-sacred-sites-some-dating-before-the-ice-age-could-be-destroyed-by-mining-companies (accessed 1 October 2020); Gary-Jon Lysaght, 'Indigenous Sacred Site Lake Torrens Faces Exploratory Drilling for Resources', ABC News, ABC North and West SA, available online: https://www.abc.net.au/news/2020-09-28/lake-torrens-sacred-site-faces-exploratory-mining/12696750 (accessed 1 October 2020).

of 'the sacred'. The English word 'sacred' derives through French from the Latin *sacer*, to be 'sacred, holy; dedicated for sacrifice', also, in some contexts, 'forfeited', even to be 'criminal' or 'accursed'.[10] In the NRSV the English word 'sacred' most commonly translates the Hebrew words קדשׁ and קדושׁ referring to the 'apartness, sacredness, or holiness' of G-d.[11] But 'sacred' rarely appears in the NRSV translation of the Second Testament; more common is the English 'holy' translating the Greek ἅγιος, 'a cultic concept, of the quality possessed by things and persons that could approach a divinity'.[12] The concepts of the sacred and the holy, and the adjectives deriving from these, contain the senses of being set apart (for) and sometimes also being close to the divine. The ambiguity in the pre-Christian etymology of the English 'holy' suggests not only a sense of 'wholeness', that resonates with the cultic use of the Hebrew קדשׁ, but also a link with health and good fortune, something which echoes the biblical notion of beatitude.[13]

Beyond dictionary definitions and concordance searches, 'the sacred' is a denser concept and experience. Aspects of wholeness, health and beatitude have resonance with an ecological thinking that emphasizes the interconnectedness and interdependence of things. As noted earlier, such ecological thinking resonates with and is in debt to First Nations whose understandings of land, kinship and law have informed ecological philosophies invoking the concept of the sacred. To this ecological sense, I bring the character of being 'set apart', inherent in biblical notions of the sacred. Such should not be taken to affirm a hyper-separation between spirit and matter but rather to indicate that an alterity must be accounted for in any consideration of a material sacred.

A number of ecologically focused scholars speak of a material sacred. For example, writing of a 'Presence permeating' Earth, Habel values the 'spiritual dimensions of nature' as 'mysteries'.[14] Gottlieb hopes his volume *This Sacred Earth* 'may fuel our awareness of what needs to be done even as it also helps remind us of our simple joy in the divinity of the earth'.[15] Berry refers to the 'spirit dimension of the Earth', as 'a quality of the Earth itself, not a human spirituality with special reference to the planet Earth'.[16] The qualification of the nouns Earth and cosmos with the adjective 'sacred' need not mean that Earth or cosmos should be identified with divinity, but that the sacred is characteristic of Earth.

---

10. 'sacer', *Collins Latin GEM Dictionary* (London: Collins, 1957), p. 294.

11. BDB, p. 871.

12. BAGD, pp. 9–10.

13. 'holy, adj. and n.', OED Online, June 2021, Oxford University Press, available online: https://www.oed.com/view/Entry/87833?isAdvanced=false&result=1&rskey=nuUqLS& (accessed 15 June 2021).

14. Habel, *Rainbow of Mysteries*, p. 9.

15. Roger S. Gottlieb, 'Introduction: Religion in an Age of Environmental Crisis', in *This Sacred Earth: Religion, Nature, Environment* (ed. Roger S. Gottlieb; New York: Routledge, 1996), pp. 3–14 (13).

16. Berry, *Sacred Universe*, p. 70.

Writing of the concept of the sacred in an Australian context, Lyn McCredden says, 'the contemporary sacred seeks to recognize and reconstruct what Luce Irigaray has often referred to as the incarnate, "sensible transcendent"…, a refusal to separate the corporeal and the spiritual, but a languaged, creative proposing of the one with the other'.[17] The corporeal is a subset of the material. Moreover, through the senses, bodies are sites of interagency and co-relation of matter with matter, of experiencing the self-in-relation materially.[18] When speaking of a material sacred, rather than imaging the divine as purely immanent in matter, and its organized forms including human bodies, I propose that matter itself has a quality of transcendence, a material transcendence.[19] Matter is not fully graspable or knowable and carries in its otherness – even the otherness that is the material constituency of human beings – a calling forth and an openness to its being otherwise, that is, to its becoming-other.[20] Matter, whether it is the matter that founds an image, the matter of a writing such as a poem, or the matter of the entire Earth or cosmos, is always matter-in-becoming. In this frame, divine transcendence is a kind of uncanny immanence at the point where a material transcendence and the alterity of the divine meet in things, from the subatomic realm to the macro-organization of a forest, a mountain or a star system. What I am suggesting here is subtler I think than the notion of panentheism, and closer to what has been described as 'deep incarnation'.[21]

---

17. Lyn McCredden, 'Contemporary Poetry and the Sacred: Vincent Buckley, Les Murray and Samuel Wagan Watson', *Australian Literary Studies* 23, no. 2 (October 2007), pp. 153-67 (154). See also, Luce Irigaray, *An Ethics of Sexual Difference* (trans. Carolyn Burke and Gillian C. Gill; Ithaca, NY: Cornell University Press, 1993 [Fre. 1984]), p. 148.

18. On the multiplicity of the body's sensory engagement with its material surrounds, see Michel Serres, *The Five Senses: A Philosophy of Mingled Bodies (I)* (trans. Margaret Sankey and Peter Cowley; London: Continuum, 2008 [Fre. 1985]), p. 306. I take issue, however, with the racially charged example Serres gives on the following page to describe the multiplicity of the body.

19. Anne Elvey, 'Material Elements: The Matter of Women, the Matter of Earth, the Matter of God', in *Post-Christian Feminisms: A Critical Approach* (ed. Lisa Isherwood and Kathleen McPhillips; Aldershot: Ashgate, 2008), pp. 53-69.

20. Anne Elvey, 'Ashes and Dust: On (not) Speaking About God Ecologically', in *Eco-Theology* (ed. Elaine Wainwright, Luiz Carlos Susin and Felix Wilfred; *Concilium* 2009, no. 3; London: SCM Press, 2009), pp. 33-42.

21. On 'deep incarnation', see Niels Henrik Gregersen, 'The Cross of Christ in an Evolutionary World', *Dialog* 40, no. 3 (2001), pp. 192-207; Niels Gregersen (ed.), *Incarnation: On the Scope and Depth of Christology* (Minneapolis: Fortress, 2015); Denis Edwards, *Deep Incarnation: God's Redemptive Suffering with Creatures* (Maryknoll: Orbis, 2019); idem, *Ecology at the Heart of Faith: The Change of Heart that Leads to a New Way of Living on Earth* (Maryknoll: Orbis Books, 2006), pp. 58-60; Deborah Guess, 'Deep Incarnation: A Resource for Ecological Christology', in *Climate Change – Cultural Change: Religious Responses and Responsibilities* (ed. Anne Elvey and David Gormley-O'Brien; Preston, Vic.: Mosaic Books, 2013), pp. 107-17.

Discussing the sacred and nature in contemporary thinking, Vine Deloria distinguishes between 'intuiting the sacred in nature and proclaiming a site to be sacred to an individual'.[22] The experience (rather than the construction) of the sacred or holy can be described through the concept of the *mysterium tremendum fascinans*: 'It is mysterious, upsets our intellectual beliefs with a devastating display of energy, and remains with the individual as a fascinating, attractive presence and reminder that there are dimensions to life we cannot possibly imagine.'[23] This experience of the sacred can be described as a counter-experience, an instance (perhaps a paradigmatic instance) of what Jean-Luc Marion calls 'the saturated phenomenon'.[24]

The experience of the sacred as saturated phenomenon cannot be separated from the human interpreter of the experience.[25] The material sacred, embedded in Earth and cosmos, calls forth, even 'demands', a response that 'rises from the wild unconscious depths of the human soul', a mutual response such as an artist or a poet might make co-creatively with other matter.[26] For the poet William Wordsworth's such an experience – 'And I have felt / A presence that disturbs me with the joy / Of elevated thoughts... ' – is a kind of pantheism: 'A motion and a spirit, that impels / All thinking things, all objects of all thought, / And rolls through all things'.[27] The intuition of the sacred follows on the poet's evocation of 'The still, sad music of humanity' that has the 'power/To chasten and subdue'. In the poem, the speaker's orientation to tragedy is part of the experience of the disturbing immanence it describes. The sacred does not come as a 'coup', a blow on a screen, but is part of a saturated communion.[28] The intuition of phenomena through sensation implies a hermeneutic communion between the thing presenting itself and its interpreter.

---

22. Vine Deloria Jr, 'The Sacred and the Modern World', in *Encyclopedia of Religion and Nature* (ed. Bron R. Taylor; London: Thoemmes Continuum, 2005), pp. 1446–8 (1446).

23. Deloria, 'Sacred', p. 1446.

24. Jean-Luc Marion, 'The Saturated Phenomenon', *Philosophy Today* 40, no. 1 (1996), pp. 103–24.

25. See Shane Mackinlay, *Interpreting Excess: Jean-Luc Marion, Saturated Phenomena, and Hermeneutics* (New York: Fordham University Press, 2009), p. 36.

26. Thomas Berry, 'The Wild and the Sacred', in *Religions and Environments: A Reader in Religion, Nature and Ecology* (ed. Richard Bohannon; London: Bloomsbury, 2014), pp. 73–8 (73, 78), excerpted from Thomas Berry, *The Great Work: Our Way into the Future* (New York: Bell Tower, 1999), pp. 48, 55.

27. William Wordsworth, 'Lines Written a Few Miles Above Tintern Abbey' [1798], in *Selected Poems* (ed. with an introduction and notes by Stephen Gill and Duncan Wu; Oxford World's Classics; Oxford: Oxford University Press, 1997), pp. 57–61. See further Kate Rigby, *Reclaiming Romanticism: Towards an Ecopoetics of Decolonization* (Environmental Culture Series; London: Bloomsbury, 2020), pp. 35–6.

28. Anne Elvey, *The Matter of the Text: Material Engagements between Luke and the Five Senses* (BMW, 37; Sheffield: Sheffield Phoenix, 2011), pp. 61–4. Cf. Jean-Luc Marion, *Being Given: Toward a Phenomenology of Givenness* (trans. Jeffrey L. Kosky; Stanford: Stanford University Press, 2002), p. 151.

While in some respects I am departing from Marion, I want to affirm his notion of the 'banality of saturation'.[29] If interpretation is part of the appearance of the phenomenon, that is, if the phenomenon in its appearing gives itself to interpretation, then the orientation of the interpreter is crucial for the apprehension of saturation and by extension of the sacred.[30] So, the notion of the sacred as a saturated phenomenon allows me to posit the possibility that the sacred *both* addresses us uniquely through the disturbance felt in its alterity, even otherworldliness, in the here and now of Earth and cosmos, *and* that the sacred might be utterly banal, but not entirely immanent, if only we had the capacity to pay attention. A person might as Kevin Hart's narrator does in parentheses in his poem 'Mud' encounter the sacred in the 'you', 'the Dark One', who smells of the mud of the mangroves by the Brisbane River.[31]

An Earth voice?

The Earth Bible Team's ecojustice principle of voice is about paying attention in a particular way to something that might yet smell of the sacred: 'Earth is a subject capable of raising its voice in celebration and against injustice.'[32] The hermeneutic of retrieval asks interpreters to retrieve or recover an Earth voice in biblical texts, and this interpretive practice can be extended to other texts:

> Discerning Earth and members of Earth community as subjects with a voice is a key part of the retrieval process. In some contexts their voices are evident but have been traditionally ignored by exegetes. In other contexts the voice of Earth and Earth community is not explicit, but nevertheless present and powerful. These subjects play roles in the text that are more than mere scenery or secondary images. Their voice needs to be heard. It is a voice that need not correspond to the languages of words we commonly associate with human voices.[33]

---

29. Jean-Luc Marion, 'The Banality of Saturation', in *Counter-Experiences: Reading Jean-Luc Marion* (ed. Kevin Hart; Notre Dame: University of Notre Dame Press, 2007), pp. 383–418.

30. On the relation of the phenomenon to interpretation, see Mackinlay, *Interpreting Excess*.

31. Kevin Hart, *Young Rain: New Poems* (Artarmon, NSW: Giramondo, 2008), p. 85. See further on a phenomenological poetics of revelation of the sacred, Kevin Hart, *Poetry and Revelation: For a Phenomenology of Religious Poetry* (London: Bloomsbury Academic, 2017).

32. Norman C. Habel (ed.), *Readings from the Perspective of Earth* (Earth Bible, 1; Sheffield: Sheffield Academic, 2000), p. 24.

33. Norman C. Habel, 'Introducing Ecological Hermeneutics', in *Exploring Ecological Hermeneutics* (ed. Norman C. Habel and Peter L. Trudinger; Atlanta: Society of Biblical Literature, 2008), pp. 1–8 (5).

As I discussed in Chapter 2, the hermeneutic of retrieval comes as the last in a series of three, of which the first two are suspicion and identification. A hermeneutic of suspicion concerns alertness to the anthropocentrism of biblical texts and interpretations, and awareness that other-than-human experience and interests are frequently ignored or elided in these writings or their interpretations.[34] A hermeneutic of identification requires readers to recognize and experience their 'deep ecological connections', their 'kinship with Earth', and to exercise sympathy and empathy in relation to Earth and its myriad creatures.[35] The hermeneutic of identification is a necessary step between suspicion and retrieval, one requiring of the interpreter an ecological conversion to the other, to Earth as other.[36] Identification with Earth entails a recognition of human difference from and continuity with Earth others. Interpreters are prompted to know themselves otherwise, to be 'converted' to an ecological frame of reference, where they understand themselves as enmeshed and sharing habitation with many others, and acting in accord with this understanding.[37] Vicky Balabanski argues that identification requires of readers an ability to draw connections, to exercise imagination, self-reflection, critique and, cautiously, a 'self-transcendence' where transcendence means going beyond 'the narrowly defined individualized self'.[38] As I noted in Chapter 2, such identification requires an ecological conversion, a re-orientation of understanding and behaviour occasioning an active and attentive respect for difference while deeply affirming connection. Such attentiveness is a prerequisite for hearing, responding to and speaking an Earth voice.

While affirming the focus on retrieving an Earth voice as the 'most distinctive and innovative' part of the Earth Bible project, however, David Horrell sees two problems with this approach beyond 'the unavoidable anthropomorphism involved'.[39] First, the concept of 'an' or 'the' voice of Earth can elide the plurality of the Earth community whose constituents may or may not have voices of their own.[40] For those who have voice (birds, frogs, whales) or that sound to our ears (seas, rivers, leaves shifting in the wind, branches falling to ground), the voices are not singular. A second concern relates to creative constructions of an Earth voice that exceed or intervene in the text rather than arising from the text itself,

---

34. Habel, 'Introducing Ecological Hermeneutics', p. 4.

35. Habel, 'Introducing Ecological Hermeneutics', p. 4.

36. Vicky Balabanski, 'The Step of "Identification" in Norman Habel's Ecological Hermeneutics: Hermeneutical Reflections on "Ecological Conversion"', in *Where the Wild Ox Roams: Biblical Essays in Honour of Norman C. Habel* (ed. Alan H. Cadwallader with Peter L. Trudinger; HBM, 59; Sheffield: Sheffield Phoenix, 2013), pp. 20–31.

37. On ecological conversion, see, e.g., Edwards, *Ecology at the Heart of Faith*, pp. 2–4; see also Balabanski, 'Step of "Identification"', pp. 23–9.

38. Balabanski, 'Step of "Identification"', pp. 22–3, 31.

39. David G. Horrell, 'Ecological Hermeneutics: Reflections on Method and Prospects for the Future', *Colloquium* 46, no. 2 (November 2014), pp. 139–65 (156). Cf. Elaine M. Wainwright's response to Horrell *Colloquium* 46, no. 2 (November 2014), pp. 166–9.

40. Horrell, 'Ecological Hermeneutics', p. 156.

for example when interpreters imagine 'the cries of Earth' protesting or lamenting 'the injustice perpetrated against it, by humans or by God'.[41] For Horrell, the practice of identifying with Earth is a useful 'thought-provoking' exercise, but should not be constitutive of ecological hermeneutics.[42] What Horrell underplays in his second critique is the way in which texts written from an anthropocentric perspective frequently elide other-than-human beings and their interests. Such others are often necessary to the existence of the text as a material thing or they are elements essential to, but ignored in, the text's telling. Without Earth there is no text. To retrieve the voices of Earth and its constituents, therefore, need not be to bring them in as if from outside the text but to attend to them in, and draw them out from, the text itself through a process of identification and retrieval, and sometimes reconstruction, using creative imagination.[43]

As Gene Tucker notes, although the principle of voice seems to 'personify the earth in human terms', this principle is effectively 'a summons to respect… to listen again to the earth', an invitation 'to pay attention'.[44] Alphonso Lingis takes a similar approach: 'Today we have become aware once again that we share this planet with innumerable other living things, whose voices summon our attention and must also direct our lives.'[45] This notion extends beyond 'living things' to include so-called 'inert matter', which may affect even order 'our material bodies in ways that biochemists have not yet been able to trace'.[46] The notion of attention to the voice (or better voices) of Earth shifts towards an attentiveness that is already a response to a summons occurring through the material-corporeal interchange between humans and the multiple others (both inside and outside the body) whose proximity (or perhaps also distance) has effects in the body. These effects call forth a response (that is at the least biochemical but may also become philosophical, ethical and theological).[47] This sense of a summons that is both prior to human volition and

41. Horrell, 'Ecological Hermeneutics', pp. 156-7.
42. Horrell, 'Ecological Hermeneutics', p. 163.
43. This hermeneutic of creative imagination, and the related recovery (rather than invention) of voice in the reading of a text, parallels a feminist approach that recognizes the silencing of women's voices in androcentric texts and the interpretive task of reconstruction, to account for and bring to voice the stories and interests of the elided 'other' whose absent presence was essential to the text. On creative imagination in a feminist frame, see Elisabeth Schüssler Fiorenza, *But She Said: Feminist Practices of Biblical Interpretation* (Boston: Beacon, 1992), p. 73.
44. Earth Bible Team, 'Conversations with Gene Tucker and Other Writers', in *The Earth Story in Genesis* (ed. Norman C. Habel and Shirley Wurst; Earth Bible, 2; Sheffield: Sheffield Academic, 2000), pp. 21-33 (29). See further, idem, 'The Voice of the Earth: More Than Metaphor?', in *The Earth Story in the Psalms and the Prophets* (ed. Norman C. Habel; Earth Bible, 4; Sheffield: Sheffield Academic, 2001), pp. 23-8.
45. Alphonso Lingis, 'The Voices of Things', *Senses and Society* 4, no. 3 (2009), pp. 273-81 (280).
46. Lingis, 'Voices of Things', p. 281.
47. Lingis, 'Voices of Things', p. 281.

part of human being echoes Jean-Louis Chrétien's understanding of the *call to be* as the first vocation, to which the response is already a 'yes'; this 'yes', I suggest, includes the body's assent to its complex being-in-relation: as matter with other matter.[48] I propose that my corporeal response to the summons of material things, including but not exclusive to those I understand as living things, underscores attention to the myriad voices of Earth. Readers' prior participation in the material exchange of being needs to inform the principle of voice.

The assertion of the principle of voice, by the Earth Bible Team, echoes Berry's claim that the spirituality he attributes to Earth is not about human spirituality extended; rather it is about something Earthy/Earthly in which humans might participate, which they cannot own but to which they might attend as to a cry.[49] Jan Morgan reads ecological destruction as a form of oppression analogous to the experience of the Hebrews at the beginning of the book of Exodus. They cry out. This paradigmatic 'cry' is sacred.[50] It becomes a prophetic task 'to find a way to bring the cry, the hurt, to the surface, to public expression'.[51] Aware of the conceptual difficulties in attributing a cry to Earth, Morgan argues that 'Earth's cry requires human mediation' and that this mediation responds to an existing more-than-human agency.[52] Moreover, no human articulation of an Earth voice will be complete; many are needed, individually and in concert.[53]

For the Earth Bible Team, while the ecojustice principles and the related ecological hermeneutics arise from the sense of Earthy/Earthly cries of oppression, the Earth voice to be retrieved is not limited to this notion of cry. Voice for the Earth Bible Team expresses subjecthood, something to which the careful writer/reader need attend in order to make space for the interests of Earth to be announced. 'Voice' is one of the mysteries of Earth.[54] An Earth voice may not only lament or cry out in agony, but also celebrate or proffer a vision of an alternative to the present.[55] The point is that human writers understand themselves and their productions as only part of the multiplicity of co-beings, co-relations and co-agencies of Earth, and that they speak from this understanding with an ear attuned to the alterity with which they are enmeshed.

If human interpreters of texts are to speak a voice in some senses other than their own, they need imagination, employing what Elisabeth Schüssler Fiorenza

---

48. Jean-Louis Chrétien, *The Call and the Response* (trans. Anne A. Davenport; New York: Fordham University Press, 2004 [Fre. 1992]), p. 18.

49. Berry, *Sacred Universe*, p. 70.

50. Jan Morgan, *Earth's Cry: Prophetic Ministry in a More-than-human World* (Preston, Vic.: Uniting Academic Press, 2013), pp. 62, 66–70.

51. Morgan, *Earth's Cry*, p. 49.

52. Morgan, *Earth's Cry*, pp. 64, 66.

53. Morgan, *Earth's Cry*, p. 66.

54. Habel, *Rainbow of Mysteries*, pp. 119–38.

55. See Morgan, *Earth's Cry*, p. 151; Nonie Sharp, 'Being True to the Earth – in Peril: Finding a Voice to Touch the Heart', *PAN*, no. 5 (2008), pp. 47–58.

describes in a feminist context as a hermeneutics of creative imagination.[56] There can be no unmediated recovery of an Earth voice, but only the approximation or hint that the interpreter might, for example, 'hear Earth as the narrator of the story'.[57] In a biblical text such as the parable of the Good Samaritan (Lk. 10.25-37), which I discuss in Chapters 7 and 8, a reader might note, for example, the way other matter is co-agent with humans in the act of compassion, through the healing properties of wine and oil and the capacity for the pack animal to carry the wounded person.[58] While the material co-agency of oil and wine, animal and place can be described discursively, another and often more difficult step remains: to tell the story with Earth, oil or animal as narrator. The resulting writing may or may not be effective literature, however much its author has identified sympathetically and empathically with Earth and its constituents. Part of the practice of Earth Bible readings that focus on the principle of voice and the related hermeneutic of retrieval is a kind of creative writing in this mode. A moving example of Earth Voice occurs in Habel's 'Scorched Earth Sites: The Mystery of Voice', where the 'Earth-Voice' speaks of destruction of specific sites and the 'People' respond: 'We hear you. And we feel your pain.'[59] The power of this rite lies less in the mediated 'Earth-Voice' on its own, more in the gathering around a bowl filled with material symbols of destruction (e.g. a chain from a chainsaw); the litany-like build-up of imagery; and the structure of call-response, including a final symbolic action and blessing. The moving voice in this rite, and in any effective retrieval of Earth voice, is always a human voice. How is this human voice also a more-than-human Earth voice?

The matter of voice

For humans and other animals, voice is already produced materially through the interplay of corporeal processes and qualities of air, and can be understood as a material mediation of the breath (itself material) producing sound that is picked up by the organ of hearing. Voice also has a wider meaning and takes us into that space where the inner life is produced in, and produces, certain material transformations. If humans have something that might be called voice, in all its layers of meaning, this is an instance of an attribute that is already Earthy/Earthly. In writing and reading the materiality of voice intersects with, perhaps inhabits, the materiality of a text.

---

56. Schüssler Fiorenza, *But She Said*, p. 73.

57. Habel, 'Introducing Ecological Hermeneutics', p. 5.

58. See Michael Trainor, *About Earth's Child: An Ecological Listening to the Gospel of Luke* (Earth Bible Commentary, 2; Sheffield: Sheffield Phoenix, 2012), pp. 174–5. See also, Anne Elvey, 'To Bear the Other: Toward a Passionate Compassion (An Ecological Feminist Reading of Luke 10:25-37)', *Sea Changes* 1 (2001), available online: https://www.wsrt.asn.au/seachanges (accessed 22 October 2020).

59. Habel, *Rainbow of Mysteries*, pp. 214–18.

Poets and literary critics speak of voice in ways that have resonance for understanding the material relations between text and voice. For example, Susan Stewart writes of 'the particular timbre, tone, hesitations, and features of articulation by which all the voices subject to [the poet's] own history have shaped [the] voice's instrument'.[60] In listening, the reader or hearer attends to 'the material history' of the poet's connection to her more-than-human genealogy, where ancestry is understood widely to include familial, cultural, educational and occupational lineages enmeshed in a wider Earth community.[61] Around the notion of poetic voice, Seamus Heaney makes a distinction between craft and technique. Craft 'is what you can learn from other verse', whereas technique 'involves not only a poet's way with words, his management of metre, rhythm and verbal texture; it involves also a definition of his stance towards life, a definition of his own reality'.[62] Voice is situated where technique emerges from craft, though some poets may have strong technique and 'wobbly' craft.[63] An important aspect of technique for considering ways in which a poet might be attuned to an Earth voice is the quality of what John Keats calls 'negative capability'.[64] The poet stands aside from herself open to the alterity of another (human or other than human) and their experience. Such a stance requires sympathy or empathy for the other, and a capacity for allowing the coexistence of ambiguities.[65] Exercising this attitude, the poet does 'not flinch or look away no matter what the arresting experience'.[66] This is particularly important for an ecological poetics, such as the Earth Bible hermeneutic of retrieval requires, because attentiveness to an Earth cry is first, though not exclusively, attention to ecological destruction.

In an ecologically oriented poetics, such a stance implies not only a standing aside from self, but an acknowledgement of the entanglement of self with that 'outside' towards which the poet attends. Poems may be 'written with' the places they evoke.[67] If the poet's technique involves a collaborative stance towards more-than-human others, this also raises questions of craft. For example, Forrest Gander asks: 'Aside from issues of theme and reference, how might syntax, line break, or

60. Susan Stewart, *Poetry and the Fate of the Senses* (Chicago: The University of Chicago Press, 2002), p. 110.

61. Stewart, *Poetry*, p. 110.

62. Seamus Heaney, 'Feeling into Words', in *Preoccupations: Selected Prose 1968–1978* (London: Faber and Faber, 1980), pp. 41–60 (47).

63. Heaney, 'Feeling into Words', p. 47.

64. John Keats, 'Letter to George and Thomas Keats', Hampstead, 22 December 1817, in *Letters of John Keats to His Family and Friends* (ed. Sidney Colvin; The Project Gutenberg eBook), available online: http://www.gutenberg.org/files/35698/35698-h/35698-h.htm#XXIV (accessed 22 October 2020).

65. Mary Oliver, *A Poetry Handbook: A Prose Guide to Understanding and Writing Poetry* (Orlando: Harcourt, 1994), pp. 80, 83.

66. R. S. White, *John Keats: A Literary Life* (Basingstoke: Palgrave Macmillan, 2010), p. 122.

67. Stuart Cooke, *Departure into Cloud* (Sydney: Vagabond Press, 2013).

the shape of the poem on the page express an ecological ethics?'[68] Is any particular form of writing more expressive of an Earth voice than any other? Is it a matter of writing/reading or both?

The text as a material thing

One possibility is to attend to Earth as expressed in the materiality of the text itself. I will consider three poems (one by Michelle Boisseau and two by Denise Levertov) which touch on Earth as subject through their foregrounding of the text as a material thing.

'Parchment' (Boisseau)

In Michelle Boisseau's 'Parchment', the speaker evokes in detail the materiality of a prayer book, its indebtedness to more-than-human (including human) creatures whose lives and labours went into its making.[69] The poet also addresses related issues of class and justice, since this fine and costly material artefact was made for private use by a monarch. Beginning 'I'm holding in my hand the skin of a calf/ that lived 600 years ago', the poem describes the animal life that was taken or gave itself for the production of a book. Respectfully, the poem evokes the two sides of the skin, the one ('the flesh side') oriented towards the dark inside the body, the other ('the hair side') exposed to sun, wind and rain. The speaker carefully details the plants and insects which supply the pigments, the birds and other creatures whose bodies provide the quill and bindings. The poem moves between describing more-than-human creatures passively and actively as they contribute to the book's production, so that the question of matter (including creaturely bodies) as taken or giving, or both at once, remains open. Description of the threads of material being and agency that contribute to the making of the singular material artefact the speaker holds in her hands interweaves with her evocation of the beauty of the illuminations themselves. Human labour and its costs appear particularly in the 'the illuminator's/boy assistants' who are 'felled' because of their work with the yellow arsenic used to colour 'flowering meadows or a lady's long braids'.

---

68. Forrest Gander, 'The Future of the Past', in Forrest Gander and John Kinsella, *Redstart: An Ecological Poetics* (Iowa City: University of Iowa Press, 2012), pp. 1–3 (2).

69. Michelle Boisseau, *Trembling Air* (Fayetteville: University of Arkansas Press, 2003), p. 21. Excerpts from 'Parchment' from *Trembling Air*. Copyright © 2003 by Michelle Boisseau. Reprinted with the permission of The Permissions Company, LLC on behalf of the University of Arkansas Press, www.uapress.com. The full poem appears at Poetry Foundation, available online: https://www.poetryfoundation.org/poetrymagazine/browse?contentId=40741 (accessed 22 October 2020). See readings of this poem in Kate Rigby, 'Ecocriticism', in *Introducing Criticism at the Twenty-first Century* (ed. Julian Wolfreys; Edinburgh: Edinburgh University Press, 2002), pp. 151–78; idem, 'Introduction', *Religion and Literature* 40, no. 1 (Spring 2008), pp. 1–8 (7–8); Elvey, *Matter of the Text*, p. 44.

Perhaps 'felled' echoes Gerard Manley Hopkins' 'Binsley Poplars' – 'All felled, felled, are all felled.'[70] The poem registers human damage both to other humans and to other than humans.

The reader could leave this poem as a witness to the complex material interdependencies of a particular ancient book, and the inter-human relations of power that went into its production. But the poem that highlights the materiality of the artefact speaks back to itself, reminding the reader of the material relations of the poem's production in multiple material artefacts, on a printed page in the journal *Poetry*, in the author's collection *Trembling Air* and online, together at least hundreds if not thousands of material instances of this one poem. For each individual instance of Boisseau's poem, a reader could tell a narrative of interdependencies and relations of power. In the poem, the stretched calf skin, flesh side and weather side, is 'all inscribed/with the dark brown ink of prayer'. This 'all' that comes towards the end of the first stanza includes not only the skin but the labour of 'someone' who 'stretched' and 'scraped' the skin, described earlier in the same stanza. At one level, the reference to prayer explains that this is a prayer book, but at another level, the 'ink of prayer' implies that the sacred is embedded in the materiality of the book itself, and in all its layers of indebtedness to more-than-human life and labour. The deaths and injustices that contributed to this book, and by implication to the multiple material instances of Boisseau's poem itself, become a sacred cry to which the poem both responds and witnesses, but which it also prompts again and again by the cost of its own material existence.

'O Taste and See' (Levertov)

Questions of matter and justice appear differently in Denise Levertov's 'O Taste and See', where the speaker comes upon a material artefact, a subway Bible poster with the words 'O taste and see' recalling Psalm 34, 'O taste and see that the Lord is good.'[71] The poem shifts quickly from the biblical text to 'all that lives/to the imagination's tongue', followed by a list that travels from 'grief and mercy' through language to the materiality of things and human engagement with them, for which eating and digestion are symbols. With reference to Wordsworth's 'The world is too much with us', the poem takes the reader into a world that is 'not with us enough', progressing from nouns to verbs: from 'tangerine' and 'weather' to the first action 'to breathe them' then a list of infinitives, 'to bite,/savor, chew, swallow'. The poem celebrates the taking-in and transformation of matter; through breathing and eating 'to transform // into our flesh'. Without further punctuation, 'our flesh' flows

---

70. Gerard Manley Hopkins, *Poems and Prose* (selected and edited by W. H. Gardner; Middlesex: Penguin, 1953), p. 39.
71. Denise Levertov, *Poems 1960–1967* (New York: New Directions, 1983), p. 125. Quotations reprinted by permission of New Directions Publishing Corp and Bloodaxe Books.

into 'our/deaths'. Tasting and seeing, breathing and eating are reminders of the interdependent materiality of embodied, mortal human beings.

The poem does not leave the reader with 'our deaths'. The next phrase 'crossing the street' enacts a crossing. By way of the names of fruit – 'plum' and 'quince' – the poet has humans 'living in the orchard'. '[B]eing hungry' returns the reader to the subway and its associated poverty. A tension remains between the divine goodness the psalmist enjoins the reader 'taste and see', and to which the fruit of the orchard and human material engagement with things witness, and the reality of human hunger. Finally, with the reference to 'plucking the fruit', the poem recalls the primeval forest garden of Genesis 2 and 3. The poem's invitation 'taste and see' evokes the goodness of both the divine and matter, suggesting that they cannot be fully separated. Moreover, in the interplay of nouns and verbs, by the movement and variation through the list of being and doing and the phrases 'transform // into our flesh our/deaths' and 'living in the orchard', the poem performs the interrelatedness between humans and the Earth community of which we are part, and on which we depend for sustenance.[72] In hunger and death, in living and being fed, the 'grief and mercy' of the middle stanza resonate.

'To Live in the Mercy of God' (Levertov)

'To Live in the Mercy of God' celebrates the mercy the poet experiences by way of her embeddedness in and attentiveness to a more-than-human world.[73] Divine mercy is a passion, 'a vast flood' that is 'flung on resistance'. At one level the poem performs the speaker's resistance to this mercy through responses to the repeated phrase 'to live in the mercy of God'. At the outset, the responding image is pastoral: 'to lie back under the tallest/oldest trees'. The next time, the phrase 'to live in the mercy of God' provokes a critique (of itself or of writing): 'The complete/ sentence too adequate, has no give.' The third time the phrase evokes a waterfall – which echoes in the 'vast flood' that the reader meets at the end – in constant motion, a torrent 'flinging itself/unabating down and down/to clenched fists of rocks'. The resistance here is more-than-human, part of the interplay of water and the environs it pushes against and shapes. Water has a voice that intersects with the human voice of the poem: 'Oh or A/uninterrupted, voice/many stranded.' 'Stranded' not only suggests the multiple weavings of material voices to which the poet attends, but together with the images of 'the clenched fist', the 'smoke' of the spray, 'steelwhite' foam, 'the fugitive jade' and the final 'resistance', the poem subtly evokes the violence and industrialization that both fissure and inhabit the pastoral

---

72. This reading of Levertov's 'O Taste and See' is drawn in part from a slightly longer reading of the poem in Elvey, *Matter of the Text*, pp. 170–1.

73. Denise Levertov, *Sands of the Well* (New York: New Directions, 1996), pp. 127–8. Quotations reprinted by permission of New Directions Publishing Corp. The full poem appears at Poetry Foundation, available online: https://www.poetryfoundation.org/poems/48710/to-live-in-the-mercy-of-god (accessed 2 August 2021).

images of an ecologically embedded divine mercy. For Levertov this interplay of exploitation and beauty, praise and shame, was an integral part of her poetic imaginary, of, in Heaney's terms, her technique.[74]

Reading 'as if it is holy'

What of the technique of the reader? The Earth Bible principle of voice is a hermeneutic principle. As such it concerns a mode of reading as much as a mode of writing. In the ninth part of Heaney's sequence 'Station Island' a confessor tells the narrator: 'Read poems as prayers'.[75] For Simone Weil, 'Absolutely unmixed attention is prayer.'[76] Such attention, she holds, is necessary for creative work: 'The poet produces the beautiful by fixing his [or her] attention on something real.'[77] Study – learning, reading and interpretation – is also marked by this capacity to attend; such attention needs to 'be a looking and not an attachment'.[78] It is a kind of sensory engagement including but not exclusive to the sense of sight.

A long Christian tradition of *lectio divina* applies to scripture. In the Divine Office this practice pertains also to the inclusion of poems as prayers. A long, but neglected, Christian tradition of two books of revelation also exists: alongside the Book of Scripture is the Book of Nature. A parallel practice of *lectio divina* can be applied to the Book of Nature.[79] Perhaps it might also be applied to the materiality of the text in a kind of saturated communion with texts as materially embedded not only by way of the materiality of the artefact in which they present themselves (even so-called virtual presentations are material), but also by way of the materiality that underlies image, word and voice.

Jennifer Harrison's poem 'Book Sculptor' picks up this possibility of reading as touching on the sacred through folding, interpreting, sculpting matter and words, artefact and image.[80] In Harrison's poem, 'Paper birds fly from unread pages./

---

74. John Felstiner, *Can Poetry Save the Earth? A Field Guide to Nature Poems* (New Haven: Yale University Press, 2009), pp. 266–74.

75. Seamus Heaney, *Opened Ground: Poems 1966–1996* (London: Faber and Faber, 1998), p. 265.

76. Simone Weil, *Gravity and Grace* (trans. Emma Crawford; Routledge Classics; London: Routledge, 2002 [French 1947]), p. 201.

77. Weil, *Gravity and Grace*, pp. 201, 204.

78. Weil, *Gravity and Grace*, p. 205.

79. Robin Pryor and Cath James, 'Addressing Change through the Two Books of God: Education for Cultural Change in Religious Communities', in *Climate Change – Cultural Change: Religious Responses and Responsibilities* (ed. Anne Elvey and David Gormley-O'Brien; Preston, Vic.: Mosaic Books, 2013), pp. 176–90 (185).

80. Jennifer Harrison, 'Book Sculptor', *Salt Lick Quarterly* (Autumn 2003), p. 9. For me the poem calls to mind Elizabeth Presa's 2000 exhibition of kimonos and wedding dresses sculpted from a manuscript of Jacques Derrida's *Le Toucher Jean-Luc Nancy*, entitled 'The Four Horizons of the Page', to which Kevin Hart responded in his 'Horizons and Folds: Elizabeth Presa', *Contretemps* no. 2 (May 2001), pp. 171–5.

Stories ruffle in the wind's stealth'. While the poem is sculpted in a fairly regular fashion, the poet's 'hands make a book into something/other' and 'the godly wealth' of words becomes 'a tinderbox of origami flowers'. The poem moves between the poiesis of writing and its undoing, which occurs through the poiesis of book sculpting. Book sculpting transforms a material artefact – a book, or perhaps a poem on a page – into a material artefact that is something else, 'a fan,... a dragon'. This undoing reverses the undoing of the thing that occurs through metaphor. Through this undoing, the poet evokes a poiesis of reading:

> All is discipline you see. Concentrate.
> Fold and fold. Press and fold. Then, be able –
> free your pleated creatures! Read as if it's holy.[81]

A later version of this poem, much changed, appears in Harrison's collection *Colombine* and ends:

> All is discipline, you see. Concentrate.
> Fold and fold. Press and fold. Then, be able—
> free your creatures. You cannot make them holy.[82]

The first version concludes with an imperative although without the exclamation mark that precedes it: 'Read as if it's holy'. Both versions of the poem are written for the paper sculptor Nicholas Jones, but the address is wider. The imagery of making and unmaking a text through attentive sculpting becomes a summons to a reader to attend in a certain way, with an ear perhaps to a text's sacred cry as a material thing. But in the second instance, the focus shifts to suggest that no matter how careful the attention to the unmaking and making of the text – through the processes in this case of sculpting – these 'creatures' cannot be made holy. The later version draws back from the sacred.

In Australia, where Harrison is writing, the sacred is a contested category. Andrew McCann, for example, critiques what he sees as a ubiquitous appeal to the sacred in Australian cultural and literary discourse, first because the notion of the sacred is so fluid, untied to particular religious traditions, but more particularly because its use can become an aesthetic substitute for ethical and political action.[83] Functioning in this way to gloss over the realities of colonial Australian history, '[t]he sacred... underwrites the social order it promises to transform'.[84]

---

81. Harrison, 'Book Sculptor' (*Salt Lick Quarterly* version). Quoted with permission of the author.

82. Jennifer Harrison, 'Book Sculptor', in *Colombine: New and Selected Poems* (North Fitzroy: Black Pepper, 2010), p. 223. Quoted with permission of the author and publisher.

83. Andrew McCann, 'The Obstinacy of the Sacred', *Antipodes* 19, no. 2 (December 2005), pp. 152–8 (152).

84. McCann, 'Obstinacy of the Sacred', p. 153.

In the Australian history of invasion/settlement, the colonial and the ecological are interconnected, as mutually reinforcing sites of damage and dispossession. Harrison's later version of 'Book Sculptor' calls into question the possibility of the sacred or holy in a situation where 'when everything strung unstrings? / The tree's corpse dissected for the violin // how beautiful that music. How haunted'.[85] Here again is an interplay of praise and shame such as Levertov offers. But I do not want to dispose of the earlier ending entirely, rather to let the two finales inform each other. What might it mean to develop a technique of reading 'as if it's holy' in a situation where 'everything strung unstrings', where ecological interconnectedness means connection sometimes more with and through damage (much of it human-induced) than with sustenance and wholeness?

Conclusion

The material sacred arrives as an alterity at the heart of things. Famously, poet William Carlos Williams states, 'No ideas/but in things'.[86] This much quoted, parenthetical split line comes from his poem, 'A Sort of a Song'. As Michael Hamburger observes: 'To begin with this is a dynamic poem of discovery; and the words in brackets are not a prescription, but part of an experience – a part of the experience, incidentally, which could not be rendered in terms of the two "images" or things dominant in the poem, the snake and the saxifrage.'[87] 'No ideas [and then the line break] but in things' emerges from the encounter with the thing of a snake which gives itself as a metaphor for writing, the writing of the poem. In turn the poem expresses an intention through an idea, rather than an image: 'through metaphor to reconcile/the people and the stones'. Such reconciliation of human and other than human is central to Williams' poetry, and happens not by enlisting 'nature' to explain human experience through simile, but by understanding human imagination as sharing in the materiality of Earth.[88] Sharply at the end – and the poem itself proposes the writing should be sharp – the poem returns from ideas to image: 'Saxifrage is my flower that splits/the rocks'. The word that arrests me in those two lines is 'my'. A flower splitting a rock is almost a cliché for the power of a fragile thing over a stronger. Not only does the possessive pronoun avoid the cliché but also through the 'my' the line enacts a possible reconciliation of poet and thing. Such a reconciliation is always already fissured – split – because the alterity of the material thing – Earth, material artefact, poem – towards which I might

---

85. Harrison, 'Book Sculptor', in *Colombine*, p. 223.

86. William Carlos Williams, 'A Sort of a Song', in *The Collected Poems of William Carlos Williams Volume II: 1939-1962* (ed. Christopher MacGowan; New York: New Directions, 1991), p. 55. Quotations reprinted by permission of New Directions Publishing Corp. and Carcanet Press.

87. Michael Hamburger, *The Truth of Poetry: Tensions in Modernist Poetry Since Baudelaire* (London: Anvil Press Poetry, 1996), p. 32.

88. Felstiner, *Can Poetry Save the Earth?*, pp. 150-1.

orient myself as if towards the holy is like Derrida's impossible, simultaneously approachable and unapproachable.

In his 1962 sermon 'The Care of the Earth', Joseph Sittler speaks of how his reading Richard Wilbur's poem 'Advice to a Prophet', which questions what it means to be human under the threat of nuclear and ecological destruction, pushed his mind back against a wall and forced him to ask about what his religion, Christianity, could offer to such a reality.[89] The use of poetry or other creative writing as part of an ecological hermeneutic of retrieval needs at best to work with such impetus, bringing craft and technique together, to push the reader to ask such questions. But the hermeneutic of retrieval is also a challenge to read biblical and other texts with an ear to their materiality, as if in their material embeddedness through voice, breath and medium, they are holy. At the same time, such an orientation towards the sacred is already fissured by settler uses in order to ease what ought continually to unsettle us. The final line break in *A Sort of a Song* falls after 'splits' and what might have been a 'nice' poem, *read as if its holy*, may leave its reader 'rocked'. How often does biblical interpretation leave us as rocked as nightly news or scientific reports may do? In the next chapter, I take up the disturbances of climate change. With a focus again on breath, I reconsider the capacity of breath, air and atmosphere to call us forth to new possibilities, as I sketch a performative inter-contextual reading of Lk. 4.16-30.

---

89. Joseph Sittler, *The Care of the Earth* (Facets edn; Minneapolis: Fortress, 2004 [1964]), p. 52.

Chapter 4

STRAINED BREATH AND OPEN TEXT: EXPLORING THE MATERIALITY OF BREATH IN RELATION TO LUKE 4.16-30

Breathing becomes strained when bushfire smoke blankets towns and cities, as it did in the 2019–20 Australian summer in Victoria and New South Wales.[1] With the Victorian Environment Protection Agency registering air quality as hazardous, P-2 and N-95 masks sold out. In 2020 and 2021, in Australian houses and across the globe, masks have become commonplace, sometimes mandatory, as a precaution against the spread of Covid-19, a virus carried on the breath, a virus that strains the breath when those worst affected need ventilators to breathe. As cities, states and whole nations shut down, and domestic and international flights are a small fraction of their former numbers, National Geographic reports that some once highly polluted cities have clearer air; moreover, pollution itself may be a factor in Covid-19 deaths.[2] Will the global discipline of physical distancing, including staying at home, have a lasting mitigating effect on climate change or will the push for 'business-as-usual' forestall this?

As ecological hermeneutics has long done, the current situation highlights the ecological reality of interconnectedness, one of the ecojustice principles of the Earth Bible Project: 'Earth is a community of interconnected living things that are mutually dependent on each other for life and survival.'[3] Material connections cross

---

1. This chapter is a revised version of an essay, Anne Elvey, 'Strained Breath and Open Text: Exploring the Materiality of Breath in Relation to Reading Luke 4.16-30', *BCT* 16, no. 1–2 (2020), pp. 1–14. In a related essay, I explore the materiality of breath in the context of climate change, through readings of three poems from Australian women poets, Jill Jones, Natalie Harkin and Susan Hawthorne. See Anne Elvey 'Climate Embodied: Exploring a Poetics of Strained Breath', *Axon* 10, no. 1 (May 2020), available online: https://www.axonjournal.com.au/issue-vol-10-no-1-may-2020/climate-embodied (accessed 12 November 2020).

2. Beth Gardiner, 'Pollution Made COVID-19 Worse. Now Lockdowns Are Clearing the Air', *National Geographic* (8 April 2020), available online: https://www.nationalgeographic.com/science/2020/04/pollution-made-the-pandemic-worse-but-lockdowns-clean-the-sky/ (accessed 12 November 2020).

3. Norman C. Habel (ed.), *Readings from the Perspective of Earth* (Earth Bible, 1; Sheffield: Sheffield Academic, 2000), p. 24.

species and continents. One corporeal facet and sign of this connectedness is breath. Building on Chapters 2 and 3, and with the strained breath of climate change in view, in this chapter I explore the materiality of breath and its relation to both ecological hermeneutics and corporealities of resistance. My focus is on material co-agencies, intertextualities and voice. Against contemporary contexts of strained breath, I apply my exploration of breath in an intertextual, performative reading of Lk. 4.16-30, where the Lukan Jesus is materially engaged with biblical texts in multiple ways.

The materiality of air and breath

Air surrounds us. As animals, humans breathe air. In the processes of inhalation and exhalation, air transforms us through fleshy, organic agencies of tissue and blood, and we, too, transform it. We are part of its breathy circulation. Mostly, the air and its relation to our breath go unremarked. Mostly, our breathing goes unnoticed unless it is strained in some way, through illness or violence, or unless we consciously attend to it, for example, in meditation, playing a wind instrument or singing, or when on a cold morning breath becomes visible as we exhale warm vapour into chill. Mostly, many of us take air for granted. What is at stake when air and breath are unremarked?

For Luce Irigaray, a forgetting of air plays into a philosophical privileging of solidity and certainty, of thinking based on firm ground.[4] The air itself offers a different medium for philosophical becoming by way of a complex, life-sustaining materiality that echoes and affirms 'the feminine'.[5] Air is a gift given in the flesh of the maternal body.[6] I am not altogether comfortable with the terminology of 'the feminine', because of its tendency to a problematic essentialism, but Irigaray situates the feminine in the context of sexual difference.[7] Sexual difference is not based in, but rather resists, patriarchal binaries while retaining a trace of what it resists; a writing of sexual difference reaches towards a becoming otherwise for women, a 'becoming divine' in the feminine.[8] A focused remembering of the breath as enfleshed is necessary for woman's becoming, beyond both the patriarchal constraints around the names, *woman, she, feminine* and the conventional, remarkably durable, imagery of masculine divinity.[9] Irigaray does

---

4. Luce Irigaray, *The Forgetting of Air in Martin Heidegger* (trans. Mary Beth Mader; Austin: University of Texas Press, 1999), p. 2.

5. Irigaray, *Forgetting of Air*, p. 28.

6. Irigaray, *Forgetting of Air*, p. 28.

7. Luce Irigaray, *An Ethics of Sexual Difference* (trans. Carolyn Burke and Gillian C. Gill; Ithaca: Cornell University Press, 1993).

8. Luce Irigaray, *Sexes and Genealogies* (trans. Gillian C. Gill; New York: Columbia University Press, 1993), pp. 62, 71.

9. Luce Irigaray, 'The Age of the Breath' (trans. Katja van de Rakt, Staci Boeckman and Luce Irigaray), in *Key Writings* (ed. Luce Irigaray; London: Continuum, 2004), pp. 165–70; Luce Irigaray, 'The Redemption of Women' (trans. Jennifer Wong, Jennifer Zillich with Luce Irigaray), in *Key Writings* (ed. Luce Irigaray; London: Continuum, 2004), pp. 150–64.

not substitute a feminine divinity for a male one; rather 'divinity' represents a 'process of mediation between nature and culture (between body and word, for example), a process that destroys neither but enables those two principal aspects of our being to relate in a manner that cultivates *well*-being'.[10] A recollection of air in its relation to the 'feminine' not only unsettles patriarchal hegemony but also promotes an alternative epistemology that privileges life and its flows. In challenging the binaries of earth and heaven through its fluidity, air resists the dematerialization of the sacred.[11]

In the context of the strained breath of climate change, the forgetting of air remains problematic, as David Abram suggests: 'What is climate change if not a consequence of failing to respect or even to notice the elemental medium in which we are immersed?'[12] Risking hyperbole, he continues, 'Is not global warming, or global weirding, a simple consequence of taking the air for granted?'[13] Although climate change is hardly 'simple', behind Abram's questions is a recognition that air connects us, that climate change already inhabits our bodies because humans are breathing beings who, normally, are in constant touch with Earth's atmosphere. Exceptions, where the breather is separated from Earth's atmosphere under a diving helmet or beyond Earth in a space suit, for example, are indeed exceptional and point to the normality of breathing as an immediate material exchange of animal and plant bodies with a wider Earth community sharing the same atmosphere.

When I breathe, I am a coagent in vast processes of material exchange that connect creatures across species, continents and times in the circulation of air. William Bryant Logan, for example, describes air as 'the restless shaper of the world'.[14] The atmosphere itself 'is regulated by the living', so that 'breath is being', and 'creatures are the expressions of its existence'.[15] For Earthly beings, including humans, 'air is about as close as it gets to an unconditional good', as Kate Rigby explains.[16] Moreover, it is a good that can be withdrawn.[17] Air, with its energetic exigencies of weather, its agencies in relation to climate, pollution, contamination and storm, is not only a material necessity for human existence, but its necessity also places air and our relation to it at the nexus of death and life. Air is an instance of what I describe as 'the material given', for which bodies, pregnant bodies and

10. Julie Kelso, 'Irigaray's Madonna', *Feminist Theology* 23, no. 2 (2015), pp. 171–85 (174), emphasis in original.

11. Irigaray, *Forgetting of Air*, p. 2.

12. David Abram, 'Afterword: The Commonwealth of Breath', in *Material Ecocriticism* (ed. Serenella Iovino and Serpil Oppermann; Bloomington: Indiana University Press, 2014), pp. 301–14 (301).

13. Abram, 'Afterword', p. 301.

14. William Bryant Logan, *Air: The Restless Shaper of the World* (eBook; New York: Norton, 2012).

15. Logan, *Air*, p. 321.

16. Kate Rigby, *Dancing with Disaster: Environmental Histories, Narratives, and Ethics for Perilous Times* (Charlottesville: University of Virginia Press, 2015), p. 148.

17. Rigby, *Dancing with Disaster*, p. 149.

Earth are paradigms – a gift-life necessity.[18] The material given has a quality of 'prepropriation' and can be described in Derridean terms as 'aneconomic', that is, the material given embodies, or I could say en-matters, a logic of being as 'encounter' in which self and other are enmeshed.[19] The logic of the material given precedes and unsettles a logic of capitalist exchange even where bodies themselves, for example, are subject to trafficking and other forms of coerced labour. Air, too, has these qualities of economic unsettlement even as global consumerist capitalism and its meta-industries impact Earth's atmosphere in ways that engage multiple more-than-human agencies.[20] In an interview with Maude Barlow, Helen Caldicott contrasts the privatization of water, through bottling for example, with capitalism's failure thus far to privatize the air; Barlow replies that 'carbon-emission trading' is a form of privatization of the air.[21] Nonetheless, attempts of capital to 'own' the air are unsettled by the fluid agencies of air itself and our bodily enmeshments with air as we breathe.

Ecologies of breath and corporealities of resistance

In the eighteenth century, the way breathing transformed air into life in the body came under scrutiny, and scientists tested the ancient linguistic links between breath and spirit in devastating experiments on other animals, for example, involving drownings.[22] Poets, too, such as Samuel Taylor Coleridge and John Keats, examined the relation of breath to life.[23] Not only corporeal life but 'the life of *art*' was 'figured as a matter of breathing'.[24] The notion of a breathing *art* was not a reaffirmation of ancient links between breath and divinity; rather poetic speech itself was seen as a 'creative exhalation', a controlled shaping of the air.[25]

18. Anne Elvey, *An Ecological Feminist Reading of the Gospel of Luke: A Gestational Paradigm* (Studies in Women and Religion, 45; Lewiston, NY: Edwin Mellen, 2005), p. 101.

19. Elvey, *Ecological Feminist Reading*, p. 98; Gayatri Chakravorty Spivak, *Outside in the Teaching Machine* (London: Routledge, 1993), p. 148; Jacques Derrida, *Given Time: 1. Counterfeit Money* (trans. Peggy Kamuf; Chicago: University of Chicago Press, 1992), p. 7; Freya Mathews, *For Love of Matter: A Contemporary Panpsychism* (Albany: State University of New York Press, 2003), pp. 83–8.

20. Deborah Guess, 'Oil Beyond War and Peace: Rethinking the Meaning of Matter', in *Ecological Aspects of War: Religious and Theological Perspectives* (ed. Anne Elvey, Deborah Guess and Keith Dyer, *A Forum for Theology in the World* 3, no. 2; Adelaide: ATF Theology, 2016), pp. 73–93 (79–84).

21. Helen Caldicott, 'Maude Barlow', in *Loving This Planet: Leading Thinkers Talk about How to Make a Better World* (ed. Helen Caldicott; New York: The New Press. Proquest Ebook Central, 2011), pp. 1–13 (9).

22. Francis O'Gorman, 'Coleridge, Keats, and the Science of Breathing', *Essays in Criticism* 61, no. 4 (2011), pp. 365–81 (365–6).

23. O'Gorman, 'Science of Breathing', p. 366.

24. O'Gorman, 'Science of Breathing', p. 367.

25. O'Gorman, 'Science of Breathing', p. 368.

As a literary genre, poetry provides a potent example of the material relations between breath and written language. In Chapter 2 I focused on a Lukan poetic text, the song of Mary. In Chapter 3 I turned to late modern or contemporary poets. In the context of ecological feminist hermeneutics, I am especially interested in poetry immersed in and responsive to the situated materialities, especially post the Second World War, prompting ecological, feminist, anti-racist, counter-colonial and related responses. Furthermore, I am interested in poetic practices that show consciousness of the relation of matter and text, and which may inform a hermeneutics inclined towards the material givenness of things.[26]

In the mid-twentieth century, for example, Charles Olson described a practice of 'projective' or 'OPEN' verse, focused in the materiality of the breath.[27] Material energies propel the writer towards constructing a poem, in which these energies are transformed in both the poem's composition and its reading.[28] Type opens a way towards the shaping of the breath on the page as a projection of characters and space; the length of a space in a poem signals a timed breath, a pause to be held.[29] This poetics of breath has purpose; it is meant to be useful in the world, because it takes seriously 'a stance toward reality outside a poem as well as a new stance towards the reality of a poem itself'.[30] A practice of attentiveness connects a poet's inner world to Earth, even in its destruction. Breath is the medium of this attentiveness and a human's 'special qualification as animal'.[31] The 'corporeality of the poet' is essential to the poem's shaping of breath.[32]

Recollecting our corporeal enmeshments with air and the way they might be expressed in written poetic form prompts for me a thinking of the breath in biblical literature, through the relation of a text to the embodied capacities of speech and voice. Speaking and hearing, writing and reading are material, embodied acts. Speaking and hearing are mediated by breath and air. Writing and speaking, and

26. Jane Bennett, *Vibrant Matter: A Political Ecology of Things* (Durham: Duke University Press, 2010); Serenella Iovino and Serpil Oppermann (eds), *Material Ecocriticism* (Bloomington: Indiana University Press, 2014).

27. Charles Olson, 'Projective Verse', Poetry Foundation ([1950] first published online 13 October 2009), available online: https://www.poetryfoundation.org/articles/69406/projective-verse (accessed 7 May 2020).

28. The method and form for this poetic transfer of material energies is 'FIELD COMPOSITION' in which form extends and coheres with content. Olson revives a focus on breath where the line is not defined by the foot, but by its spaces and endings. Olson, 'Projective Verse'.

29. Olson, 'Projective Verse'.

30. Olson, 'Projective Verse'.

31. Olson, 'Projective Verse'.

32. Affirming that the 'breathing body' is porous 'in relation to atmosphere', Olsen's poetics finds echoes in the contemporary turn towards understanding material agencies and their enmeshments. Sarah Daw, '"If He Chooses to Speak from These Roots": Entanglement and Uncertainty in Charles Olson's Quantum Ecopoetics', *Green Letters* 23, no. 4 (2019), pp. 350–66 (355–6, 363); Chantelle Mitchell, 'Airy Matters: Turning toward a Contemporary Breath Poetics', lecture, Free Association and Bus Projects, 1 August 2019.

likewise reading and hearing, are sibling processes where the priorities of one over the other shift and circle. Arguably orality precedes writing, though perhaps the uses of language in speaking may be understood as a form of writing, perhaps a writing with the breath on the air.[33] Oral or vocal composition, which may be described as a kind of storytelling, is more-than-human, and places the human as animal in a breathing world. Storytelling is a material act, mediated 'by chemical signals, by odors, scents, perfumes, stenches', or by waves that act on the air to form sounds.[34] Human oral performances also come to us through the medium of air. Written language, too, encodes breath.[35]

Orality and performance studies remind me that biblical texts are full of breath. Through rhythms and pauses, repetitions and punctuation, a text encodes the breath. Richard Horsley suggests that this encoding of breathy oral performance in a text can be approximated by the way a text is set out on a page, as I have attempted in Chapter 2.[36] A seemingly intangible voice or voices emerge in the interplay of text and reader, recitation and audition. The reader's breath becomes the medium of a biblical text, as it is also for the reader of a poem.[37]

Voice connotes more than speech. Voice can also be understood as a breathy relation to freedom. A focus on breath, argues Irigaray, is a necessity for women in coming to voice in their own bodies and beyond patriarchal identification of women with bodies.[38] This breathy necessity pertains not only to women under patriarchy but especially also to any persons who are subject to the complex intersectionality of racist, classist, sexist, heteronormative violence. Multiple emergences and exercises of voice, of voices, can be performances of resilience and resistance, unfolding in a claim for freedom from oppression.[39]

As I explored in previous chapters, for the Earth Bible Team, Earth itself is voiced: 'Earth is a subject capable of raising its voice in celebration and against injustice.'[40] This ecojustice principle underlies the ecological hermeneutic of retrieval, the third of three key ecological hermeneutics.[41] Applying an ecological hermeneutic of suspicion, the reader is alert to the anthropocentric (including androcentric) biases

33. Walter J. Ong, *Orality and Literacy* (Milton Park, Abingdon: Methuen, 1982), p. 115.
34. Logan, *Air*, p. 18.
35. David Abram, *The Spell of the Sensuous* (New York: Vintage Books, 1997), p. 99.
36. Richard A. Horsley, 'Oral Communication, Oral Performance, and New Testament Interpretation', in *Method and Meaning: Essays on New Testament Interpretation in Honor of Harold W. Attridge* (ed. Andrew B. McGowan and Kent Harold Richards; Atlanta: SBL, 2011), pp. 125-55 (151).
37. Robert Pinsky, *The Sounds of Poetry: A Brief Guide* (New York: Farrar, Straus and Giroux, 1998), p. 8.
38. Irigaray, 'Redemption of Women', pp. 159-60.
39. See, e.g., Ashon T. Crawley, *Blackpentecostal Breath: The Aesthetics of Possibility* (New York: Fordham University Press, 2017).
40. Habel (ed.), *Readings from the Perspective of Earth*, p. 24.
41. Norman C. Habel, 'Introducing Ecological Hermeneutics', in *Exploring Ecological Hermeneutics* (ed. Norman C. Habel and Peter Trudinger; SBL Symposium Series, 46; Atlanta: SBL, 2008), pp. 1-8 (3-8).

of a text and the ways a text represses or elides Earth and human enmeshments in Earth.[42] With an ecological hermeneutic of identification, the reader engages empathically with Earth through a conversion to a wider sense of ecological self.[43] Using an ecological hermeneutic of retrieval, the reader attempts to write creatively *with* Earth, foregrounding an Earthy subjectivity and voice, through a process of recollection and imaginative reconstruction.[44] Voice is communal, social, ethical, Earth-breathed; it is part of hermeneutic, poetic becoming in the space of colonialism and climate emergency. Voice is embodied, and human voice relates to Earth voice through the material givenness of bodies and Earth, air and breath.

A hermeneutic focus on air and breath, moreover, connects readers with histories marked by ecological and social violence enacted on bodies and Earth. In this moment of ongoing colonialism, race-based violence and anthropogenic climate change, interpreters need to think beyond the individualized body to reckon with both the entanglements of human oppressions and the scale of climate change, globally, geologically, across species and into a deep future.[45] This reckoning can inform an understanding of corporeal enmeshments and solidarities both ecologically and socially. The material interplay of atmosphere under climate change with breathing bodies offers a way of considering the co-agencies at work in this moment, and their capacities for productive resistance.

Breath taken violently can provoke such resistance. Eric Garner's dying words repeated, 'I can't breathe', on 17 July 2014, Staten Island, New York, become a prompt for Ashon T Crawley writing in witness and resistance to the murders of African Americans.[46] This is not simply an issue in the United States; in Australia, hundreds of Indigenous people have died in police custody since the Royal Commission into Aboriginal Deaths in Custody, whose 'final report, signed on 15 April 1991, made 339 recommendations, mainly concerned with procedures for persons in custody, liaison with Aboriginal groups, police education and improved accessibility to information'.[47] In November 2015, 26-year-old Dunghutti man,

42. Habel, 'Introducing Ecological Hermeneutics', p. 4.

43. Habel, 'Introducing Ecological Hermeneutics', pp. 4–5; Vicky Balabanski, 'The Step of "Identification" in Norman Habel's Ecological Hermeneutics: Hermeneutical Reflections on "Ecological Conversion"', in *Where the Wild Ox Roams: Biblical Essays in Honour of Norman C. Habel* (ed. Alan H. Cadwallader with Peter L. Trudinger; HBM, 59; Sheffield: Sheffield Phoenix, 2013), pp. 20–31 (25–7).

44. Habel, 'Introducing Ecological Hermeneutics', p. 5.

45. Timothy Clark, *Ecocriticism on the Edge: The Anthropocene as a Threshold Concept* (London: Bloomsbury, 2015), pp. 72–3.

46. Crawley, *Blackpentecostal Breath*, p. 1.

47. 'Deaths Inside', *The Guardian* (24 August 2019), available online: https://www.theguardian.com/australia-news/ng-interactive/2018/aug/28/deaths-inside-indigenous-australian-deaths-in-custody (accessed 17 November 2020); National Archives of Australia, 'Royal Commission into Aboriginal Deaths in Custody', available online: https://www.naa.gov.au/explore-collection/first-australians/royal-commission-aboriginal-deaths-custody (accessed 17 November 2020).

David Dungay, said 'I can't breathe' twelve times before he died restrained by five prison guards.⁴⁸ Dungay's family has expressed solidarity with the family of George Floyd, whose death at the hands of police in Minneapolis on 25 May 2020 sparked widespread protests.⁴⁹ Countering the constriction and taking of the breath in violent deaths authorized by racism, Crawley sees breath and its performance, especially in the 'Blackpentecostal' tradition, a term he coins to emphasize Black agency, as a form of survival-resistance, what Anishinaabe scholar Gerald Vizenor terms 'survivance'.⁵⁰ Through shouting, howling, preaching and riffing, the act of breathing is an embodied performance of survival in the face of racism, an enunciation of a community's freedom producing a critical disruption that expands to what he calls 'otherwise possibilities' which alter 'the normative worlds of juridical violence and violation'.⁵¹

This writing of breath as a performative of disruptive remembrances and possibilities, echoes for me in Paul Celan's description of the capacity of poetry to 'turn the breath'.⁵² In contemporary encounters with the impossibility of adequately addressing the strained breath of climate change, air pollution and toxic social orders, can my readings of biblical texts also work poetically and performatively to turn the breath towards 'otherwise possibilities'? Attention to the way texts encode multiple possibilities through intertextuality provides one reading strategy for such poetic and performative hermeneutic practices.

Breath as intertext

Intertextuality is not only a practice of citation and allusion, it is also the complex relation of textuality to the semiotic space of the maternal and the material.⁵³ Through the breath of other times and places, the interplay with other bodies and other texts, a text is multiple; it carries traces of its relation to the material given, through both its materiality and its relation to the cross-temporal, more-

---

48. Lorena Allam, '"Deaths in Our Backyard": 432 Indigenous Australians Have Died in Custody since 1991', *The Guardian*, 1 June 2020, available online: https://www.theguardian.com/australia-news/2020/jun/01/deaths-in-our-backyard-432-indigenous-australians-have-died-in-custody-since-2008 (accessed 17 November 2020).

49. Allam, '"Deaths in Our Backyard"'.

50. Crawley, *Blackpentecostal Breath*; Gerald Vizenor, *Manifest Manners: Narratives on Postindian Survivance* (Lincoln: University of Nebraska Press, 1994), p. 4.

51. Crawley, *Blackpentecostal Breath*, pp. 2, 85.

52. Paul Celan, 'The Meridian' (trans. Rosemarie Waldrop), in *Selections* (ed. and with an introduction by Pierre Joris; Berkeley: University of California Press, 2005), pp. 154–69 (162).

53. Julia Kristeva, *Revolution in Poetic Language* (trans. Margaret Waller; New York: Columbia University Press, 1984), pp. 43–51, 57–71; Anne Elvey, *The Matter of the Text: Material Engagements between Luke and the Five Senses* (BMW, 37; Sheffield: Sheffield Phoenix, 2011), pp. 28–43.

than-local interconnectedness of air. The category of 'auratic citation' is useful for understanding processes of intertextuality in relation to the material interplay of breath and text.[54] 'Auratic' derives from the word 'aura', a concept linking breath and atmosphere.[55] The notion of auratic citation expands the concept of intertextuality by focussing on the way intertexts in their plurality are each connected to creaturely breath. Practices of auratic citation provide 'language with the means to fracture the impermeable carapace of the present, opening it to a breath of other times and other forms of time'.[56] What could then be called an 'auratic' intertextuality calls forth the repressed voices of Earth in the multiplicities of existence and agency across place, space and time. This recollection allows for the unsettling of the oppressions encoded in the text when breath (πνεῦμα) flows, even 'through the tightest texts'.[57]

In my performative reading below, I listen for the breath when (1) breath (πνεῦμα) is announced in the text itself; (2) breath is embodied in the character of the Lukan Jesus; (3) breath arrives in the direct citation of other texts; (4) the matter of Earth's air and the body's breath are remarked where the text alludes to its own materiality; (5) breath enters in the repressed bodies of women; (6) it is interpolated in the contemporary strained breaths of racist violence and climate change; (7) breath (πνεῦμα) is unsettled by and unsettles violence, social and systemic, that would take the breath. These instances of a breath-filled text do not suggest inspiration in the traditional sense so much as an aspiration to interpret as an exercise of attending to the breath.

Some matters of biblical breath

The Hebrew word רוח bears multiple, interrelated meanings, as I noted in Chapter 2; it is 'the air of both atmospheric winds and animal respiration'.[58] Through its connotations as breath, spirit or divine breath, wind and air, רוח links the human breath of life, inhalation and exhalation, and spirit – the 'sacred' breath of creatures – with Earth's atmosphere marked in our time by global warming/heating or, more commonly now, climate change. Appearing in Gen. 1.2, as primeval wind, breath, air and atmosphere, רוח, is for Theodore Hiebert 'the first sacred thing'.[59]

---

54. On 'auratic citation', see Thomas H. Ford, 'Aura in the Anthropocene', *symplokē* 21, no. 1–2 (2013), pp. 65–82.

55. Ford, 'Aura in the Anthropocene'.

56. Ford, 'Aura in the Anthropocene', p. 76.

57. Catherine Keller, *Apocalypse Now and Then: A Feminist Guide to the End of the World* (Boston: Beacon, 1996), p. 37.

58. Theodore Hiebert, 'Air, the First Sacred Thing: The Conception of רוח in the Hebrew Scriptures', in *Exploring Ecological Hermeneutics* (ed. Norman C. Habel and Peter Trudinger; SBL Symposium Series, 46. Atlanta: SBL, 2008), pp. 9–19 (13).

59. Hiebert, 'Air', p. 15.

When the word רוח is poorly translated with an over-emphasis on spirit and read as immaterial, this can have problematic otherworldly, Earth-subordinating connotations.[60] In contrast, as Luise Schottroff suggests, in Gen 1.2 רוח can be characterized as 'a giant mother-bird'; the wind or breath is the movement of her wings.[61] In this verse, an originary matter vibrates with sacred breath.[62] In the Hebrew Bible, רוח 'almost always appears in connection with verbs of motion' where wind, storm and the 'life force' of animal respiration are associated with 'divine power', life and death.[63] Recovering the material meanings of breath, wind, air and atmosphere becomes significant for an Earth community under the sign of climate change, air pollution and the strained breath of creatures suffering loss of habitat, the failing breath of oceans and the excision of breathing forests such as the Amazon.

In the book of Job, life and breath stand in parallel: 'In his hand is the life (נפש) of every living thing and the breath (רוח) of every human being' (Job 12.10). The divine relation to breathy life (which is more than human) is associated with discernment: 'Does not the ear test words as the palate tastes food?' (Job 12.11). An interplay of divine breath and creaturely life underscores Job's assurance or oath that he speaks truthfully (Job 27.3-4). This assurance echoes in the way prophetic speech is signed with the divine breath (e.g. Isa. 61.1). The concept of רוח in the Hebrew Bible suggests a non-dualistic understanding of humankind in a more-than-human world and contains 'a deep appreciation for the interrelatedness of human life, other life, and the atmosphere upon which all life depends.'[64] The understanding embedded in the word רוח and its usages in the Hebrew Bible affirms the 'correspondence between the respiration of all living beings and the atmosphere they inhabit'.[65] This affirmation, I suggest, functions intertextually when Second Testament writers, such as the Lukan composer, use the word πνεῦμα.

As noted in Chapter 2 above, in biblical Greek the Hebrew word רוח is commonly rendered πνεῦμα, with a similar range of meanings: 'blowing', 'breathing', 'breath', '(life-)spirit' and sometimes also 'wind'.[66] Although western readers have inherited

---

60. Theodore Hiebert, 'The Human Vocation: Origins and Transformations in Christian Traditions', in *Christianity and Ecology: Seeking the Well-Being of Earth and Humans* (ed. Dieter T. Hessel and Rosemary Radford Ruether; Cambridge, MA: Harvard University Press, 2000), pp. 135-54 (141-3); Anne Elvey, 'Beyond Culture? Nature/Culture Dualism and the Christian Otherworldly', *Ethics & the Environment* 1, no. 2 (2006), pp. 63-84 (69).

61. Luise Schottroff, 'The Creation Narrative: Genesis 1:1-2:4a', in *A Feminist Companion to Genesis* (ed. Athalya Brenner; Sheffield: Sheffield Academic, 1993), pp. 24-38 (24).

62. Catherine Keller, *Face of the Deep: A Theology of Becoming* (London: Routledge, 2003), p. 238.

63. Silvia Schroer and Thomas Staubli, *Body Symbolism in the Bible* (trans. Linda M. Maloney; Collegeville: Liturgical Press, 2001), pp. 214-15.

64. Hiebert, 'Air', p. 18.

65. Hiebert, 'Air', p. 18.

66. BAGD, pp. 674-5.

a problematic dematerialization of πνεῦμα when rendered 'spirit' or 'Spirit', Second Testament writings are more likely steeped in material understandings.[67] For example, Troels Engberg-Pedersen holds that for Paul, πνεῦμα is 'a material entity'; in Pauline cosmology earth and heavens are constituted by material realities (water and earth; fire and air), and the materiality of earth and heavens/skies/cosmos resonates in the materiality of spirit/breath and flesh/body.[68] Stanley Stowers argues, too, for the substantial material grounding of the concept of πνεῦμα. The question is not one of opposition but of hierarchy. In the Pauline world, '*pneuma* (wind, air, breath, spirit)… is a refined, qualitatively higher substance with its own power of movement and intelligence'.[69] Paul's understanding of πνεῦμα is steeped in traditions of ancestry and concrete thinking about the interplay of divine breath in the physical body.[70] Nonetheless, Paul's thinking remains indebted to a tradition in which breath/spirit (πνεῦμα) is the active element in relation to 'passive matter'.[71] From an ecocritical perspective, both the hierarchy and the contrast of active-passive in relation to spirit/breath (πνεῦμα) over flesh/matter (σάρξ) remain a concern. But the exercise of breath/spirit (πνεῦμα) in flesh/matter (σάρξ) in Paul's Christology represents a deepening of the materiality of the Christian's corporeality and their bodily participation in/with Christ.[72]

In the Gospel of Luke, where the word πνεῦμα appears, it is usually translated 'spirit', often with a capital. But ecologically the ancient resonances may be better served by rendering τὸ πνεῦμα τὸ ἅγιον as 'sacred breath' rather than 'holy spirit'. In the Lukan narrative, while the promised child John will share the prophetic character denoted by the presence of breath/spirit (πνεῦμα, 1.15, 17), and a sacred breath (πνεῦμα ἅγιον) will arrive on Mary of Nazareth (1.35), it is Luke's Elizabeth who, the narrator tells, is first 'filled' with a sacred breath (πνεύματος ἁγίου; 1.41). Mary, too, in her encounter with Elizabeth is engaged with this breathing life (1.46-47) as she sings out in the Magnificat (1.46-55). As Barbara Reid explains in relation to 1.46-55, breath/spirit (πνεῦμα) and life/soul (ψυχή) are not opposed to either body (σῶμα) or flesh (σάρξ).[73] Rather these terms work together to describe the fleshy material subjectivity of the whole person. This breathy sacred engages, too, with the male characters, Zechariah, John, and Simeon (1.67, 80; 2.25-27). As the narrative turns to the Lukan Jesus as an adult, the focus of the sacred breath shifts to him (3.16, 22; 4.1, 14), arriving in bodily form as a dove (3.22) recalling

67. Stanley Stowers, 'Matter and Spirit, or What Is Pauline Participation in Christ?', in *The Holy Spirit: Classic and Contemporary Readings* (ed. Eugene F. Rogers, Jr.; Chichester: Wiley-Blackwell, 2009), pp. 91–105 (93–4).

68. Troels Engberg-Pedersen, 'The Material Spirit: Cosmology and Ethics in Paul', NTS 55 (2009), pp. 179–97 (179).

69. Stowers, 'Matter and Spirit', p. 94.

70. Engberg-Pedersen, 'Material Spirit', pp. 187–9.

71. Stowers, 'Matter and Spirit', p. 99.

72. Stowers, 'Matter and Spirit', pp. 99–100.

73. Barbara E. Reid, *Choosing the Better Part? Women in the Gospel of Luke* (Collegeville: Liturgical Press, 1996), pp. 76–7.

the hovering birdy breath-wind (רוח) of Gen. 1.2.⁷⁴ Thus, when the Lukan Jesus comes into the synagogue of Nazareth (4.16) the reader knows already that Luke's Jesus is enmeshed with the breathing life of Earth. Nonetheless, just as the Lukan narrative retreats from an affirmation of the maternal (11.27-28), the corporeal, airy, material resonances of the Hebrew רוח could be said to be forgotten when in 24.39 – where the NRSV translates πνεῦμα as 'ghost' – πνεῦμα is contrasted with the corporeal, the tactile, the material.⁷⁵ Πνεῦμα becomes a breath that has no body. But the materiality of this sacred breath returns in the first chapter of Acts (1.2, 5, 8, 16), with the arrival of breath/wind/spirit (πνεῦμα) at Pentecost signalled by a violent gust (2.2, 4), an Earthy breath. With these multiple associations in mind, I turn to a performative reading of Lk. 4.16-30.

*A performative reading of Luke 4.16-30*⁷⁶

And he came into Nazareth, where he had been nourished, and went, according to his custom on the Sabbath, into the synagogue.
   Should we assume this to be a male-only space? Perhaps not. But if it were, the recollection of nourishment in οὗ ἦν τεθραμμένος is a reminder of the material givenness of the maternal body and Earth, including its atmosphere, which sustains life, and of his mother Mary of Nazareth whose dynamic connection with a sacred breath precedes and enables his own.

---

74. Cf. Edward P. Dixon, 'Descending Spirit and Descending Gods: A "Greek" Interpretation of the Spirit's "Descent as a Dove" in Mark 1:10', *JBL* 128 (2009), pp. 759-80.

75. On retreat from the maternal, see Elvey, *Ecological Feminist Reading*, pp. 141-2. To what extent was the Lukan narrative also echoing Plato's or Aristotle's distinctions between spirit and matter and the relation of the body to the cosmos? On the influence of Greek philosophy on Luke's understanding of the body, see Michael Trainor, *About Earth's Child: An Ecological Listening to the Gospel of Luke* (Earth Bible Commentary, 2; Sheffield: Sheffield Phoenix, 2012), pp. 121-3.

76. This reading references the following: American Public Health Association, 'Climate Change Decreases the Quality of the Air We Breathe', Fact Sheet, available online: https://apha.org/-/media/files/pdf/factsheets/climate/air_quality.ashx (accessed 26 November 2020); The Breathe Project, available online: https://breatheproject.org/ (accessed 26 November 2020); Bernadette Brooten, *Women Leaders in the Ancient Synagogue: Inscriptional Evidence and Background Issues* (Chico: Scholars Press, 1982); Crawley, *Blackpentecostal Breath*; Elvey, *Matter of the Text*, pp. 44-67; idem, *Reading the Magnificat in Australia: Unsettling Engagements* (BMW, 75; Sheffield: Sheffield Phoenix, 2020); Allen Ginsberg, *Howl, Kaddish and Other Poems* (Melbourne: Penguin, 2010 [1956]), p. 5; Robert Pogue Harrison, *Forests: The Shadow of Civilization* (Chicago: The University of Chicago Press, 1992), pp. 51-2; William H. Lamar, IV, 'It's Not Just the Coronavirus – Bad Theology Is Killing Us', Faith & Leadership (Tuesday, 26 May 2020), available online: https://faithandleadership.com/william-h-lamar-iv-its-not-just-coronavirus-bad-theology-killing-us (accessed 26 November 2020);

He stood up to read.
    HE TAKES A BREATH.

    The American Public Health Association reports that due to increases in air pollutants exacerbating 'increased allergens associated with climate change' persons who have 'existing pollen allergies may have increased risk for acute respiratory effects'.

    In a media release on Tuesday 10 December 2019, The Thoracic Society of Australia and New Zealand declares climate change 'a medical emergency'.

The scroll
    βιβλίον – a material thing, made of papyrus or parchment, plant or animal skin
    Hear the wind through the papyrus reeds, the warm breath in the nostrils of a sheep.
of the prophet Isaiah was given to him and he unrolled the scroll
    He touches the matter of the text.
and found the place
    Is it several places?
where it is written
    inscribed, matter to matter, ink on papyrus or parchment, a place that is several places

    HE TAKES A BREATH

    Air carries the sound of the voice from his mouth to the ears of those in the synagogue.

    Tripled, the breath of Isaiah (42.7; 58.6; 61.1-2) breathes in the text
    AURATIC CITATION

Amy-Jill Levine and Ben Witherington III, *The Gospel of Luke* (New Cambridge Bible Commentary; Cambridge: Cambridge University Press, 2018), p. 113; Laura Poppick, 'The Ocean Is Running Out of Breath Scientists Warn', *Scientific American* (25 February 2019), available online: https://www.scientificamerican.com/article/the-ocean-is-running-out-of-breath-scientists-warn/ (accessed 26 November 2020); Sharon H. Ringe, *Luke* (Westminster Bible Companion; Louisville: Westminster John Knox, 1995), p. 183; The Thoracic Society of Australia and New Zealand, 'Declaration on Climate Change' (10 December 2019), available online: https://www.thoracic.org.au/documents/item/1800 (accessed 26 November 2020); Elaine M. Wainwright, 'Unbound Hair and *Ointmented* Feet: An Ecofeminist Reading of Luke 7.36-50', in *Exchanges of Grace: Festschrift for Ann Loades* (ed. Natalie K. Watson and Stephen Burns; London: SCM, 2008), pp. 178–89.

the breath of ha shem is on me
> breath speaks like wind against hair and skin, a voice that moves through air brushing an ear, yes metaphor, for material relation with the divine
> an echo too of a woman
> my whole bodied self (ψυχή) makes great
> my breath (πνεῦμα) rejoices (1.46-47)

on account of who anointed me
> oil to skin, yes metaphor again, but grounded in matter to matter, plant oil, the animal skin of a human

to bring the good news to the poor
> material situations of want, welcome news of needs met
>> hear his mother sing of an overturning and the hungry sated while the rich go hungry (1.54)

who has sent me to announce/proclaim freedom (ἄφεσις) to captives
> a material situation of confinement, that might mean slavery as a result of war or debt
> and the otherwise possibility of ἄφεσις

and to the blind recovery of sight
> the return of a lost sense
> but what of the senses of the blind, senses as modes of fleshy engagement with matter, matter to sense

to send the oppressed/broken down/violated in freedom (ἄφεσις)
> material situations of trauma
> and the otherwise possibility of ἄφεσις

> a co-agency with Earth recalled
>> For as the earth brings forth its shoots,
>>> and as a garden causes what is sown in it to spring up,
>> so Adonai Yhwh will cause righteousness and praise
>>> to spring up before all the nations (Isa. 61.11).

to announce/proclaim the year of ha shem acceptable (δεκτόν)
> a period of material undoing
> a period of renewal
> an otherwise possibility of material relation that is Jubilee, imagined or real
>> an acceptable day is a day of critique
>> of the oppression of workers
>> and the enslavement of other creatures
>> a day of imagining yokes broken (Isa. 58.3-6)

Hear in the background: Rome and empire, the felling of breathing forests, a colonial cultural invasion effected though destroying the forested bounds that enabled story and rite to grow in their own unique habitats, a totalizing force to be resisted.

> a co-agency with Earth recalled
>> you shall be like a watered garden,
>>> like a spring of water,
>> whose waters never fail. (Isa. 58.11)

AURATIC CITATION

A co-agency with Earth in a Sabbath observance predicated on more-than-human engagement in alleviating oppressions of hunger, disease, debt and imprisonment.

And he closed/rolled up the scroll
> touching the matter of the text

gave it back to the assistant/attendant/servant and sat down.
And the eyes of everyone in the synagogue were fixed on him.
> from hearing to sight

HE TAKES A BREATH
> Air carries the sound of his voice from his mouth to the ears of those in the synagogue from sight to hearing

But (δέ)
> Is this a turning of the breath?

he began to say to them that today this writing is fulfilled/has been fulfilled in your ears
> the body, the senses, the matter of a text from the air to the body's ear

And all were witnessing to him and were admiring the words of grace coming out of his mouth and said is this not Joseph's son?
> Do you hear the body language?

> The Ocean Is Running Out of Breath Scientists Warn. (*Scientific American* 2019).

It appears he does not want to be admired for the grace of his words – the howl, the shout, the breath exhaled in protest, these are not gracious words, but words of resistance, of otherwise possibility; so, he provokes them…

And he said to them 'By all means, you will tell me this parable, "Physician, cure yourself, as much as we have heard you did in Capernaum do also here in your homeland/hometown"' (ἐν τῇ πατρίδι σου).
And he said, 'Amen I say to you that no prophet is acceptable (δεκτός)
> hear the echo of 4.19

in his/their homeland/hometown' (ἐν τῇ πατρίδι αὐτοῦ).
> The place where he was nourished (οὗ ἦν τεθραμμένος) is now πατρίς from πατήρ (father) and presumed inhospitable.

He has the conversation with himself, from himself: Listen, beneath what
seems like grace to the otherwise possibility: 'I am howling'.

Written between 1955 and 1956, in the 49th and 50th stanzas/units of
the first part of Allen Ginsberg's 'Howl', breathing and lung disease bump
up against theology amid flames that suggest apocalypse.

*But according to the truth I say to you many widows were in the days of Elijah
in Israel when the sky was shut up for three years and six months and there was
famine over all the land/earth*
    A material situation of want, and need met; recognition of a group of
    women vulnerable to privation in patriarchal economies
*And to none of them was sent Elijah except to Sarepta in Sidon to a woman
widow. And many lepers were in Israel in the time of Elisha, and none of them
were cleansed except Naaman, the Syrian.*
    Are you holding your breath at the injustice of the divine choice? Is this
    what the hometown (πατρίς) crowd are doing?
*And all were filled with anger (sorrow, soul, spirit, mind) in the synagogue when
they heard this.*
    A soul deep sorrowful rage they will not bear…
    instead seek to quell their distress through annihilation…
And rising up, they threw him out
    expelled him, exorcised him
from the town and led him to the brow
    scorn, pride
of the hill on which their town
    It is no longer *his* hometown. Is it still the place of nurturance – repressed?
was built, in order to throw him over the cliff
    TO TAKE HIS BREATH.

William Lamar describes intersections of racism and the impacts of
COVID-19 in poor communities as 'the American empire in viral form'
which is supported by 'bad theology'. He closes with an allusion to Lk.
4.18-30 and describes the response of the Lukan Jesus to the lethal
violence threatening him as one of inclusivity.

But he passed through their midst and kept going on.
    HE TAKES A BREATH,
    goes on to Capernaum… as the story goes…

In Pennsylvania there is 'a coalition of citizens, environmental
advocates, public health professionals and academics' called The Breathe
Collaborative who through The Breathe Project are 'working to improve
air quality, eliminate climate pollution and make [their] region a healthy
and prosperous place to live'.

Conclusion

Beyond breath shared across millennia of atmospheric unfoldings, no easy conjunctions exist between ancient text and contemporary context, between the otherwise possibilities of freedom (ἄφεσις) breathed into and out of a text and its meaning amid our contemporary howls. While it might be satisfying to decide that a text is either unambiguously useful to our time or irredeemably toxic, neither is true of Lk. 4.16-30. Read with an ear to its breathy engagements – and I have not considered its oral properties fully – intertextual voices and situations speak into and out of the text both through citation and in the materialities on which the text depends and to which it alludes. The breathy energies of the drama of the text, its intersections with the atmospheric energies of Earth, its situation in relation to empire, and its approach towards and temporary escape from the final breath of its protagonist taken violently allow the text to be read in parallel with contemporary systemic situations of strained breath, as part of breathy voicings of 'otherwise possibilities'.[77]

Freedom to act for an imagined future that is otherwise than the promise of destruction that haunts contemporary ecological thinking is key to the following section. Section 2 begins with a focus on feminisms and materialisms, as a basis for responding to a present and future where more-than-human communities struggle under ecological pressure. I discuss freedom to act in hope towards 'otherwise possibilities' for collective more-than-human being and living. In the remainder of the section, I address climate change as a sign of the times and human responsibility for a deep future, and I argue for the ecological energy of neighbour love in a context of more-than-human material agencies.

---

77. Crawley, *Blackpentecostal Breath*, p. 2.

Section 2

SITUATING ECOLOGICAL MATERIALISM

Chapter 5

REFRAMING FEMINIST APPROACHES ECOLOGICALLY:
MATTER, FREEDOM AND THE FUTURE

In previous chapters I highlighted the need to attend to material situation and focused on the materiality of shared breath.[1] New materialism (or the material turn) challenges me to consider not only that matter as a concept can be the focus for the unfolding of ecological feminist thinking but also that materialities of situation and breath are foundational to thought. In western political and social thought key approaches to the scholarly search for 'truth', namely objectivity and relativism, are inadequate from the perspective of the breadth of women's situated materialities.[2] For example, Patricia Hill Collins argues that Black women's social conditions shape both situated and specialist knowledges, formed in 'the interdependence of the everyday'.[3] Knowledge arising from material situation contributes to critiques of domination not through decentring one subject in order to recentre another but by allowing the centre of discourse to 'pivot'.[4] While the dominant group must be decentred, models of sharing the centre can emerge from women's subjugated knowledges; for example, 'the Afrocentric call-and-response tradition' offers a model for discourse where each voice is affirmed and 'everyone must listen and respond to other voices in order to be allowed to remain in the community'.[5] The affirmation of subjugated ways of knowing is crucial, too, for First Nations women.

Regrettably, white settler approaches in colonial settings such as Australia are often incommensurable with 'Indigenous women's subjugated knowledges', as Aileen Moreton-Robinson shows.[6] Central to Indigenous women's knowledges are 'relationality' and 'spirituality'; for Indigenous women 'spirituality permeates

---

1. This chapter builds on and revises, Anne Elvey, 'Matter, Freedom and the Future: Reframing Feminist Theologies through an Ecological Materialist Lens', *Feminist Theology* 23, no. 2 (2015), pp. 186–204. First published by SAGE.

2. Patricia Hill Collins, *Black Feminist Thought: Knowledge, Consciousness, and the Politics of Empowerment* (Perspectives on Gender, 2; New York: Routledge, 1991), p. 235.

3. Collins, *Black Feminist Thought*, pp. 235–6.

4. Collins, *Black Feminist Thought*, p. 236.

5. Collins, *Black Feminist Thought*, pp. 236–7.

6. Aileen Moreton-Robinson, *Talkin' Up to the White Woman: Indigenous Women and Feminism* (St. Lucia, Qld: University of Queensland Press, 2000), p. 15.

life' and 'the universe is aware and organic', so that relationships are collective, intergenerational and 'underpinned' by connections with Country and 'the spirit world'.[7] This is materially meaningful: 'the spirit world is immediately experienced because it is synonymous with the land', and so 'spirituality is a physical fact because it is experienced as part of one's life'.[8] Such lived knowledges challenge rationalist approaches, including or especially where these inform western systems of belief and white feminist thought.[9]

For the kind of ecological feminist hermeneutics I propose in this book, with sympathy towards new materialist approaches, my focus in Section 1 on the materiality of breath includes its relation to spirit. This focus on breath not only unsettles matter-spirit binaries but also provides a necessary condition for thinking that offers an alternative to rationalist approaches. Non-violence scholar and activist, Chandra Satha-Anand provides a striking example. He shifts the rationalist Cartesian *cogito ergo sum*, 'I think therefore I am', to the more materially embodied and interconnected *spiro ergo sum*, 'I breathe therefore I am'.[10] As breathing beings, humans are already in relationship, open to empathy with, and able to grieve for, others: past, present and future others.[11] Breathing, as I have suggested in previous chapters, embeds us in genealogies of breathing beings. In this book such networked lineages include not only the ancestral deep time materialities and more-than-human corporealities of Earth and Earth beings, but also the genealogies of more recent feminists, Earth Bible scholars and environmental humanities researchers, especially exponents of the new materialism, who through their work have breathed into this work.[12]

Over the past half-century, feminist theologians, including feminist biblical scholars, have taken a variety of approaches to discourse and experience, from critiques of patriarchy and androcentrism, to emphases on women's bodies and experience, to more subtle affirmations of the possibility of divine becoming in the feminine. From the presumption of their mostly western (white) liberal beginnings, feminist theologies have become multidimensional, recognizing their place and limits alongside liberationist, womanist, mujerista, postcolonial and First Nations perspectives, in approaches that note the multiple dimensions of women's experience, where race, ethnicity, class, gender, sexuality and location

---

7. Moreton-Robinson, *Talkin' Up*, p. 16.

8. Moreton-Robinson, *Talkin' Up*, p. 19.

9. Moreton-Robinson, *Talkin' Up*, p. 19.

10. Chaiwat Satha-Anand, 'Breathing the Others, Seeing the Lives: A Reflection on Twenty-First-Century Nonviolence', in *Towards a Just and Ecologically Sustainable Peace: Navigating the Great Transition* (ed. Joseph Camilleri and Deborah Guess; Singapore: Palgrave Macmillan, 2020), pp. 229–48 (243).

11. Satha-Anand, 'Breathing', p. 242.

12. See, e.g., Niamh Moore, 'Eco/feminist Genealogies: Renewing Promises and New Possibilities', in *Contemporary Perspectives on Ecofeminism* (ed. Mary Phillips and Nick Rumens; Routledge Explorations in Environmental Studies; Milton Park, Abingdon: Routledge, 2016), pp. 19–37.

intersect.[13] The focus on intersectionality is not new, but can be traced to both the lived experience of women of colour and the theory of scholars such as bell hooks.[14] Ecological feminism adds a further dimension, exploring critical links not only between women's embodiment and the materiality of Earth and cosmos, but also between oppression of women and First Nations and ecological destruction, including violence towards other animals.[15]

An ecological focus, however, is not one more perspective to add to a multidimensional approach to feminist theologies. Rather it requires a fundamental shift of perspective, so that the focus of feminism, traditionally a human focus, is rethought within the frame of the materiality that constitutes not only humans but Earth and the cosmos we inhabit. Writing from an ecological feminist perspective informed by the new materialism and its affirmative turn towards the shared materiality of the cosmos, I imagine myself already sympathetic to Indigenous ways of knowing, but I need to hear the ways in which both western rationality and late capitalist individualism have infected the kinds of feminist thinking in which I have been schooled. In this chapter, as a way of situating feminist theological discourses and experiences ecologically, drawing on the new materialism I focus

13. This can be classified as a third wave. See, e.g., Anita J. Monro, 'A Kaleidoscopic Vessel Sailing a Kyriarchal Ocean: The Third Wave Feminist Theologies of *Women-Church* (1987–2007)', in *Theological and Hermeneutical Explorations from Australia: Horizons of Contextuality* (ed. Jione Havea; Lanham: Lexington Books, 2021), pp. 25–42 (28–9).

14. See, e.g., bell hooks, *Talking Back: Thinking Feminist, Thinking Black* (Boston: South End Press, 1989); see also Patricia Hill Collins and Sirma Bilge, *Intersectionality* (ProQuest Ebook Central; Cambridge, UK: Polity, 2016); IWDA, 'What Does Intersectional Feminism Actually Mean?', International Women's Development Agency (11 May 2018), available online: https://iwda.org.au/what-does-intersectional-feminism-actually-mean/ (accessed 2 February 2021).

15. See, e.g., Chris J. Cuomo, *Feminism and Ecological Communities: An Ethic of Flourishing* (London: Routledge, 1998); Heather Eaton and Lois Ann Lorentzen, *Ecofeminism and Globalization: Exploring Culture, Context, and Religion* (Lanham, MD: Rowman & Littlefield, 2003); Susan Griffin, *The Eros of Everyday Life: Essays on Ecology, Gender and Society* (New York: Anchor Books, 1995); Ronnie Zoe Hawkins, 'Ecofeminism and Nonhumans: Continuity, Difference, Dualism and Domination', *Hypatia* 13, no. 1 (1998), pp. 158–97; Susan Hawthorne, *Wild Politics* (North Melbourne: Spinifex Press, 2002); Mary Mellor, *Feminism and Ecology* (Cambridge: Polity, 1997); Maria Mies and Vandana Shiva, *Ecofeminism* (North Melbourne: Spinifex Press, 1993); Mary Phillips and Nick Rumens (eds), *Contemporary Perspectives on Ecofeminism* (Routledge Explorations in Environmental Studies; Milton Park, Abingdon: Routledge, 2016); Ariel Salleh, *Ecofeminism as Politics: Nature, Marx and the Postmodern* (London: Zed Books, 1997); Ariel Salleh (ed.), *Eco-sufficiency and Global Justice: Women Write Political Ecology* (North Melbourne: Spinifex Press, 2009); Noël Sturgeon, *Ecofeminist Natures: Race Gender Feminist Theory and Political Action* (London: Routledge, 1997); Lara Stevens, Peta Tait and Denise Varney (eds), *Feminist Ecologies: Changing Environments in the Anthropocene* (Cham, Switzerland: Palgrave Macmillan, 2018).

on a shared materiality as a basis for reframing human being, dwelling, agency and labour, in terms of co-being, habitat, co-agency and more-than-human labour. I acknowledge that to most First Peoples this is not new, and that there is still much for me to both learn and unlearn. My modest exploration in this chapter implies for western feminists a rethinking of human freedom with implications for how we frame feminist theologies in relation to the future of Earth and humankind. I suggest that material situation and freedom exist in tensive correlation.

Matter, materialities and materialisms

Ecological thinking and the new materialism intersect in their affirmation of the materiality of Earth (and cosmos) as lively and to be cherished. The 'ecological thought' upholds our interconnectedness with and embeddedness in a wider community of coexistent others, who or which are particular in space, time and relation to us.[16] Is 'matter' too general a term for this particularity and plurality of things?[17] While, as I argue below, 'nature' is a homogenizing term, the term 'matter', however, is not in the same sense problematic. 'Matter' pertains not to some overarching other-than-human category, but to 'stuff' in its minutiae and indeterminacy (in its intangibility at a subatomic level). 'Matter' refers to the stuff which constitutes each element and their complex agglomerations in the universe (stars, trees, water, air, individual animals, including human beings, and plants, minerals, tables, computers), each instance of these in their peculiar specificity and interrelatedness. 'Matter' is a term that supports the 'ecological thought'. Matter is the stuff that both connects us and constitutes each as uniquely itself. Several ways of theorizing matter and materiality may be useful for the task of describing an ecological materialism. I adopt this term ecological materialism to signal the intersection between ecological thinking, the new materialism and what I have called in earlier chapters situated materialities, which I seek to elucidate through ecologically informed Marxist and feminist lenses.

The rise of materialist views in science and philosophy in eighteenth- and nineteenth-century England and France was often seen at the time to be in conflict with Christian views of G-d.[18] These materialists understood that the physical universe operated under its own laws, and that these laws, adequately comprehended, could offer sufficient explanation, for example, for the operation of mind, without appeal to a supernatural end for humankind. Among such

---

16. Timothy Morton, *The Ecological Thought* (Cambridge, MA: Harvard University Press, 2010).

17. See, Timothy Morton, 'Ecological Awareness as Blindness' (Keynote address presented at Regarding the Earth: ASLEC-ANZ Conference, 1 September 2012, Monash University, Caulfield), available online: http://ecologywithoutnature.blogspot.com.au/2012/09/ecological-awareness-as-blindness-mp3.html (accessed 3 February 2021).

18. John Bellamy Foster, *Marx's Ecology: Materialism and Nature* (New York: Monthly Review Press, 2000), pp. 21–31.

potentially 'heretical' materialists was Charles Darwin, whose articulation of the theory of evolution unsettled notions of humankind as the end of a great chain of being, and affirmed connections between humankind and other species.

Karl Marx took this scientific and philosophic materialism in a different direction. Writing of Marx and ecology, John Bellamy Foster describes an Epicurean materialism that was more than mechanistic, but 'pointed to human cultural evolution as representing a kind of freedom for rational organization of historical life, building on constraints first established by the material world'.[19] Working with, but departing from, this Epicurean approach, Marx and Engels developed a practical (or historical) materialism in response to the oppressive labour practices of the industrial revolution.[20] In their view, labour constitutes an interactive or metabolic relation between humans and 'nature'.[21] Under capitalism, the worker is a commodity alienated from the product of her or his labour, since 'capital is stored-up labour'; moreover, it is labour stored up as private property.[22] While there seems to be more focus on the human than on matter *per se*, the emphasis on the relationality of labour, and its meaning within economic and social institutions, suggests a framework for rethinking human engagement with materiality. Importantly, central to ecological thinking in a Marxist frame is 'the issue of the relation of the materialist conception of nature to the materialist conception of history (that is, of the alienation of labor to the alienation of nature)'.[23] This linking of the alienation of labour and the alienation of 'nature' pertains not only to questions of when and how 'nature' is dominated and abused for 'narrow human ends'.[24] It also asks whether human existence can in a sense transcend these alienations so that 'the alienation of human beings from nature and from each other will be no longer the precondition for human existence'.[25] But the primary issue is that the alienations of labour and of 'nature' imply the alienation of 'all that is human'.[26] By implication, an ecological materialism requires a rethinking of what it is to be human.

A focus on embodiment is crucial for such rethinking. In her investigation of relations between historical materialism and feminism, for example, Gillian Howie

---

19. Foster, *Marx's Ecology*, p. 53.
20. Foster, *Marx's Ecology*, p. 53.
21. Foster, *Marx's Ecology*, p. 158.
22. Karl Marx, *Economic and Philosophical Manuscripts of 1844* (trans. M. Milligan; Moscow: Progress Publishers, 1959), first manuscript; William Cavanaugh applies this concept of alienation to contemporary consumerist economies, in which consumers are alienated from the things they consume or use in three ways: from products, production and their producers. See William T. Cavanaugh, *Being Consumed: Economics and Christian Desire* (Grand Rapids: Eerdmans, 2008), pp. 35–47.
23. Foster, *Marx's Ecology*, p. 254.
24. Foster, *Marx's Ecology*, p. 254.
25. Foster, *Marx's Ecology*, p. 254.
26. Foster, *Marx's Ecology*, p. 254.

affirms the notion of 'a sensuous subject situated within a web of social relations' as in accord with an 'idea of body-consciousness'.[27] Body-consciousness offers a way of thinking about or through the body situationally, considering 'perspectives, projects, situations, habits, interests, capacities, and pleasures... [and]... about the located character of an always projecting and engaged subject: affecting and being affected in the world'.[28] The body is the locus of the subject's situated materiality, including her relation to systems of power. Her materially grounded, corporeal subjectivity is not singular but complex and relational, both vulnerable and potentially resilient in the face of systemic injustices.

A paradigm for thinking about the situated material conditions of embodied human experience arises in Simone de Beauvoir's work on 'old age'.[29] Material conditions – such as the corporeal limits of an ageing body, the production (or construction) of ageing bodies in discourse and a society's treatment of aged persons – work together to produce the experience of 'old age'.[30] An ecological materialism attends non-reductively to the inter-constituencies of such material conditions. Such attentiveness takes account not only of the interdependence of humans and other animals with a wider Earth community for their sustenance and flourishing, but also of the toxic effects of materials such as asbestos and lead, and the intersections of harm on humans with, for example, their economic and socio-cultural status. Moreover, it goes beyond these interrelationships (beneficial and dangerous) to consider a wider materialist frame in which relationship to human well-being is one aspect of the inter-relationality of matter.

A materialist frame and matter-spirit dualism

Germane to this ecological materialism is ecophilosophical critique of a system of mastery.[31] A logic of colonization has characterized a dominant mode of western rationality, where women, enslaved persons, the body, animals and matter are opposed to, and hyper-separated from, men, master, the mind-soul-and-spirit, humans and spirit (again) in a system of thought and practice that valorizes the latter set. In each set the elements are identified with one another: *women* with

---

27. Gillian Howie, *Between Feminism and Materialism: A Question of Method* (New York: Palgrave Macmillan, 2010), p. 32; Simone de Beauvoir, *The Second Sex* (ed. and trans. H. M. Parshley; London: Random House, 1953).

28. Howie, *Between Feminism and Materialism*, p. 14.

29. Sonia Kruks, 'Simone de Beauvoir: Engaging Discrepant Materialisms', in *New Materialisms: Ontology, Agency, and Politics* (ed. Diane Coole and Samatha Frost; Durham: Duke University Press, 2010), pp. 258–80 (269–75); Simone de Beauvoir, *The Coming of Age* (trans. Patrick O'Brian; New York: Norton, 1996).

30. Beauvoir, *Coming of Age*; Kruks, 'Simone de Beauvoir', pp. 262, 276.

31. Val Plumwood, *Feminism and the Mastery of Nature* (Feminism for Today; London: Routledge, 1993).

enslaved persons, bodies, animals and matter, and *men* with mastery, mind, soul, human being and spirit.³² Mapped onto this is the theological presupposition that the divine creator and heaven are on the male side; the created and Earth are on the female side. The historical rise of technological control over nature occurred at the same time as European colonization; a logic of domination and deceit (parallel to the patriarchal logic of colonization) is linked with a denial of death, narratives of world destruction and especially the ecological and social destructiveness of war.³³ Moreover, a constitutive erotophobia underpins the colonizing structures of dualism.³⁴

Addressing the tradition of western philosophy and rationality in which she was trained, Val Plumwood describes further aspects of this system, which I will outline briefly in relation to the master/enslaved paradigm, but master/enslaved could be replaced with man/woman or human/nature or spirit/matter:

1. *backgrounding* occurs when the work of enslaved persons and the master's dependence on the enslaved are kept in the background or denied;
2. *radical exclusion* constructs an enslaved person as the other, excluded from the category human which is defined by, and as, the category of the master;
3. *incorporation* means that the enslaved person is assimilated to the master's worldview as 'lack', as describing necessity and lacking the masterly quality of freedom;
4. *instrumentalization* serves to value enslaved persons only in terms of their use by, or for, the master;
5. *homogenization* casts enslaved persons as alike and interchangeable; this alikeness can be reinforced by stereotyping or demonization.³⁵

When applied to 'nature', homogenization and stereotyping entail a denial of the complexity of nature, of the difference within nature and of human continuity with nature. In this regard the word 'nature' is problematic in itself, as a generalizing term which masks differences between the many constituents of Earth and cosmos, species, kinds, ecosystems, galaxies and so on. Because the system of mastery fails to account for the multiple more-than-human others on which the 'master' depends it will collapse, since it neglects and/or denies the things which sustain the 'master'.³⁶

Suspicious of spirituality in a framework of matter-spirit dualism, Plumwood writes of 'achieving more earth-friendly and counter-hegemonic forms of

---

32. Plumwood, *Feminism*, pp. 41–68. This mapping resonates with Elisabeth Schüssler Fiorenza's description of kyriarchy. Elisabeth Schüssler Fiorenza, *But She Said: Feminist Practices of Biblical Interpretation* (Boston: Beacon, 1992), p. 117.

33. Rosemary Radford Ruether, *Gaia and God: An Ecofeminist Theology of Earth Healing* (San Francisco: HarperCollins, 1992), pp. 198–9.

34. Greta Gaard, 'Towards a Queer Ecofeminism', *Hypatia* 12, no. 1 (1997), pp. 114–37.

35. Plumwood, *Feminism*, pp. 47–55.

36. Plumwood, *Feminism*, p. 195.

spirituality' that honour 'the material and ecological bases of life'.³⁷ Such spirituality will be 'counter-centric in affirming continuity and kinship for earth others as well as their subjecthood, opacity and agency. It will be dialogical, communicative, open to the play of more-than-human forces and attentive to the ancestral voices of place and of earth'.³⁸ Relationship to place is multiple; humans are not only interrelated with (and responsible to) the place or places each inhabits, but all those places and their constitutive agents (including humans) on whose productive and reproductive labour people depend must also be accounted for in human attentiveness to place.³⁹ When I ignore the complexity of my relationships to multiple places, I participate in the 'dematerialization' of commodity culture, that is, the process of alienation (of becoming less and less in touch with) the material conditions that support my life.

The analysis of systems of mastery and the related logic of colonization, I have sketched from Plumwood, and her foray into discussion of spirituality in the context of matter-spirit dualism, are both compelling and limited. In an Australian context, First Nations women and girls were indentured to labour for white settler women, a form of slavery, as part of the colonial project of invasion and assimilation. In this context, too, as Moreton-Robinson and many other Indigenous scholars affirm, First Nations women continue to live modes of sisterhood, kinship and spirituality based in material relations to lands, waters and skies.⁴⁰ Settler analyses of a logic of colonization and considerations of the possibility of a spirituality that does not reinforce a matter-spirit dualism must acknowledge the situated knowledges of Indigenous women and many others, including the experience of enslavement, that underpin such philosophical critiques. Understandings of more-than-human agency are likewise indebted to Indigenous ways of knowing.⁴¹

Material agency

Considerations of other-than-human agency are crucial for an ecological materialism. A problematic dematerialization extends to the ways in which colonial perspectives and late capitalist consumerist ideologies ignore the complex factors involved in human agency and act as if humans act alone. In her influential new materialist work, Jane Bennett questions assumptions that other-than-human things are without agency, or that their impacts and acts should be described as qualitatively

---

37. Val Plumwood, *Environmental Culture: The Ecological Crisis of Reason* (Environmental Philosophies; London: Routledge, 2002), p. 229.

38. Plumwood, *Environmental Culture*, p. 229.

39. Val Plumwood, 'Shadow Places and the Politics of Dwelling', *Australian Humanities Review* 44, Ecological Humanities (March 2008), available online: http://australianhumanitiesreview.org/2008/03/01/shadow-places-and-the-politics-of-dwelling/ (accessed 3 February 2021); see also, Howie, *Between Feminism and Materialism*, p. 203.

40. Moreton-Robinson, *Talkin' Up*, p. 16.

41. Jeanine Leane, 'Voicing the Unsettled Space: Rewriting the Colonial Mythscape', paper given at Unsettling Ecological Poetics Conference, University of Sydney, Thursday 24 October 2019.

different from human impacts and agency.⁴² The focus on material agency echoes First Nations' perspectives, not only in Australia. Sensitized by his Native American Seminole experience, theologian Mark Wallace links the animism of ancient and living First Nations with the return to animism of the new materialism and his own theological affirmation of biblical and Christian animism.⁴³ Modernist western disavowals of animism and devaluations of animist beliefs coincide with imperialist ideologies of European supremacy over colonized peoples.⁴⁴ In the material turn, emphasis on more-than-human agency may be a counterpoint to this colonizing ideology that devalues Indigenous knowledges. For Wallace, while the affirmation of animism in the academy after a colonial history of neglect of Indigenous knowledges can be hurtful for First Nations, there are productive parallels between Indigenous knowledges and a philosophical turn towards animism, especially as it works to decentre western modes of understanding the human as exceptional.⁴⁵ As Linda Hogan comments, 'animism' is not a word First Peoples use to describe their knowledge systems which are in fact more complex than the term itself suggests.⁴⁶ So, rather than appropriating Indigenous knowledges, Bennett, for example, engages European cultural histories of animist thought as she describes 'vibrant matter' and material agency.⁴⁷ This trajectory of a western animism resonates with the 'panpsychism' Freya Mathews recovers 'to characterize a metaphysic in which mentality in some sense is restored to materiality'.⁴⁸ While introduction to and respect for Indigenous knowledges may have informed their interest in material vibrancy, both Bennett and Mathews also draw on western traditions undervalued in the objectifying economies of late capitalism.

To speak of 'material agency', thus, is 'counter to human-exceptionalism'; that is, the concept of 'material agency' resists 'the human tendency to understate the degree to which people, animals, artifacts, technologies, and elemental forces

---

42. Jane Bennett, *Vibrant Matter: A Political Ecology of Things* (Durham: Duke University Press, 2010), p. 34.

43. Mark I. Wallace, *Finding God in the Singing River: Christianity, Spirit, Nature* (Minneapolis: Fortress, 2005), p. 1; idem, *When God Was a Bird: Christianity, Animism, and the Re-Enchantment of the World* (New York: Fordham University Press, 2019), pp. 5–10.

44. Wallace, *When God Was a Bird*, p. 7.

45. Wallace, *When God Was a Bird*, pp. 5, 11–13. Linda Hogan, 'We Call It Tradition', in *The Handbook of Contemporary Animism* (ed. Graham Harvey; Milton Park, Abingdon: Routledge, 2014), pp. 17–26 (21).

46. Hogan, 'We Call It Tradition', p. 18.

47. Bennett, *Vibrant Matter*, pp. 18–19.

48. Freya Mathews, *For Love of Matter: A Contemporary Panpsychism* (Albany: State University of New York Press), p. 4. On the western philosophical tradition of panpsychism, see Philip Goff, William Seager and Sean Allen-Hermanson, 'Panpsychism', in *The Stanford Encyclopedia of Philosophy* (ed. Edward N. Zalta; Summer 2020 edn), available online: https://plato.stanford.edu/archives/sum2020/entries/panpsychism/ (accessed 9 March 2021).

share powers and operate in dissonant conjunction with each other'.⁴⁹ The action of writing a book, for example, occurs within complex assemblages of matter and material agencies, including the breath that I take in as I write, the food I ate recently for lunch, bacteria in my gut, the wattlebird calling in the garden, the hum of the next door heating unit, the whirr of the computer fan, the dust from my book shelves, light from the computer screen, sun filtered through curtains and falling on my notes, and the long genealogy of more-than-human ancestors that brought me to this here, this now.⁵⁰ As I have discussed elsewhere, in an ecological context, the question of agency needs to be understood in a wider more-than-human framework, where particular human social structures intersect with the sociality of the more-than-human habitats in which those structures subsist.⁵¹

When a human acts, for example, to form a pot on a potter's wheel, the action of making the pot occurs within a contextual field in which the qualities of the clay, the technology of the wheel and the place of work are integral to the making of a particular pot.⁵² The intention to form a pot is elicited from, and actualized by, a 'world of things' as an engagement with the possibilities their materiality and material situation affords.⁵³ More negatively, for example, when a human or a company acts to pollute a river, the properties of the waste and the water and the geography and flow of the river, each contribute to the 'world of things' in which the pollution is actualized. Moreover, the polluting act may be a by-product of an act of which the governing intention was not to pollute but to dispose of waste. While the intention is not tied directly to the effect, the responsibility for the action *is*, precisely because the intending agent does not adequately account for the more-than-human contextual field of the action. With more complex actions, the intending agent may be unable to wholly account for the more-than-human contextual field of the action. In all these contexts, from an ecological perspective, the concept of agency finds a focus not in an individual entity that acts, but in the process of enactment, distributed in 'collectives of humans

49. Bennett, *Vibrant Matter*, p. 34.
50. Bennett, *Vibrant Matter*, p. 23.
51. See Anne Elvey, 'Can There Be a Forgiveness That Makes a Difference Ecologically? An Eco-materialist Account of Forgiveness as Freedom (ἄφεσις) in the Gospel of Luke', *Pacifica* 22, no. 2 (2009), pp. 148–70 (153–4), from which the following paragraph in large part comes. See further idem, *The Matter of the Text: Material Engagements between Luke and the Five Senses* (Sheffield: Sheffield Phoenix, 2011), pp. 12–14, 179. On the 'material turn' in ecocriticism, see Serenella Iovino and Serpil Oppermann (eds), *Material Ecocriticism* (Bloomington: Indiana University Press, 2014). For feminist engagements with the 'material turn', see Stacy Alaimo and Susan Hekman (eds), *Material Feminisms* (Bloomington: Indiana University Press, 2008) and Susan Hekman, *The Material of Knowledge: Feminist Disclosures* (Bloomington: Indiana University Press, 2010).
52. Lambros Malafouris, 'At the Potter's Wheel: An Argument for Material Agency', in *Material Agency: Toward a Non-Anthropocentric Approach* (ed. Carl Knappett and Lambros Malafouris; New York: Springer, 2008), pp. 19–36 (33).
53. Malafouris, 'At the Potter's Wheel', p. 33; see also Bennett, *Vibrant Matter*, pp. 365–7.

and nonhumans'.[54] This focus on agency as process unsettles the active/passive dualism that maps onto the master/slave dynamic, because an entity that is acting can at the same time be acted upon. Moreover, every action of an elite is already a complex process of enactment by multifaceted (usually unacknowledged) more-than-human collectives.

A materialist freedom

If human agency is already a process of more-than-human agency, how am I to understand human freedom to act, especially to act in relation to eco-social justice? Elizabeth Grosz argues helpfully for a move from a focus on 'freedom from' that is strived for within political and social contexts of oppression such as patriarchy, to a focus on 'freedom for', understood 'not only or primarily as the elimination of constraint or coercion but more positively as the condition of, or capacity for, action in life'.[55] 'Freedom from', Grosz argues, 'remains tied to the options or alternatives provided by the present'.[56] In this regard, to rethink freedom I need to rethink my relation to time. 'Freedom for' becomes a capacity to act and in acting to transform the self, even while my action is constrained to greater or lesser extents by external factors, such as social situation and past experience.

The idea of 'freedom for' has links with Luce Irigaray's notion of becoming, so that the subject who enacts freedom for, is a 'subject-to-be', a subject-in-becoming.[57] 'Freedom for' – and the subject-in-process enacted in this sense 'freely' – is always an exercise of more-than-human agency.[58] Occurring in processes of material co-agency, free acts are free insofar as 'they are integral to who or what the subject is'.[59] They both express and transform the subject, and express that transformation as a process of the subject-in-becoming.[60] 'Freedom for' does not deny the conditions

54. Carl Knappett, 'The Neglected Networks of Material Agency: Artefacts, Pictures and Texts', in *Material Agency: Toward a Non-Anthropocentric Approach* (ed. Carl Knappett and Lambros Malafouris; New York: Springer, 2008), pp. 139–56 (140, 143); see further John Law and Annemarie Mol, 'The Actor-Enacted: Cumbrian Sheep in 2001', in *Material Agency: Toward a Non-Anthropocentric Approach* (ed. Carl Knappett and Lambros Malafouris; New York: Springer, 2008), pp. 57–77; Owain Jones and Paul Cloke, 'Non-Human Agencies: Trees in Place and Time', in *Material Agency: Toward a Non-Anthropocentric Approach* (ed. Carl Knappett and Lambros Malafouris; New York: Springer, 2008), pp. 79–96.

55. Elizabeth Grosz, 'Feminism, Materialism, and Freedom', in *New Materialisms: Ontology, Agency, and Politics* (ed. Diane Coole and Samatha Frost; Durham: Duke University Press, 2010), pp. 139–57 (140).

56. Grosz, 'Feminism, Materialism, and Freedom', p. 141.

57. Luce Irigaray, 'Divine Women' (trans. Stephen Muecke; Local Consumption Paper, 8; Sydney: Local Consumption, 1986); idem, 'Equal to Whom?' (trans. Robert L. Mazzola), *Differences* 1 (1989), pp. 59–76.

58. Grosz, 'Feminism, Materialism, and Freedom', p. 142.

59. Grosz, 'Feminism, Materialism, and Freedom', p. 144.

60. Grosz, 'Feminism, Materialism, and Freedom', p. 146.

of difficulty or oppression that constrain thought and action but operates within these material conditions refusing the logic of oppression through, for example, collaboration and nonviolent resistance.[61]

Integral to this notion of 'freedom for', the capacity for transformation is a characteristic of matter, of the material organization of things, including human bodies. This freedom is not limited to humans, but can be recognized in the capacity for choice exhibited in even 'the most elementary forms of mobile life', expressing 'both the particularity of each species and the specificity of individuals within them'.[62] Thus, as Grosz explains, materiality 'is also the field in and through which free acts are generated through the encounter of life with matter and the capacity of each to yield to the other its forms and forces, both its inertia and its dynamism'.[63] Matter has aspects of both determination and indetermination.[64] Matter is both necessary to planetary, cosmic existence and its unfolding as we know it, and not wholly determinative of the future, thus providing a condition of possibility for 'freedom for'.

Freedom should be understood not only through historical materialism, but also in a context where bodies are engaged materiality in both time and space. This broad context of situated materiality contrasts with a limited liberal feminist agenda that has focused on 'freedom from' the constraints of patriarchy; instead 'freedom for' is 'not primarily a capacity of mind but of body… linked to the body's capacity for movement, and thus its multiple possibilities of action'.[65] For Grosz freedom is attained 'through the struggle with matter, the struggle of bodies to become more than they are, a struggle that occurs not only on the level of the individual but also of the species'.[66] What she calls a 'struggle with matter' is, nonetheless, a material co-agency in which matter itself is 'matter-in-becoming'. A materialist framework suggests that freedom is consequent on indetermination; through matter's indetermination, life is freed 'from the constraints of the present', so that 'the world itself comes to vibrate with its possibilities for being

---

61. E.g., this exercise of 'freedom for' occurred in the November 2017 nonviolent action of asylum seekers and refugees detained on Manus Island (Manus Prison). See, Behrouz Boochani, 'A Letter from Manus Island', *The Saturday Paper* 186 (9–15 December 2017), pp. 1, 4; Anne Elvey, 'From Cultures of Violence to Ways of Peace: Reading the Benedictus in the Context of Australia's Treatment of Asylum Seekers in Offshore Detention', in *Things That Make for Peace: Traversing Text and Tradition in Christianity and Islam* (ed. Anthony Rees; Lanham: Lexington Books, 2020), pp. 41–57 (44–6).

62. Grosz, 'Feminism, Materialism, and Freedom', p. 149.

63. Grosz, 'Feminism, Materialism, and Freedom', p. 150. Immediately preceding this quotation, Grosz comments that '[m]ateriality tends to determination; it gives itself up to calculation, precision, and spatialization'. At a subatomic level, however, I would argue that matter seems to give itself to indeterminacy and unpredictability, as Grosz hints in her reference to the 'dilating expression of indetermination'. I would extend Grosz's comments about choice beyond what she terms 'mobile *life*' (emphasis added).

64. Grosz, 'Feminism, Materialism, and Freedom', pp. 150-1.

65. Grosz, 'Feminism, Materialism, and Freedom', p. 151.

66. Grosz, 'Feminism, Materialism, and Freedom', p. 151.

otherwise'.⁶⁷ From a feminist perspective, the challenge becomes 'how to enable women to partake in the creation of a future unlike the present'.⁶⁸ What kind of future might women 'partake' in creating?

Summary

Before I turn to this question of a future, let me summarize the preceding discussion. First, I am discussing two basic materialisms: (1) the material conditions of human lives understood in terms of just distribution of, and access to, goods such as food, shelter, clothing and adequate life-giving social networks and culture, and the alienation or otherwise of labour; (2) the materiality that describes human embeddedness in, interconnectedness and interdependence with, a more-than-human sociality. These two materialisms are not entirely separate, but the first resonates more with historical or practical materialism and allows an ecological extension from social justice to environmental or ecological justice. The second is the wider frame which potentially decentres the 'human' and understands the material embeddedness of humankind as one instance of wider more-than-human materialities and material agencies. While Grosz does not take a specifically ecological perspective, her discussion of freedom, like Bennett's discussion of agency, fits this second frame. In this second materialism social justice becomes an instance of ecological justice, notwithstanding the tensions that arise when deciding who or what might benefit from, and who or what would be harmed by, a particular action for ecological justice.

Second, the notion of the material basis of human being and action has social, political and theological implications precisely in regard to the question of 'freedom for' raised by Grosz, and its relation to a future unlike the present. An ecological materialism expands my thinking through inviting me to recognize both my relation to the necessity of material givenness and my capacity to choose cooperatively, within these necessary material parameters, *for* the well-being of Earth and the future more-than-human generations.⁶⁹ In Plumwood's description of dualism, necessity appears on the side of matter and freedom on the side of spirit.⁷⁰ An ecological materialist approach destabilizes this hyper-separation of necessity and freedom and sees choice emerging in and through material relations, choice as a capacity of matter.

Freedom and a future unlike the present

In a particular way, climate change concerns human freedom and the possibility of a future unlike the present. Notions of both the future and human freedom are unsettled by the capacity of humans to effect the Earth on a geological, not only

67. Grosz, 'Feminism, Materialism, and Freedom', pp. 152–3.
68. Grosz, 'Feminism, Materialism, and Freedom', p. 154.
69. Cf. Morton, *The Ecological Thought*, p. 135.
70. Plumwood, *Feminism*, p. 43.

a biological, scale through human-induced (anthropogenic) climate change.[71] Dipesh Chakrabarty argues that human history and 'natural' history can no longer be separated, because while humans have always affected other than humans, it is now the case that as a species humans have the capacity to affect Earth itself on a geological or planetary scale, through human-induced climate change.[72] Stratigraphers as well as many scholars in the humanities are calling the current age the Anthropocene, an epoch characterized by the geological agency of humans, because as a kind we are acting as a geological agent of mass extinction.[73]

The flow-on effects of extinctions of species, and changes in climate, on the human species itself cannot be predicted with any degree of certainty. These uncertain effects nonetheless highlight the finitude of both the species and the planet; thus, the way we think of the future is changing.[74] Moreover, the geological agency of humankind is to a significant extent related to Enlightenment, colonial, industrial, technological – and their 'post' (e.g. post-colonial) – pursuits in the name of human freedom. While the actions of converting fossils, stored in the Earth's crust, into fuels then into greenhouse gases in the atmosphere have been undertaken by elite humans more than others, it is as a species that humans have become capable of a kind of geological agency. This is complicated by the fact that this geological agency has a feedback effect in that it will exacerbate the rich-poor divide, and the aspiration towards freedom from injustice, that in part accompanies it.

Globalization and capitalism, in its changing forms over recent centuries, are implicated with anthropogenic climate change, but the issue is bigger than capitalism; the impacts of climate change may long outlast contemporary forms of global capitalism.[75] While capitalism and climate change are entwined, a critique of capitalism is insufficient 'for addressing questions relating to human history once the crisis of climate change has been acknowledged', because in the Anthropocene,

71. Dipesh Chakrabarty, 'The Climate of History: Four Theses', *Critical Inquiry* 35, no. 2 (2009), pp. 197–222.

72. Chakrabarty, 'Climate of History'.

73. See, e.g., Jan Zalasiewicz, Paul Crutzen and Will Steffen, 'The Anthropocene', in *The Geological Time Scale* 2012 (ed. Felix M. Gradstein, James G. Ogg, Mark D. Schmitz and Gabi M. Ogg; Boston: Elsevier, 2012), pp. 1033–40, available online: https://doi.org/10.1016/B978-0-444-59425-9.00032-9; Jan Zalasiewicz, Will Steffen, Reinhold Leinfeld, Mark Williams and Colin Waters, 'Petrifying Earth Process: The Stratigraphic Imprint of Key Earth System Parameters in the Anthropocene', *Theory, Culture & Society* 34, no. 2–3 (2017), pp. 83–104; Clive Hamilton, *Defiant Earth: The Fate of Humans in the Anthropocene* (Sydney: Allen & Unwin, 2017). For further discussion of climate change and the terminology of 'the Anthropocene', see chapter 6.

74. Chakrabarty, 'Climate of History'.

75. Chakrabarty, 'Climate of History', p. 212.

planetary geology and human history are entangled.⁷⁶ Chakrabarty defends the use of the generalizing term 'species' as being helpful in understanding what it is to have the collective capacity to act as a geological agent.

What does this enacted capacity, already 'entangled with the now of human history', and thus the 'now' of women that comes under the purview of feminist theories and theologies, mean for our understanding of freedom for life?⁷⁷ What does this collective capacity mean for the possibility of a future unlike the present, when what climate change already promises is a future tragically unlike the present?⁷⁸ What frameworks might suffice to describe this, to see human freedom for life as also a freedom within the limits of the matter humans are individually and uniquely, but also co-existentially, collectively?

The materiality of who we are

In a contemporary context, the divide between nature and culture breaks down and the 'possibilities of life and death for everyone are at stake'; in articulating a notion of humanity adequate to the time, I need to resist 'reductionist accounts of self-contained, rational, decision making subjects'.⁷⁹ My theological and humanist questions about 'meaning, value, ethics, justice and the politics of knowledge production' must be brought into environmental domains.⁸⁰ Writers, readers, thinkers and activists are entangled in more-than-human 'patterns of cultural and historical diversity' which shape us as subjects-in-becoming-with others.⁸¹ A number of aspects of materiality inform my understanding of humankind as formed of and enmeshed, 'entangled', in the 'stuff' of the cosmos as we 'become with' others: material givenness; material agency; the materiality of texts, language and voice; material transcendence; the materiality of habitat; and the materiality of vocation.⁸²

76. Chakrabarty, 'Climate of History', p. 212.
77. Chakrabarty, 'Climate of History', p. 212.
78. This future is in many respects already here and for many is a continuation of the logic of European imperialism and colonization. See Kyle Powys Whyte, 'Is It Colonial *Déjà vu*? Indigenous Peoples and Climate Injustice', in *Humanities for the Environment: Integrating Knowledge, Forging New Constellations of Practice* (ed. Joni Adamson and Michael Davis; London: Routledge, 2017), pp. 88–105.
79. Deborah Bird Rose, Thom van Dooren, Mathew Chrulew, Stuart Cooke, Matthew Kearnes and Emily O'Gorman, 'Thinking through the Environment: Unsettling the Humanities', *Environmental Humanities* 1, no. 1 (2012), pp. 1–5 (2), available online: https://doi.org/10.1215/22011919-3609940 (accessed 9 March 2021).
80. Rose et al., 'Thinking through the Environment', p. 2.
81. Rose et al., 'Thinking through the Environment', p. 2.
82. Anne Elvey, 'The Material Given: Bodies, Pregnant Bodies and Earth', *Australian Feminist Studies* 18, no. 4 (2003), pp. 199–209; idem, *An Ecological Feminist Reading of the Gospel of Luke: A Gestational Paradigm* (Studies in Women and Religion, 45;

Briefly, as introduced in Chapter 1, material givenness describes the materiality of bodies, pregnant bodies and Earth as material necessities for human life. This givenness resists a naïve essentialism because the underlying materiality of human life, even when bought and sold through organ trading and human trafficking, retains a quality that is 'prepropriative' and 'aneconomic'.[83] These necessities exist both prior to, essential for, and as the often-unacknowledged ground of, the economic systems in which they might be afforded a fiscal value.

Rarely, if ever, is the reproductive labour associated with the life-giving aspects of these grounds (Earth, bodies, pregnant bodies) afforded economic worth.[84] In contrast, even when kept below a just value, the productive labour that relies on these grounds for its raw materials, and the maintenance and renewal of its labour force, is included in economic accounting. Social justice and socialist movements for freedom from exploitative labour seldom include reproductive labour along with a revaluation of productive labour. Feminist accounting for reproductive labour needs to include not only the reproduction of the work force, but also the production and reproduction of the wider material conditions that make any work possible. If ecological feminists are not to continue a necessity/freedom dualism mapped on to passive/active, woman/man, nature/human dualisms, we need all the more to account for the wider reproductive materialities of labour, not only the productive ones.[85]

This rethinking of material grounds represents a nuanced essentialism where givenness is gift-like, giving itself to myriad less and more complex forms of organization which are sometimes delineated as inorganic and organic. Both kinds of organized matter (organic and inorganic) – and they may not be as easy to delineate as I once imagined – are involved in processes of agency, such as human labour (reproductive and productive, noting that some labour, such as the writing of a poem or the planting of a garden, may be both). The notion of material agency, or co-agency, discussed above, recognizes that human productive and reproductive labours occur in the context of

---

Lewiston, NY: Edwin Mellen, 2005); idem, 'Material Elements: The Matter of Women, the Matter of Earth, the Matter of God', in *Post-Christian Feminisms: A Critical Approach* (ed. Lisa Isherwood and Kathleen McPhillips; Aldershot: Ashgate, 2008), pp. 53–69; idem, *The Matter of the Text*; Elaine M. Wainwright, 'Images, Words, Stories: Exploring their Transformative Power in Reading Biblical Texts Ecologically', *BibInt* 20 (2012), pp. 280–304; Jean-Louis Chrétien, *The Call and the Response* (trans. Anne A. Davenport; New York: Fordham University Press, 2004).

83. Gayatri Chakravorty Spivak, *Outside in the Teaching Machine* (London: Routledge, 1993), p. 148; Jacques Derrida, *Given Time: 1. Counterfeit Money* (trans. Peggy Kamuf; Chicago: University of Chicago Press, 1992), p. 7.

84. Salleh, *Ecofeminism as Politics*.

85. Plumwood, *Feminism*, p. 22.

agency understood as a process shared across human and other-than-human constituencies, so that every work has multiple producers, some human, some other than human. One aspect that I have considered is the question of the materiality of texts. Enmeshed with this question are far broader questions of the relationship between matter and language, including the materiality of the voice, its corporeal production.

Language carries a trace of the maternal. The severance (which is also a continuing connection) of child and mother becomes encoded uncannily in language (and texts) through the 'semiotic'.[86] The maternal is one instance and aspect of the material given. The separation from, and connection to, the mother, encoded in language as the semiotic, is part of a wider severance/connection of humans and their material milieus. The givenness of 'the material' may also remain as a trace in language, precisely through the trace of the maternal.[87] Through this uncanny quality of language and texts, the material ground of production and reproduction (including of language and texts) – the materiality of 'stuff', of human bodies, Earth and cosmos – can be traced (and may indeed actively 'push up' through a text).[88]

The underlying principle is this: the material ground and human material milieus precede and remain as traces in human constructions of them, even as they and we both exercise co-agency and are mutually transformed in our interactions, including discursive ones. The notion of habitat, which includes built as well as so-called 'natural' environments, becomes important for situating humans in our particular local material contexts.[89] The senses connect us as humans with our material milieus. As I discussed in Chapter 3, voice, for example, is produced materially through the interplay of corporeal processes and qualities of air, and could be understood as a material mediation of the breath (itself material) producing sound that is picked up by the ear. Voice also has a wider meaning and takes me into that space where the inner life is produced in, and produces, certain material transformations.

In this focus on materiality, is there room for spirituality, for theology, for something like a divine other? As I suggest in Chapter 3, rather than imaging the divine or the sacred as purely immanent in matter and its organized forms, matter itself has a quality of transcendence, a material transcendence. Attentiveness to a material transcendence is a calling forth that resonates with the notion of vocation I extrapolate from Jean-Louis Chrétien, who speaks of a human being's existence

---

86. Julia Kristeva, *Revolution in Poetic Language* (trans. Margaret Waller; New York: Columbia University Press, 1984).

87. Elvey, *Matter of the Text*, pp. 28–43.

88. Wainwright, 'Images, Words, Stories', p. 293; Kate Rigby, 'Earth, World, Text: On the (Im)possibility of Ecopoiesis', *New Literary History* 35 (2004), pp. 427–42.

89. Wainwright, 'Images, Words, Stories'.

itself as already a 'yes' to a call: 'I have already responded when I respond.'[90] Human response occurs within a world, 'the inexhaustible chorus of which I am only one voice'.[91] In the ecological materialist frame I am sketching, I extend the notion of a 'yes', that humans already are in their being, to the mutuality of a 'yes' between things.[92] The material interplay in which species cooperate for their mutual survival and flourishing is a joint affirmation, a response of 'yes' to 'yes'. The description of a mutual responsiveness for the flourishing of each draws on two tasks: 'to resituate the human within the environment, and to resituate nonhumans within cultural and ethical domains'.[93] Moreover, the notion of freedom, as a capacity to respond *for* a future imagined otherwise, may helpfully be understood in this frame of mutuality where human materiality and material embeddedness ground the possibility and practice of cooperative call and response. I need also to recognize the complexities of more-than-human interactions, where mutual survival and flourishing are not necessarily the outcome, at least at the level of the individual.

Conclusion

In this chapter I have outlined some bases for a materialist reframing of feminist theology for an ecological feminism. A combined and extended practical materialism, while resisting the alienation of human labour, affirms and accounts for both other-than-human labour (often elided) and the reproductive labour (frequently unacknowledged) which has more-than-human aspects. In this practical materialist frame, the labour involved in producing feminist theological outputs is more than human. An underlying materiality supports any human enterprise, including the making of theology. This could be a trite observation, but I hope I have indicated that in concepts such as material organization and co-agency, habitat and vocation, the material basis of our being anything, including ecological feminist theologians and biblical scholars, has profound implications for our worldviews as theologians.

In this chapter, freedom emerged as an important uniting concept. In other work, I discuss freedom in the context of the Lukan concept of liberation and forgiveness (ἄφεσις); I point towards a kind of material grace, as a 'capacity of things to shift toward freedom... the freedom to act as we are... to know ourselves as participants in a more-than-human *ecos* where we continue to learn what it

90. Chrétien, *Call and the Response*, p. 19.
91. Chrétien, *Call and the Response*, p. 19.
92. Deborah Bird Rose gives the example of a 'yes' between bats and flowering gums. Deborah Bird Rose, 'The Goodness of Creation and the Darkening World of Extinctions', paper presented at the Climate Change – Cultural Change: Religious Responses and Responsibilities Symposium, 29 October 2011, Centre for Theology and Ministry, Parkville, Victoria, Australia.
93. Rose et al., 'Thinking through the Environment', p. 3.

means to exercise our co-agency well'.[94] This concept of a materially based freedom can be developed more fully.

For those of us enmeshed in systems that profit (in the short term) from the hyper-separation of humans and nature, *to act as we are* means to understand ourselves as already materially engaged, as called forth, as already implicated in all kinds of reproductive and productive labour, some of it unacknowledged, some of it alienated, some of contributing to a mutual 'yes' with other things, a 'yes' oriented towards mutual sustenance and flourishing. The freedom to respond in chorus, acting as we are, resisting false ideologies of human separation from Earth, links us to the future in several ways. Two important ones are these: (1) the future of climate change, which will likely be other than we intended and perhaps beyond our capacity to redress, and which tells us that humankind have become, as a species, an agent on the scale of Earth's climatic and geological systems themselves; (2) the future we might yet hope for or imagine, towards which we might exercise the kind of transformative 'freedom for' that Grosz explores.[95]

Collegially, theological enterprises need to take into account both futures. The first describes the habitat in which scholars will labour to produce theology, as members of a species in cooperation with other species. Ecological feminist theological and biblical scholars will continue to be cognizant of the dynamics of gender, social and cultural situation and bring this understanding to an analysis of the unequal impacts of climate change on particular human groups as well as on other species. We will also need, in taking account of this first aspect of the future, to do theology contemplatively, attending to matter, bodies, senses, habitat, texts and so on, in ways that enable us to know ourselves otherwise, not only as members of a species that is a geological agent, but recognizing what this means in terms of our connectedness with other things, a connectedness that is vulnerable and interdependent, as well as powerful. The second takes us in the direction of thinking the collegiality of theology as a more-than-human collectivity oriented towards 'new possibilities' not only for 'collective life', but for how humans as a kind engage with the world.[96]

Feminist theology is, in my view, no longer an 'endpoint', if it ever was, for theological engagement. Rather feminist theology has opened up ways of being towards the world that enable ecological feminist theologians and biblical scholars to see and imagine ourselves and our world otherwise, to affirm humankind as one species among many with particular gifts and challenges. While feminists will continue to strive to 'dream forward'; while we will continue to enact transformations for humans, especially women unjustly and violently treated; while we will continue to intervene in discourses that frame women and many others as available to be abused, we must also recognize the partiality of feminist

94. Elvey, 'Forgiveness', p. 170.
95. Grosz, 'Feminism, Materialism, and Freedom'.
96. The term 'new possibilities for collective life' is borrowed from Eric Santner, *On Creaturely Life: Rilke, Benjamin, Sebald* (Chicago, IL: University of Chicago Press, 2006), pp. 58, 133.

theories and theologies as situated human projects.[97] We can then also appreciate the gift feminist ecological approaches are to a wider Earth community as modes of discourse that open spaces for thinking beyond themselves, for thinking, loving, engaging in the web of material relations in which we are who we are. Ecological materialism – at the intersection of ecological thinking, the new materialism and situated materialities, understood through practical/historical and feminist frames – thus informs a transformative ecological feminist hermeneutics for this moment. The next chapter focuses on climate change as a sign of the long moment we inhabit. In conversation with Lk. 12.54-56, I explore kinds of discernment and cultural change our more-than-human co-inhabitants call forth in us.

---

97. Rosi Braidotti uses the term 'dream forward' when she evokes an 'ethics of nonprofit' at the level of being. Rosi Braidotti, 'The Politics of "life itself" and New Ways of Dying', in *New Materialisms: Ontology, Agency, and Politics* (ed. Diane Coole and Samatha Frost; Durham: Duke University Press, 2010), pp. 201–18 (217).

Chapter 6

CLIMATE CHANGE AS MATERIAL SITUATION:
INTERPRETING THE PRESENT PERIOD (ΚΑΙΡΟΣ)
ALONGSIDE LUKE 12.54-56

The future intersects with the present in a particular way in the global situation of climate change, calling forth a choral responsibility of 'freedom for' and opening towards new possibilities out of the material realities of the here and now.[1] Two biblical tropes from Luke 12 may be useful for developing ecological feminist theological responses to this complex and urgent situation, namely, the biblical notion of season, time or period (καιρός) and the hermeneutic impetus to interpret or understand the signs of the time.[2] Anthropogenic (human-induced) climate change is a 'sign of the time'. I take the best scientific evidence to be that climate change is occurring, is in large part induced by human activity and requires a response. Nonetheless, the so-called 'climate debate' is also a 'sign of the time', but is not my focus in this chapter.[3] Rather I am interested in the way the 'sign of the time' that is climate change is both simple and complex, requiring nuanced and dedicated responses.

Signs of the time – and climate change is a case in point – may be and often are particular to their time. Thus, biblical texts will not address such signs directly. How might biblical interpreters and theologians discern what it is that reading

---

1. This chapter builds on and revises Anne Elvey, 'Interpreting the Time: Climate Change and the Climate in/of the Gospel of Luke', in *Climate Change – Cultural Change: Religious Responses and Responsibilities* (ed. Anne Elvey and David Gormley O'Brien; Preston, Vic.: Mosaic Press, 2013), pp. 78–91.

2. The Vatican II *Pastoral Constitution on the Church in the Modern World* refers to 'signs of the time': 'At all times the Church carries the responsibility of reading the signs of the time and of interpreting them in the light of the Gospel, if it is to carry out its task' (*GS* 4). Vatican II, *Gaudium et Spes* (7 December 1965), in *Vatican Council II: The Conciliar and Post Conciliar Documents* (ed. Austin Flannery, O.P.; Collegeville: Liturgical Press, 1975), p. 905.

3. On this feature, from a US perspective, see Laurel Kearns, 'Cooking the Truth: Faith, Science, the Market, and Global Warming', in *Ecospirit: Religions and Philosophies for the Earth* (ed. Laurel Kearns and Catherine Keller; New York: Fordham University Press, 2007), pp. 99–124 (108–16).

ancient texts can contribute in response to a contemporary sign such as climate change? This chapter first discusses climate change and its relation to the future as a sign of the time. Second, the chapter explores the way in which Lk. 12.54-56 images the notion of the 'signs of the time' taken up in *Gaudium et Spes*, especially how it does this in relation to meteorological, social and theological signs. The third part of the chapter asks in what ways this reading of the Lukan time, period or season (καιρός) might speak to our contemporary material situation of climate change.

The Anthropocene and a deep future

The stratigraphic description of the current geological epoch as the Anthropocene is a sign of the time. The Anthropocene follows from the Holocene epoch which both saw on planet Earth the flourishing of myriad forms of living organisms, including humans, and provided the conditions for the current situation of human dominance affecting the entire more-than-human Earth community. From a systems perspective – where Earth is understood as a complex, not necessarily sentient, system which includes the planet and the moon under the influence of the sun – the Anthropocene describes a 'rupture' in human relationship with Earth.[4] Some privileged humans are far more implicated than many others in planetary harm and ecological destruction; however, while humans individually and communally are not equally responsible for the Anthropocene, humans as a kind are capable of occasioning this damaging shift in relationship between humans and the Earth system.[5] The contemporary 'rupture' is this: that humans have impacted Earth in such a way that humankind is a geological force, so that, human history and Earth history are entwined in an unprecedented way.[6]

As I argued in the previous chapter, this situation requires for many a shift in our understanding of what it means to be human.[7] For Clive Hamilton, it means this also, but in a particular way. Several practices of thinking shaped in response to ecological crisis are inadequate or inappropriate, he argues, for this unique situation of climate change: namely, ecocentric (Earth-focused approaches that reject anthropocentrism); new materialist; the collapsing of distinctions between humans and other creatures; and the more problematic ecomodernist (where a technological consumer capitalist business-as-usual 'fix' is envisaged); as well as

---

4. Clive Hamilton, *Defiant Earth: The Fate of Humans in the Anthropocene* (Sydney: Allen & Unwin, 2017), pp. 1–5.

5. Hamilton, *Defiant Earth*, pp. 27–35.

6. Hamilton, *Defiant Earth*, p. 8; Dipesh Chakrabarty, 'The Climate of History: Four Theses', *Critical Inquiry* 35, no. 2 (2009), pp. 197–222.

7. Deborah Bird Rose, Thom van Dooren, Mathew Chrulew, Stuart Cooke, Matthew Kearnes and Emily O'Gorman, 'Thinking through the Environment: Unsettling the Humanities', *Environmental Humanities* 1, no. 1 (2012), pp. 1–5, available online: https://doi.org/10.1215/22011919-3609940 (accessed 9 March 2021).

cosmological evolutionary approaches.[8] Instead, for Hamilton, a renewed, humble, even humbled anthropocentrism is required that recognizes the reality of (potent but doomed) human domination of a (damageable but untameable) planet, as the ground for a new ethic of human responsibility.[9] Nonetheless, human agency must be understood as under the constraints of human embeddedness in the natural world.[10] Despite Hamilton's dissatisfaction with the new materialism, any 'renewed' anthropocentrism, if such is warranted, needs to be undertaken on the basis of the shared materiality of more-than-human (including human) co-agents.

Designations for the current epoch need to take due account of the geological scale of the rupture.[11] They should also offer hope. Among alternative eco-social designations to the Anthropocene, two suggest positive alternatives that might call forth response and responsibility: the Symbiocene and the Holoreflexive epoch. The Symbiocene marks a time of companionship or symbiosis with all things living together for mutual benefit.[12] The Holoreflexive epoch is marked by inclusion and the 'entanglements' of more than humans, with broad implications for more-than-human flourishing and peace-making.[13] The concept of entanglement not only suggests interconnectedness and interdependence of humans with other than humans and our more-than-human habitats, but also includes the tangled exercises of power and the complex material inter-agencies that shape these and Earth itself.

Another term, Chthulucene, brings together two ideas, through Donna Haraway's melding of the Greek words χθών and καινός, the former referring to Earth, particularly its surface; the latter translated as now or fresh.[14] The word καινός evokes the thick present with its myriad entangled 'temporalities and materialities', enmeshed with past and future.[15] The word, χθών evokes Earth beings in their plurality and materiality, ancient and contemporary; an emphasis on 'chthonic

8. Hamilton, *Defiant Earth*, pp. 36–75.

9. Hamilton, *Defiant Earth*, esp. pp. 50–1. Hamilton rightly, I think, prefers the term 'humankind' to that of 'species', to signal the particular world-making capacity of humans, though I would not go as far as Hamilton towards a Heideggerian construct of humans, animals and stones concerning their respective relations to 'world' (62). See Martin Heidegger, *The Fundamental Concept of Metaphysics* (trans. William McNeill and Nicholas Walker; Bloomington: Indiana University Press, 1995), p. 196; cf. Jean-Luc Nancy, *The Sense of the World* (trans. Jeffrey S. Librett; Minneapolis: University of Minnesota Press, 1997), pp. 59–63.

10. Hamilton, *Defiant Earth*, p. 51.

11. Hamilton, *Defiant Earth*, p. 28.

12. Glenn Albrecht, 'Exiting the Anthropocene and Entering the Symbiocene', Psychoterratica blog (17 December 2015), available online: https://glennaalbrecht.wordpress.com/2015/12/17/exiting-the-anthropocene-and-entering-the-symbiocene/ (accessed 15 March 2021).

13. Joseph Camilleri and Jim Falk, *Worlds in Transition: Evolving Governance across a Stressed Planet* (Cheltenham, UK: Edward Elgar, 2009), pp. 530–1.

14. Donna Haraway, *Staying with the Trouble: Making Kin in the Chthulucene* (Durham: Duke University Press, 2016), p. 2.

15. Haraway, *Staying with the Trouble*, p. 2.

ones' opens to and affirms the kinds of material agency and animism, I introduced in previous chapters.[16] As Haraway argues, the disposition of the Anthropocene, and its economic-political counterpart the Capitolocene, towards extermination of the life-force of Earth is scandalous.[17] In answer, she evokes 'kin' as a 'wild category', a relation of 'living-with and dying-with each other'.[18] From the perspective of an ecological feminist hermeneutic practice, the evocation of 'kin' resonates with both scholarly readings of kinship in the biblical notion of the reign (βασιλεία) of G-d, and First Nations' understandings of more-than-human kinship relations with community and Country, where climate change and colonization intersect.

Colonization is an ongoing violent complex of agencies that must be acknowledged as entangled with both climate change and hope for more-than-human flourishing. For First Nations in Australia, the Anthropocene may be less a new epoch and more of the colonizing same.[19] Eschatological apocalyptic 'end time' stories about climate catastrophe are not new to Indigenous Australians, who have been living their own invasion catastrophe for Country and its peoples for over two centuries.[20] Invasion is an ongoing process, in which 'colonisation was and to some extent remains a conflict dependent on violence for its success'.[21] This ongoing invasive colonial ideology is a dual war against Earth, Country and First Peoples, 'that includes both genocide and ecocide'.[22] Turning to the history of

---

16. Haraway, *Staying with the Trouble*, p. 2.

17. Haraway, *Staying with the Trouble*, p. 2.

18. Haraway, *Staying with the Trouble*, p. 2.

19. The remainder of this paragraph draws with permission from Anne Elvey, 'Reimagining Decolonising Praxis for a Just and Ecologically Sustainable Peace in an Australian Context', in *Towards a Just and Ecologically Sustainable Peace: Navigating the Great Transition* (ed. Joseph Camilleri and Deborah Guess; Singapore: Palgrave Macmillan, 2020), pp. 275–95 (285–6, 288). Writing on 'protection of Indigenous Country and climate justice', Birch borrows the title, 'We've Seen the End of the World and We Don't Accept It' from Murrawah Johnson a young Indigenous spokesperson for the Wangan and Jagalingou people, who have been resisting the Adani (Bravus) mega-coal mine in the Galilee Basin in far north Queensland. Tony Birch, '"We've Seen the End of the World and We Don't Accept It": Protection of Indigenous Country and Climate Justice', in *Places of Privilege: Interdisciplinary Perspectives on Identities, Change and Resistance* (ed. Nicole Oke, Christopher Sonn and Alison Baker; Leiden: Brill, 2018), pp. 139–52 (148); Wangan and Jagalingou Family Council, available online: https://wanganjagalingou.com.au/ (accessed 26 July 2021).

20. Birch, '"We've Seen the End of the World"', p. 140. Birch quotes Kyle Powys Whyte, 'climate injustice for Indigenous peoples is less about the spectre of a new future and more like the experience of déjà vu'. Kyle Powys Whyte, 'Is It Colonial *Déjà vu*? Indigenous Peoples and Climate Injustice', in *Humanities for the Environment: Integrating Knowledge, Forging New Constellations of Practice* (ed. Joni Adamson and Michael Davis; London: Routledge, 2017), pp. 88–105.

21. Birch, '"We've Seen the End of the World"', p. 141.

22. Deborah Bird Rose, *Reports from a Wild Country: Ethics for Decolonisation* (Sydney: UNSW Press, 2004), p. 34, cited in Birch, '"We've Seen the End of the World"', p. 141.

British invasion of Australia, Tony Birch sees the current climate situation as built on successive capitalist extractive colonizations of land – deemed *terra nullius* precisely so that it could be invaded and utilized – first for the wool industry, then gold, and later agribusiness and mining; he describes the 'beatification of mining'.[23] This extractive praxis is of a piece with the contemporary invasion of Wangan and Jagalingou Country for mega coal mines like Adani's, in the process of which the Queensland Government has resisted the people's sovereignty by undermining that weakest of land rights in law: Native Title.[24] Climate justice requires '[g]reater recognition of the knowledge maintained within Indigenous communities relative to localized ecologies and the effects of climate change'.[25] For settler scholars such as myself, it requires a transformed decolonizing or better counter-colonial praxis, including in the development and use of ecological feminist hermeneutics.

Hermeneutic questions

Climate change forms part of, and often a focus for, a range of ecological concerns in the present time. As a starting point for biblical interpretation, climate change raises a number of issues including fundamental questions about the status of the biblical text. If the interpreter addresses the text on its own terms, not only is it a document of faith, with particular social, cultural and theological influences and interests, it is a historical document from times in which climate change was not a notable concern. Why read the biblical text at all? Why not read contemporary scientific, psychological and literary works that describe both climate change as an imminent concern and suggest ways in which humans might change their behaviour to address it?

Some scholars read biblical texts to uncover the roots of the ecological crisis in biblical religion; others read biblical texts apologetically to show their pro-Earth stance, to rescue the Bible for today. Other readings seem to assuage concern for the present through appeals to personal salvation in the promised resurrection of believers.[26] Taken as a sacred text for Jews and Christians, biblical texts can also be read as offering modes of situated interpretations of the relationship between G-d,

---

23. Birch, '"We've Seen the End of the World"', pp. 144–6.

24. 'Traditional Owners Continue to Resist Adani's "Invasion"', Wangan and Jagalingou Family Council, Latest News (25 January 2019), available online: https://wanganjagalingou.com.au/traditional-owners-continue-to-resist-adanis-invasion/ (accessed 15 March 2021).

25. Tony Birch, 'Climate Change, Mining and Traditional Knowledge in Australia', *Social Inclusion* 4, no. 1 (2016), pp. 92–101 (92).

26. For a useful appraisal of critical, apologetic and similar approaches to reading biblical texts in the context of contemporary ecological concern, see David G. Horrell, 'Introduction', in *Ecological Hermeneutics: Biblical, Historical and Theological* Perspectives (ed. David G. Horrell, Cherryl Hunt, Christopher Southgate and Francesca Stavrakopoulou; London: T&T Clark, 2010), pp. 1–12 (1–8).

humans and their social, cultural and ecological contexts that might suggest modes of situated interpretations of such relationships today. Such dialogue enacts cross-cultural conversations, between contemporary cultures and the ancient worlds and worldviews of the biblical texts, and requires a kind of cultural sensitivity. What would make such conversations fruitful for today's context of anthropogenic climate change?

As I outlined in the Introduction to this book, since the mid-1990s there have been several major projects in ecological hermeneutics that suggest ways forward for conversations between ecological concerns such as climate change and biblical studies, notably the Earth Bible Project and the Uses of the Bible in Environmental Ethics Project (UBEE).[27] Both projects acknowledge that biblical texts cannot be read as uncritically ecologically friendly in a contemporary sense, but should be understood within their contexts and traditions of interpretation, as generally addressing questions different from those we bring to them with climate change in mind. At their best ecological hermeneutics uncover, for example, more-than-human relationships readers may not otherwise have noticed in the text and set up questions, such as what models of relationship between G-d, humans and the wider Earth and cosmic communities does the text suggest? Does the text have inbuilt assumptions or overt images/paradigms that are counter to/unhelpful for an effective engagement with the challenge of climate change today? More specifically, for the purposes of this chapter, can the contemporary context of climate change call forth questions about climate in Luke, where there is direct reference to understanding the signs of the weather (12.54-56)? How might the climates of Luke speak back to this contemporary context of climate change?

Modes of biblical interpretation matter. Does the mode of interpretation, its genre, expression and tone, support or unsettle colonial praxis in relation to Earth and its atmosphere? In what ways does anthropogenic climate change intersect with modes of biblical reading? Novelist Amitav Ghosh asks about kinds of writing (e.g. the human-focused literary novel) dominant in the time of the Anthropocene and the way the materialities of fossil fuels (e.g. coal and oil, their different properties and propensities) intersect with writing.[28] The same questions could be asked of the way the material agencies (including human agencies) producing climate change intersect with different modes of reading in ways that are collusive with or resistant to ecological destruction. This issue echoes in Chapter 9 where I consider readings of Isa. 40.4 in the context of Mountaintop Removal Mining. In the current chapter, I address the climate in/of Lk. 12.54-56; how might the agencies of wind and weather co-inform my reading; how might a reading be braided with more-than-human ways of knowing?

---

27. See, e.g., Norman C. Habel (ed.), *Readings from the Perspective of Earth* (Earth Bible, 1; Sheffield: Sheffield Academic, 2000); David G. Horrell, Cherryl Hunt, Christopher Southgate and Francesca Stavrakopoulou (eds), *Ecological Hermeneutics: Biblical, Historical and Theological Perspectives* (London: T&T Clark, 2010).

28. Amitav Ghosh, *The Great Derangement: Climate Change and the Unthinkable* (Berlin Family Lectures; Kindle eBook; Chicago: The University of Chicago Press, 2016), pp. 73–8.

Interpreting the time: Climate in Luke

Luke 12.54-56 reads:

> But he also said to the crowds, 'When you see the clouds rising in the west, immediately you say, "A rainstorm is coming and it happens thus." And when the south wind blows, you say, "There will be scorching heat and it happens." Hypocrites, you know how to interpret the face of the earth and the sky, but how is it that you do not know how to interpret this present period (τὸν καιρὸν... τοῦτον)?' (my translation).

This short passage, which has a 'remote' parallel in Mt. 16.2-3 and a partial parallel in the Gospel of Thomas 91, juxtaposes knowledge of meteorological signs with another kind of knowledge, knowledge of what Luke calls this period (καιρός) and which the NRSV translates 'the present time' and Joseph Fitzmyer 'the season that is here'.[29] For the purposes of the comparison in this short speech, the Lukan Jesus assumes that weather prediction is unproblematic.[30] The background to the meteorological 'signs' can be explained as follows: 'In Israel, clouds coming from the direction of the Mediterranean Sea to the west mean approaching showers. Conversely, a south wind blowing from the Negeb desert brings sudden scorching heat.'[31] In a largely peasant culture the ability to read or interpret these meteorological signs may be assumed.[32]

The comparison with the ability to interpret this present period (τὸν καιρὸν... τοῦτον) can be read in at least two ways. Is it that the crowds are incapable of interpreting this time or is it that they correctly interpret this time but pretend otherwise? The word 'hypocrites' links the crowds at this point with others in the Lukan narrative, against whose 'hypocrisy' the Lukan Jesus warns the disciples in the presence of the pressing crowds (12.1). While the term 'hypocrite' can refer to one who acts a part, who pretends, it seems to carry in Luke a resonance of judgement.[33] By their inability, willed or otherwise, to interpret rightly 'this present period' the crowds are judged. Moreover, in the Lukan Jesus' judgement on the crowds, the reader, too, hears a call to interpret this time (καιρός).

---

29. Joseph A. Fitzmyer, *The Gospel According to Luke X–XIV: Introduction, Translation, and Notes* (The Anchor Bible; New York: Doubleday, 1985), pp. 998-9.

30. Robert C. Tannehill, *Luke* (Abingdon New Testament Commentaries; Nashville: Abingdon, 1996), p. 215.

31. Sharon H. Ringe, *Luke* (Westminster Bible Companion; Louisville, Westminster John Knox, 1995), p. 182.

32. Ringe, *Luke*, p. 182.

33. See Ringe, *Luke*, p. 182; Fitzmyer, *Gospel According to Luke X–XIV*, p. 1000.

What does the capacity to interpret this present period (καιρός) effectively entail for Luke? I will explore three aspects of this question. First, the local narrative context of 12.54-56 suggests a tone of judgement. Second, both the local and wider narrative context give content to the term καιρός. Third, the repetition and placement of words in 12.56, stemming in part at least from the oral character of the Gospel (its being written to be heard or recited rather than read), emphasize the verb 'to interpret' (δοκιμάζω) and prompt the hearer to ponder what the Greek word δοκιμάζω means in this context.

Narrative context and judgement

Luke 12.54-56 occurs immediately after a section describing the division the Lukan Jesus will bring to the Earth: 'I came to bring fire to the earth, and how I wish it were already kindled. I have a baptism with which to be baptized, and what stress I am under until it is completed. Do you think that I have come to bring peace to the earth? No, I tell you, but rather division!' (12.49-51). Images of crisis and stress pick up a Lukan thread of violent upheaval (e.g. 2.34-35; 3.9; possibly also 16.16) in tension with a promise of peace (2.14; cf. 19.41-44). This tension is important to a Lukan understanding of the divine purpose and I will return to this point when discussing the 'present period' (τὸν καιρὸν... τοῦτον, 12.56) below. In 12.49-53, the primary example of division is division within families or households (12.52-53). Prompted by the advent and reception of 'good news to the poor' that marks the liberation brought by the Lukan Jesus (4.18-19), this familial division forms the context for the sayings to the crowd concerning interpreting the 'present period'. Household division is a metaphor, and likely a lived reality, that highlights the way in which not only the disciples and the religious authorities but also the crowds are judged by their response to this advent of 'good news to the poor'. Because reception of the divine purpose is so critical (7.30; 19.44), this purpose occasions division between those who reject and those who welcome the divine visitation, even within the same household.

As 12.54-56 implies, the focus is not on the division itself, but on interpreting 'the present period'. For Joel Green, the present period is marked by this family division.[34] Sharon Ringe focuses, however, on what follows in 12.57: 'And why do you not judge (κρίνετε) for yourselves what is right (τὸ δίκαιον)?'[35] The verb 'to judge or discern' (κρίνω) is used here with a meaning like 'to interpret' (δοκιμάζω) in the previous verse.[36] The present period (καιρός) also stands in relation to the social structures of debt set out in 12.58-59:

---

34. Joel B. Green, *The Gospel of Luke* (NICNT; Grand Rapids, MI: Eerdmans, 1997), p. 511.

35. Ringe, *Luke*, pp. 182–3.

36. I. Howard Marshall, *The Gospel of Luke* (NIGTC; Grand Rapids: Eerdmans, 1978), p. 551; Tannehill, *Luke*, p. 215.

The social and economic context for the saying is the rampant debt that was destroying families and communities throughout Palestine. If disputes about debt reached the Roman legal system, one of two verdicts would greet the debtor. Either the debtor would be forced into indentured service to work off the debt, or the debtor would be thrown into prison until family members managed to scrape together the needed money to pay off the debt (usually by selling off any remaining lands).... In order to avoid playing into such blatant injustice, the only solution would be to settle cases before they went to court.[37]

In Luke for justice to occur and for the visitation of G-d to be welcomed, the situation of debt and credit, its impacts on relations in families and households, 'must be brought to an end', in the liberation promised as 'good news to the poor' (4.18-19).[38] Release from debt forms in Luke not only a metaphor for forgiveness (see, e.g., 7.40-48), but its material expression in the present period (καιρός).[39]

Time, season, period (Καιρός)

Context matters for understanding the meaning of the Greek word καιρός in Luke and Acts. In the Second Testament, καιρός sometimes refers to a 'right or decisive time' and sometimes simply 'time'; in the latter case καιρός is similar to χρόνος.[40] For Luke, as Kylie Crabbe maintains, 'history comes divided into times and periods, which have been set by divine authority'.[41] Καιρός can denote for Luke both 'periods of duration and significant punctiliar moments'.[42] In 12.56, καιρός refers to a 'period of significance' which 'may be contrasted with the coming αἰών [age]'.[43] At one level, the present period (καιρός) is a time marked by Roman occupation, debt slavery and divisions within families these political and social conditions may bring.[44] Luke does not stop here, but interprets the political, social, cultural and religious conditions of the time theologically. So, at another level, the present period (καιρός) occurs within the 'final period of history', or 'end', in which

37. Ringe, *Luke*, pp. 182-3; cf. Judith Lieu, *The Gospel of Luke* (Epworth Commentaries; Peterborough: Epworth, 1997), p. 106. Lieu suggests that 12.57-59 does not fit well after 12.54-56, but Ringe makes a good case for coherence between the units.

38. Ringe, *Luke*, p. 183.

39. See further, Anne Elvey, 'Can There Be a Forgiveness That Makes a Difference Ecologically? An Eco-Materialist Account of Forgiveness as Freedom (Ἄφεσις) in the Gospel of Luke', *Pacifica* 22 (2009), pp. 148-70.

40. James Barr, *Biblical Words for Time* (2nd revised edn; Naperville, IL: A. R. Allenson, 1969), p. 55; Kylie Crabbe, *Luke/Acts and the End of History* (BZNW, 238; Berlin: De Gruyter, 2019), pp. 119-20. Cf. Amy-Jill Levine and Ben Witherington III, *The Gospel of Luke* (New Cambridge Bible Commentary; Cambridge: Cambridge University Press, 2018), pp. 356-7.

41. Crabbe, *Luke/Acts and the End of History*, p. 121.

42. Crabbe, *Luke/Acts and the End of History*, pp. 119, 346.

43. Crabbe, *Luke/Acts and the End of History*, p. 346.

44. For discussion of Roman empire and Luke, see Chapter 7 below.

Luke's hearers/readers 'are exhorted to urgent repentance' whereby they '[align] their priorities with those of the divine purpose'.[45] The Lukan divine purpose or plan (βουλή) is not deterministic but functions according to its own logic where situational materialities, such as the socio-religious political forces in opposition to Jesus and the exercise of Roman power that lead to his execution, cannot curtail a divine will oriented towards life and its flourishing.[46] This orientation shows itself both in Earth's sustenance of more-than-human creatures, including ravens, lilies and human disciples (12.24-30), and in the way the execution of the Lukan Jesus is not the final word in the story.[47]

In earlier chapters, I described breath, bodies, pregnant bodies, Earth and its atmosphere as material givens insofar as they are necessities for more-than-human mammalian life in particular. The notion of the material given extends beyond the category of what is necessary for the living animal to what is necessary for all Earthy and cosmic co-existents. There are other types of material necessity, associated with what I have called situational materialities, that is, with the working and impact of social, political, cultural and religious forces on more than humans (including humans), their communities and habitats. This kind of situational materiality, including as it does multiple failures to recognize the divine visitation and accept the divine plan, produces such a material necessity. For Luke the tragic suffering and death of Jesus is a necessity (δεῖ; 9.22; 17.25; 24.5-7, 25-26) not because it is divinely willed but because it is a necessary consequence of the situational materiality in which Jesus of Nazareth is enmeshed.[48] This necessity relates to the Lukan divine purpose or plan (βουλή), not as something divinely intended, rather as foreseen by G-d, and incorporated into an unfolding purpose that is not obstructed by violence and its tragic outcomes, such as the death of Jesus or the destruction of Jerusalem, though these remain causes for grief (see esp. 13.31-35; 19.41-44).

These two events are critical for the Lukan gospel: the death of Jesus and the destruction of Jerusalem. Luke interprets both through the lens of the divine purpose, so that the 'present period' (12.56) is identified with the 'time of your

---

45. Crabbe, *Luke/Acts and the End of History*, p. 335.

46. As Crabbe notes, Acts 4.27-28 is nonetheless a counter-example to Luke's general non-deterministic presentation of the divine purpose, *Luke/Acts and the End of History*, pp. 196–7.

47. As I noted in Chapter 2, Lk. 12.24-30 needs also to be read with a hermeneutic of suspicion in relation to the classical hierarchies it reaffirms between humans and other kind.

48. Crabbe, *Luke/Acts and the End of History*, p. 158 n.108; pp. 163–4. See further, Charles H. Cosgrove, 'The Divine Δεῖ in Luke-Acts', *NovT* 26 (1984), pp. 168–90; Mark Reasoner, 'The Theme of Acts: Institutional History or Divine Necessity in History?', *JBL* 118 (1999), pp. 635–59; cf. John T. Squires, *The Plan of God in Luke-Acts* (Cambridge: Cambridge University Press, 1993). For a preliminary discussion of the necessity associated with the material given and Lukan use of necessity (δεῖ) and its relation to the logic of divine purpose, see Anne Elvey, *An Ecological Feminist Reading of the Gospel of Luke: A Gestational Paradigm* (Studies in Women and Religion, 45; Lewiston, NY: Edwin Mellen, 2005), pp. 69–110.

visitation' (19.44), a visitation of both liberation and judgement.[49] Although these events are understood as a consequence of failure to respond to the divine visitation (see esp., 19.41-44), they are not pre-determined.[50] An interplay occurs between the material events of the present period and the time of divine purpose, that extends into the 'end of history'. The Lukan divine purpose takes history seriously as the place of encounter with G-d, in a divine visitation enacted by the Lukan Jesus. A two-way movement exists between divine purpose and history, so that even in the unfolding of an oppressive rule, the interwoven and enfolding divine reign and rule (ἡ βασιλεία τοῦ θεοῦ) opens a space of liberating possibility.

The Lukan juxtaposition of Roman rule and the visitation of G-d is most clearly shown in the narrative of Jesus' birth; Luke sets in parallel and contrast the reign of peace claimed by the 'saviour', Caesar, and the peace announced at the birth of the 'saviour', Jesus (2.1-14).[51] The 'present period' intersects with the 'today' of salvation (2.11; 19.9). A time of fulfilment (1.20; 4.21), the present period (καιρός) also marks seasonal time, the time of sowing, harvesting and feeding (12.42; 20.10; Acts 14.17), the period of the imminence of the reign (βασιλεία) of G-d (10.2, 9, 11), requiring response. What does it mean to interpret this time?

To interpret (Δοκιμάζω)

While the Greek verb δοκιμάζω occurs twenty times in the Second Testament outside Luke (in Pauline and other letters), it occurs in Luke only at 12.56 and 14.19. Where in 12.56 it appears in relation to interpreting both the 'face of the earth and the sky' and 'the present period', in 14.19 it relates to 'trying out' a new group of oxen. From these two instances, it seems that the Lukan usage relates to a kind of physical discernment, probably related to agriculture, through the discernment of the weather and of the ways of animals to serve human purposes. It may be that this linking of physical everyday signs with the present period is not simply a contrast but says something about 'the present period' as a material reality that needs to be interpreted not in opposition to, but in close association

---

49. Tannehill, *Luke*, p. 215; Luke Timothy Johnson, *The Gospel of Luke* (SP; Collegeville: Liturgical Press, 1991), p. 299. The repetition of the word καιρός in 13.1 and the image of the fruitless fig tree in 13.6-9, a tree that should be ready for harvest in season, also signal judgement as a context for interpreting this present period (καιρός) in 12.56.

50. I do not wish to gloss over the tragic and insupportable violence against Jews that has appealed for warrant to Christian writings, including the presentation of the Jewish religious authorities in the Gospel of Luke, and have discussed this in other contexts. See, e.g., Anne Elvey, 'Legacies of Violence toward the Other: Toward a Consideration of the Outsider within the Lukan Narrative', *Colloquium* 34, no. 1 (2002), pp. 21-34. I argue that the Pharisees and scribes in particular become 'outsiders within' the Lukan narrative; I critique a Lukan characterization of them as rejecting the divine purpose and failing to welcome the divine visitation (see esp. Lk. 7.29-30; 19.41-44).

51. See, e.g., Raymond E. Brown, *The Birth of the Messiah: A Commentary on the Infancy Narratives in Matthew and Luke* (Garden City, NY: Doubleday, 1979), p. 424.

with the signs of earth, sky, and human political and social institutions, as Ringe has suggested in relation to ancient structures of credit and debt.[52]

An ecojustice approach to Lk. 12.54-56 focuses on the winds, earth and sky and asks whether the face of earth and sky appears in the saying solely as a point of reference for a more important spiritual point. Or does the capacity to read the movements of earth and sky, the shifts of wind for example, show an interconnectedness between G-d's time (the time of visitation), and the physical climate which might encompass not only meteorological states, but also political and social ones? In both cases, the Lukan narrative world is one in which just as the divine is active in opening the storehouses of the skies for wind and rain to come (Ps. 135.7), G-d is also active in opening a space within the oppression of Roman occupation and the related intransigence of some of the religious authorities, for the visitation of peace (1.79; 2.14; cf. 19.42) and liberation (ἄφεσις) (1.77; 4.18-19) in the reign (βασιλεία) of G-d. The capacity to interpret this present period (καιρός) is, for Luke, evident in a quality of responsiveness to the unsettling, but liberating, visitation of G-d. With implications for social relations in the present, this quality of responsiveness implies the capacity to discern, and presumably act on, what is just.[53]

The meteorological metaphor enables the 'interpreting the times' pericope to function. Use of this metaphor suggests that social relations in Luke's world are embedded in wider more-than-human relations. Weather matters to the crowds, because it has implications not simply for their comfort but for their sustenance, for the conditions under which their food supply is grown, harvested and their households subsist, if not flourish. The social reality of credit and debt matters to the crowds because it, too, has implications for their survival. The visitation of G-d in the present period should, the Lukan Jesus argues, therefore also matter to the crowds because it speaks to these conditions of their survival in such a way as to open up the possibility of liberation from life-denying systems not through war but through a kind of 'grace', though Luke does not use the word in this context. This 'grace' stands in the present with the capacity to enact a shift towards a promised future, such as that described in Acts 2.44-47 and 4.32-37, whether experiment, ideal or both. This present focus has an eschatological dimension; the present period is 'a space for conversion before the storm of judgement arrives', the final year in which the fig tree might be productive (13.9).[54] Eschatology is integral to Luke's understanding of history and shapes the Lukan narrative crucially, through its affirmations that 'divine faithfulness in the past' assures that divine authority guides 'all of history'.[55] Moreover, this guidance is not deterministic; rather 'the unstoppable divine βουλή adapts to the tragic consequences of opposition' and situational materialities more generally.[56] Whether an ancient eschatological focus,

---

52. Ringe, *Luke*, pp. 182–3.

53. Ringe, *Luke*, pp. 182–3.

54. Brendan Byrne, *The Hospitality of God: A Reading of Luke's Gospel* (Strathfield, NSW: St Pauls, 2000), p. 119.

55. Crabbe, *Luke/Acts and the End of History*, p. 339.

56. Crabbe, *Luke/Acts and the End of History*, p. 339.

especially an apocalyptic one such as found in parts of Luke 17 and 21, is helpful for contemporary discourse around climate change needs further consideration, but it is important to understand that in 12.56 the Greek καιρός has both present and future orientations that are entwined and together arrive with a sense of urgency.

Re-framing climate change

The discourse around climate change itself has present and future orientations, and concerns not only observed changes in climate in the recent past and the present but also, and more particularly, carefully judged scientific predictions about future climate, its changes and the impacts of these changes on atmosphere, seas, lands, biological communities and species, including humans. Catherine Keller uses Lk. 12.56 as an epigraph to her 1993 essay 'Talk about the Weather', where she writes: 'Talk about the weather has lost its innocence.'[57] Many descriptions of 'the ecological crisis' bear an eschatological tone.[58] Eschatology 'is the doctrinal lens through which Christian culture, consciously or not, imagines any "end of the world"'.[59] But the identified 'end of nature' signals not that Earth and its constituents will disappear; rather what we call 'nature' is under stress because of, and no longer exists separate from, human actions.[60] Therefore, the distinction between 'natural' and 'human-made' conditions collapses. While both biblical and contemporary perspectives present a variety of eschatologies, there remains a challenge: to reconstruct the 'end' or 'ends' (of habitats and homelands, communities and species) that climate change presses us to imagine.[61] This entails a kind of cultural change: 'We will still talk about the weather, just because we are in it together. That's what weather talk always did. But now the damage to the earth-home binds us all together as never before, as members of a species, indeed members of a planet.'[62] This new or renewed sense of what it is to be human contains a hope that calls forth 'the green ecumenacy'.[63] But what might this 'green ecumenacy' be like?

The theme of apocalypse resurfaces in Keller's recent work, where she energetically laments the deeply interconnected contemporary political-social-religious powers for destruction supported by an apocalyptic imaginary.[64] Against this destructive slant, she holds tentatively the (im)possibility of healing, situated

---

57. Catherine Keller, 'Talk about the Weather: The Greening of Eschatology', in *Ecofeminism and the Sacred* (ed. Carol J. Adams; New York: Continuum, 1993), pp. 30–49 (esp. 30–1).

58. Keller, 'Talk about the Weather', pp. 32–5.

59. Keller, 'Talk about the Weather', p. 36.

60. Bill McKibben, *The End of Nature* (New York: Random House, 1989).

61. Keller, 'Talk about the Weather', pp. 37–47.

62. Keller, 'Talk about the Weather', p. 48.

63. Keller, 'Talk about the Weather', p. 48.

64. Catherine Keller, *Facing Apocalypse: Climate, Democracy, and Other Last Chances* (Kindle eBook; Maryknoll, NY: Orbis Books, 2021).

incarnationally in the co-relation of creator and creation.[65] While Keller focuses on the Book of Revelation, perhaps this co-relation might be read as an aspect of what Luke characterizes as divine visitation, understood as both ongoing and singular event. If what Luke offers is a holding together of ecological, social and theological contexts in a way that is determined by the logic of divine visitation, which enables liberation from (or better within) oppressive modes of relating in the present, how might this speak to our contemporary context of climate change and the slowness with which humans as a kind seem to be addressing it?

While different, the first-century CE context of the Lukan narrative and our contemporary experience of climate change are situations of grief. In the Lukan context, grief accompanies the material consequences of Roman domination, the system of debt and more particularly the Jewish war and the destruction of Jerusalem (see esp. 13.31-35; 19.41-44). Luke relates this grief to the inadequate response of some of the religious authorities and the crowds to the present period, the time of visitation. Our contemporary experience of climate change is framed by grief, when climate change is described in terms of loss (of biodiversity, habitat, home), as both experienced and imminent disaster. It is also framed as a question of social justice (where more marginal communities are likely to be most adversely or first affected by climate change). At another level, like empire, climate change is 'bigger than us' and appears simultaneously resolvable (if we have the will to change our behaviour individually, communally, nationally and internationally) and unresolvable (because we seem not to have the will, or because global systems, such as markets, are too complex, or because we have not acted adequately and in time). It is something we as humans accept, fear, ignore, deny and act on, sometimes at the same time in the same person or community. Into this complex of action, inaction and grief, the Lukan motif of interpreting the present period suggests a different mix of action, inaction and grief.

The litany of climate change effects, present and to come, is cause for grief, prompt for action and something more. Ecological, feminist and First Nations theologians and biblical scholars take up the notion of the present period (καιρός) to describe the urgent call of climate change.[66] Framed by the knowledge that this is 'bigger than us', our present period warrants interpretation, not only in the mode of scientific research, although this is crucial, but also in the mode of theological understanding. Luke does not identify the signs of the weather with the signs of the time. To interpret contemporary climate change as the visitation of G-d, as if it were divinely ordained, would be counter to the subtlety of the Lukan presentation of this present period (καιρός).

65. Keller, *Facing Apocalypse*, pp. 176-80, 186.

66. Sean McDonagh, *Climate Change: The Challenge to All of Us* (Blackrock, Dublin: The Columba Press, 2006), p. 194; see also Barbara Rossing, 'God Laments with Us: Climate Change, Apocalypse and the Urgent *Kairos* Moment', *The Ecumenical Review* 62 (2010), pp. 119-30; Seforosa Carroll, 'Reimagining Home: Migration and Identity in a Changing Climate', in *Theological and Hermeneutical Explorations from Australia: Horizons of Contextuality* (ed. Jione Havea; Lanham: Lexington Books, 2021), pp. 167-79 (173).

When I look at Lk. 12.54-56 from the perspective of climate change, however, I find an irony: rather than arising as a contrast with interpreting the weather, interpreting the present period requires today that we interpret the weather as a priority. The challenge of Luke is not to stop here, but to ask in what ways response to this present material situation – like the release from debt that is not only a metaphor for a theological concept of forgiveness but also material good news to the poor – can be understood as cooperation with a liberating visitation that might make another future possible.

Conclusion

To exercise 'freedom for' another possible future entails both an embodied relation to the entanglements – interconnectedness, interdependency and material co-agencies – of our present period, and a sense of relation with a deep future. Both are part of an 'ecological conversion' such as Pope John Paul II evoked and Pope Francis reaffirmed. Interconnectedness is a keynote of *Laudato Si'*.[67] Francis rejects capricious human dominion over other creatures (*LS* 82), writing: 'The biblical accounts of creation invite us to see each human being as a subject who can never be reduced to the status of an object. / Yet it would also be mistaken to view other living beings as mere objects subjected to arbitrary human domination' (*LS* 81-82). Humans are creatures among creatures, in relationships of mutual responsibility (*LS* 67). While it displays a lingering anthropocentrism, the encyclical affirms that other creatures are our kin – sisters and brothers (*LS* 11). This does not mean that humans are the same as other creatures (*LS* 81, 90). Each species has its own characteristic qualities and humankind holds a particular place of dignity and responsibility in relation to the rest of creation by virtue of its divinely given character as human (*LS* 119). While in many places the encyclical's focus on and return to human beings seem to reinforce an anthropocentrism common to religious social teaching, *Laudato Si'* is both subtle and far-reaching in its approach to other creatures and affirms their worth in themselves (*LS* 140, 190). The interconnectedness of humans and other creatures and their embeddedness in Earth pertains not only to a mutual sustaining but to a shared grief or trauma at the tragedies of cruelty to other creatures and ecological damage more generally (*LS* 89). Humans as creatures are recipients of a divine gift vis-à-vis the rest of creation, which is not only a 'being given' to the human other but also a (prior) being given in itself. Such affirmations are grounded in an ecological relational Trinitarian theology.[68]

67. Pope John Paul II, 'General Audience' (17 January 2001), available online: http://www.vatican.va/holy_father/john_paul_ii/audiences/2001/documents/hf_jp-ii_aud_20010117_en.html (accessed 29 August 2014); Pope Francis, *Encyclical Letter Laudato Si' of the Holy Father Francis on Care for Our Common Home* (Australian edn; Strathfield, NSW: St Pauls, 2015) (abbreviated as *LS*).

68. Denis Edwards, '"Everything Is Interconnected": The Trinity and the Natural World in *Laudato Si'*', *ACR* 94, no. 1 (2017), pp. 81–92; *LS* 240.

The underlying focus on creaturely interconnectedness found in *Laudato Si*, while necessary for an ecologically informed understanding of what it is to be human, may be insufficient to the Anthropocene situation of rupture – an ontological shock requiring a radical shift in worldview, towards which it seems even thinkers like Hamilton can only scrabble, mixing science and polemic with philosophy and mythic symbolism. While ecological and new materialist thinking challenges the notion of human exceptionalism, in the Anthropocene situation humankind is an exception in terms of the extent of human power to affect the Earth system.[69] Supposing this claim is true, what are the implications for understanding human creatureliness theologically?

It is arguable that *Laudato Si'* fails to address the question of the 'deep future' of Earth, where current and relatively recent human activity will have effects not only for the next several human generations (which is the usual time frame discussed in relation to climate change) but for over a hundred thousand years.[70] How can theology empower people to respond to this deep future? For Richard W. Miller an answer lies in linking creation, incarnation and eschatology.[71] This has promise in a mainstream theological mode, but remains inadequate, I suspect, to empower a shift in human relation and responsibility to the deep future.

Climate scientist Peter Rayner suggests we shift from seeing climate change as marker of human immorality/hubris to focusing on 'climate protection as a transcendent value'.[72] This resonates with Pope Francis's description of climate as a 'common good' (*LS* 23). Nonetheless, climate change challenges our thinking about G-d, ourselves and our religious practices.[73] When John Paul II spoke of an ecological conversion, he acknowledged that such a metanoia was already at work outside the churches.[74] In 'the great derangement' that is anthropogenic climate change, perhaps Earth itself is pressing humans towards what might be called an ecological conversion.[75] The climatic events that surprise us, such as the catastrophic bushfire season of Spring-Summer 2019-20 in South Eastern Australia, that come to us again and again as 'unprecedented', have the force of the uncanny. Their uncanniness lies in their turning humankind towards something that many but not all of us had forgotten or ignored, namely 'the presence and

---

69. Hamilton, *Defiant Earth*, pp. 1-8.

70. Richard W. Miller, 'Deep Responsibility for the Deep Future', *TS* 77, no. 2 (2016), pp. 436-65. Miller takes a similar starting point to Hamilton but from a theological perspective.

71. Miller, 'Deep Responsibility'.

72. Peter Rayner, 'On the Science and Ethics of Climate Change: Why Utilitarian Responses Are Not Enough', in *Climate Change – Cultural Change: Religious Responses and Responsibilities* (ed. Anne Elvey and David Gormley-O'Brien; Preston, Vic.: Mosaic Press, 2013), pp. 21-34 (31-4).

73. Anne Primavesi, *Gaia and Climate Change: A Theology of Gift Events* (London: Routledge, 2009), pp. 3-5; Sigurd Bergmann, 'Climate Change Changes Religion: Space, Spirit, Ritual, Technology – through a Theological Lens', *ST* 63 (2009), pp. 98-118.

74. John Paul II, 'General Audience'.

75. Ghosh, *Great Derangement*.

proximity of nonhuman interlocutors'.[76] This turning towards, as Ghosh suggests, has 'stirred a sense of recognition, an awareness that humans were never alone'.[77] Such awareness, already a feature of First Nations' epistemologies, is evidenced in the humanities by attention to panpsychism, process thought, the material turn, the chthonic and the interest in forms of animism that these philosophies (broadly understood) describe.[78]

What then does it mean to be a creature among creatures in this period of time? In the next chapter I turn to a notion of 'creaturely life', expounded by Eric Santner who explores the relation of the human being to the political.[79] While human beings are creatures among creatures, they are not just this, he holds, but humans 'are in some sense *more creaturely* than other creatures' because of 'an excess that is produced in the space of the political and that, paradoxically, accounts for their "humanity"'.[80] Humans are distinct from other animals due to their 'biopolitical *animation*'.[81] A key point of his analysis is the notion of 'the cringe': the excess of creaturely life is characterized not by connectedness with other creatures, though this is there, but by the 'cringe', the abjection of the human in the face of the power of humankind to enact unconscionable harm on others on a massive scale.[82] The cringe is manifest in human thraldom to a certain trajectory of socio-political violence, which is now evident ecologically even geologically.[83] The cringe that occurs in the face of this socio-political violence is answered by a reclaiming and expansion of traditions of 'neighbour love' in a framework of material agency. Events triggered by climate change are uncanny; they are cases 'of the uncanny intimacy of our relationship with the nonhuman' and of more-than-human agency.[84] In an ecological materialist frame, I ponder the thought that there are material agencies, including Earth itself, who/which are also prompting shifts of worldview, capable as they are of 'inserting themselves into our processes of thought'.[85] Might such more-than-human agents of ecological conversion prompt a kind of ecologically compelling 'neighbour love' sufficient to the time? I take this up in the next chapter with a focus on Lk. 10.25-37.

76. Ghosh, *Great Derangement*, p. 30.
77. Ghosh, *Great Derangement*, p. 30.
78. Ghosh, *Great Derangement*, p. 30.
79. Eric Santner, *On Creaturely Life: Rilke, Benjamin, Sebald* (Chicago: The University of Chicago Press, 2006).
80. Santner, *On Creaturely Life*, p. 26.
81. Santner, *On Creaturely Life*, p. 39, emphasis in original.
82. There is a melancholic aspect to Santner's understanding of creaturely life and its 'immersion in stranded objects' particularly those artefacts of the extermination camps of the Second World War. See Dominic LaCapra, *History, Literature, Critical Theory* (Ithaca: Cornell University Press, 2013), p. 66.
83. The cringe is typified in characters such as Shakespeare's Caliban and Sebald's Austerlitz and that novel's narrator. W. G. Sebald, *Austerlitz* (trans. A. Bell; reissued with a new introduction by J. Wood; eBook; London: Penguin, 2011 [2001]).
84. Ghosh, *Great Derangement*, pp. 32-3.
85. Ghosh, *Great Derangement*, p. 31.

Chapter 7

RETHINKING NEIGHBOUR LOVE: POLITICAL THEOLOGY, SOVEREIGNTY AND AN ECOLOGICAL MATERIALIST READING OF LUKE 10.25-37

Contemporary political and theological systems have been unreliable at best in addressing environmental damage, both locally and on planetary scales, nationally and internationally. But these are systems in which I am entangled and alongside which I ask what ethical praxis is sufficient to this time. In this chapter I consider two notions arising in recent political theology which have important biblical resonances: sovereignty and neighbour love.[1] The notion of political theology suggests not only that religious institutions are political institutions with the concomitant issues of power relations and sovereignty that this implies, but also that theology, especially Christian theology, remains as a trace, or more than a trace, in contemporary politics, particularly in or informed by the West. The parable of the Good Samaritan, for example, is not simply a religious text from the Gospel of Luke, but has entered culture through both art and everyday usage, where someone can be described as a 'good Samaritan'. The entry into culture of this religious image is part of a wider interplay between 'secular' culture and theology that touches on political theology. In this chapter I look at the notions of sovereignty and neighbour love as they pertain to Lk. 10.25-37, and suggest how an ecological materialist approach to this well-known text can amplify an ecological ethical worldview.

---

1. This chapter revises and builds on, Anne Elvey, 'Rethinking Neighbour Love: A Conversation between Political Theology and Ecological Ethics', in *'Where the Wild Ox Roams': Biblical Essays in Honour of Norman C. Habel* (ed. Alan H. Cadwallader and Peter L. Trudinger; HBM, 59; Sheffield: Sheffield Phoenix, 2013), pp. 58–75, with permission of the publisher. The political theology I am engaging with derives from Eric L. Santner, *On Creaturely Life: Rilke, Benjamin, Sebald* (Chicago: The University of Chicago Press, 2006), esp. pp. 75–80, 206–7; idem, 'Miracles Happen: Benjamin, Rosenzweig, Freud, and the Matter of the Neighbor', in *The Neighbor: Three Inquiries in Political Theology* (ed. Slavoj Žižek, Eric L. Santner and Kenneth Reinhard; Chicago: The University of Chicago Press, 2005), pp. 76-133.

Political theology, ecological ethics and ecological feminist hermeneutics

My interest in political theology is primarily in relation to ecological ethics. I understand the ecojustice principles and the ecological hermeneutics, discussed in previous chapters, to be projects in ecological or environmental ethics.[2] The principles of intrinsic worth, interconnectedness, voice, purpose, mutual custodianship and resistance open interpreters to a world in which humans are learning, relearning or continuing to acknowledge, that we are part, not the centre or pinnacle, of a much wider Earth community which has its own interests and purposes and can act in its own right.[3] They are ethical principles in that they shift interpreters towards listening for the ways of Earth, towards hearing Earth's ecological mores as informing human ethical behaviour.

Earth and its systems, however, should not be sentimentalized.[4] Rather ecological thinking challenges interpreters both to be converted from anthropocentrism, prevailing especially in western cultures, and to recognize ways in which notions of ecology and ecological thinking are themselves shaped by ideological interests.[5] 'Ecological thinking' is oriented particularly towards unsettling the oppressive dominations of western capitalism.[6] Nonetheless, oppressive masteries are not unique to western capitalism. Biblical texts in their ancient social, cultural and political contexts are already engaged in a kind of political theology.[7] As explorations of empire and slavery in biblical studies show, imperial sovereignty, systems of debt and master-slave relations need to be accounted for when studying ancient biblical texts.[8] How are biblical theologies enmeshed with and/or resistant

---

2. For an outline of the ecojustice principles and the ecological hermeneutics of suspicion, identification and retrieval, see Norman C. Habel (ed.), *Readings from the Perspective of Earth* (Earth Bible, 1; Sheffield: Sheffield Academic, 2000), p. 24; idem, 'Introducing Ecological Hermeneutics', in *Exploring Ecological Hermeneutics* (ed. Norman C. Habel and Peter L. Trudinger; SBL Symposium Series, 46; Atlanta: SBL, 2008), pp. 3–8.

3. See Norman Habel, 'Introducing the Earth Bible', in *Readings from the Perspective of Earth* (ed. Norman C. Habel; Earth Bible, 1; Sheffield: Sheffield Academic, 2000), pp. 25–37. For an Indigenous perspective, see, e.g., Tyson Yunkaporta, *Sand Talk: How Indigenous Thinking Can Save the World* (Melbourne: Text Publishing, 2019).

4. Lorraine Code, *Ecological Thinking: The Politics of Epistemic Location* (New York: Oxford University Press, 2006), p. 6.

5. Code, *Ecological Thinking*, pp. 28–9.

6. Code, *Ecological Thinking*, p. 15.

7. See, e.g., Elaine M. Wainwright, *Women Healing/Healing Women: The Genderization of Healing in Early Christianity* (London: Equinox, 2006), pp. 24–31.

8. See, e.g., Allen Dwight Callahan, Richard A. Horsley and Abraham Smith, 'Introduction: The Slavery of New Testament Studies', *Semeia* 83/84 (1998), pp. 1–15, and other essays in that joint volume; Elizabeth Dowling, *Taking Away the Pound: Women, Theology and the Parable of the Pounds in the Gospel of Luke* (London: T&T Clark International, 2007), pp. 11–18; idem, 'Slave Parables in the Gospel of Luke', *AusBR* 56 (2008), pp. 61–8; idem,

to these masteries? The notion of the reign (βασιλεία) of G-d, a theological concept in debt to, and potentially critical of, political notions of sovereignty provides perhaps the most obvious test case.

In contemporary political life the notion of divine sovereignty – to which the concept of the reign (βασιλεία) of G-d might be understood to refer in its ancient gospel contexts – re-emerges in the bourgeois individual as sovereign.[9] This is a skewed sovereignty. This displaced or replaced sovereignty has material effects, not only in the way human corporeality is understood and experienced, but also in the ways material things are commodified. Commodification of Earth beings, for example, minerals, women, enslaved persons, DNA, cattle, elephants, forests and fish, is in tension with the principle of intrinsic worth. Moreover, such commodification tends to ignore the other principles, by assuming that (or acting as if) other than humans and some humans are properly without voice and agency. There is an interplay between sovereignties, collective and individual (noting, for example, that companies can be deemed persons), so that the individual is both sovereign over that which is commodified and a commodity, subject to other sovereignties.[10]

At the point of subjection, 'life becomes a matter of politics and politics comes to inform the very matter and materiality of life'; for Eric Santner, this is precisely where the human is rendered 'creaturely'.[11] The notion of a divine creator's sovereignty over creation both informs the problematic political and power relations of contemporary sovereignties and is displaced by a creatureliness marked not by embeddedness in a more-than-human created world but by subjection to a bourgeois individualism. 'Cringed bodies' mark the shamefulness of subjection

---

'Luke-Acts: Good News for Slaves?', *Pacifica* 24 (June 2011), pp. 123–40; J. Albert Harrill, *Slaves in the New Testament: Literary, Social, and Moral Dimensions* (Minneapolis: Fortress, 2006); Mitzi J. Smith, 'Review of J. Albert Harrill, *Slaves in the New Testament: Literary, Social, and Moral Dimensions* (Minneapolis: Fortress, 2006)', *JAAR* 75, no. 1 (2007), pp. 219–23; Judy Diehl, 'Anti-Imperial Rhetoric in the New Testament', *CurBR* 10, no. 1 (2011), pp. 9–52; Richard A. Horsley (ed.), *In the Shadow of Empire: Reclaiming the Bible as a History of Faithful Resistance* (Louisville: Westminster John Knox, 2008); David Rhoads, David Esterline and Jae Won Lee (eds), *Luke-Acts and Empire: Essays in Honor of Robert L. Brawley* (Princeton Theological Monograph Series, 151; Eugene: Pickwick, 2011); and the earlier Richard J. Cassidy, *Jesus, Politics and Society: A Study of Luke's Gospel* (Maryknoll: Orbis, 1978).

9. Santner, *On Creaturely Life*, pp. 76–80.

10. Happily, and in contrast, in 2017 the Whanganui River in Aotearoa (New Zealand) has been afforded the legal status of person and has in law human guardians. See Aikaterini Argyrou and Harry Hummels, 'Legal Personality and Economic Livelihood of the Whanganui River: A Call for Community Entrepreneurship', *Water International* 44, no. 6-7 (2019), pp. 752–68, doi: 10.1080/02508060.2019.1643525

11. Santner, *On Creaturely Life*, p. 12.

and become an 'emblem' of creaturely life.[12] Ironically, it is the 'cringe' that allows for an intervention in the destructive nexus of sovereign-subject-commodity relations, because the 'cringed body' of the creature is the point at which neighbour love may open up 'new possibilities for collective life'.[13]

A conversation

The parable of the Good Samaritan seems an apt text for a biblical interpreter to explore these ideas. On face value the parable offers an example of compassionate attention to a stranger in need. The Samaritan attends to the neighbour, even or especially where the neighbour is a stranger. Some ecological theologians have suggested extending the notion of neighbour to other than humans in need or to Earth itself.[14] Two points need to be made at this juncture, one biblical critical and one ecological critical. First, from a biblical studies perspective, interpretation of the parable is not as simple as the everyday usage 'good Samaritan' suggests. Second, from an ecological perspective, there are problems with simply extending the application of the parable to a more-than-human context. These problems relate to the way in which human paradigms need to be rethought ecologically. Extending paradigms of compassionate human relationships (such as neighbour love) to a more-than-human context is insufficient. Interpreters need to rethink human relationships in a more-than-human framework of interconnectedness, interdependence and material co-agency.

An ecological materialism

As discussed in Chapter 5, at least two materialisms are useful here, the first being the material conditions of human lives understood in terms of just distribution of and access to goods such as food, shelter, clothing and adequate life-giving social networks and culture; the second being the materiality that describes human embeddedness in, interconnectedness and interdependence with, a more-than-human sociality. These two materialisms are not entirely separate but the first resonates more with Marxist approaches and allows an ecological extension from social justice to environmental or ecological justice. The second is the wider frame which potentially decentres the human and understands the material embeddedness of humankind as one instance of wider more-than-human materialities and material agencies. In this latter setting social justice becomes an instance of ecological justice, notwithstanding the tensions that arise when deciding

---

12. Santner, *On Creaturely Life*, pp. 29–30, 130–1. It is beyond the scope of this chapter to explore Santner's thought in detail, especially as it explores the role of the unconscious in the production of creaturely life.

13. Santner, *On Creaturely Life*, pp. 58, 133.

14. See, e.g., James A. Nash, 'Toward the Ecological Reformation of Christianity', *Int* 50, no. 1 (1996), pp. 5–15 (9); Sallie McFague, *Blessed Are the Consumers: Practicing Restraint in a Culture of Consumption* (Minneapolis: Fortress, 2013).

who or what might benefit and who or what be harmed by a particular action for ecological justice. An ecological materialist approach takes these frameworks seriously and asks questions about relationships between texts, bodies, matter and political conglomerates such as empires.

The Earth Bible principles inform my ecological materialist approach, as do the ecological hermeneutics, of suspicion, identification and retrieval, as I work not only to question the ways in which biblical texts and interpretations have effaced their material bases, but also to open a space for affirming the co-agency of Earth others in biblical interpretation.[15] An interplay exists between suspicion and reconfiguration, as Elaine Wainwright explains: 'Ecological reading will… critically evaluate biblical methodologies and interpretations not just to see if they include an ecological focus or attention to the environment but to determine ways in which they might be *reconfigured* to participate in an ecological reading that is a process within ecological thinking'.[16] An ecological materialist approach derives from and is situated at the intersection of ecological thinking, the new materialism and situated materialities.

Ecological materialism resonates with a multidimensional approach that both attends to ecological, postcolonial and feminist concerns and studies the layered textures of the text: material, social, embodied, ecological and their embeddedness in their multiple habitats.[17] The multidimensionality of reading becomes an instance of the multidimensionality of readers and texts as materially embedded in the multiplicity of Earth. More than context or setting, the complexity of habitat offers a way of accessing this material embeddedness.[18] When encountered in the text, Earth is not only a construct of writers and readers, but is more particularly its haptic and inspired self (tangible and breathing: in the materialities of medium, voice and language).

In my reading of the parable of the Good Samaritan, I focus on two aspects of an ecological materialism. First, when I come to a text, which is a writing in a specific material artefact, my senses are engaged as mediators of both materiality and meaning.[19] A focus on the senses offers a point of entry into the layers of materiality and material agency mediated in the story world of the text in its ancient context. In my reading of the parable of the Good Samaritan, I focus on the sense of sight. Second, I inquire into the situational materiality meditated in the story world of the text in its ancient context, particularly as it concerns the

---

15. See Anne Elvey, *The Matter of the Text: Material Engagements between Luke and the Five Senses* (BMW, 37; Sheffield: Sheffield Phoenix, 2011), esp. pp. 12–14.

16. Elaine M. Wainwright, 'Images, Words, Stories: Exploring Their Transformative Power in Reading Biblical Texts Ecologically', *BibInt* 20 (2012), pp. 280–304 (289); emphasis in original.

17. See Elaine Wainwright, *Habitat, Human, and Holy: An Eco-Rhetorical Reading of the Gospel of Matthew* (Earth Bible Commentary, 6; Sheffield: Sheffield Phoenix, 2016), pp. 18–21, 49; idem, *Women Healing*, pp. 11–23.

18. Wainwright, 'Images, Words, Stories', esp. p. 286 and p. 294 n. 43.

19. See Elvey, *Matter of the Text*, esp. p. 189.

social and political, through examination of the material spaces of the narrative. Categories of public and private as they pertain to space, action and speech have political implications and inform an understanding of the political theological impact of a text. The category of habitat encompasses, but is broader than notions of public and private space, and offers a frame from which to examine and unsettle constructions of space that are potentially socially divisive.[20] The parable of the Good Samaritan in its narrative context offers an example of a complex interplay of public and private agendas and agencies that should be accounted for in its relation to the multiple sovereignties that appear in the Lukan gospel.

Lukan sovereignties

Politically the Gospel of Luke is both produced and set in, and under, the sovereignty of the Roman empire; there is in effect no outside to this empire, so that even where mention of the empire is not explicit, it is assumed and engaged in every pericope.[21] Informed by contemporary postcolonial perspectives, many biblical scholars understand the Roman empire as functioning for the benefit of elites by 'exerting material domination' to extract resources, for example, in the form of labour and taxation, from its provinces.[22] Luke makes the ubiquity of Roman empire evident with reference to a decree (concerning a census) that

---

20. On the textures of a text, and habitat as part of the ecological texture of a text, see Wainwright, *Habitat, Human, and Holy*, pp. 21–5. For a nuanced consideration of the categories of public and private in relation to Luke and its political, social and cultural contexts, see Bart B. Bruehler, *A Public and Political Christ: The Social-Spatial Characteristics of Luke 18:35-19:43 and the Gospel as a Whole in Its Ancient Context* (Princeton Theological Monograph Series, 157; Eugene: Pickwick, 2011), pp. 31–134.

21. Warren Carter, *The Roman Empire and the New Testament: An Essential Guide* (Nashville: Abingdon, 2006), p. 1; Diehl, 'Anti-Imperial Rhetoric in the New Testament', p. 23. Karl Galinsky, arguing for a nuanced approach to the religious plurality of the Roman empire, comments that within the comprehensiveness of the empire there was an 'elastic order of things', under which many flourished. Karl Galinsky, 'The Cult of the Roman Emperor: Uniter or Divider?' in *Rome and Religion: A Cross-Disciplinary Dialogue on the Imperial Cult* (ed. Jeffrey Brodd and Jonathan L. Reed; WGRWSup, 5; Atlanta: SBL, 2011), pp. 1–22 (7). It is likely, nonetheless, that the flourishing of Greek cities under Rome did not extend to the poor and indebted within and outside their walls.

22. Leo G. Perdue and Warren Carter, *Israel and Empire: A Postcolonial History of Israel and Early Judaism* (London: Bloomsbury T&T Clark, 2015), p. 291. See also, Adam Winn, 'Striking Back at the Empire: Empire Theory and Responses to Empire in the New Testament', in *An Introduction to Empire in the New Testament* (ed. Adam Winn; Atlanta: SBL, 2016), pp. 1–14.

is obeyed (2.1-5); imperial rulers and local leaders in collaboration with them (3.1-2); Pilate's power to execute a person he deems innocent (23.4, 15, 25); the collaboration with Pilate of local leaders (both Herod and the religious leaders, 23.6-25; Acts 4.27); and the destruction of Jerusalem by Roman armies (19.43-44; 21.20-24).[23] Luke draws an unmistakable contrast between Caesar Augustus and Jesus, claiming implicitly that 'Jesus is the true *kyrios* and *sōtēr*'.[24]

One debate in Lukan studies concerns the force of this contrast between the emperor and Jesus, and the extent to which the Gospel is resistant to, or an apology to (and for), Roman rule.[25] Does Luke deal with the oppressive effects of Roman rule, such as poverty, not by resistance to the structures that create, maintain or exacerbate poverty, but by calling forth a different way of living in community? Luke and Acts are directed not only to insiders but, centred on the divine plan, the double narrative both encourages faithful communities even in face of opposition and gives witness to the good news before the empire.[26] The ambiguity available

---

23. See, e.g., Barbara E. Reid, 'Women Prophets of God's Alternative Reign', in *Luke-Acts and Empire: Essays in Honor of Robert L. Brawley* (ed. David Rhoads, David Esterline and Jae Won Lee; Princeton Theological Monograph Series, 151; Eugene: Pickwick, 2011), pp. 44–59 (45-7); Jae Won Lee, 'Pilate and the Crucifixion of Jesus in Luke-Acts', in *Luke-Acts and Empire: Essays in Honor of Robert L. Brawley* (ed. David Rhoads, David Esterline, and Jae Won Lee; Princeton Theological Monograph Series, 151; Eugene: Pickwick, 2011), pp. 84–106 (105–6). I am not here concerned with the historicity of the census, but with its symbolic and indicative functions.

24. Seyoon Kim, *Christ and Caesar: The Gospel and the Roman Empire in the Writings of Paul and Luke* (Grand Rapids: Eerdmans, 2008), pp. 79–81. Galinsky points out that terms like *sōtēr* and son of god predate Roman usage ('The Cult of the Roman Emperor', p. 6). On the imperial propaganda around peace and salvation, and the reality of living under Roman empire, see Bruce W. Longenecker, 'Peace, Prosperity, and Propaganda: Advertisement and Reality in the Early Roman Empire', in *An Introduction to Empire in the New Testament* (ed. Adam Winn; Atlanta: SBL, 2016), pp. 15–45.

25. Writing in the 1970s, Richard Cassidy disagrees with Hans Conzelmann that there is a political apologetic in Luke's gospel. More recently, Steve Walton argues carefully that Luke and Acts take a nuanced approach to the empire, based on how Roman authorities behave, for example, towards the Lukan Jesus, the apostles and Paul. Bart Bruehler holds that Luke is epideictic rather than apologetic: without ignoring reception by outsiders Luke's gospel is written primarily for insiders. In this epideictic style, two contrasting perspectives are possible: (i) accommodation to (perhaps even support) of the empire; (ii) 'a radical new social ethic inaugurated by Jesus and carried out by the disciples that threatens the oppressive political order of the Roman Empire'. Cassidy, *Jesus, Politics and Society*, esp. pp. 32–3, 128; Steve Walton, 'The State They Were in: Luke's View of the Roman Empire', in *Rome in the Bible and the Early Church* (ed. Peter Oakes; Carlisle: Paternoster, 2002), pp. 1–41 (33–5); Bruehler, *Public and Political Christ*, p. 5.

26. Walton, 'The State They Were in', p. 35.

to interpreters of Luke's attitude to empire may be indicative of the structures of imperial sovereignty themselves; rather than being directly confrontational, resistance and strategies of survival in a colonial situation are encoded in texts that can be understood subversively.[27] As I discussed in Chapter 2, there is a strong case for reading the hymns of the Lukan infancy narratives as songs of protest.[28] Furthermore, while neither 'overtly' criticizing the Roman empire, nor portraying it 'in a positive light', Luke and Acts 'can be said to be counter-imperial inasmuch as [they] presents a wisdom or strategy for renewal that is set in contrast to key claims of Greco-Roman society'.[29]

This wisdom or strategy for renewal can be found in the way divine sovereignty and human responsive participation in the reign (βασιλεία) of G-d is depicted through two Lukan tropes: purpose and visitation, the latter having the dual aspects of hospitality (through table fellowship; compassion; and forgiveness or release from debt) and judgement.[30] For Luke the destructive effects of Roman power, as exemplified in the death of Jesus (9.22; 17.22-25; 22.36-37; 24.5-7, 25-26) and the destruction of Jerusalem, are subsumed, not without grief (13.31-35; 19.41-44), under the sovereignty of G-d which makes another future possible. This divine sovereignty and the possibilities it evokes are captured for Luke in the notion of the visitation of G-d (see esp. 1.76-79; 4.18-19; 19.44), a liberating divine hospitality calling forth welcome (see esp. 10.1-11). Visitation only becomes

27. See, e.g., Diehl, 'Anti-Imperial Rhetoric', pp. 21–4; Reid, 'Women Prophets', pp. 48–9; Gary Gilbert, 'Luke-Acts and the Negotiation of Authority and Identity in the Roman World', in *The Multivalence of Biblical Texts and Theological Meanings* (ed. Christine Helmer and Charlene Higbe; Atlanta: Society of Biblical Literature, 2006), pp. 83–104 (100, 104); Brigitte Kahl, 'Reading Luke against Luke: Non-Uniformity of Text, Hermeneutics of Conspiracy and the "Scriptural Principle" in Luke 1', in *A Feminist Companion to Luke* (ed. Amy-Jill Levine with Marianne Blickenstaff; London: Sheffield Academic, 2002), pp. 70–88 (71–6); idem, 'Acts of the Apostles: Pro(to)-Imperial Script and Hidden Transcript', in *In the Shadow of Empire: Reclaiming the Bible as a History of Faithful Resistance* (ed. Richard A. Horsley; Louisville: Westminster John Knox, 2008), pp. 137–56 (149–51); Eric D. Barreto, 'Crafting Colonial Identities: Hybridity and the Roman Empire in Luke-Acts', in *An Introduction to Empire in the New Testament* (ed. Adam Winn; Atlanta: SBL, 2016), pp. 107–21. Cf. Mary Rose D'Angelo, 'Women in Luke-Acts: A Redactional View', *JBL* 109 (1990), pp. 441–61.

28. Warren Carter, 'Singing in the Reign: Performing Luke's Songs and Negotiating the Roman Empire (Luke 1–2)', in *Luke-Acts and Empire: Essays in Honor of Robert L. Brawley* (ed. David Rhoads, David Esterline and Jae Won Lee; Princeton Theological Monograph Series, 151; Eugene: Pickwick, 2011), pp. 23–43; see also, Reid, 'Women Prophets', p. 44.

29. Raymond Pickett, 'Luke and Empire: An Introduction', in *Luke-Acts and Empire: Essays in Honor of Robert L. Brawley* (ed. David Rhoads, David Esterline and Jae Won Lee; Princeton Theological Monograph Series, 151; Eugene: Pickwick, 2011), pp. 1–22 (6, 12).

30. Brendan Byrne, *The Hospitality of God: A Reading of Luke's Gospel* (Strathfield, NSW: St Pauls, 2000); Robert C. Tannehill, *Luke* (Abingdon New Testament Commentaries; Nashville: Abingdon, 1996), p. 215; Luke Timothy Johnson, *The Gospel of Luke* (SP; Collegeville: Liturgical Press, 1991), p. 299.

judgement as a consequence of a failure to welcome or receive (10.11; 19.41-44), and so participate in, the hospitality of G-d.

This brief sketch of an alternative sovereignty, that in the concept of the reign (βασιλεία) of G-d employs the political language of kingdoms and empires, recalls the ambiguity of survival-resistance under empire. The embeddedness of Second Testament writings in the imperial world in which they were produced contributes to the re-inscription of the language of empire, even where these texts may be resisting empire.[31] Rehabilitation of such texts as anti-imperial needs to be matched with an ongoing critique of the kyriarchal imaginary they continue to purvey. Ironically, use of the language and imagery of empire to describe the visitation of G-d reinforces imperial power while at the same time protesting its multiple oppressions by offering in the reign (βασιλεία) of G-d a different mode of social inclusion. The Lukan parable of the Good Samaritan contributes to this alternative worldview.

The parable of the Good Samaritan

The parable appears in Luke 10 which begins with an episode concerning welcoming or refusing to welcome the visitation of G-d in the person of the disciples sent out by the Lukan Jesus (10.1-11). The consequence of reception or rejection of this divine hospitality is met as respectively the advent of peace or its lack, each enmeshed with the imminence of the reign (βασιλεία) of G-d (10.5-6, 8-11). For Luke, this is not simply inner peace, or peace in the local community; recognizing the time of divine visitation (as hospitality and judgement) is allied with what makes for peace as opposed to the kinds of violence that result in the destruction of Jerusalem by Roman forces (19.41-44).[32] It is possible to read Luke here, especially in the light of the contrast between the peace announced by the

---

31. Elisabeth Schüssler Fiorenza, *The Power of the Word: Scripture and the Rhetoric of Empire* (Minneapolis: Fortress, 2007), p. 5.

32. John Dominic Crossan argues that 'the program of Roman imperial theology incarnated in Caesar was the sequence of religion, war, victory, and peace or, more succinctly, peace through victory'; in contrast, Jesus offers an alternative vision of 'peace through nonviolent justice'; see John Dominic Crossan, 'Roman Imperial Theology', in *In the Shadow of Empire: Reclaiming the Bible as a History of Faithful Resistance* (ed. Richard A. Horsley; Louisville: Westminster John Knox, 2008), pp. 59–73 (73). Joseph Grassi argues for a reading of Luke as a Gospel of nonviolence, which may nonetheless suggest a certain accommodation to Roman rule. Joseph Grassi, *Peace on Earth: Roots and Practices from Luke's Gospel* (Collegeville: Liturgical Press, 2004), esp. pp. 92–4. David Neville considers the tension in Luke between an impetus towards peaceful restoration and violent judgement for those who reject the Lukan Jesus. For Neville, an analysis of the retributive and restorative eschatology of Luke-Acts is key to understanding this pervasive tension; his hope is that Luke's paradigm of reversal extends to the violence of divine judgement with a preference for peace. David J. Neville, *A Peaceable Hope: Contesting Violent Eschatology in New Testament Narratives* (Grand Rapids: Baker Academic, 2013), pp. 91–173.

heavenly multitude in 2.14 and the 'peace' brought by the order of Rome, as writing an alternative and resistant theopolitics where receptivity to the divine visitation has material effects in peace on Earth.

The theme of reception or otherwise is carried through in various ways in 10.12-24, both in the pronouncement of judgement on cities (10.12-15) and in the metaphor of sensual receptivity for responsiveness to the divine visitation in Jesus (10.16, 23-24). An interplay exists between public and private discourse; while the crowds are not explicitly mentioned in the settings of Luke 10, the woes on the cities (10.13-15) assume a wider audience than the disciples. That the Lukan Jesus turns privately to his disciples at 10.23 suggests that this turning aside to temporarily private space occurs within a wider more public discourse. This private conversation is in effect interrupted by a lawyer when he stands up (presumably in the more public space) 'to test Jesus' asking 'what must I do to inherit eternal life?' (10.25).

The parable (10.30-35) occurs in response to the ensuing dialogue between the lawyer and the Lukan Jesus where the hearer is reminded of the material text in the questions, 'what is written? how do you read?' (10.26).[33] The lawyer's reference to Deuteronomy and Leviticus provides the dual command that links love of G-d and love of neighbour (10.27). The lawyer quotes two passages from the Hebrew Bible:

Hear O Israel. The Lord is our God, the Lord alone [the Lord is one]. You shall love the Lord your God with all your heart, and with all your soul, and with all your might. (Deut. 6.4-5)
You shall love your neighbour as yourself. (Lev. 19.18)

The second, the command of neighbour love, appears in a wider context of familial, social and communal justice, more-than-human agricultural and social engagement that shows a concern for keeping species boundaries (Lev. 19.15-19). In its Levitical context, it is not simply an isolated inter-human ethic. The dual ethic is indispensable.[34] Love of G-d, divine love for the whole person, is incomplete without love of neighbour. The mystic, for example, remains closed in, unethical even, without neighbour love. Neighbour love has both particular and universal aspects that are constitutive of it, aspects which imply its connectedness with the created world.[35]

Three questions central to interpretation of the Levitical command are: 'What is love?' 'What is meant by loving your neighbour as yourself?' 'Who is my neighbour?'[36] Luke's gospel addresses each of these questions through the parable

33. See Elvey, *Matter of the Text*, p. 161.

34. As Franz Rosenzweig likewise asserts: Franz Rosenzweig (1886–1929), *The Star of Redemption* (trans. Barbara E. Galli; Madison, WI: The University of Wisconsin Press, 2005).

35. Rosenzweig, *Star of Redemption*, esp. pp. 221–36.

36. Rodney S. Sadler, Jr., 'Guest Editorial: Who Is My Neighbor? Introductory Explorations', *Int* 62, no. 2 (April 2008), pp. 115–21.

of the Good Samaritan in the context of the wider Lukan narrative. In this broader narrative context, the appeal to love reminds the reader of the earlier admonitions of the Lukan Jesus:

> love your enemies (6.27a)
> do good to those who hate you (6.27b, 35a)
> bless those who curse you (6.28).

In Luke 10, Jesus responds to the lawyer's citation of the dual command: 'Rightly you have answered; do this and you will live' (10.28). In other words, the dual commandment of love is resonant with the Hebrew command to 'choose life' (Deut. 30.19). That this might entail 'love of enemies' resonates with a kind of reversal integral to Luke's rhetoric and theology, where for example poor are blessed and rich cursed; sight is restored to the blind; the indebted are liberated (1.46-55; 4.18-19; 6.20-26; 7.22; 16.19-31).

This last example addresses the socio-political reality of debt, land debt, forfeit of land, imprisonment for debt and forms of debt slavery under Roman rule.[37] Theology and politics are interconnected when forgiveness of sins, a theological concept, is described in the same words and symbols as release from debt (see particularly 7.40-48). In the traditions shared by Matthew and Luke, facing the impact of Roman oppression on the social fabric of village life, 'Jesus declares a renewal of covenantal community'; this is a 'renewal of cooperation and solidarity in local communities' to resist 'the effects of Roman imperial domination that was driving families into debt, loss of land, and reduction to low-paid wage labourers completely dependent on the wealthy'.[38] The emphasis of the discourse around love of enemies pertains, argues Richard Horsley, primarily to fellow villagers not to outsiders.[39] While this may hold for the shared tradition, within the context of the Lukan narrative, love of enemies has a wider application. Immediately following Luke's sermon on a level place (6.17-49) which includes both blessings and woes, on poor and rich respectively, and the discourse on love of enemies,

---

37. While debt slavery is not unique to Roman rule, but was part of Hebrew biblical tradition, it is telling that the reality of debt formed one focus of resentment towards the Roman occupiers. Sharon Ringe makes the important point: 'It is little wonder that when the Zealots entered Jerusalem at the start of the war in 66 C.E., the first thing they did was to burn the debt records!' Sharon H. Ringe, *Luke* (Westminster Bible Companion; Louisville: Westminster John Knox, 1995), p. 183.

38. Richard A. Horsley, 'Jesus and Empire', in *In the Shadow of Empire: Reclaiming the Bible as a History of Faithful Resistance* (ed. Richard A. Horsley; Louisville: Westminster John Knox, 2008), pp. 75–96 (94–5); see also, idem, 'Jesus-in-Movement and the Roman Imperial (Dis)order', in *An Introduction to Empire in the New Testament* (ed. Adam Winn; Atlanta: SBL, 2016), pp. 47–69 (53).

39. Horsley, 'Jesus and Empire', pp. 93–4.

Jesus encounters a representative of Roman occupation, a centurion (7.1-10), and heals his servant.[40]

Considering 'love of enemies', however, Alan Kirk identifies a problem: the golden rule 'do to others as you would have them do to you' (6.31) 'introduces a note of reciprocity into Luke 6.27-35 that seems dissonant with the instruction's inaugural command to "love your enemies"' (6:27).[41] Two logics appear in tension: the golden rule's 'logic of equivalence' and the 'logic of superabundance' that underscores the call: 'love your enemies'.[42] In the juxtaposition of the two imperatives is a 'dialectic crucial for ethics'.[43] The dynamics of reciprocity are important; so too are the ways in which the two commands serve to either inculcate or transform existing social, economic and religious patterns.[44] In classical Greek reciprocity ethics, three kinds of reciprocity characterize social relations: general reciprocity ('open-ended exchange of benefits among friends'); balanced reciprocity; and negative reciprocity.[45] Similar ethics of reciprocity apply in the Hellenistic and Roman periods.[46] Where gift (χάρις, also, grace, favour or credit) describes a kind of general reciprocity, the experience with enemies is likely to be a history or expectation of negative reciprocity – enemies are unlikely 'to return favors', and in this case reciprocity ought be, at the very least, abandoned.[47]

---

40. Grassi, *Peace on Earth*, pp. 80-1. It is beyond the scope of this chapter to engage with Alan Cadwallader's subtle reading of this episode in the light of Roman occupation, but it seems likely that the adulation of the centurion by the Jewish elders (7.4) is part of processes of collaboration between local leaders and occupying forces. Moreover, the affirmations of Jesus' authority by the centurion (7.8) and the centurion's faith by Jesus (7.9) may need to be read with irony. Most likely in my opinion Luke is writing a layered text with the amazement of Jesus (7.9) signally both a recognition of the action of God in the encounter, and the ongoing bewilderment of the colonized at the short-sightedness of their colonizers. Alan Cadwallader, 'The Roman Army as a Total Institution and the Implications for Gospel Interpretation', paper given at the Bible and Critical Theory Seminar, Brisbane, 5-6 November 2011.

41. Alan Kirk, '"Love Your Enemies," The Golden Rule, and Ancient Reciprocity (Luke 6.27-35)', *JBL* 122 (2003), pp. 667–86 (667).

42. Kirk, '"Love Your Enemies"', p. 669. The 'logic of superabundance' echoes the 'economy of the gift'. The modern notion of 'the economy of the gift' has many strands, from Marcel Mauss to Jacques Derrida; for my staging of a conversation between these notions of 'gift', and Lukan understandings of gift and gifts, see Anne Elvey, *An Ecological Feminist Reading of the Gospel of Luke: A Gestational Paradigm* (Studies in Women and Religion, 45; Lewiston, NY: Edwin Mellen, 2005), pp. 84–91.

43. Kirk, '"Love Your Enemies"', p. 670.

44. Kirk, '"Love Your Enemies"', p. 673.

45. Kirk, '"Love Your Enemies"', pp. 674, 675–7.

46. Kirk, '"Love Your Enemies"', p. 678.

47. Kirk, '"Love Your Enemies"', pp. 678–9.

Luke 6.27-29 gives examples of such negative reciprocity, but the command to love one's enemies and the examples of doing good that accompany this are, as Kirk suggests, 'stunningly liberal acts of general reciprocity, not abandonment of reciprocity in principle'.[48] The golden rule grounds the exhortation to 'love one's enemies' in reciprocity, connecting 'the programmatic love command to the social realia of human relations'.[49]

When the lawyer asks: 'Who is my neighbour?' (Lk. 10.29), the Lukan Jesus focuses on the social world of human relations and tells the parable known as the Good Samaritan. While the interchange with the lawyer appears to take place in a kind of space of public Jewish discourse, the parable draws the reader into a different relation to space and place. A person of unspecified ethnicity, but it would be reasonable to assume the person to be a Judaean/Jew, on the road from Jerusalem to Jericho is set upon, stripped, beaten and left half dead (ἡμιθανῆ, 10.30). The Roman road from Jerusalem to Jericho 'descends from over 2500 feet above sea level (Jerusalem) to 770 feet below it (Jericho)' and takes the traveller through '"desert and rocky" country' over about 'eighteen miles'.[50] The robbers were possibly 'some of the roving terrorists staging their own form of protest against various types of official and unofficial exploitation of the poor'.[51] To the extent that the wild country surrounding the road was habitat for any of the humans in the story world of the parable, it was likely the place that hid, and to a certain extent sustained, these violent and resistant characters. For the religious leaders on the road, and even for the Samaritan carrying wine, oil and coins (10.34-35), this was not a hospitable place. For the characters, other than the 'robbers' who are quickly off-stage, the road while public space is potentially isolated enough to carry a sinister kind of privacy, where a passer-by might be attacked and left half-dead.

Setting up a contrast between the lawyer's desire for life – what must I do to have life?[52] – and a traveller's looming death, the parable displays a pattern in which seeing is the dominant sense. *See* the person lying near death on the way, the parable seems to be saying. The implied command to see becomes more explicit as the story progresses; in succession a priest, a Levite and a Samaritan happen to be going down the same road and each sees:

---

48. Kirk, '"Love Your Enemies"', pp. 682.

49. Kirk, '"Love Your Enemies"', p. 686. Debt is part of this social reality and liberation from debt, a key practical and symbolic relation for Luke, is another example of general reciprocity, where the logic of negative reciprocity might be anticipated but is undone.

50. Joseph A. Fitzmyer, *The Gospel According to Luke X–XXIV: A New Translation with Introduction and Commentary* (AB, 28A; New York: Doubleday, 1985), p. 886.

51. Ringe, *Luke*, p. 158. For Ringe, however, Luke's city-bound audience may not have picked up this nuance of the parable (p. 159).

52. The lawyer specifies 'eternal life' (10.25), Jesus simply says 'do this and you will live' (10.28).

and seeing him, passed by on the other side (καὶ ἰδὼν αὐτὸν ἀντιπαρῆλθεν, 10.31)
and seeing [him], passed by on the other side (καὶ ἰδὼν ἀντιπαρῆλθεν, 10.32)
and seeing [him], was moved with compassion (καὶ ἰδὼν ἐσπλαγχνίσθη 10.33).[53]

The repetition of a traveller's seeing followed by a response highlights the contrast with the first two characters and emphasizes the call of the visible. It is as if what is seen has a voice, necessitating a response.[54] The visible voice of the one who is half dead prompts compassion, a movement in the gut, signalled by the verb 'to be moved with compassion' (σπλαγχνίζομαι, 10.33) which in Luke echoes the gut-felt movement of divine mercy (διὰ σπλάγχνα ἐλέους θεοῦ ἡμῶν) in the visitation of G-d (1.78). This pattern occurs twice elsewhere in Luke. In each case, the protagonist sees – in 7.13 the Lukan Jesus, titled lord, sees the bereaved widow; in 15.20 a father sees his disgraced son returning; in 10.33 the Samaritan sees the wounded person on the road – and each, moved in the guts with compassion, acts in such a way as (through touch) to bring life from death.[55]

At the end of the parable, the original question, 'Who is my neighbour?' (10.29), shifts to: 'Which of these three acted as neighbour to the person who fell into the hands of the robbers?' (10.36). The lawyer's original question is an important one. The emphasis is on the cultivation of virtues that dispose one towards recognizing the neighbour in the one in need, such that one is disposed to act as neighbour.[56] In answer to Jesus' question 'who acted as neighbour?', the lawyer does not use the word Samaritan, but responds 'the one who showed mercy' (10.37a).

Despite the temptation to read the Samaritan as an enemy, the situation is subtler. The shift in the question may signal not that the Samaritan is an enemy who in the praxis of neighbour love has shown up the Israelite religious authorities

---

53. My translations.

54. For the concept of a visible voice, see Jean-Louis Chrétien, *The Call and the Response* (trans. Anne A. Davenport; New York: Fordham University Press, 2004), pp. 33–43. The eye 'listens' to both beauty and suffering (43). To borrow Jean-Luc Nancy's term, one is 'sounded' by the visible. Jean-Luc Nancy, *Listening* (trans. Charlotte Mandell; New York: Fordham University Press, 2007), p. 12.

55. See Further, Anne Elvey, 'Love and Justice in the Gospel of Luke: Ecology, the Neighbour and Hope', *AusBR* 60 (2012), pp. 1–17 (14–15), in which elements of this paragraph appear as part of a longer discussion.

56. Samuel K. Roberts, 'Becoming the Neighbor: Virtue Theory and the Problem of Neighbor Identity', *Int* 62, no. 2 (April 2008), pp. 146–55.

but that the Samaritan is kin, responding to kin.⁵⁷ At another level, in turning the question, the Lukan Jesus challenges the lawyer to place himself in the position of the one left half-dead on the road.⁵⁸ The half-dead one receives the compassionate attention of the Samaritan. To see oneself as neighboured by the Samaritan, who exhibits the compassionate quality of divine hospitality, is to be challenged in turn to receive and respond to the divine visitation. When Jesus says, 'Go and do likewise' (10.37b), that is, do good, the lawyer and Luke's hearers/readers are invited to participate in the visitation of divine mercy. Such action is an expression of love for both other humans and G-d.⁵⁹

Towards an ecological materialist conversation

How might this pattern of compassionate neighbour love be understood in an ecological materialist framework? First, when I look at the parable, I note that the action of the Samaritan is not a lone action:

> Going to him he bandaged his wounds, pouring oil and wine (on them), and placing him on his own pack animal, he brought him to an inn and took care of him. And the next day, taking out two denarii he gave them to the innkeeper, and said, 'Take care of him, and whatever you spend in addition, on my return I will give you' (10.34-35, my translation).

---

57. In earlier work, I accepted the scholarly view of the Samaritan as 'other' within the socio-religious world of first century CE Judaism. Elvey, *Ecological Feminist Reading*, p. 239. Love R. Sechrest argues cogently that the Lukan Jesus views Samaritans as insiders. Love L. Sechrest, 'Double Vision for Revolutionary Religion: Race Relations, Moral Analogies, and African-American Biblical Interpretation', in *Ethnicity, Race, Religion: Identities and Ideologies in Early Jewish and Christian Texts, and in Modern Biblical Interpretation* (ed. Katherine M. Hockey and David G. Horrell; paperback edn; London: T&T Clark, 2020), pp. 202-18 (209-11). Questioning racialized readings of supposed Jewish-Samaritan enmity, Matthew Chalmers, too, makes a strong argument that the Samaritan is better described as a 'Samaritan Israelite', whose behaviour in the parable offers a model for Israelite renewal within the broader community of Israel. Matthew Chalmers, 'Rethinking Luke 10: The Parable of the Good Samaritan Israelite', *JBL* 139 (2020), pp. 543-66. Roberts, 'Becoming the Neighbor', pp. 146-55.

58. Alan H. Cadwallader, 'The Fall, the Samaritan and the Wounded Man: An Example of Multiple Readings of Scripture (Lk. 10:25-37)', in *Lost in Translation?: Anglicans, Controversy and the Bible* (ed. Scott Cowdell and Muriel Porter; Thornbury, Vic.: Desbooks, 2004), pp. 155-84.

59. Amanda C. Miller, 'Good Sinners and Exemplary Heretics: The Sociopolitical Implications of Love and Acceptance in the Gospel of Luke', *RevExp* 112, no. 3 (2015), pp. 461-9 (465).

The loving action occurs within a community of agency, in which the material elements of oil and wine, the cloth for bandages, the plants from which this cloth was produced, the animal who bears the wounded person, the environment and hospitality of the inn, the human labour to extract oil, make wine and weave bandages, and another human, namely the innkeeper, even the metals of the coins, are all necessary for the Samaritan's act of mercy, of doing good to another human. From the inhospitable habitat of the wild place surrounding the road, the Samaritan brings the person to the hospitable place of the inn, a more-than-human place where the public and the private intersect. This is not an unusual situation; every act for ill or good occurs within a wider network of more-than-human assemblages and agencies. The interrelatedness of Earthkind makes no act solo. Ecological materialism challenges me to imagine myself, my subjectivity and agency, my capacity to act, within a framework of material agency in which my individual corporeality is already engaged.

Secondly, at a human level, the parable is unsettling. Instead of the religious figures, a priest and a Levite, who might be expected to act in accord with the command to love the neighbour, it is a 'Samaritan Israelite', who acts compassionately, recognizing the wounded person as neighbour, and demonstrating an ethic of 'communal obligation' that applies in Luke to Israelite religious leaders, Jews and Samaritans.[60] This communal obligation extends the notion of neighbour beyond the immediate kinship group and is resonant with Jewish teaching, especially with regard to treatment of the stranger. This in turn has allowed ecological readers to extend the object of neighbour love to other Earthkind, and ask how each of us might conduct ourselves as good neighbours towards the more-than-human Earth community in which we are enmeshed.[61] In the context of the parable, is it possible that the Samaritan's compassionate attention to the needs of the one half-dead on the side of the road was part of a pattern of action which included his attentiveness to the needs of the animal with which he shared his journey?

As noted above, the question 'who acted as neighbour?' prompts the lawyer, not only to act as neighbour, but also to see himself receiving the attention of the neighbour, that is, to see himself in the one who was set upon by robbers, one tended by the Samaritan. This, too, is unsettling. Recollecting the category of creaturely life I described earlier in this chapter, when I ask with the lawyer 'who is my neighbour?' I am challenged to recognize in myself my subjection in sovereign-subject-commodity relations, as if I were 'left half-dead'. In their subjection Luke's hearers/readers may find themselves tended by another. Extending this, readers may ask: when are we tended by the neighbour? Where and when we have found ourselves tended not only by human others but by other Earthkind? When has Earth – its soils, seas and atmosphere, places, plants and other animals – acted as neighbour to us?

60. Chalmers, 'Rethinking Luke 10', p. 563.

61. Taking this route, James Nash argues that if I accept that 'God is love'; 'creation itself is an act of love'; and Christians are called to care for all that G-d loves. Nash, 'Ecological Reformation of Christianity', p. 9.

Thirdly, in Luke neighbour love is part of a structure of divine visitation, where both hospitality and judgement together characterize divine sovereignty. Lukan hospitality is evident in compassion and forgiveness – the latter is both metaphorically and literally liberation from debt, a symbol of oppression or subjection. Together with the directive to love one's enemies, neighbour love shares in a pattern of divine hospitality; it disrupts destructive patterns of behaviour, such as the system of debt (that destroys links with family and land) and perhaps also the violence brought about by resistance to Roman rule. The one left half-dead may be one privileged enough to be the target of an attack by 'robbers' violently resistant to imperial oppression. To see oneself in this position is similar to knowing oneself as both colonized and colonizer, as both sovereign and commodity. The shifts in the parable can be read as challenges to be loved in, and to love from, this position of uncomfortable (even shameful) ambiguity.

Who is 'the one neighboring on me'?[62] What are the material foundations and effects of compassionate neighbourly/neighbouring action? I have hinted at three aspects: the simplest is that every human action already occurs as a more-than-human action, as a material co-agency. The second is that not only are human beings matter, complexly organized, but as human animals we are neighboured on by other matter, which is always in complex material exchanges with other matter. In some of these exchanges we may find ourselves treated with compassion or something like compassion. The third is more difficult. I have argued elsewhere that the notions of hospitality and sacrifice that are central to the Christian practice and theology of Eucharist are already part of the way a more-than-human Earth community and cosmos engages; Eucharist describes, or focuses, qualities or capacities of material life and processes of consumption that are necessarily both death-dealing and life-giving.[63] Does the human value of compassion, expressed in so many cultures particularly in the notion of neighbour love, also express a quality of material being? Is the Earth in its orientation towards sustaining life already enacting a kind of neighbour love to humans and other animals?[64]

This suggests to me two further questions. First, if neighbour love disrupts oppressive networks of relation, does the Earth's life-sustaining capacity also disrupt networks of oppressive relation such as those humans have co-engaged in, with fossil fuels, to produce the current climate crisis? Second, does this human co-engagement with fossil fuels, for example, disturb the capacity of Earth to

62. Rosenzweig, *Star of Redemption*, p. 234.

63. See further Anne Elvey, 'Living One for the Other: Eucharistic Hospitality as Ecological Hospitality', in *Reinterpreting the Eucharist: Explorations in Feminist Theology and Ethics* (ed. Anne Elvey, Carol Hogan, Kim Power and Claire Renkin; Sheffield: Equinox, 2013), 186–205.

64. As noted earlier, it is important not to sentimentalize Earth, but the evolution of the conditions for the production, reproduction and maintenance of plant, fungal, animal (including human) and microbial life on Earth suggests that it is not overly romantic to speak of a sustaining Earth.

sustain life, by straining the conditions of possibility for Earth, and its atmosphere, to act as neighbour to many species, including humankind? These two questions describe a tension between co-existent possibilities for Earth's enmeshed material agencies in relation to this period of anthropogenic climate change.

Conclusion

Together, these questions inform an experience of the 'cringe', the abjection of the human being in the face of our power to enact ecocidal harm. In this moment, the skewed sovereignty of the individual in the face of the complex entanglements of more-than-human agencies producing climate change is called into question by a kind of Earth sovereignty. Already enmeshed in cosmic material interrelations and in its own multiplicity of being and agency, Earth should not only be the ethical subject-object of human neighbour love, but more particularly Earth has the capacity to enact a kind of neighbour love towards all Earth kind, not necessarily even primarily humankind.

How is such Earth sovereignty related to divine sovereignty, presuming divinity itself is supposed? Divine sovereignty for Luke is enmeshed with the hospitality of compassion that prompts neighbour love. From a Lukan perspective, considered through the lens of an ecological materialism, such divine sovereignty is inter-agential with Earth's sovereign being *for life*. That this being on the side of life is not coextensive with the life of any particular individual, and their skewed sovereignty, is not the issue. Rather, in the materiality of Earth and cosmos, divine sovereignty quivers with and in the material possibilities of Earthy openness to life. Divine sovereignty is enmeshed with Earthy sovereignty at the point not only where eco-social trauma calls forth compassion, but also where receptivity to what might be called the compassionate visitation of the material sacred (mediated, for example, by another human being, a companion animal or familiar, a forest, a mountain or an ocean) prevails over the skewed sovereignty of the individual. The following section turns to the shared vulnerabilities of a more-than-human world undergoing ecological trauma, with a focus on road kill, mined landscapes and bleached corals. In the next chapter, in a context where animals are left to die on roadsides, I explore the interplay of compassion and material vulnerability through an ecological feminist emphasis on relatedness.

Section 3

SHARED VULNERABILITIES

Chapter 8

AN ECOLOGICAL FEMINIST APPROACH TO CROSS SPECIES RELATEDNESS: COMPASSION AND LUKE 10.30-37

Bodies and texts intersect in ways that are not fully definable.[1] The kind of ecological feminism I am working with in this book foregrounds the material givenness of bodies, pregnant bodies, Earth, air and breath, and the materiality of texts, as sites and products of multiple more-than-human agencies. In this context, words such as interconnectedness, interdependence, embeddedness and entanglement resonate in ecological and feminist theological understandings of relationality and relatedness. A relational emphasis on material agencies decentres human hegemony, while a focus on racialization calls into question the limits of the construct 'human'. In the interplay between matter and the maternal, both as denied sources of value and as affirmed necessities for creaturely life, is a material vulnerability that is en-mattered and embodied (not only in human bodies) and that acts in the mode of a call, or multiple calls.

Material vulnerability shares the character of the 'face' that calls, making an ethical demand.[2] Material vulnerability becomes visible, for example, in animals left as road kill, mountains levelled for coal, forests razed for paper products and bodies subject to nuclear fallout. The mutuality of a material vulnerability is at the crux of understanding not only compassionate action as an ethical response but also the way actions of hospitality and service rely on more-than-human

---

1. The core of this chapter appeared in Anne Elvey, 'Roadsides: Toward an Ecological Feminist Theology of Cross-Species Compassion', in *Contemporary Feminist Theologies: Power, Authority, Love* (ed. Kerrie Handasyde, Cathryn McKinney and Rebekah Pryor; London: Routledge, 2021), pp. 133-44. Copyright © Anne Elvey 2021. Reproduced by permission of Taylor & Francis Group.

2. On the ethical call of the 'face', see Emmanuel Lévinas, 'Is Ontology Fundamental?', (1951) (trans. Peter Atterton, Simon Critchley and Graham Noctor), in *Basic Philosophical Writings* (ed. Adriaan T. Peperzak, Simon Critchley and Robert Bernasconi; Bloomington: Indiana University Press, 1996), pp. 1–10 (10). Extending and critiquing Lévinas in a more-than-human frame, see Deborah Bird Rose, *Wild Dog Dreaming: Love and Extinction* (Under the Sign of Nature: Explorations in Ecocriticism; Charlottesville: University of Virginia Press, 2011), pp. 13, 30, 97.

agencies. In the Gospel of Luke, compassion and hospitality are characteristics of a divine visitation.[3] In this chapter, the mutuality of material vulnerability is focused in cross-species relatedness, as I engage further with Lk. 10.30-37 around the practical exercise of compassion. I begin with the material vulnerability represented by the road.

Roadsides

News media regularly publish statistics on human fatalities on our roads, although these reports have gone into the background somewhat as hourly news in 2020 charts the impact of coronavirus disease 2019 (Covid-19) statistically. At any time, the number of other creatures killed on Australian roads does not feature as part of the road toll. Before Covid-19, I need only have travelled from Devonport to Launceston, sections of the Kings Highway between Canberra and the East Coast, the Princes Highway from Melbourne to Mount Gambier or many other roads on the outskirts of, and outside, major Australian cities to see the multiple daily deaths of other creatures because of road trauma.[4] This trauma impacts not only the individual animals but also, for example in the case of kangaroos, the communities to which they belong.[5] In the 2019–20 summer, the deaths of other creatures entered my consciousness afresh as news outlets detailed at least a billion other animals killed as a result of the devastating bush fire season.[6] In 2020, as cities, states and whole nations shut down, and domestic and international flights became a small fraction of their former numbers, National Geographic reported that some once highly polluted cities had clearer air, although the long-term impacts on climate change are not yet known.[7] It is possible that stay-at-home directives have, in the short term, also mitigated the impact on other animals from

---

3. Brendan Byrne, *The Hospitality of God: A Reading of Luke's Gospel* (Strathfield, NSW: St Paul's Publications, 2000).

4. See, e.g., Natasha Fijn, 'Impacts on the Kings Highway: A Photo Essay', *Plumwood Mountain* 1, no. 2 (August 2014), available online: http://plumwoodmountain.com/photo-essay-by-natasha-fijn/ (accessed 14 May 2020).

5. See Daniel Ramp, 'Roads as Drivers of Change for Macropods', in *Macropods: The Biology of Kangaroos, Wallabies and Rat-Kangaroos* (ed. Graeme Coulson and Mark Eldridge; Collingwood: CSIRO Publishing, 2010), pp. 279–91.

6. See, e.g., Emma Elsworthy, 'NSW Bushfires Lead to Deaths of over a Billion Animals and "hundreds of billions" of Insects, Experts Say', ABC News (9 January 2020), available online: https://www.abc.net.au/news/2020-01-09/nsw-bushfires-kill-over-a-billion-animals-experts-say/11854836 (accessed 13 May 2020).

7. Beth Gardiner, 'Pollution Made COVID-19 Worse. Now Lockdowns Are Clearing the Air', *National Geographic* (8 April 2020), available online: https://www.nationalgeographic.com/science/2020/04/pollution-made-the-pandemic-worse-but-lockdowns-clean-the-sky/ (accessed 12 November 2020).

traffic on Australian highways.[8] What the current novel coronavirus situation highlights – as ecophilosophy, ecopoetics and ecocriticism have long done – is the ecological reality of interconnectedness. As climate change and Covid-19 both show, material connections cross continents and species.

In the first part of this chapter, I consider road kill in Australia as an example of trauma to other creatures that highlights a kind of human species supremacism which many in settler cultures (and I include myself) share. The legal requisite to stop to assist at the scene of an accident applies principally where humans are victims. That this is so indicates a disjunction between our behaviour towards other creatures and our behaviour towards our own kind.[9] Organizations such as WIRES provide wildlife rescue services for animals, or their offspring in pouches, after an accident.[10] But the issue is not principally about what to do in the aftermath of an accident. Rather, the question is what are the routine conditions, such as speed and time of day, that in our economies of road transit privilege human lives over the lives of other kind? This privileging, while to an extent unavoidable, even at times necessary, needs to be brought to consciousness. In this chapter, it forms a context for reimagining compassion in an ecological feminist theological framework as a cross-species ethic.

In Chapter 1, I offered a brief genealogy of ecological feminist approaches. Here, I consider Ivone Gebara's focus on relatedness. I follow this with discussion of an ethic of compassion and describe an ecological feminist basis for compassion in the link with the maternal and the material. Then I offer reflections on a Lukan road text introduced in the previous chapter: Lk. 10.30-37 (the parable of the Good Samaritan) in relation to formulations of compassion across species. What are the implications for refiguring the road as a way of compassion, that spills over from cross-species compassion to human relatedness and vice versa?

Relatedness

As Latin American ecological feminist theologian Ivone Gebara argues, not only is relatedness 'the most basic characteristic of the human person', but it also reflects contemporary understandings of ecological interconnectedness and interdependence, as well as the global experience of the enmeshments and

---

8. *The Weekly Times* reports that in Victoria, insurance claims for kangaroo damage to vehicles have declined during Covid-19 lockdowns. Peter Hunt, 'Insurance Claims for Kangaroo Damage Down, Says RACV', *The Weekly Times* (6 May 2020), available online: https://www.weeklytimesnow.com.au/news/victoria/insurance-claims-for-kangaroo-damage-down-says-racv/news-story/de93df81cb7a099b5fd06e7737ed7019 (accessed 13 May 2020).

9. Ecotheologian Heather Eaton commented as we drove to a conference in Adelaide in 2015 that this behaviour is one of the clearest pieces of evidence for our devaluation of other animals in relation to humans.

10. WIRES: Wildlife Rescue, available online: https://www.wires.org.au/ (accessed 13 May 2020).

entanglements of oppressions that are both social and ecological.[11] Relatedness, as a philosophical-theological concept and material reality, challenges the dualism of matter and spirit, immanence and transcendence. Ecological feminist critiques of such dualistic and matter-subordinating thinking in malestream theologies have a substantial history.[12] Gebara offers an alternative theological trajectory where the divine can be described as relatedness, with the implication that the divine is 'concomitant' with creation.[13] Relatedness, which opens to the mysterious alterity of the material, is such that creatures are both 'created within and creators of this relatedness'.[14] Relatedness is 'a human condition', 'an earthly condition', 'an ethical reality', 'a religious experience' and 'a cosmic condition'.[15] For the purposes of this chapter, its status as an ethical reality is my focus.

As Gebara comments, 'the ethical dimension… implies respect for all kinds of living beings'; the ethical reality of relatedness can be understood in action as a 'welcoming' of the 'relatedness that animates all living things'.[16] This ethical dimension of relatedness is part of its and our earthly, cosmic situation, but kyriarchal conditioning means many of us need to relearn this reality in our bodies and in our communities.[17] The road, where the lives of other animals are taken in the wake of human interests, is a place of often unacknowledged relatedness, except in the negative when a collision with another animal threatens a human's well-being. The relatedness of the more-than-human users of the road suggests a different ethical reality from that of individuals, or small groups of humans, in their auto-bubbles. Compassion is an expression of the ethical reality of this relatedness.

Compassion

Compassion is not simply a feeling of sympathy or even empathy, nor is compassionate action purely or even primarily an individual act. Ash Barker, founder of Urban Neighbourhoods of Hope, writes of 'risky compassion' when he tells the story of his and his family's experience of compassion in the Klong Toey slum in Bangkok where they made their home for twelve years.[18] Central for

---

11. Ivone Gebara, *Longing for Running Water: Ecofeminism and Liberation* (Minneapolis: Fortress, 1999), pp. 103–4.

12. See especially Rosemary Radford Ruether, *Gaia and God: An Ecofeminist Theology of Earth Healing* (San Francisco: HarperSanFrancisco, 1992), pp. 26–31, 61–84, 173–201.

13. Gebara, *Longing*, p. 105.

14. Gebara, *Longing*, p. 103.

15. Gebara, *Longing*, pp. 84–5.

16. Gebara, *Longing*, p. 90.

17. Gebara, *Longing*, p. 90.

18. Ash Barker, *Risky Compassion* (Kindle eBook; Bournville, Birmingham: Urban Life Together Publishing, 2014).

Figure 3 John Reid, *Performance for 25 Passing Vehicles. Australia. Newell Highway, 23 July 1989*. 1989, 48.0 × 134.0 cm. Silver gelation photographic print © John Reid. Reproduced by permission of the artist.

Barker is not so much the risk to himself, although he is honest about the dangers he and his family faced, and the choices he and his partner, Anji, made for their children; rather, the keynote for Barker is the transformation that compassion brings. Compassion, and compassionate solidarity, is an experience of liminality and finitude accompanied by joy. Compassion is communal rather than individual; it is mutual, exposing the one who would exercise compassion to the potentiality and surprising resilience of the other. Compassion necessitates and prompts honesty in relation to self and others. It occasions both lament and hope, and it could be said to be an eschatological act towards the vision of the reign of G-d and its possibilities in the here and now. It is material but not materialistic. Compassion is situated in place and is enmeshed with and responsive to the complex social and political exigencies of place. Barker shared place with the urban poor, and sharing place called forth for him not only limited individual acts of compassion but also passionate analyses of the social, political, economic, global and cultural structures of injustice that keep people in extreme poverty. Compassion places the person quite literally in the place of, or as neighbour to, another.

In relation to my example of the road, I am reminded of a piece of artwork by John Reid, *Performance for 25 Passing Vehicles. Australia. Newell Highway, 23 July 1989* (1989).[19] On noticing a dead kangaroo near a road sign, Reid decided to pull over, undress and place himself naked on the side of the road with his body in the same orientation as the kangaroo but at the opposite end of the sign. He maintained this pose while the performance was documented visually until twenty-five vehicles had passed by. This was more than an individual act of empathy. It was a performance of solidarity with the kangaroo and all those killed on the road. Reid writes: 'For me, the work addresses our high-energy, high-speed careless life

---

19. John Reid, 'Spotlight: Road Kill', *Plumwood Mountain* 1, no. 1 (February 2014), available online: https://plumwoodmountain.com/spotlight-road-kill/ (accessed 12 May 2020).

style and reasserts the proposition that our fate is bound to the fate of other life around us.'[20] The performance was also a critique of systems and practices that deny human interconnectedness with other creatures. The image was made into a postcard as a reminder to others and, ultimately, to the artist himself because artists (and theologians) are enmeshed in the structures they (and we) critique. Analyses such as Barker's and artworks such as Reid's shift compassion towards critical engagement with the structures of oppression themselves.

For Maureen O'Connell, this critical compassionate engagement with the structures of oppression takes on a particular nuance.[21] O'Connell writes to a white (Christian) North American constituency and argues that compassion can no longer, if it ever could, be limited to individual acts for individuals or groups. Rather, in an era of globalization, rich Christians need to practise a compassion that recognizes their own complicity in, and advantage derived from, the global economic structures that oppress the majority and keep millions in extreme poverty.[22] From a different context, like Barker, O'Connell sees compassion as transformative, not only for those in need but more particularly for those who would act with compassion but are, in fact, by their very standard of living and unacknowledged privilege reinforcing the oppressive situation they wish to redress. For both Barker and O'Connell, compassion requires a shift of perspective, not only to see the reality of our own involvement in oppressive systems but also to learn to interpret that reality from the perspective of those suffering.

It might seem problematic that I am discussing compassion in relation to road trauma for other creatures with reference to writers attending to extremes of human poverty. Surely, the latter ought to take priority. Carol Adams addresses a similar dilemma concerning whether care for suffering humans should take precedence over care for other animals.[23] She comments that the dilemma 're-erects the species barrier and places a boundary on compassion while enforcing a conservative economy of compassion; it splits caring at the human-animal border, presuming that there is not enough to go around'.[24] Compassion is figured as scarce, and there is a 'war on compassion' that is enacted not only in relation to other animals but also to any group of humans, such as asylum seekers in mandatory detention, who can be dismissed as part of a group outside the borders of our

---

20. Reid, 'Road Kill'.

21. Maureen H. O'Connell, *Compassion: Loving Our Neighbor in an Age of Globalization* (Kindle eBook; Maryknoll: Orbis Books, 2009).

22. In some ways, this argument reprises the earlier insights of Ronald J. Sider whose *Rich Christians in an Age of Hunger* first published in the mid-1970s is in its fifth updated edition: *Rich Christians in an Age of Hunger: Moving from Affluence to Generosity* (5th edn; Nashville: Thomas Nelson, 2005 [1977]). Nonetheless, O'Connell's focus on globalization as context for compassion is significant, and her argument builds on a sustained attention to philosophical and theological traditions.

23. Carol J. Adams, 'The War on Compassion', in *The Animal Catalyst: Towards Ahuman Theory* (ed. Patricia MacCormack; London: Bloomsbury, 2014), pp. 15–25.

24. Adams, 'War on Compassion', p. 16.

care.²⁵ Through a failure of imagination, the 'war on compassion' resists feelings of vulnerability, fear, culpability and futility that might arise should we care.²⁶ But, argues Adams, the way we say of humans who are grievously oppressed that they are 'treated like animals' is a reminder of the obverse, that in the treatment of animals as 'animals' – a category presumed to exclude humans – 'both the treatment and the concept will legitimize the treatment of humans like animals'.²⁷ In relation to the road, the acceptance of the deaths of other animals as routine or unavoidable perhaps also allows the acceptance of a certain level of, although far fewer, human deaths as part of the business of road travel and transport. To simply extend compassion for humans to other animals is to reinforce a separation between humans and animals; rather, compassion needs to be understood as a more-than-human capacity. As human animals, we exercise compassion.

A basis for this exercise of compassion is the body. In Hebrew, the root רחם refers to both compassion and womb.²⁸ In koine Greek, the verb σπλαγχνίζομαι (to have compassion or feel sympathy for) situates compassion in relation to the intestines, σπλάγχνον/σπλάγχνα.²⁹ These etymological links between compassion, the maternal and the corporeal are not incidental. Rather, they point to an understanding of the materiality of compassion; its roots in bodily encounter, subject to subject, rather than subject to object; and its material givenness in relatedness with another.³⁰ This co-subjectivity occurs in a particular way in the pregnant body, as a corporeal encounter mediated by the organ of the placenta.³¹ It is not simply a one-to-one relation, as if on the road only the injured animal and I were subjects in the moment. Rather, the exercise of compassion, as a participant in and an emergent from the material givenness of relatedness, reaffirms and enacts that relatedness as an earthly, ethical reality.

A Lukan Story of the Road: Luke 10.30-37

Three stories in the Gospel of Luke (7.11-17, 10.25-37, 15.11-32) portray a pattern of compassionate responsiveness in which seeing prompts compassion (7.23; 10.33; 15.20). These are moments of encounter with another person who is dead, near death or socially dead (7.14; 10.30; 15.24). In each instance, the protagonist (Jesus; the Samaritan; the father) is moved by compassion to act to restore the

25. Adams, 'War on Compassion', p. 18.
26. Adams, 'War on Compassion', pp. 24–5.
27. Adams, 'War on Compassion', pp. 19, 25.
28. BDB, p. 933.
29. BAGD, pp. 762–3.
30. On 'encounter', see Freya Mathews, *For Love of Matter: A Contemporary Panpsychism* (Albany: SUNY Press, 2003), pp. 83–8.
31. Jane-Maree Maher, 'The Promiscuous Placenta: Crossing Over', in *Contagion: Historical and Social Studies* (ed. Alison Bashford and Claire Hooker; London: Routledge, 2001), pp. 201–16.

person to life.³² This movement of compassion is gut-felt (7.13; 10.33; 15.20). Compassion, like forgiveness and hospitality, is an aspect and evidence of the Lukan divine visitation.³³ In the parable of the Good Samaritan, this compassionate action occurs on a road where another is left half dead; this is a dangerous habitat. The compassionate action of the Samaritan occurs within a more-than-human community which includes the pack animal and the innkeeper, the wine, oil and even coins, whose material agencies work together to support and make possible the enactment of compassion.³⁴ So it is not simply a matter of extending the narrative to imagine another creature rather than the implied human person near death on the side of the road. Rather, the story suggests that already compassionate responsiveness is materially a more-than-human act.

Moreover, the road itself and the characters who pass along it point to its relatedness to systemic inequalities, conflicts and resistances. The parable is situated in the wider Lukan programme of good news, of liberation and healing set out in Luke 4 when the Lukan Jesus proclaims at least two texts from Isaiah (Lk. 4.18-19; Isa. 58.6, 61.1-2). The longed-for liberation has in its sights not (or not only) a spiritual liberation but also forgiveness (ἄφεσις) that is first release from the kinds of debt suffered under the economic and social systems of imperial Rome.³⁵ What this suggests among other things is that in addition to the two who looked and passed on (10.31-32), retaining their relative privilege, there is a hidden character or set of characters in the parable of the Good Samaritan and that is the Roman empire, which promotes and makes possible the particular situation of inequality that renders the road to Jericho so risky for its travellers.³⁶

The narrative setting for the parable suggests moreover that compassion requires several shifts of perspective. In telling the parable, the Lukan Jesus shifts the focus of the lawyer's question that prompted it: 'Who is my neighbour?' (10.29) becomes, 'Who acted as neighbour?' (10.36). To this, the lawyer rightly answers that the Samaritan acted as neighbour, but then, as Alan Cadwallader has noted

---

32. Anne Elvey, *An Ecological Feminist Reading of the Gospel of Luke: A Gestational Paradigm* (Studies in Women and Religion, 45; Lewiston, NY: Edwin Mellen, 2005), pp. 237–42.

33. Byrne, *Hospitality of God*.

34. Anne Elvey, 'Rethinking Neighbour Love: A Conversation between Political Theology and Ecological Ethics', in *'Where the Wild Ox Roams': Biblical Essays in Honour of Norman C. Habel* (ed. Alan H. Cadwallader and Peter L. Trudinger; Sheffield: Sheffield Phoenix, 2013), pp. 58–75 (73).

35. See, e.g., Richard A. Horsley, 'Jesus and Empire', in *In the Shadow of Empire: Reclaiming the Bible as a History of Faithful Resistance* (ed. Richard A. Horsley; Louisville: Westminster John Knox, 2008), pp. 75–96 (94–5); Martin Goodman, 'The First Jewish Revolt: Social Conflict and the Problem of Debt', *JJS* 33, nos. 1–2 (Spring–Autumn 1992), pp. 417–27; Sharon H. Ringe, *Luke* (Louisville: Westminster John Knox, 1995), p. 183.

36. On the dangerous nature of the road between Jerusalem and Jericho, see, e.g., Amy-Jill Levine and Ben Witherington III, *The Gospel of Luke* (New Cambridge Bible Commentary; Cambridge: Cambridge University Press, 2018), p. 291.

and I discussed in the previous chapter, the questioner (and so the reader or hearer of the story) is left not in the Samaritan's shoes but on the side of the road receiving the Samaritan neighbour's compassion.[37] It is on this basis of shared vulnerability that the command 'Go and do likewise' is based (10.37).

Itself an exercise in compassion for the questioner (10.29), the parable invites a transformation where the basis of compassion is a gut-felt response to vulnerability shared (albeit unequally) under systems of oppression. What if we were to read the parable of the Good Samaritan and see the roadside littered with the bodies of other animals, killed or near dead from last night's trucks carrying goods long distances from state to state? Would we understand our vulnerability in the way John Reid's performance art suggests? In the Tarkine in Tasmania, recommended dusk-to-dawn speed limits are set to protect endangered wildlife; is this indicative of broader societal and church attitudes? For most of us, the sight of corpses by the side of the road can be distressing, and were they human, we would stop, indeed be obliged to stop, every time we saw one. The sheer numbers make this a practical impossibility on a long drive, unless our frameworks change drastically.

A fleshy space of solidarity

As ecofeminist theologian Rosemary Radford Ruether argues, a trajectory of western Christian theology has inscribed matter- and body-subjugating oppressions in the flesh of women and the house or household (οἶκος) of Earth.[38] She argues that one element necessary for the development of 'an ecological culture and society' is 'an overcoming of competitive alienation and domination for compassionate solidarity'.[39] An ecological feminism shaped around the reality of a material givenness that encompasses not only bodies, pregnant bodies and Earth but also the relatedness that is an ethical reality offers a framework for understanding compassion as shared vulnerability. This shared vulnerability is not an end itself, but the risky possibility of being on the side of the road together. To be vulnerable on the side of the road is not to lie down passively. Rather, it is to feel in our bodies the structures of oppression that rely on the dead bodies of animals, including humans, structures for which trauma is constitutive rather than accidental. Compassion in this context, where structural trauma causes impacts unequally across race, class, gender and species, recalls us to the corporeal, the material, as a fleshy space of solidarity and resistance.

---

37. Alan H. Cadwallader, 'The Fall, the Samaritan and the Wounded Man: An Example of Multiple Readings of Scripture (Lk. 10:25–37)', in *Lost in Translation?: Anglicans, Controversy and the Bible* (ed. Scott Cowdell and Muriel Porter; Thornbury, Vic.: Desbooks, 2004), pp. 155–84.
38. Ruether, *Gaia and God*, pp. 173–201.
39. Ruether, *Gaia and God*, p. 201.

Entanglements and ecological conversion

In this fleshy space, entangled exercises of power and compassion are more than human. In Lk. 10.34 an animal (κτῆνος, often translated as 'pack animal') is effectively a co-agent in the Samaritan's act of compassion to the wounded traveller. Unnamed and silent, this pack animal is characterized as owned by the Samaritan and presumably subject to his will. In the time of Luke's narrative, some humans can be 'owned' as enslaved persons, and from the perspective of empire they 'were viewed as bodies, not as full persons'.[40] In different ways, a logic of possession, entitlement or use value and a denial of personhood encompassed enslaved persons and domestic or service animals, although the status in the Roman empire of the owners varied from a Samaritan on a road to Jericho, perhaps a merchant with his pack animal (κτῆνος), to a Roman paterfamilias with many enslaved persons engaged in the upkeep and sustenance of his elite household. In each case, through their labour the pack animal (κτῆνος) or the enslaved person (δοῦλος/δούλη) contributed as coagent (willing or otherwise) to the way the Samaritan or the Roman paterfamilias was able to act for the benefit of another.

To risk this analogy between relations of ownership and use of other animals and the possession of enslaved human persons is both problematic and necessary. Where in the modern world 'animal' can function as a racial slur, a complex relation of enslavement, animalization and racialization forms a background for considerations of material co-agencies. An exhibition of confederate currency at the Martin Luther King Jr Historical Centre in Atlanta, Georgia, when I visited in 2003, displayed banknotes with images of enslaved persons working in the fields. The economic dependence of the owning classes on enslaved persons was hidden in plain sight. The forced displacement of African peoples through enslavement and the ongoing racialization of bodies in the United States is entangled with a violent trajectory of western thought concerning both the human and the animal.[41] Zakiyyah Iman Jackson's analysis suggests that notions of species; the limits of humanism; and feminist discourses of sex, gender and sexual difference participate in a 'failed metaphysics'.[42] The 'burden' of this 'failed metaphysics' has been pressed on 'those marginalized' through their 'being abjectly animalized'.[43] Rather than disavowing human co-relation with other animals, Jackson interrogates 'humanism by identifying our shared being with the nonhuman without suggesting that some members of humanity bear the burden of "the animal"'.[44] As she demonstrates, 'racialized gender and sexuality' is central to the human-animal binary that

---

40. Christy Cobb, *Slavery, Gender, Truth, and Power in Luke-Acts and Other Ancient Narratives* (Cham, Switzerland: Palgrave Macmillan, 2019), p. 6, https://doi.org/10.1007/978-3-030-05689-6_1.

41. Zakiyyah Iman Jackson, *Becoming Human: Matter and Meaning in an Antiblack World* (New York: New York University Press, 2020), p. 14.

42. Jackson, *Becoming Human*, p. 12.

43. Jackson, *Becoming Human*, p. 12.

44. Jackson, *Becoming Human*, p. 12.

ecological feminism and the new materialism seek to call into question.[45] For white settler scholars such as myself, this analysis requires that I reconsider the entangled exercises of power and language assumed in the discourses with which I work. My universalizing presumptions need to be disturbed whenever I write the word 'human'. I need to recognize, too, that the quality of relatedness I seek to affirm is for many already a lived strategy for survival and flourishing.

Entangled life and kin

As noted in previous chapters, relatedness, community-focus, cross-species kinship and entanglements of beings and place are part of First Nations' self-understanding. From a western perspective, twentieth-century sciences, sometimes drawing on or echoing Indigenous perspectives, have contributed to a renewed understanding of such entanglements.[46] Contemporary environmental and science writings on trees and fungi demonstrate that the lives of forest systems, fungi, trees and animals (including humans) exemplify material entanglements and co-agencies that extend beyond the individual.[47] Every making is already a co-making, a process of *sympoiesis*, a making with many material others.[48]

Bodies themselves are (in) processes of sympoiesis. Creatures do not exist prior to their relatedness; rather 'they make each other', through co-involvement.[49] Where species of orchid and bee, for example, partner, involving themselves in each other's lives, the mimicry through which an orchid attracts a bee persists beyond those bees' scarcity or extinction.[50] The orchid's material memorialization of its partner species becomes a model for human making amid the entangled damages of the Anthropocene.[51] On this model, human making or poiesis (artistic, poetic, scholarly) eschews the problematic responses of simplistic technofixes or despairing resignation, for 'staying with the trouble' in humble ways, through

---

45. Jackson, *Becoming Human*, p. 12.

46. Elizabeth A. Johnson, *Ask the Beasts: Darwin and the God of Love* (Kindle eBook; London: Bloomsbury, 2014), p. 267; Úrsula Oswald Spring, Hans Günter Brauch and Keith G. Tidball, 'Expanding Peace Ecology: Peace, Security, Sustainability, Equity, and Gender', in *Expanding Peace Ecology: Peace, Security, Sustainability, Equity and Gender. Perspectives of IPRA's Ecology and Peace Commission* (ed. Úrsula Oswald Spring, Hans Günter Brauch and Keith G. Tidball; Springer Briefs in Environment, Security, Development and Peace, Peace and Security Studies, 12; Cham, Switzerland: Springer, 2014), pp. 1–30 (6).

47. See, e.g., Peter Wohlleben, *The Hidden Life of Trees: What They Feel, How They Communicate* (trans. Jane Billinghurst; Carlton, Vic.: Black Inc., 2016); Merlin Sheldrake, *Entangled Life: How Fungi Make Our Worlds, Change Our Minds, and Shape Our Futures* (London: The Bodley Head, 2020).

48. Donna Haraway, *Staying with the Trouble: Making Kin in the Chthulucene* (Durham: Duke University Press, 2016), p. 58.

49. Haraway, *Staying with the Trouble*, p. 60.

50. Haraway, *Staying with the Trouble*, p. 69.

51. Haraway, *Staying with the Trouble*, pp. 69–71.

'worldings committed to partial healing, modest rehabilitation, and still possible resurgence'.[52] A conscious human engagement on the model of sympoiesis suggests for me a change of perspective and practice, a kind of turning or conversion (μετάνοια).

Ecological conversion

In his General Audience of 17 January 2001, Pope John Paul II spoke of an 'ecological conversion': 'We must therefore encourage and support the "ecological conversion" which in recent decades has made humanity more sensitive to the catastrophe to which it has been heading.'[53] The appeal to 'ecological conversion' was not primarily a call from Rome for Christians to be converted in their relation to the community of Earth, though it was also this; rather it was first a recognition that in the wider society there were already signs of a change of attitude with respect to human place in the Earth community of which humans are inescapably part. As I have noted earlier, this relatedness of humans in a more-than-human world is already part of First Nations' epistemologies and experience. For many others, an 'ecological conversion' involves not only a change of behaviour but also a kind of cultural change, that involves changes in worldview, in how we understand what it means to be human, where this category is not limited to liberal humanist understandings. Nonetheless, the cultural change signalled by 'ecological conversion' requires not only a suspicion of and turning from anthropocentrism, but also a repudiation of its underlying androcentric and kyriarchal entanglements, which remain a dominant feature of Roman Catholic hierarchy, embedded not only in John Paul II's ecological sensibility but in the more recent writing of Pope Francis in *Laudato Si'*.[54]

For Christians, an ecological conversion includes both a suspicion of the residual kyriarchal enculturation of their communities and a realization that Christian communities are also already ecological communities, by which I mean that they are more-than-human (other-than-human and human) communities. They are composed of humans in relation to many other-than-human entities (especially those that sustain human lives and worship for example, and even the bacteria that inhabit our bodies). Human beings, as individuals and communities as well as at the level of species or kind, therefore, live and die enmeshed with the living and being of other kind – both those I understand conventionally as living (e.g. fleas, whales, mushrooms and eucalypts) and those I may understand

---

52. Haraway, *Staying with the Trouble*, pp. 3, 71.

53. Pope John Paul II, 'General Audience', 17 January 2001, available online: http://www.vatican.va/holy_father/john_paul_ii/audiences/2001/documents/hf_jp-ii_aud_20010117_en.html (accessed 29 August 2014). See also, Denis Edwards, *Ecology at the Heart of Faith: The Change of Heart that Leads to a New Way of Living on Earth* (Maryknoll: Orbis, 2006), pp. 2–4.

54. See Agnes M. Brazal, 'Ethics of Care in Laudato Si': A Postcolonial Feminist Critique', *Feminist Theology* 29, no. 3 (2021), pp. 220–33.

otherwise (e.g. glaciers, sand and air). This recognition at the very least calls into question pure notions of human pre-eminence over other creatures.

Conclusion

This chapter began with the reality of animals dead or dying on the roadside, a signal of both more-than-human (including human) shared vulnerability and human indifference to other-than-human suffering. The questions 'who is my neighbour?' and 'who acted as neighbour?' resonate with material vulnerability both in extending compassion for other humans towards other kind and in recognizing the cross-species and material agencies at work in any act of compassion, its fleshy solidarities and resistances. These solidarities and resistances amplify the problematic inheritances of contemporary situation where animalization and racialization are entangled with western constructions of the human. The way Luke shifts a question – from 'who is neighbour' to 'who acted as neighbour' – is a prompt for a transformation of worldview, a conversion that in our time must be ecologically informed in a way that consents to our shared vulnerability as a basis for both scholarship and activism. The following chapters focus on two scenes of material vulnerability, namely, Mountaintop Removal Mining and the impacts of climate change on the Great Barrier Reef, in braided ecological feminist materialist conversations with Isa. 40.4 and Lk. 9.28-36 respectively.

Chapter 9

MOUNTAINTOP REMOVAL MINING (MTR) AND ISAIAH 40.4 (AND LUKE 3.5): RESISTING THE VIOLENCE OF HOMOGENIZATION

Through a history of extractive conquest, the Appalachian region in the United States is a scene of more-than-human vulnerability. The coalfield of the Appalachians occurs in Earth's oldest mountains.[1] Coal mining began in the region in the mid-eighteenth century as an accompaniment of colonial settlement (invasion) and its spread.[2] The practice of Mountaintop Removal Mining (MTR) itself began in the late 1950s, undergoing 'significant expansion during the 1990s'.[3] MTR has occurred in six Appalachian states, namely Kentucky, West Virginia, Virginia, Tennessee, Pennsylvania and Ohio, in an area of around 12 million acres. Through MTR mountains are levelled and valleys filled in, and the vast diversity of more-than-human communities comes under the stress of homogenizing violence. Because of its echoes with the reality of MTR, the biblical text of Isa. 40.4 – 'Every valley shall be lifted up, and every mountain and hill be made low' – has been taken up both by proponents of, and resisters to, MTR.

With appeal to an ecological feminist critique of homogenization, in this chapter I explore ways in which the imagery of Isa. 40.4 carries homogenizing tendencies; I ask how the Isaian metaphors of valleys raised/exulted and hills/mountains levelled operate in relation to MTR. The question is not whether there are better or worse readings of Isa. 40.4 from the perspective of critical biblical studies, but how the metaphors employed in the text enable violent uses of the text. How does the text also empower resistance? Which critical principles can

---

1. Carl E. Zipper, Mary Beth Adams and Jeff Skousen, 'The Appalachian Coalfield in Historical Context', in *Appalachia's Coal-Mined Landscapes* (ed. Carl E. Zipper and Jeff Skousen; Cham, Switzerland: Springer Nature, 2021), pp. 1–26 (3). This is not to claim that the Appalachian range as a whole is the oldest range of mountains on Earth. The current chapter revises and updates Anne Elvey, 'Homogenizing Violence, Isa 40:4 (and Luke 3:5) and MTR (Mountaintop Removal Mining)', *Worldviews* 19, no. 3 (2015), pp. 226–44.

2. Zipper, Adams and Skousen, 'Appalachian Coalfield in Historical Context', pp. 10–11.

3. Jeff Skousen and Carl E. Zipper, 'Coal Mining and Reclamation in Appalachia', in *Appalachia's Coal-Mined Landscapes* (ed. Carl E. Zipper and Jeff Skousen; Cham, Switzerland: Springer Nature, 2021), pp. 55–83 (63).

help a hearer/reader discern between violent (homogenizing) readings of Isa. 40.4 and readings empowering resistance to the practice of MTR? My proposal is that the principles are not those of historical criticism, though these may be of use, but rather reside in the liveliness underlying metaphor. The dynamism of the valleys and hills of Isa. 40.4, affirming and in conversation with the liveliness of the mountains, valleys and their communities subject to MTR, stands in contrast to the homogenizing ethos of capitalist extractivism.

Mountaintop Removal Mining (MTR)

The extractive practice of MTR displaces 'an entire ridge or summit of overburden to access underlying coals'; frequently 'multiple seams' of coal are mined and mountaintops are removed 'to depths of 100 meters or more'.[4] MTR can extend into bedrock and disturbs both the former mountaintop area and valleys where 'crushed rock is deposited'; thousands of miles of rivers and streams have been filled with debris; and MTR has 'cascading effects' on both the immediate location of the disturbances and downstream, for example, affecting water quality.[5] While catchment hydrology in the area is complex, it is compromised by MTR.[6] Aquatic life is affected, often adversely.[7] Geophysical effects of mining disturb forest communities.[8] There are significant adverse health impacts for human communities, including through sulphide and sulphate in water supply, direct mining-related injuries, as well as challenges to social cohesion due to conflict over the value of MTR itself.[9] One feature of weakened personal health and communal

---

4. Skousen and Zipper, 'Coal Mining and Reclamation', p. 63.

5. Fabian Nippgen, Matthew R. V. Ross, Emily S. Bernhardt and Brian L. McGlynn, 'Creating a More Perennial Problem? Mountaintop Removal Coal Mining Enhances and Sustains Saline Baseflows of Appalachian Watersheds', *Environmental Science & Technology* 51 (2017), pp. 8324–34 (8324–5, 8331–2), available online: http://dx.doi.org/10.1021/acs.est.7b02288; Matthew R. V. Ross, Brian L. McGlynn and Emily S. Bernhardt, 'Deep Impact: Effects of Mountaintop Mining on Surface Topography, Bedrock Structure, and Downstream Waters', *Environmental Science & Technology* 50 (2016), pp. 2064–74, available online: http://dx.doi.org/10.1021/acs.est.5b04532.

6. Andrew J. Miller and Nicolas Zégre, 'Landscape-Scale Disturbance: Insights into the Complexity of Catchment Hydrology in the Mountaintop Removal Region of the Eastern United States', *Land* 5, no. 3 (2016), pp. 1–23 (19–20), available online: https://doi.org/10.3390/land5030022.

7. George T. Merovich Jr., Nathaniel P. Hitt, Eric R. Merriam and Jess W. Jones, 'Response of Aquatic Life to Coal Mining in Appalachia', in *Appalachia's Coal-Mined Landscapes* (ed. Carl E. Zipper and Jeff Skousen; Cham, Switzerland: Springer Nature, 2021), pp. 245–85.

8. Thomas A. Maigret, John J. Cox and Jian Yang, 'Persistent Geophysical Effects of Mining Threaten Ridgetop Biota of Appalachian Forests', *Frontiers in Ecology and the Environment* 17, no. 2 (March 2019), pp. 85–91, doi:10.1002/fee.1992.

9. Abee L. Boyles et al., 'Systematic Review of Community Health Impacts of Mountaintop Removal Mining', *Environment International* 107 (2017), pp. 163–72 (170), available online: https://doi.org/10.1016/j.envint.2017.07.002.

stress has been opioid addiction and abuse.[10] Studies have considered the fallacy of economic arguments for MTR in the United States, its link with cancers, analyses of the affects along gender lines, including the deleterious effects on women's reproductive health and on infants, and the loss not only to species whose primary habitat is water but also to the biodiversity of terrestrial life, and the likely overall negative impact in relation to climate change.[11] Even best practices of reclamation do not fully mitigate the environmental and social effects of MTR.[12]

On the ground, lives and livelihoods, life habits and habitats, are entangled for Appalachian co-inhabitants.[13] The damage and ensuing ecological and social

---

10. See, e.g., Harrison Jacobs, 'Here's Why the Opioid Epidemic Is So Bad in West Virginia – the State with the Highest Overdose Rate in the US', *Business Insider* (2 May 2016), available online: https://www.businessinsider.com.au/why-the-opioid-epidemic-is-so-bad-in-west-virginia-2016-4?r=US&IR=T (accessed 31 May 2021); M. Katie Marberry and Danilea Werner, 'The Role of Mountaintop Removal Mining in the Opioid Crisis', *Journal of Social Work Practice in the Addictions* 20, no. 4 (2020), pp. 302–10, available online: https://doi.org/10.1080/153325 6X.2020.1821539; Paula Gallant Eckard, 'Queerness, Opioids, and Mountaintop Removal: The Politics of Destruction in *The Evening Hour*', *South Atlantic Review* 83, no. 3 (2018), pp. 24–43.

11. Shirley Stewart Burns, *Bringing Down the Mountains: The Impact of Mountaintop Removal Surface Coal Mining on Southern West Virginia Communities, 1970–2004* (Morgantown: West Virginia University Press, 2007); Brad R. Woods and Jason S. Gordon, 'Mountaintop Removal and Job Creation: Exploring the Relationship Using Spatial Regression', *Annals of the Association of American Geographers* 101, no. 4 (2011), pp. 806–15; Joyce M. Barry, *Standing Our Ground: Women, Environmental Justice, and the Fight to End Mountaintop Removal* (Athens: Ohio University Press, 2012); David C. Holzman, 'Mountaintop Removal Mining: Digging into Community Health Concerns', *Environmental Health Perspectives* 119, no. 11 (November 2011), pp. 476–83; Cancer Weekly News Reporter-Staff News Editor, 'Asthma, Heart Disease, Cancer and General Illness Found in Kentucky Mountain Top Removal Community', *Cancer Weekly* (2 April 2013), p. 173; Onleilove Alston, 'Faultlines in Coal Country: An Interview with Allen Jones, Cofounder of Christians for the Mountains', *Sojourners Magazine* 39, no. 6 (June 2010), p. 21; Matt Wasson, 'Study Shows Steep Decline in Fish Populations near Mountaintop Removal', *The Appalachian Voice* (10 August 2014), available online: http://appvoices.org/2014/08/10/study-shows-steep-decline-in-fish-populations-near-mountaintop-removal/ (accessed 31 May 2021); James Wickham et al., 'The Overlooked Terrestrial Impacts of Mountaintop Mining', *BioScience* 63, no. 5 (2013), pp. 335–48; J. Elliott Campbell, James F. Fox, and Peter M. Acton, 'Terrestrial Carbon Losses from Mountaintop Coal Mining Offset Regional Forest Carbon Sequestration in the 21st Century', *Environmental Research Letters* 7, no. 4 (2012), pp. 1–6, available online: http://iopscience.iop.org/1748-9326/7/4/045701 (accessed 3 August 2021). This last article is cited in IPCC, 'Chapter 7 Energy Systems', Fifth Assessment Report (AR5), Working Group III, Mitigation (2014), pp. 48, 92, available online: http://report.mitigation2014.org/drafts/final-draft-fgd/ipcc_wg3_ar5_final-draft_fgd_chapter7.pdf (accessed 31 May 2021).

12. Skousen and Zipper, 'Coal Mining and Reclamation', p. 56.

13. Ann Pancake's novel, *Strange as This Weather Has Been* (Berkeley: Counterpoint, 2007), set in West Virginia and told from several perspectives, demonstrates this well.

trauma for individuals and communities require that I recognize that I am writing as an outsider to MTR in the Appalachians. I do so because this tragic example of extractivism is bigger than the primary more-than-human communities it affects directly.

More-than-human communities co-inhabit threatened and despoiled habitats, where practices of extractivism, such as major industrialized coal mining enterprises, exemplify the shared vulnerability of human communities and other kind. In Australia, the mega open-cut and underground coal mines proposed for the Galilee Basin in North Queensland on Wangan and Jagalingou Country, for example, have already had effects in denying the Native Title of traditional owners, bankrupting a First Nations anti-mining campaigner, and are anticipated to adversely affect waterways, including for agriculture, as well as habitat for endangered species, in particular the black-throated finch.[14] In this situation, the politics of extraction, international trade and late capitalism coincide to override local environmental values and national responsibilities attendant on global climate change.[15]

In a similar vein, the embodiment and enmeshments of subjects in relation to the situational materialities of MTR require an ecologically sensitive class as well as counter-colonial analysis.[16] Coal extractivism is driven by capital, and MTR reflects and materializes 'the ultimate destructiveness of capitalism' as well as 'the dire need for a sustainable human alternative'.[17] The 'metabolic rift' of late capitalist extractivism occurs through the removal of food and other so-called 'resources',

---

14. See Wangan and Jagalingou Family Council, available online: https://wanganjagalingou.com.au/ (accessed 26 July 2021); Quentin Beresford, *Adani and the War over Coal* (Sydney: NewSouth Publishing, 2018); Tor Hundloe, *Adani versus the Black-Throated Finch* (Pampleteer Series, 6; North Melbourne: Australian Scholarly Publishing, 2018); Lindsay Simpson, *Adani, Following Its Dirty Footsteps: A Personal Story* (North Geelong: Spinifex, 2018). While the development of many of the proposed mines in the Galilee Basis has been slowed, the Adani Carmichael mine sent its first coal to port in late 2021. Graham Readfearn, 'After Adani: Whatever Happened to Queensland's Galilee Basin Coal Boom?', *The Guardian* (9 January 2022), available online: https://www.theguardian.com/australia-news/2022/jan/09/after-adani-whatever-happened-to-queenslands-galilee-basin-coal-boom (accessed 14 January 2022).

15. Beresford, *Adani and the War over Coal*, ch. 4; Romana Coêho de Araujo, Jorge Madeira Nogueira and Paul Martin, 'Biodiversity Risk Management in Mining', in *Achieving Biodiversity Protection in Megadiverse Countries: A Comparative Assessment of Australia and Brazil* (ed. Paul Martin, Márcia Dieguez Leuzinger, Solange Teles da Silva, and Gabriel Leuzinger Coutinho; Abingdon: Routledge, 2020), pp. 47–66.

16. William Ryan Wishart, 'Underdeveloping Appalachia: Toward an Environmental Sociology of Extractive Economies' (PhD thesis, Department of Sociology and the Graduate School, University of Oregon, 2014), p. 165.

17. Wishart, 'Underdeveloping Appalachia', pp. 163, 181. See further, Kelly Austin and Brett Clark, 'Tearing Down Mountains: Using Spatial and Metabolic Analysis to Investigate the Socio-Ecological Contradictions of Coal Extraction in Appalachia', *Critical Sociology* 38, no. 3 (2011), pp. 437–57.

such as coal, from the earth and their transport long distances to cities, thereby 'preventing [their] recirculation in the soil, and resulting in urban pollution'.[18] The term 'metabolic rift' derives from Marx's theory of metabolism, which describes the process by which labour connects human communities with the materiality of the more-than-human world of which they are part.[19] A rift occurs in the metabolic eco-social relations proper to labour, when under capitalism the commodification of the worker and the commodification of 'nature' coincide, and both are alienated.[20] The crisis of climate change itself 'is part of a larger and still differentiating metabolic rift between capitalist society and natural systems that threatens their resilience'.[21] As C. Parker Krieg holds, '[c]limate change exposes the unlivability of a world sustained by coal'.[22] A coal-based world makes more-than-human communities, such as those in the Galilee Basin in North Queensland and those in MTR-affected regions of Appalachia 'sacrifice zones'.[23]

Led by traditional owners, environmental activists, including faith-based activists, have been resisting coal-mining in the Queensland Galilee Basin since 2016 or earlier.[24] Resistance to MTR in the United States dates to at least the 1990s. At a Coalfield Justice Rally in February 1999, Denise Giardina said: 'You are flattening our mountains and filling in our hollows, and this is the last evil you will do.'[25] In 2009, John McQuaid wrote: 'Since the mid-1990s, coal companies have pulverized Appalachian mountaintops in West Virginia, Kentucky, Virginia and Tennessee. Peaks formed hundreds of millions of years ago are obliterated in months. Forests that survived the last ice age are chopped down and burned.'[26] On 12 September 2014, a small group of protesters rallied at the White House Council on Environmental Quality to call on the Obama administration to act on its then five-year-old Memorandum of Understanding to address the destructive impacts

---

18. Wishart, 'Underdeveloping Appalachia', p. 163.

19. John Bellamy Foster, *Marx's Ecology: Materialism and Nature* (New York: Monthly Review Press, 2000), pp. 155–63.

20. Foster, *Marx's Ecology*, pp. 158–9. See further, John Bellamy Foster, Brett Clark and Richard York, *The Ecological Rift: Capitalism's War on the Earth* (New York: Monthly Review Press, 2010).

21. Wishart, 'Underdeveloping Appalachia', p. 167.

22. C. Parker Krieg, 'Coal Optimism: Carbon Ideologies and the Good Lives of Extraction', *Textual Practice* 35, no. 3 (2021), pp. 431–48 (445).

23. Krieg, 'Coal Optimism', p. 445.

24. Wangan and Jagalingou Family Council; Stop Adani, available online: https://www.stopadani.com/ (accessed 27 May 2021); Australian Religious Response to Climate Change (ARRCC), available online: https://www.arrcc.org.au/ (accessed 27 May 2021).

25. From epigraph to Barry, *Standing Our Ground*.

26. John McQuaid, 'Mining the Mountains', *Smithsonian Magazine* 39, no. 10 (January 2009), pp. 74–85, available online: https://www.proquest.com/magazines/mining-mountains/docview/236861789/se-2?accountid=12528 (accessed 28 May 2021).

of MTR in the Appalachian region.[27] In 2021, Appalachian Voices reports that MTR continues 'despite the decline in coal'.[28]

Biblical religion is not neutral in relation to these coal-mining situations. While many publicly professed Christians hold seats in Australian Federal Parliament, including the current Prime Minister Scott Morrison who famously brought a lump of coal into the House of Representatives to demonstrate its innocuousness, biblical religion is less to the fore in Australian discourses of extractivism and resistance, than in the United States.[29] In the case of MTR in the United States, the Bible has been harnessed to both support and resist extractive economies of thinking and practice. Because of its resonance with the material reality of mountains levelled, one text in particular claims my hermeneutic interest, namely, Isa. 40.4, also cited in Lk. 3.5. As I will argue below, the text of Isa. 40.4 employs and supports a homogenizing imaginary, the limits of which need to be understood in the context of the material agency of the mountains and their inhabitants.

An ecological feminist analysis of homogenization

From an ecological feminist perspective, homogenization is akin to stereotyping, where it is necessary that an oppressed class appear homogenous so that its members can be identified with, and assimilated to, their 'nature' as subordinate.[30] Homogenization applies in relation to race, ethnicity and gender, and is a feature of colonial relationships including relationships between humans and other than humans. Homogenization is one of the conceptual structures supporting dualism, and its logic of colonization.[31] Critique of dualism is not a critique of difference per se: 'Dualism should not be seen as creating difference where none exists. Rather it tends to capitalise on existing patterns of difference, rendering these in ways which ground hierarchy.'[32] Homogenization renders difference in two ways that

---

27. See Claudia Copeland, *Mountaintop Mining: Background on Current Controversies*, Congressional Research Services, CRS Report for Congress 7.5700 (2 December 2013; updated 13 December 2016), p. 1, available online: https://crsreports.congress.gov/product/pdf/RS/RS21421 (accessed 28 May 2021); McQuaid, 'Mining the Mountains'; Appalachian Voices, 'End Mountaintop Removal Coal Mining', available online: http://appvoices.org/end-mountaintop-removal/ (accessed 28 May 2021); ilovemountains.org, 'Successful Rally at the White House Council on Environmental Quality', News (12 September 2014), available online: http://ilovemountains.org/news/5012 (accessed 2 August 2021).

28. Appalachian Voices, 'End Mountaintop Removal Coal Mining'.

29. 'Scott Morrison Brings a Chunk of Coal into Parliament' (video), *The Guardian* (Thursday 9 February 2017), available online: https://www.theguardian.com/global/video/2017/feb/09/scott-morrison-brings-a-chunk-of-coal-into-parliament-video (accessed 27 May 2021).

30. Val Plumwood, *Feminism and the Mastery of Nature* (Feminism for Today; London: Routledge, 1993), p. 53.

31. Plumwood, *Feminism*, pp. 53–5.

32. Plumwood, *Feminism*, p. 55.

are problematic: (1) all members of a (usually dominated) group are characterized as the same, as their difference from each other is denied or minimized; (2) this rendering of sameness enables the dominated group and its members to be seen as completely other than, and open to exploitation by, the dominant group. This kind of colonizing operation works to keep the dominant group at the centre.[33]

Centrisms, among these, androcentrism, Eurocentrism and anthropocentrism, work to maintain the power and privilege of an elite centre, through homogenization of others. In the case of anthropocentrism, nature and animals are assimilated to each other when all are characterized as lacking consciousness, which is understood to be exclusively human.[34] This anthropocentric paradigm homogenizes other than humans promoting 'insensitivity to the marvellous diversity of nature, since differences in nature are attended to only if they are likely to contribute in some obvious way to human welfare'.[35] The term 'nature' itself is problematic in that it can also exacerbate this homogenizing tendency where the word 'nature' collapses the vast diversity of things. For example, particular mountains, valleys, rivers, lions, sheep and so on are encompassed in a single category ('nature') that is often construed as distinct from, and in opposition to, human culture.

In contrast, biological and cultural diversity are interwoven especially through the entanglements of co-inhabitants (human and other kind), their habits and their habitats.[36] From this perspective of intermeshed biological and cultural diversity, the concept of embodiment applies not only to humans and other animal kin, but to Earth itself, and 'the Earth body... needs an "eco-medicine" that takes into account biological-ecological, anatomic-geographic, cultural, philosophical, and spiritual dimensions in complementary ways'.[37] The essential (rather than essentialist) inter-relationality of these dimensions echoes in the understanding of First Nations' perspectives described by Aileen Moreton-Robinson, as well as in what I have called in earlier chapters 'situational materialities'.[38] Biocultural homogenization occurs when the diversity proper to interconnected biological and cultural systems is minimized or denied, and a place such as the Galilee

33. Plumwood, *Feminism*, p. 55. Even the language of 'dominated' serves a homogenizing agenda by eliding the agency of other than a dominant elite.

34. Val Plumwood, *Environmental Culture: The Ecological Crisis of Reason* (Environmental Philosophies; London: Routledge, 2002), p. 107.

35. Plumwood, *Environmental Culture*, p. 107.

36. Ricardo Rozzi, 'Biocultural Homogenization: A Wicked Problem in the Anthropocene', in *From Biocultural Homogenization to Biocultural Conservation* (ed. Ricardo Rozzi et al.; Ecology and Ethics, 3; Cham, Switzerland: Springer Nature, 2018), pp. 21–48 (22–4), available online: https://doi.org/10.1007/978-3-319-99513-7_2.

37. Angelina Paredes-Castellanos and Ricardo Rozzi, 'Biocultural Exoticism in the Feminine Landscape of Latin America', in *From Biocultural Homogenization to Biocultural Conservation* (ed. Ricardo Rozzi et al.; Ecology and Ethics, 3; Cham, Switzerland: Springer Nature, 2018), pp. 167–83 (181), available online: https://doi.org/10.1007/978-3-319-99513-7_10.

38. Aileen Moreton-Robinson, *Talkin' Up to the White Woman: Indigenous Women and Feminism* (St. Lucia, Qld: University of Queensland Press, 2000), pp. 15–21.

Basin in North Queensland is defined by one characteristic – the prevalence of coal – in order to exploit it.[39] With a focus on embedded experience, ecological feminists can listen to First Peoples and recognize the embodiment of subjects in their situational materialities, as a starting point for countering biocultural homogenization. Actants' own recognition of their embodied enmeshments in social, cultural and political systems of damage to life habits, habitats and co-inhabitants forms a foundation for the exercise of resilience and resistance in the face of homogenizing violence.[40]

Homogenization, MTR and Isaiah 40.4

In MTR not only are mountains and valleys homogenized as simply resources to serve coal production and its waste, but homogenization also affects human communities. Rebecca Scott, for example, observes the homogeneity of MTR 'mining town economies' where most men worked either as 'miners or managers'.[41] This homogeneity is reinforced by stereotypical gender, class and racial expectations, that, she argues, also occur in some coal company practices.[42] Such homogenizing transfers into biblically based Christian communities of the region as Allen Jones, cofounder of Christians for the Mountains, puts it: 'You have someone who is driving a coal truck in one pew, and in another pew you have someone whose life is being messed up by the effects of mining. What do you do as a pastor? You ignore that issue and just pray for people to get to heaven.'[43] In this homogenizing gesture, immediate differences in the economic, social, health and ability status of humans are subsumed into the sameness of souls destined for an otherworldly heaven, eliding the claims for dialogue concerning social and ecological justice in the here and now.

Homogenization takes on a particular nuance when it appears in biblical texts to support prophetic accounts of an ancient people's aspirations and G-d's longed for actions on their behalf. That predator and prey might lie down together has been read as a sign of an age of peace, a 'peaceable kingdom' (Isa. 11.6-9; 65.25). The image both relies on the specific behaviours of members of different species

---

39. The term 'biocultural homogenization' comes from Rozzi, 'Biocultural Homogenization'.

40. Patitapaban Das, 'Hearing the Unheard: Voices of the Silent', *Tattva Journal of Philosophy* 12, no. 2 (2020), pp. 59–70 (68); Jennifer McWeeny, 'Topographies of Flesh: Women, Nonhuman Animals, and the Embodiment of Connection and Difference', *Hypatia* 29, no. 2 (Spring 2014), pp. 269–86 (270, 284).

41. Rebecca R. Scott 'Dependent Masculinity and Political Culture in Pro-Mountaintop Removal Discourse: Or, How I Learned to Stop Worrying and Love the Dragline', *Feminist Studies* 33, no. 3 (Fall 2007), pp. 484–509 (489).

42. Scott, 'Dependent Masculinity', 489.

43. Alston, 'Faultlines', p. 21.

and seems to promote the dissolution of these characteristic behaviours into a singular peaceable relationality. Wryly, John J. Collins observes: 'After all, it is only in the utopian future that the wolf is supposed to live with the lamb, and even then the wolf will probably feel the safer of the two.'[44] That the image is directed towards a utopia only adds to its homogenizing dynamic.[45] This trope appears in colonial and later contexts, for example in the paintings of Edward Hicks and in animal theologies, as one that has both positive and negative aspects for its uses in theological politics and ethics.[46] The imagery in Isa. 40.4, taken up in Lk. 3.5, has a similar homogenizing quality:

> Every valley shall be lifted up,
> and every mountain and hill be made low;
> the uneven ground shall become level,
> and the rough places a plain. (Isa. 40.4)

> Every valley shall be filled
> and every mountain and hill shall be made low
> and the crooked shall be made straight
> and the rough ways made smooth. (Lk. 3.5)

Rather than principally reading these verses from any number of critical approaches to biblical studies, I propose to look at the kind of homogenization suggested by the image of valleys lifted up/filled and mountains made low. On the surface, these texts gesture towards the roughness of terrain and the specific altitudes of high and low places being smoothed out, so that everything is level ground or plain. This differs in one respect from the homogenization I described earlier that erases difference in order to stereotype. Nonetheless, it entails a smoothing out of difference between two categories (valley and hill) to create a third category (plain). The material characters of valleys as low places (through which rivers or streams may run) and of mountains or hills as high places are together reduced to the level character of a plain, and subordinated to the anticipated coming or intervention of Yhwh, promising 'comfort' to the people. While historical and literary critical readings of the text can give context and nuance to the homogenizing aspect of the image (and I will consider some important contextual aspects below), there is evidence these verses have had impact outside biblical studies at this surface level. As I will explain below, the text of Isa. 40.4 has been employed in relation to MTR.

---

44. John J. Collins, 'The Zeal of Phineas: The Bible and the Legitimation of Violence', *JBL* 122 (2003), pp. 3–21 (20).
45. See the brief critique in Norman Habel, *An Inconvenient Text: Is a Green Reading of the Bible Possible?* (Adelaide: ATF Press 2009), p. 102.
46. Anne Elvey, 'Desiring the "Peaceable Kingdom"? Use/Respect Dualism, the Enigma of Predation and Human Relationships to Other Animals', *PAN* 3 (2005), pp. 31–40.

The Bible and MTR

The Bible has been used by Christians to resist MTR in the United States.[47] Epigraphs to Andrew R. H. Thompson's *Sacred Mountains: A Christian Ethical Approach to Mountaintop Removal* (Isa. 11.9) and to its first chapter (Job 28.9, 12) show the potency of biblical imagery in relation to MTR:[48]

> They will not hurt or destroy
> on all my holy mountain;
> for the earth will be full of the knowledge of Yhwh
> as the waters cover the sea. (Isa. 11.9)

> They put their hand to the flinty rock,
> and overturn mountains by the roots.
> But where shall wisdom be found?
> And where is the place of understanding? (Job 28.9, 12)

There are three main religious trajectories of resistance to MTR in the Appalachians: an Earth-based spirituality situating 'inherent value in the landscape of Appalachia itself'; a Catholic and mainstream Protestant approach based in environmental and social justice; an evangelical approach founding creation care and Christian stewardship in biblically based ethics.[49] This last was the approach of evangelical Christian Julia (also known as Judy) Bonds who died in 2011. Bonds was an outreach worker of the Whitesville, West Virginia-based Coal River Mountain Watch.[50] In 2003, she was one

---

47. See, Andrew R. H. Thompson, *Sacred Mountains: A Christian Ethical Approach to Mountaintop Removal* (Lexington: The University of Kentucky Press, 2015); Joseph D. Witt, *Religion and Resistance in Appalachia: Faith and the Fight against Mountaintop Removal Coal Mining* (Lexington: The University of Kentucky Press, 2016). See also, e.g., Christians for the Mountains (CFTM), 'Coal', available online: https://christiansforthemountains.org/coal/ (accessed 28 May 2021); Megan Fincher, 'Christian Stewardship Group Seeks to Blow Top Off Mountaintop Removal', National Catholic Reporter (4 February 2014), available online: http://ncronline.org/blogs/eco-catholic/christian-stewardship-group-seeks-blow-top-mountaintop-removal (accessed 28 May 2021); John S. Rausch, 'The Cross in the Mountains: Mountaintop Removal in Appalachia', in *Sacred Acts: How Churches Are Working to Protect Earth's Climate* (ed. Mallory McDuff; Gabriola Island, BC: New Society Publishers, 2012), pp. 149–62.

48. Thompson, *Sacred Mountains*, pp. v, 1.

49. Witt, *Religion and Resistance*, pp. 8, 13. My own early background is Roman Catholic, and I resonate with an ecological social justice perspective, informed in the last thirty years by my learning from First Nations Christians, poets, ecological feminists and deep ecologists, who have helped me shape an Earth-based, ecological materialist perspective. As a biblical reader, I am interested in uses and reception of biblical texts in relation to MTR, evident in the biblically based ethical approaches of evangelical Christian activists in the Appalachians.

50. Beth Newberry, 'Mountain Defender', *Sojourners Magazine* 34, no. 3 (March 2005), pp. 26–30 (26).

of seven activists from across the world to win the Goldman Environmental Prize. Beth Newberry comments on Bonds: 'Whether she is testifying before congressional committees, speaking at a rally, or leading a lawsuit to strengthen environmental protections, her source for renewal and unwavering dedication to her cause is her relationship with God, grounded in a critical reading of the Bible.'[51] Newberry highlights Bonds' appeal as an evangelical Christian to biblically based creation and covenant theologies to uphold her resistance to MTR. A network of evangelical Christians in the Appalachians, Christians for the Mountains (CFTM), of which Bonds was a member, also adduces covenant theology, a covenant with G-d and a covenant with creation, to support their resistance to MTR. CFTM cites Ps. 24.1 – 'The earth is the Lord's' – in support of its mission.[52] Bonds and her evangelical co-activists take a theocentric approach to MTR; that is, the environmental creation ethics they espouse have as a primary focus divine interests in and purposes for creation.[53]

On Mountain Sunday in 2012 during the Season of Creation, Erik Christensen delivered a sermon resisting MTR. He situated MTR in the context of the rich mountain imagery of biblical texts from both testaments and made the telling link between sacred place and care for place: 'Perhaps it is because we have, in our religious imaginations, removed God from the mountaintops and relocated God into our sanctuaries, that we no longer care so deeply for the real-life mountaintops here at home and around the world.'[54] He reminded his congregation that while some mountains have become holiday resorts, others are being destroyed.[55]

MTR and Isaiah 40.4

A 1999 article by Kevin Clarke in *U.S. Catholic* is titled 'And Every Mountain Brought Low', with a summary line which reads: 'Hiding behind economic development, King Coal is making molehills out of mountains.' The article points

---

51. Newberry, 'Mountain Defender', p. 26.

52. Dwight Billings and Will Samson analyse the way 'name calling', a mode of homogenization or stereotyping, works to devalue the name 'environmentalists' among many 'evangelicals'. The opposite could also be said to be true, that 'evangelical' or 'fundamentalist' becomes a homogenizing term among those who see these sectors of Christians as opposed to environmental protection. The CFTM prefers the term 'Creation Care' to 'Environmentalism' to avoid the negative stereotype. Dwight B. Billings and Will Samson, 'Evangelical Christians and the Environment: "Christians for the Mountaintops" and the Appalachian Movement against Mountaintop Removal Coal Mining', *Worldviews* 16, no. 1 (2012), pp. 1–29; see also, CFTM, 'Our Mission'.

53. Witt, *Religion and Resistance*, p. 98.

54. Erik Christensen, 'Sermon: Sunday September 23, 2012: Season of Creation – Mountain Sunday', *By Proclamation* (23 September 2012), available online: http://byproclamation.wordpress.com/tag/mountaintop-removal-mining/ (accessed 1 June 2021).

55. Christensen, 'Sermon'.

out that in the process of MTR, used to extract what is a comparatively 'cleaner' form of coal (namely low sulphur coal), '[e]ntire mountaintops are blown up, cut up and ground into dust as the coal is extracted. The rubble left over is dumped into nearby valleys – over the last few years obliterating hundreds of mountain streams'.[56] He points out the ecojustice implications of a situation in which residents of Kentucky and West Virginia ultimately pay, in terms of health and loss of environmental amenity, such as fresh waterways, for some local economic benefit and for cleaner air for others outside their locality. Sacrificially some humans pay in poor working conditions and local environmental degradation and other creatures pay through loss of habitat to benefit other, usually richer, urban populations.[57] While depicting the levelling of mountains and filling in of valleys as the physical reality of MTR, Clarke appeals to Isa. 40.4 as an implied critique of this extractive process.

Against growing resistance to MTR, coal companies tried for several years to play up the benefits of MTR.[58] In response to Christian resistance to MTR, more than one coal association referred to Isa. 40.4. For example, on the Kentucky Coal Association website in 2013, I could read: 'Under most circumstances, we are of the opinion religion should not play a role in political debate. Recently, however,

---

56. Kevin Clarke, 'And Every Mountain Brought Low', *US Catholic* 64, no. 9 (September 1999), p. 23.

57. This observation resonates with an ecological feminist critique of unacknowledged reliance on 'shadow places' for our local sustenance and comfort. See Val Plumwood, 'Shadow Places and the Politics of Dwelling', *Australian Humanities Review* 44, Ecological Humanities (March 2008), available online: http://australianhumanitiesreview.org/2008/03/01/shadow-places-and-the-politics-of-dwelling/ (accessed 3 February 2021).

58. See, e.g., West Virginia Coal Association, *Coal Facts: West Virginia Coal: Building a Future for Our People* (Charleston, WV: West Virginia Coal Association, 2012), available online: http://www.wvcoal.com (accessed 1 June 2021). It would seem that the resistance to MTR was successful enough to be threatening to mining interests. The Senior Vice President of West Virginia Coal testified on 10 October 2013, to the Subcommittee on Energy and Mineral Resources of the Natural Resources Committee oversight hearing: 'EPA v. American Mining Jobs: The Obama Administration's Regulatory Assault on the Economy', US House of Representatives, Washington DC, that coal miners are facing from the Obama Administration 'A War on Coal': Chris R. Hamilton, 'Testimony of Chris R. Hamilton, Senior Vice President, West Virginia Coal Association and Chairman, West Virginia Business and Industry Council before the Subcommittee on Energy and Mineral Resources of the Natural Resources Committee Oversight Hearing: "EPA V. American Mining Jobs: The Obama Administration's Regulatory Assault on the Economy"', *West Virginia Coal Association* (11 October 2013), available online: https://wvcoalassociation.wordpress.com/current-events/page/16/ (accessed 1 June 2021). On successes in the campaign against MTR, see, e.g., Penny Loeb, *Moving Mountains: How One Woman and Her Community Won Justice from Big Coal* (Lexington: The University Press of Kentucky, 2007).

we've learned some religious leaders are railing against mountaintop mining and, as we hear it, invoking the Almighty to bring an end to the mining method.'[59] The comment continued with an appeal to 1 Tim. 5.8 and the onus on people 'to provide for their households', then turned to Isaiah citing the New American Bible version of Isa. 40.4-5 as support for the practice of MTR.[60] An attorney representing the West Virginia Coal Association has reportedly also used Isa. 40.4 to support MTR.[61]

Responses to mining companies' uses of Isaiah sometimes appeal to the tools of biblical studies, whether accurately or otherwise is not the precise point, to argue that Isa. 40.4-5 does not refer to valleys being 'filled in', but rather to their being 'exalted'. One argument then proffers: 'It would require the most cynical misreading of the Bible to assert that we would be adhering to the will of God by destroying a valley with fill, according to religious experts.'[62] In a similar vein Kenn Hermann writes: 'It is so comforting to know that the good Christian owners, operators, and stockholders of Hobet 21, the 12k sq. mile strip mine in West Virginia owned by Arch Coal Company, take their Bibles so seriously. How could I have missed the meaning and scope of Isaiah's prophecy?'[63] Hermann refers to an ecclesial understanding of the metaphorical nature of the passage as pertaining to the parousia and then with irony writes: 'Now we know that Isaiah was foretelling the coming of the newest advances in mountaintop mining to feed our insatiable need for coal.'[64] Anne Shelby from Clay Country, Kentucky, on a hilly seventy-acre farm inhabited by her family since the beginning of the twentieth century comments: 'The coal association takes that verse from Isaiah and uses it literally. As if the prophet were talking about MTR rather than the

---

59. Kentucky Coal Association, 'Mountaintop Mining Issues and Responses', *KCA: Kentucky Coal Association*, available online: http://www.kentuckycoal.org/index.cfm?pageToken=mtmIssues (accessed 15 October 2013). By 1 October 2014 this seemed to have been removed from the KCA website. But see, Allen Johnson, 'The Kentucky Coal Association Weighs in on Mountaintop Mining' (4 January 2010), Go Tell It on the Mountains blog, available online: https://gotell.wordpress.com/2010/01/04/ (accessed 1 June 2021).

60. Kentucky Coal Association, 'Mountaintop Mining'.

61. Keith930, '40 Years Later: The Buffalo Creek Disaster and Its Aftermath', *Daily Kos* (7 February 2012), available online: https://www.dailykos.com/stories/2012/2/7/1062372/-40-Years-Later-The-Buffalo-Creek-Disaster-Its-Aftermath (accessed 3 August 2021).

62. Bill Kovarik, 'Does the Bible Justify Mountaintop Removal Coal Mining?', *The Appalachian Voice* (1 December 2006), available online: https://appvoices.org/2006/12/01/2626/ (accessed 1 June 2021).

63. Kenn Hermann, 'Isaiah's Vision and Mountaintop Mining', Radix Perspectives blog (28 February 2006), available online: https://khermann.wordpress.com/2006/02/28/isaiahs-vision-of-mountaintop-mining/ (accessed 1 June 2021).

64. Hermann, 'Isaiah's Vision'.

coming of the Messiah.'⁶⁵ Shelby finds the assumption that Appalachians are simple-minded, insignificant people who read their Bibles literally condescending; this condescension reveals the companies' desperation as they respond to every critical prompt.⁶⁶ As noted above, allied with a biblically based theocentric ethic of Christian stewardship of creation, evangelical environmental activists place Ps. 24.1 to the fore, proclaiming, 'The earth is the Lord's'; in resistance to MTR they emphasize texts such as Ps. 72.3: 'The mountains shall bring peace to the people' (KJV).⁶⁷ For evangelical environmentalists texts are not taken in isolation but work together towards meaning, in distinction from the proof-texting employed in the MTR-promoting uses of Isa. 40.4.⁶⁸

Isaiah 40.4 uses a form of hyperbolic or exaggerated biblical language. Of such inflated language, Robert L. Plummer writes in reference to Mt. 17.20: 'Jesus is not preparing his followers to work for coal-mining companies – moving the tops of physical mountains. Rather, through faith in God, Jesus' followers will overcome seemingly impossible obstacles.'⁶⁹ Penny Loeb takes up this biblical imagery in the title of her book *Moving Mountains*, where she describes Patricia Bragg's effective campaigning against MTR.⁷⁰ Another blog shifts the Christian response a little with the theocentric approach of the title, 'Religion's View from Appalachia: Only God Should Move Mountains'.⁷¹ Nonetheless, because both advocates and opponents of MTR use the same biblical texts, 'individuals are faced with competing interpretations and translations when forming their opinions'.⁷² Although they claim that their position is biblically based, effectively 'other elements influence their interpretations beyond simply the text of the scripture'.⁷³

---

65. Silas House and Jason Howard, *Something's Rising: Appalachians Fighting Mountaintop Removal* (Lexington: University of Kentucky Press, 2009), p. 238. The point is not whether Shelby is correct in presuming that Isa. 40.5 points to Jesus Christ as Messiah; in its original context in the Hebrew Bible this is not the case but a later interpretation by Luke, other early Jesus followers and later Christians.

66. House and Howard, *Something's Rising*, p. 239.

67. Witt, *Religion and Resistance*, pp. 126–8.

68. Witt, *Religion and Resistance*, pp. 128–9.

69. Robert L. Plummer, *40 Questions about Interpreting the Bible* (Grand Rapids: Kregel, 2010), p. 225.

70. Loeb, *Moving Mountains*.

71. Stacy Morford, 'Religion's View from Appalachia: Only God Should Move Mountains', *Inside Climate News* (26 March 2009), available online: https://insideclimatenews.org/news/26032009/religions-view-appalachia-only-god-should-move-mountains/ (accessed 3 August 2021). See also the appeal to Isa. 40.12 in Neela Banjeree, 'Taking On a Coal Mining Practice as a Matter of Faith', *The New York Times* (28 October 2006), available online: https://www.nytimes.com/2006/10/28/us/28mountains.html (accessed 3 August 2021).

72. Witt, *Religion and Resistance*, p. 129.

73. Witt, *Religion and Resistance*, p. 129.

Moreover, the situational materialities of MTR are pertinent to activist readings of the Bible:

> The Bible is never read in a complete intellectual vacuum, but is interpreted within a network of other individual and communal attitudes and experiences. In the case of Appalachia, these stewardship perspectives are influenced by the presence of mountaintop removal and its related complications. Theocentric biblical interpretations among anti-mountaintop removal activists, then, point to the broader theme of reinterpreting the meaning and significance of a place through multiple interacting lenses.[74]

In his 2007 review article on three books responding to and resisting MTR creatively and critically, Norman Wirzba likens MTR to rampant robbery and violence, in which immense areas of the Appalachians resemble a lunar landscape and communities are in conflict or decimated by coal mining politics.[75] He comments that many Appalachian residents see themselves as 'throwaway people' and compares the diversity of the forests of the region with the waste and pollution of mining companies including their unsuccessful reclamation projects.[76] In conclusion, referring to the president of the Kentucky Coal Association, Bill Caylor's appeal to Isa. 40.4-5 to support MTR, Wirzba writes: 'Somehow I doubt that bulldozers and bombs, wasted lives and throwaway landscapes, are the means of the revealing of God's glory.'[77]

The question is not simply whether representatives of coal mining companies have misread the biblical text without proper attention to critical biblical studies, but whether and how the image from Isa. 40.4 repeated in Lk. 3.5 lends itself to this (abusive) reading. As noted above, there is a wider issue concerning the problematics of a particular kind of proof-texting, where a text is used out of context to support its literal enactment. What is specific to the situation of MTR is the actual mountains and valleys themselves in the Appalachians, and their relationship or otherwise to the mountains and valleys of Isa. 40.4.

The force of metaphor in Isaiah 40.4

Isaiah 40.4 appears in the opening poem of the prophetic unit that comprises Isaiah 40–55.[78] In major part likely composed shortly after the fall of the Babylonian

---

74. Witt, *Religion and Resistance*, p. 131.
75. Norman Wirzba, 'Throwaway People, Throwaway Land', *Books and Culture: A Christian Review* (December 2007), pp. 44-5 (44), available online: https://www.booksandculture.com/articles/2007/novdec/17.44.html (accessed 25 March 2022).
76. Wirzba, 'Throwaway People', p. 44.
77. Wirzba, 'Throwaway People', p. 45.
78. On Isaiah 40–55, frequently known as Deutero- or Second Isaiah, as both a distinct unit and properly part of a single biblical prophetic book called Isaiah, see John Goldingay and David Payne, *Isaiah 40–55* (vol. 1; ICC; London: T&T Clark International, 2006), pp. 1-4.

empire in 539 BCE, Isaiah 40–55 refers to events in, and concerns of, the Judean community in the preceding decade, and addresses their socio-religious needs after the exile.[79] Both during the exile and afterwards, the Judean community is aware that the Babylonian and Persian empires surpass it in power.[80] Speaking to the people's doubt concerning Yhwh's faithfulness, Isaiah 40–55 opens by recalling the covenant between Yhwh and the people:

> By commencing his oracle with the words 'My people' (עמי) and 'your God' (אלהיכם), terms that echo the well-known covenant formula (e.g., Jer. 7.23, 'I am your God and you are My people'; cf. Exod. 6.7; Lev. 26.12; Jer. 11.4; 31.33), the prophet is declaring that the covenant between God and Israel, which they thought had been broken because of their iniquities, was still intact.[81]

In Jewish liturgy, Isa. 40.1 – 'Comfort, comfort my people… ' – is recited on the first of the seven Sabbaths of comfort.[82] Comfort is a recurring motif in Isaiah 40–66.[83] Isa. 40.1-11 affirms what has become a classic theme of Judaism and Christianity, namely divine presence in human history, so much so that the Persian king Cyrus becomes the key to the future of the exiled people.[84] Is it a 'scandal' that Yhwh describes Cyrus as shepherd and anointed, Yhwh's agent, to bring blessing to the people (Isa. 45.1-8)?[85] The making of a level road parodies 'Babylonian hymnody', which honoured 'both Babylon's king and its deity' as they entered their city triumphally along its highway; Isa. 40.3 co-opts its language to describe Yhwh's leading exiles out of the city.[86] The Targum version of Isa. 40.1-5 no longer has the roadway prepared for Yhwh; it is for the people themselves returning to Jerusalem from exile.[87] The Targum interpretation highlights the human focus of the Isaian text.

In Isaiah 40–55, themes of covenant, comfort and divine presence in human history, in large part reflect anthropocentric interests. In the Hebrew Bible,

---

79. See Goldingay and Payne, *Isaiah*, p. 30; Blaženka Scheuer, *The Return of YHWH: The Tension between Deliverance and Repentance in Isaiah 40–55* (Berlin: De Gruyter, 2008), p. 12 (for discussion of the scholarly debate on the composition of Isa. 40–55, see pp. 6–13).

80. Goldingay and Payne, *Isaiah*, p. 30.

81. Shalom M. Paul, *Isaiah 40–66: Translation and Commentary* (Eerdmans Critical Commentary; Grand Rapids: Eerdmans, 2012), p. 127.

82. Paul, *Isaiah*, p. 71.

83. Isa. 49.13; 51.3, 12, 19; 52.9; 61.2; 66.13; cf. Lam. 1.2; see also, Michael Thompson, *Isaiah 40–66* (Epworth Commentaries; Peterborough: Epworth, 2001), p. 4.

84. Paul D. Hanson, *Isaiah 40–66* (IBC; Louisville: John Knox, 1995), p. 13; Goldingay and Payne, *Isaiah*, p. 30.

85. John Goldingay, *Isaiah* (Understanding the Bible Commentary Series; Grand Rapids: Baker Books, 2012), pp. 390–2.

86. Ellen F. Davis, *Opening Israel's Scriptures* (Oxford: Oxford University Press, 2019), pp. 272–3.

87. Klyne R. Snodgrass, 'Streams of Tradition Emerging from Isaiah 40:1-5 and Their Adaptation in the New Testament', *JSNT* 8 (1980), pp. 24–45 (27–8).

covenant nonetheless involves a three-way relationship between land, people and G-d. Covenant, however, is not singular. The covenant, sometimes called the Noahide covenant, after the flood, for example, is with all living creatures, and with Earth itself (Gen. 9.9-17).[88] As Rosemary Radford Ruether argues, while biblical views of relationship between people and the divine are 'highly androcentric, anthropocentric, and ethnocentric', emphasizing 'male leadership' of a particular people, the covenant tradition also has inclusive aspects.[89] At times, G-d 'relates lovingly' to other peoples and interacts directly with women and Earth, 'without [male] intermediaries' or 'human mediation'.[90] Land is a gift, part of a divine promise of intergenerational flourishing.[91] Land as gift is 'not a possession that can be held apart from relation to God'.[92] Social justice, right relationship between people and G-d, and the relationship between people and land are interconnected. Land is responsive to interhuman behaviour (e.g. Jer. 4.18, 22, 28). Emerging from traditions in which land is kin, land is a covenant partner, even the first partner to the covenant prior to the human ancestors.[93] The trauma of the exile, the loss of land, is linked to human failures in relationship to the divine, and towards the most vulnerable.[94] Isaiah 40 promises relief.

The comfort of a promised return to the land depends, however, on 'changes in the rugged desert terrain that must occur in order that a worthy and substantial highway for the great new work of the Lord may be established', even if this return requires symbolically a substantial feat of geo-engineering.[95] In Isaiah 40–55, the trauma of exile is represented by wilderness; this trauma 'will be overcome by God with radical acts of transformation'.[96] In this transformation, the desert is not

---

88. David G. Horrell, *The Bible and the Environment: Towards a Critical Ecological Biblical Theology* (eBook; Abingdon: Routledge, 2014), ch. 4.

89. Rosemary Radford Ruether, *Gaia and God: An Ecofeminist Theology of Earth Healing* (San Francisco: HarperCollins, 1992), p. 208.

90. Ruether, *Gaia and God*, p. 208.

91. In Deuteronomy, this divine gift of land is paradoxically both conditional on right action and exclusive of 'the poor, aliens, and the Canaanites'. See Norman C. Habel, *The Land Is Mine: Six Biblical Land Ideologies* (Overtures to Biblical Theology; Minneapolis: Fortress, 1995), pp. 36–53 (53).

92. Ruether, *Gaia and God*, p. 211.

93. This view of land emerges in Ellen Davis's reading of Leviticus. See Ellen F. Davis, 'Land as Kin: Renewing the Imagination', in *Rooted and Grounded: Essays on Land and Christian Discipleship* (ed. Ryan D. Harker and Janeen Bertsche Johnson; Eugene: Pickwick, 2016), pp. 3–12.

94. See, e.g., Mark G. Brett, *Political Trauma and Healing: Biblical Ethics for a Postcolonial World* (Grand Rapids: Eerdmans, 2016), pp. 112–13.

95. It would seem the desert land is not the promised land. Thompson, *Isaiah*, p. 5; Ben Witherington III, *Isaiah Old and New: Exegesis, Intertextuality, and Hermeneutics* (Minneapolis: 1517 Media and Fortress Press, 2017), p. 181, doi:10.2307/j.ctt1ggjhbz.

96. Habel, *Inconvenient Text*, p. 102.

passive; rather the call 'to prepare a way in the wilderness (Isa. 40.3) is answered by sympathetic responses from God and the wilderness itself'.[97] In response to the needs of the poor for water, G-d transforms the land, and what is properly 'a dry landscape' becomes through divine miracle 'a fertile forest' (Isa. 41.17-19).[98] The promise of Isaiah in these chapters plays on a contrast with the 'past trials in the wilderness after the exodus from Egypt'.[99] Conveyed in the Exodus narrative as ecologically destructive, these trials are reversed in Isaiah 40–55.[100] The ecosystems of the desert are transformed by divine act into an idyllic place akin to Eden. Is this a promise of divine terraforming?

If Isa. 40.4 is not to be taken to support, or at least offer an ancient preview of, contemporary practices of destructive terraforming such as MTR, then the covenant, comfort and presence Isa. 40.1-11 proclaims need to be understood in ways broader than its apparently dominant anthropocentric interests. But to point instead to the theocentric interests of the text – the divine initiative and care for the people – is frequently in effect to return to prevailing anthropocentric ones. What is needed is a shift of perspective towards framing divine-human relationships ecologically. Posing the question, '[h]ow does the land itself respond?', Norman Habel imagines the land asking: 'Why demonise my wilderness and then seek visions that transform her into a different ecosystem?'[101] Adopting this 'Earth voice', he concludes: 'Yet God bringing water to my wilderness is preferable, I suppose, to having my water turned into blood!'[102] But if I return to the verses at the start of Isaiah 40–55, reading them as the West Virginia Coal Association and Kentucky Coal have, the terraforming that occurs in MTR is anything but Edenic. It is hard to imagine that the land, should it speak, would say that the filling and levelling of MTR is preferable to other worse treatment.

Isaiah 40.3-5 is poetry.[103] The poem's dominant image is of preparing a roadway for Yhwh. The repetition of every/all (כל) 'emphasises the wondrous miracle of the straight and level highway'.[104] The overcoming of the 'obstacles to engineering', in the raising of valley and lowering of hills and mounts, and the smoothing of rugged ground, serves this metaphorical preparation of a royal highway for the divine.[105] In this metaphor the resonance of being raised and made low is broader. There is a call to valley, hill and mount to respond to the cry, to participate in the preparation

97. Habel, *Inconvenient Text*, p. 102.
98. Habel, *Inconvenient Text*, p. 102.
99. Habel, *Inconvenient Text*, p. 103.
100. Habel, *Inconvenient Text*, p. 103.
101. Habel, *Inconvenient Text*, p. 104. I prefer not to use a feminine pronoun for land or Earth, as Habel does here, but to use a gender-neutral pronoun instead.
102. Habel, *Inconvenient Text*, p. 104.
103. As Michael Thompson notes, it is satisfyingly effective poetry. Thompson, *Isaiah*, p. 5. Paul's translation captures the poetic quality well; Paul, *Isaiah*, p. 73.
104. Paul, *Isaiah*, p. 131.
105. John Goldingay, *The Message of Isaiah 40–55: A Literary-Theological Commentary* (London: T&T Clark International, 2005), p. 19.

of this thoroughfare for the divine.[106] The divine dispensation enables a response not only from humans, but from the wider Earth community, exemplified by valleys and hills. The imagery suggests that valley and mountain share both the exaltation (or attitude of praise/lifting up) and the humility summoned, when the presence or glory (כבוד) of Yhwh is revealed.

Luke 3.3-6 reprises Isa. 40.3-5 to proclaim the presence of G-d in the salvation John the Baptist is looking towards in Jesus. The prophetic preaching of John is to the fore for Luke, with a focus on warning and a call to repentance.[107] Treatment of the vulnerable and right action are at the heart of John's message (Lk. 3.10-14). Where Luke's John preaches repentance, Luke's Jesus will proclaim forgiveness and liberation (Lk. 4.18-19). The comfort Isaiah 40 foregrounds is implicit in John's address to those who have come seeking repentance.[108] Luke 3.5 not only replays Isa. 40.4 but echoes the theme of reversal found, for example, in Lk. 1.51-53 and 6.20-26. Luke's reversals, it can be argued, represent a counter-ideology to the colonizing ideology of empire.[109] But like Lk. 3.5 these texts utilize violent imagery to support their liberating vision. The imagery of mountains felled and valleys raised remains problematic from an ecological perspective.[110] At the same time, as in Isa. 40.5, in Lk. 3.5 'all flesh' – a more-than-human constituency – is subject of the divine promise. The mountains and valleys themselves are by extension not only resources for metaphors or mining, but also participants in the Isaian and Lukan worlds of divine interactivity.

A lively, responsive Earth and cosmos

While this does not diminish the problematic use of Isa. 40.4 to support MTR, the Isaian vision of terraforming occurs in the Hebrew text in part due to the volition of the things themselves, namely the valleys, hills and mounts. They are ecosystems, represented as capable of responding to the call of the divine, delivered through the prophetic voice. The metaphor contains and conveys the living character of its subject, rendering the death-dealing character of MTR all the more poignant.

The liveliness of valley and mountain – the liveliness of the particular landscape that Yhwh, Cyrus and the returning exiles might encounter on their way to Jerusalem – is prior to the road-building metaphor it supports. The transformation

---

106. Habel, *Inconvenient Text*, p. 102.

107. François Bovon, *Luke 1: A Commentary on the Gospel of Luke 1:1–9:50* (trans. Christine M. Thomas; Hermeneia, 63A; ed. Helmut Koester; Accordance electronic edn; Minneapolis: Fortress, 2002), pp. 120-2.

108. Amy-Jill Levine and Ben Witherington III, *The Gospel of Luke* (New Cambridge Bible Commentary; Cambridge: Cambridge University Press, 2018), p. 91.

109. Barbara E. Reid, 'Women Prophets of God's Alternative Reign', in *Luke-Acts and Empire: Essays in Honor of Robert L. Brawley* (ed. D. Rhoads, D. Esterline, and Jae Won Lee; Princeton Theological Monograph Series, 151; Eugene, OR: Pickwick, 2011), pp. 44-59.

110. Bovon, *Luke 1*, p. 121.

of this landscape to make a smooth way not only for Yhwh but also implicitly for the returning exiles serves the covenant recalled in Isa. 40.1. In Yhwh's faithfulness to the covenant, the people will find comfort. The liveliness of valley and mountain required for the Isaian metaphor can be understood as necessary also for the reaffirmation of Yhwh's covenant with the people. It is unsurprising then that members of CFTM (Christians for the Mountains) appeal to covenant theology to inform and support their resistance to MTR.

Where does this leave biblical readers in relation to the use of Isa. 40.4 to support MTR? The use of Isa. 40.4 by advocates of MTR might lead us not to set up biblical studies classes for mining executives, but rather to ask other questions of the text, for example, as I have suggested above: How does the primary metaphor of Yhwh processing across the land inform or influence the homogenization of valley, hill and mount? What is at work in the way metaphorical discourse touches on and/ or gives way to violence?[111] It is insufficient to find a better reading of the text in its contexts (socio-cultural, historical, literary, liturgical, theological). Rather it is necessary to recognize the violence inherent in the metaphor and, against its homogenizing tendency, to affirm the liveliness of valley, hill and mountain that precedes and underlies the metaphor.[112]

How does the imagery of a lively responsive land, even if this is subordinated to a human desire for divine intervention, speak back to the reality of a land treated as if inert and rendered passive – constructed as 'standing reserve' – even apparently deadened, in the processes of MTR?[113] For many residents of the Appalachians fighting MTR, the response to the land itself is as to their own bodies, embedded in memory and stories; the response to its destruction is 'visceral'.[114] The interplay between land and body is both evidence of the liveliness of the land and poignant witness to its deadening in MTR, but perhaps also to the capacity for land and its human inhabitants to engage together in resistance. John Rausch provides often poignant descriptions of tours and prayer in areas affected by MTR.[115] In these

---

111. On the relation of metaphor to violence, as well as its mimetic qualities, see Paul Ricoeur, *The Rule of Metaphor: The Creation of Meaning in Language* (trans. Robert Czerny, with Kathleen McLaughlin, and John Costello, SJ; Routledge Classics; London: Routledge, 2003), pp. 8–48.

112. On the liveliness underlying metaphor, see Ricoeur, *Rule of Metaphor*, p. 48.

113. The term 'standing reserve' comes from: Martin Heidegger, 'The Question Concerning Technology' (trans. William Lovitt), in *Martin Heidegger: Basic Writings: From Being and Time (1927) to The Task of Thinking (1964)* (ed. David Farrell Krell; revised and expanded edition; London: Routledge, 1993), pp. 307–41.

114. Bryan T. McNeil, *Combating Mountaintop Removal: New Directions in the Fight against Big Coal* (Urbana: University of Illinois Press, 2011).

115. Rausch, 'Cross in the Mountains'.

activities, participants witness the destruction, link their own lifestyles with the demand for cheap energy that makes MTR attractive to policy makers, commit to action and perform symbolic actions of hope. Their practices offer instances of more-than-human cooperative resistance, where people embedded in their land respond to the death-dealing of MTR through lively partnerships.

Not only can the reaffirmation of the covenant, despite its potential anthropocentric focus, offer empowerment for Christians to resist the destruction of MTR, but also – and I would argue necessarily – the liveliness underlying the problematic homogenizing metaphor of Isa. 40.4 needs to be given precedence alongside this covenant theology. There are two key reasons for this. First, the potentially anthropocentric focus on covenant needs to be understood in the context of a lively, responsive Earth and cosmos, where creator and creation are enmeshed in the mutuality of covenant to each other. Second, an affirmation of the liveliness of the specific ancient valleys, hills and mountains to which the prophet refers needs to call forth in contemporary Christians an affirmation of the liveliness of the Appalachian Mountains which are older than the biblical texts themselves.[116] Such an affirmation resists both the homogenizing tendencies of the text and the destructive homogenization of mountains and valleys through MTR. This resistance is in solidarity with the Appalachian Mountains, the destruction of which includes damage to more-than-human (including human) communities where many endure dying habitats and homes.

Conclusion

From an ecological feminist materialist approach, such as I am adopting in this book, a troubling aspect of the discourse around uses of the Bible in MTR is a theocentric ethic. What is disturbing is the way theocentrisms are so often allied with androcentric and anthropocentric language and practice. While feminists have long resisted androcentric theology, the language of lordship with its kyriarchal echoes and implications remains prevalent and potent. Moreover, while some biblical texts can support a more-than-human animism and while biblical metaphors reference the material liveliness on which they rely, a theocentric ethic may not give due attention to more-than-human material worlds. Deep incarnation, admittedly, dovetails to some extent with the new materialism, and offers a way of understanding the divine as en-mattered in creation, especially where human knowing cannot fully apprehend the material sacred.[117] An ecological feminist

---

116. Kenneth A. Eriksson and W. Lee Daniels, 'Environmental Implications of Regional Geology and Coal Mining in the Appalachians', in *Appalachia's Coal-Mined Landscapes* (ed. Carl E. Zipper and Jeff Skousen; Cham, Switzerland: Springer Nature, 2021), pp. 27–53.

117. Deborah Guess, 'Oil Beyond War and Peace: Rethinking the Meaning of Matter', in *Ecological Aspects of War: Religious and Theological Perspectives* (ed. Anne Elvey, Deborah Guess and Keith Dyer, *A Forum for Theology in the World* 3, no. 2; Adelaide: ATF Theology, 2016), pp. 73–93.

aesthetics offers a different perspective, decentring the divine and affirming the relational liveliness (and material agency) of the Appalachian mountains as more-than-human communities.

From Appalachian-based poets and novelists, such as Silas House, to Australian feminist poet of politics and power, Jennifer Maiden, come multiple examples of creative imaginings of the complex relations of power, lament, resistance and hope, in more-than-human mountain communities of the region.[118] In her 'Appalachian Elegy', bell hooks recollects First Nations' kinship with the earth of the region, and while it is not my story to tell in full, this calls to mind the trails of tears of the Cherokee people, their removal from Appalachia and determination to survive.[119]

As noted above, coal mining occurs as part of the colonial extractivist project. But the mountains themselves predate all such human relationships and projects. Resistances, activism and creative engagement need to be, and are being, understood in relation to the deep time of the mountains, both the mountains of Appalachia and of the biblical lands. These mountains are hundreds of millions of years old; they have seen the emergence of new species and the loss of others. They have responded to wind and weather, and as such are in relationship with air and sea through the processes of climate. In the case of the Appalachians, mountains have responded to the violence of MTR according to the logic of their own processes. Across continents, the passage of air breathes against the biblical mountains and the Appalachians; a creative imagining might put them in conversation as inhabitants of a deeper time than the text of Isaiah, but not entirely separate from its communities of composition and reading who share this one atmosphere.

Understood in relation to a material sacred encountered in mountains subject to MTR, a theocentric ethic can affirm an ethic of attention to the mountains themselves as voiced.[120] Activist listening to more than humans, such as mountains, is always mediated by particular cultural worlds. Resistance and protest need to be balanced with radical reverence and wonder, attendant on the

---

118. See, e.g., Patricia Youngblood, 'Two West Virginia Poems', *Vox Populi*, available online: https://voxpopulisphere.com/2017/08/08/patricia-youngblood-two-west-virginia-poems/ (accessed 5 June 2021); Crystal Good, 'Valley Girl', available online: https://crystalgood.squarespace.com/valley-girl (accessed 5 June 2021); Silas House, 'The Appalachian Trilogy', available online: https://www.silas-house.com/writing.html (accessed 7 June 2021); Jennifer Maiden, *Appalachian Fall: Poems about Poverty in Power: New Poems* (Penrith, NSW: Quemar Press, 2018).

119. bell hooks, 'Appalachian Elegy (Sections 1–6)', from *Appalachian Elegy* (Lexington: University of Kentucky Press, 2012), reproduced at Poetry Foundation, available online: https://www.poetryfoundation.org/poems/148751/appalachian-elegy-1-6 (accessed 7 June 2021); Cherokee Nation, 'Remember the Removal', Cherokee Nation, available online: https://rtr.cherokee.org/ (accessed 7 June 2021).

120. Thompson, *Sacred Mountains*, p. 146.

'elegance, astonishing diversity and complexity of life forms, entangled materiality, and stunning beauty of planetary beings and processes'.[121] Embedding more-than-human resistances in open-spirited attention to the deep time conversation of mountains, atmosphere, seas and their inhabitants, then becomes an essential ethic and aesthetic for an ecological feminist hermeneutics. In the next chapter, I turn to the material vulnerability and aesthetic pull of the Great Barrier Reef, in an ecological feminist reading braided with the disfigurations and transfigurations associated with Lk. 9.28-36.

---

121. Heather Eaton, 'Ecofeminist Theologies in the Age of Climate Crisis', *Feminist Theology* 29, no. 3 (2021), pp. 209–19 (218–19).

Chapter 10

THE GREAT BARRIER REEF AND READING TOWARDS ACTIVISM: TRANSFIGURATIONS AND DISFIGURATIONS

In Australia, scientists have wept to see huge swathes of coral in the Great Barrier Reef bleached.[1] The reef, at 2300 km long with an area of 344,400 sq. km, is roughly the size of Germany, half the size of Texas; it is Sea Country for over seventy Traditional Owner groups.[2] First Peoples carry customary stories of the Reef and continue to care for their Sea Country.[3] At odds with First Nations' epistemologies is a colonial capitalist logic of extractivism.[4] The extractivist culture of late capitalism

---

1. Crispin Hull, 'I Saw the Great Barrier Reef Die Last Weekend and I Wept', *The Age* (11 March 2017), available online: http://www.theage.com.au/comment/i-saw-the-great-barrier-reef-die-last-weekend-and-i-wept-20170310-guu0r0.html (accessed 12 November 2019).

2. Australian Government, Great Barrier Reef Marine Park Authority (GBRMPA) website, available online: http://www.gbrmpa.gov.au/ (accessed 12 November 2019), esp. the page on 'Traditional Owners of the Great Barrier Reef', GBRMPA, available online: https://www.gbrmpa.gov.au/our-partners/traditional-owners/traditional-owners-of-the-great-barrier-reef (accessed 20 July 2021).

3. Government programmes now employ Indigenous Rangers to protect the Reef, and the Great Barrier Reef Foundation, a philanthropic programme, foregrounds support programmes for First Nations as custodians of the Reef. Government and philanthropic programmes which foreground First Nations' experience and perspectives, however, remain to greater or lesser degrees within a colonial framework that limits effective recognition of Traditional Owner knowledges and sovereignty as central to the health of the Reef. Australian Government, 'Indigenous Rangers Protecting the Great Barrier Reef' (27 April 2016), National Indigenous Australians Agency, available online: https://www.indigenous.gov.au/news-and-media/stories/indigenous-rangers-protecting-great-barrier-reef-0 (accessed 15 July 2021); Great Barrier Reef Foundation, 'Traditional Owner Reef Protection', available online: https://www.barrierreef.org/what-we-do/reef-trust-partnership/traditional-owner-reef-protection (accessed 15 July 2021).

4. For a historical perspective on exploitative utilitarian attitudes to the Reef, see Rohan Lloyd, '"Wealth of the reef": The Entanglement of Economic and Environmental Values in Early Twentieth Century Representations of the Great Barrier Reef', *Melbourne Historical Journal* 43, no. 1 (January 2015), pp. 40–62.

that underscores Mountaintop Removal Mining in the Appalachians, discussed in the previous chapter, also impinges on the Reef, not only through the impacts of shipping in relation to particular mining projects, but more particularly through the flow-on effects of climate change and the resultant strain on the capacity of coral to flourish in warming oceans.[5]

The Great Barrier Reef is listed on the UNESCO World Heritage List.[6] In June 2021, a draft item for the July meeting of UNESCO World Heritage Committee recommended the Great Barrier Reef be 'inscribed' on the 'List of World Heritage in Danger'.[7] The Australian Government responded quickly to challenge the 'in danger' assessment; in turn, specialists in coral reef studies challenged the government response.[8] By late July 2021, the Federal Minister for Environment, Sussan Ley, had successfully lobbied enough nations to get the decision on the 'in

---

5. Andreas Dietzel, Michael Bode, Sean R. Connolly and Terry P. Hughes, 'Long-term Shifts in the Colony Size Structure of Coral Populations along the Great Barrier Reef', *Proceedings of the Royal Society B: Biological Sciences* 287, no. 1936 (14 October 2020), pp. 1–9, available online: https://royalsocietypublishing.org/doi/10.1098/rspb.2020.1432 (accessed 19 July 2021); Daniela M. Ceccarelli, Richard D. Evans, Murray Logan, Philippa Mantel, Marji Puotinen, Caroline Petus, Garry R. Russ and David H. Williamson, 'Long-term Dynamics and Drivers of Coral and Macroalgal Cover on Inshore Reef of the Great Barrier Reef Marine Park', *Ecological Applications* 20, no. 1 (2020), pp. 1–20 (15), available online: https://doi.org/10.1002/eap.2008. On the flow-on effects for fish of climate change disturbances on the Reef, see J. R. Lowe, D. H. Williamson, D. M. Ceccarelli, R. D. Evans and G. R. Russ, 'Environmental Disturbance Events Drive Declines in Juvenile Wrasse Biomass on Inshore Coral Reef of the Great Barrier Reef', *Environmental Biology of Fishes* 103 (2020), pp. 1279–93, available online: https://doi.org/10.1007/s10641-020-01022-2.

6. UNESCO, Great Barrier Reef, World Heritage List, available online: https://whc.unesco.org/en/list/154/ (accessed 12 July 2021).

7. UNESCO, 'State of Conservation of Properties Inscribed on the World Heritage List', World Heritage Committee, extended forty-fourth session, Fuzhou (China), online meeting, 16–31 July 2021, Item 7B of the Provisional Agenda, WHC/21/44.COM/7B.Add (Paris, 21 June 2021), pp. 83–7, available online: https://whc.unesco.org/archive/2021/whc21-44com-7B.Add-en.pdf (accessed 12 July 2021).

8. 'Environment Minister Says Government Will Challenge UNESCO Move to List Great Barrier Reef as "in danger"', ABC News (22 June 2021), available online: https://www.abc.net.au/news/2021-06-22/environment-minister-great-barrier-reef-listed-in-danger/100233088 (accessed 12 July 2021); Terry Hughes, Jon C. Day and Ove Hoegh-Guldberg, 'Is Australia Really Doing Enough for the Great Barrier Reef? Why Criticisms of UNESCO's "in danger" Recommendation Don't Stack up', *The Conversation* (30 June 2021), available online: https://theconversation.com/is-australia-really-doing-enough-for-the-great-barrier-reef-why-criticisms-of-unescos-in-danger-recommendation-dont-stack-up-163641 (accessed 12 July 2021).

danger' listing deferred until 2022.⁹ It is hard not to read this behaviour, including the lobbying of oil-rich nations, as cynical and short-sighted in the context of both the health of the Reef and the long-term effects of climate change. At a webinar on 7 July 2021, Reef campaigner David Cazzulino, with marine scientists and activists, Drs Lissa Schindler and Selina Ward defended the proposed UNESCO 'in danger' listing and appealed to love as a human response to the aesthetic quality of the Great Barrier Reef; such love, they implied, should prompt action on the Reef's behalf.[10]

For some, the story of the Reef is a story not only of precarity but also of resilience. It is a place where stories intersect: grief at damage, evidenced by mass coral bleaching, coalesces around wonder at the variety of the Reef's more-than-human lives and beings, entanglements and agencies, including its role as a teacher in a time of climate change.[11] The beauty in the colours of the Reef and the loss of colour in bleached regions appeal to our sense of sight, as both lure and petition. A focus on sight is key to this chapter, and my co-engagement between the contemporary material context of the Great Barrier Reef in a time of climate change and an ancient text, the Transfiguration episode as told by Luke (9.28-36). The linking concept for me is the changed appearances of the Reef and the Lukan Jesus, and the way these speak to each other across millennia. The chapter will move between the two by way of an ecological feminist materialist aesthetics of reading, a braided reading as outlined in my opening chapter. As discussed in previous chapters, an ecological materialist account includes not only the lively materiality of more-than-human others, but creaturely (including human) entanglements in their (and our) material situations.

9. Graham Readfearn, 'World Heritage Committee Agrees Not to Place Great Barrier Reef on "in danger" List', *The Guardian* (24 July 2021), available online. https://www.theguardian.com/environment/2021/jul/23/world-heritage-committee-agrees-not-to-place-great-barrier-reef-on-in-danger-list (accessed 26 July 2021); Michael Slezak, 'Australia Avoids Great Barrier Reef Global Embarrassment, but the Dangers of Climate Change Remain for the Reef', ABC News (24 July 2021), available online: https://www.abc.net.au/news/2021-07-24/australia-avoids-great-barrier-reef-global-embarrassment/100319950 (accessed 26 July 2021).

10. Australian Marine Conservation Society (AMCS), 'Fact Check: Reef World Heritage in Danger?' (event listing for 7 July 2021), available online: https://www.marineconservation.org.au/events/fact-check-reef-world-heritage-in-danger/ (accessed 15 July 2021); the video can be viewed via AMCS Facebook page, https://www.facebook.com/australianmarine/videos/365131468367465 (accessed 15 July 2021). In response to questions, Ward stated that bleaching events were not normal prior to 1979 and were definitely related to climate change.

11. E.g., a review of reef studies suggests the role of reefs as teachers despite, and because of, their marginal status when faced with temperature extremes: J. A. Burt, E. F. Camp, I. C. Enochs, J. L. Johansen, K. M. Morgan, B. Riegl and A. S. Hoey, 'Insights from Extreme Coral Reefs in a Changing World', *Coral Reefs* 39 (2020), pp. 495–507, available online: https://doi.org/10.1007/s00338-020-01966-y.

Towards an ecological feminist aesthetics

Ecological poetics offers insights for ecological feminist hermeneutics. For example, an 'affective ecopoetics' expresses and calls forth 'participation in the vibrant materiality of the living Earth'.[12] An ecological feminist hermeneutics can share the qualities of an 'affective ecopoetics' through a co-engagement between ancient texts and specific contemporary material situations, including scientific, activist and poetic writings that respond to these situated materialities. This co-engagement can occur through a staged conversation such as the one I made towards the close of Chapter 4. The braided conversation in the current chapter is oriented towards a 'bio-inclusive political ecology of flourishing'.[13] As the scientists speaking in the AMCS webinar suggested in their appeal to love of the Great Barrier Reef, Kate Rigby affirms that 'places have the power to elicit and entrain human affections, informing our disposition and shaping our moral sentiments, just as times of day and times of year can inflect our mood'.[14] In this respect, the Great Barrier Reef in its vibrant materiality exercises moral power over us, even at a distance.

Wonder and grief

While those First Nations living in proximity to the Reef have first-hand knowledge of its power as a moral agent, and many tourists from this continent and abroad have had immediate experience of its aesthetic pull, many more of us both locally and across the planet have viewed the wonder of the Reef through the eyes of televised documentaries, most notably by celebrated naturalist, David Attenborough.[15] Similarly, human grief at the impact of climate change on the Reef can be prompted by vision of bleached corals, in person as in the case of marine scientists, or mediated through television or social media. While Attenborough's documentaries can evoke both wonder and grief in ways that promote affective connection with the reef, they have problematic aspects. Belinda Smaill, for example, critiques Attenborough's work for its embeddedness in capitalist consumerism and its tendency to globalize specific places and their complex ecosystems in ways that elide customary First Nations' and other local knowledges.[16] For poet Bonny Cassidy the documentary camera vision of the ocean is, for the child viewer, a particular form of enculturation

---

12. Kate Rigby, *Reclaiming Romanticism: Towards an Ecopoetics of Decolonization* (Environmental Culture Series; London: Bloomsbury, 2020), p. 55.

13. Rigby, *Reclaiming Romanticism*, p. 54.

14. Rigby, *Reclaiming Romanticism*, p. 56.

15. *David Attenborough's Reef: An Interactive Journey* (interactive online; Atlantic Productions, 2018), available online: https://attenboroughsreef.com/ (accessed 13 July 2021).

16. Belinda Smaill, 'Historicising David Attenborough's Nature: Nation, Continent, Country and Environment', *Celebrity Studies* (2020), pp. 1–22 (13, 16), doi: 10.1080/19392397.2020.1855995.

that both connects and distances the viewer from the oceanic subject.[17] The poet intentionally 'write[s] out' this childhood enculturation in her work *Final Theory*.[18] In the course of a long poem sequence, Cassidy makes the relation of the camera to beauty, climate change, place, colonization and possible (post-)human futures more nuanced than the documentary form allows. The rhythms and images which she employs call forth grief, wonder and hope more subtly than the resonant-voiced, breathy enthusiasm of Attenborough, which nonetheless evokes wonder, expresses love for his more-than-human subjects and to this extent communicates their moral power.

In the genre of Attenborough's documentaries, the series *Australia Remastered* built around archives held by the Australian Broadcasting Commission is presented and narrated by Arrente and Arabana actor Aaron Pedersen.[19] The episode on the Great Barrier Reef is notable for its emphasis on more-than-human agency, importantly the agency of coral polyps in the ongoing formation of the Reef.[20] The emphasis on the agency of the coral polyps and other inhabitants of the Reef echoes epistemologies shared by First Nations throughout this continent. Such knowledges highlight relationship and reciprocity, embedded in understandings and practices of kinship, in which care for Country is shared with more than humans.[21] The kinds of ecological wonder and grief which I am considering in relation to the Great Barrier Reef are, for First Peoples, enmeshed in this more-than-human relationality.

Human self-understanding, informed by experiential, cultural and scientific knowledges of the 'reciprocity and relatedness' of all things, can evoke both wonder and activism.[22] As noted at the close of the previous chapter, ecological feminists need to partner critique and resistance with 'radical' wonder and reverence for the pulsating materiality of Earth and cosmos.[23] Wonder reflects a 'feeling for the

---

17. Bonny Cassidy, *Final Theory* (Artarmon, NSW: Giramondo, 2014), p. 1.

18. Cassidy, *Final Theory*, p. 1.

19. *Australia Remastered: Wild Treasures – Great Barrier Reef* (presented by Aaron Pedersen; produced by Wild Bear Entertainment in Association with the Australian Broadcasting Corporation, 2020), ABC iView, available online: https://iview.abc.net.au/video/DO1841H001S00 (accessed 13 July 2021). Arrente and Arabana Country is inland, in what are known colonially as South Australia and the Northern Territory, and are not to my knowledge directly related to Traditional Owner groups for the Reef.

20. *Wild Treasures – Great Barrier Reef*.

21. See, e.g., the lucid manifesto, from a lawyer and writer from the Palyku people of the Pilbara area of Western Australia: Ambelin Kwaymullina, *Living on Stolen Land* (Broome, WA: Magabala Books, 2020), esp. pp. 17–27.

22. Anne Marie Dalton, 'The Great Work in a Sacred Universe: The Role of Science in Berry's Visionary Proposal', in *The Intellectual Journey of Thomas Berry: Imagining the Earth Community* (ed. Heather Eaton; Lanham, NY: Lexington Books, 2014), pp. 173–93 (190).

23. Heather Eaton, 'Ecofeminist Theologies in the Age of Climate Crisis', *Feminist Theology* 29, no. 3 (2021), pp. 209–19 (218–19).

organism'; arising from the exercise of close attention, ecologically attuned wonder and grief occur in dynamic relation.[24]

Colour and a material ecstatics

Wonder and grief together have their ground in matter and material-corporeal perception. Through the senses, I perceive both the wonderous beauty of the Reef and its fragility. Sensory perception is a mode of participation 'in the articulated presence of things'; entering into a relationship with material things I am 'told something by them'.[25] The more than human goes out from itself, inviting more-than-human (including human) perception. An ecological aesthetics recognizes the 'ecstatics' of the natural world and, as a corollary, the perception through which I 'enter a common actuality' with things.[26]

The phenomenon of colour bridges material ecstatics and more-than-human perception, since colour is relational and has impacts on affect.[27] Colour 'is a phenomenon between subject and object'; it is a reality 'in which the visible and the seeing eye unite'.[28] The sense of sight opens me 'to the world's chromatic aliveness'.[29] But I can meet colour in its radiance or beauty as also a marker of toxicity and damage; for Serpil Oppermann the 'aesthetic experience' of colour 'transcends the passive appreciation of nature and becomes a multisensorial as well as a cognitive interaction with the material world from the human perspective'.[30] Together with, and helping shape, 'an ethical sensibility', this multivalent perception of colour can prompt moral responsibility.[31] The vibrantly colourful more-than-human community and, at times and in significant places, colour-drained corals of the Great Barrier Reef address me in such a way through colour. Aesthetic appreciation of the beauty that might evoke wonder presses me not simply to stay with the appealing. I must recognize, too, 'the maps of intersections between the beautiful and the perilously colorful [or colourless]

---

24. Evelyn Fox Keller, *A Feeling for the Organism: The Life and Work of Barbara McClintock* (New York: Freeman, 1983); Celia Deane-Drummond, *Wonder and Wisdom: Conversations in Science, Spirituality, and Theology* (Philadelphia: Templeton Foundation Press, 2006), esp. pp. 43–51. For Deane-Drummond, focused in the crucified and resurrected Christ, ecologically attuned wonder gives way to grief which in turn becomes wonder.

25. Gernot Böhme, *The Aesthetics of Atmospheres* (ed. Jean-Paul Thibaud; Abingdon: Routledge, 2017), p. 96.

26. Böhme, *Aesthetics*, pp. 95, 97.

27. Rigby, *Reclaiming Romanticism*, p. 56.

28. Böhme, *Aesthetics*, p. 93.

29. Serpil Oppermann, 'Nature's Colors: A Prismatic Materiality in the Natural/Cultural Realms', in *Ecocritical Aesthetics: Language, Beauty, and the Environment* (ed. Peter Quigley and Scott Slovic; Proquest Ebook Central; Bloomington: Indiana University Press, 2018), pp. 157–71 (158).

30. Oppermann, 'Nature's Colors', pp. 158, 166.

31. Oppermann, 'Nature's Colors', p. 158.

elements', because, as Oppermann holds, 'what is at stake is the ecological health of our planet and its naturecultures'.[32]

Beauty and alterity

Use of a term like 'natureculture' expresses two key things in the current epoch: first, an ecocritical acknowledgement that more than humans, for example, humpback whales, dugongs and green turtles, have cultures of their own, expressed in their habits of community, migration, nesting and song; second, admission that anthropogenic impacts are such that the natural world everywhere, to greater and lesser degrees, has been impacted by human habits. Moreover, while humans and our habits are not external to 'nature', most of the natural world is not itself human: there is 'the nature that we ourselves are not' and 'the nature that we ourselves are'.[33] Attention to our perceptions of the alterity of more-than-human co-beings invites recognition, too, of our embeddedness with these others in our local habitats and the wider Earth community.

Here, beauty is shared.[34] Perceptions of beauty both shift and persist, and this is not simply among human perceivers; the repeatability of floral forms that lure bees suggests that the perception of the beautiful can persist for other creatures and is not simply temporally or culturally dependant. The perception of beauty answers human transience with joy in our very existence.[35] Beauty meets us, too, in the alterity of the everyday.[36] For example, Werner Bigell explores perceptions of beauty described by organic farmers in Thailand and tenders of allotment gardens in Berlin, Germany. He finds that rather than being removed from daily life, beauty is a feature of the everyday.[37] The farmers and gardeners perceive beauty in community, in soils and plants that provide food, in the diversity of produce and in the 'community-building rituals' of meals.[38] Beauty connects his interlocutors 'to contexts of community, materiality, spirituality, and history'.[39] This occurs through 'involvement' in their more-than-human habitats, where alternative imaginaries take shape.[40] Shifting from philosophical and phenomenological discourses which emphasize the alterity of the beautiful, Bigell argues for 'a material form of transcendence', experienced, for example, when '[T]he gardens in which food is grown are themselves the afterglow of a social imaginary, as are the housing blocks in which many gardeners live'.[41]

32. Oppermann, 'Nature's Colors', p. 166.
33. Rigby, *Reclaiming Romanticism*, pp. 61–2.
34. Böhme, *Aesthetics*, p. 57.
35. Böhme, *Aesthetics*, p. 64.
36. Werner Bigell, 'Beauty as Ideological and Material Transcendence', in *Ecocritical Aesthetics* (ed. Peter Quigley and Scott Slovic; Proquest Ebook Central; Bloomington: Indiana University Press, 2018), pp. 187–200 (189, 195).
37. Bigell, 'Beauty', p. 195.
38. Bigell, 'Beauty', p. 195.
39. Bigell, 'Beauty', p. 195.
40. Bigell, 'Beauty', p. 198.
41. Bigell, 'Beauty', p. 198.

In contrast to 'a transparent world of servility' produced by capitalism, the alterity associated with beauty exists in the imagination and creation of different eco-socially nurturing futures.[42] More-than-human beauty can itself be understood as 'the locus of a radical alterity' that has resisted 'assimilation into the prevailing social order of domination'.[43] Beyond human perceptions of beauty, the relation between beauty and alterity in the material liveliness of more than humans stands in itself as both resistance to extractivist imaginaries and, as I will argue in conversation with the Lukan Transfiguration account, a summons to perceive otherwise.[44]

Ecological feminist hermeneutic weavings

The summons to perceive in ways that counter oppressive extractivist worldviews underlies the ecological materialism I have put forward in this book. Towards the close of Chapter 1, I sketched an ecological feminist hermeneutic practice that works in conjunction with new materialist perspectives as a kind of weaving or braided reading. Such hermeneutic practice draws on multiple sources to create biblical interpretations both critically and conversationally. I practise an ecological feminist hermeneutics as weaving with an ear to customs of historical and literary criticism of Lk. 9.28-36, and in conversation with social, scientific and poetic articulations of the situated materialities of the Great Barrier Reef.

A major gap is my ignorance of First Nations' knowledges in relation to the Great Barrier Reef.[45] Properly, such knowledge is not mine as a settler writer, but the centrality of Country, in this case the Sea Country of the Great Barrier Reef, as a living community, is something I hold in this reading. An article in which Bawaka Country (in North East Arnhem Land, Australia) is cited as first co-author suggests a paradigm for collaborative scholarship beyond my practice but informing the concept of braided reading as more than human.[46] For now, it is my

42. Bigell, 'Beauty', p. 199.

43. Rigby, *Reclaiming Romanticism*, p. 57. Here, Rigby is engaging with the thought of Theodore Adorno.

44. This is the summons I hear when I read Jean-Louis Chrétien's writing on beauty and suffering as a 'visible voice' that prompts in us a dedicated and enduring commitment to provide a kind of sanctuary through what he calls 'the asylum of our own voice'. Jean-Louis Chrétien, *The Call and the Response* (trans. Anne A. Davenport; New York: Fordham University Press, 2004 [Fre. 1992]), p. 43.

45. For some First Nations perspectives on the Great Barrier Reef, see Australian Earth Laws Alliance, 'Interview with Gudju Gudju about the Great Barrier Reef', YouTube, available online: https://youtu.be/ntKI2bLKRvY (accessed 13 August 2021); Seed Indigenous Youth Climate Network, 'Our Stories Are Connected to the Reef', YouTube, available online: https://youtu.be/lr1Zx2ZQ_WA (accessed 13 August 2021).

46. Bawaka Country, Sarah Wright, Sandie Suchet-Pearson, Kate Lloyd, Laklak Burarrwanga, Ritjilili Ganambarr, Merrkiyaway Ganambarr-Stubbs, Banbapuy Ganambarr and Djawundil Maymuru, 'Working with and Learning from Country: Decentring Human Author-ity', *Cultural Geographies* 22, no. 2 (2015), pp. 269–83, available online: https://doi.org/10.1177%2F1474474014539248.

hope that respect for place – the Sea Country of the Great Barrier Reef as it speaks with the mountain of Lk. 9.28-36 in my reading – carries respect for First Nations' sovereignties and knowledges in relation to the Reef.

The Lukan Transfiguration (Luke 9.28-36) and The Great Barrier Reef

Imagine for a moment, the Great Barrier Reef already tens to hundreds of thousands of years in formation when the Lukan text is taking shape around two millennia ago. What is a biblical text to a reef? What oceanic flows and sea creatures moved between the ancient Mediterranean and the southern oceans? What birds? Older still are the mountains which the Lukan author and the traditions the text draws on imagines. Origen, reading within two centuries of the formation of Lk. 9.28-36 places the mountain as Mt Tabor, as does Cyril of Jerusalem in the fourth century CE; others think Mt Hermon more likely.[47] Hebrew Bible and Septuagint traditions of Moses on Mt Sinai echo in the text (esp. Ex. 24.15-18; 34.2, 29-35). Parts of Tabor and Hermon are limestone, dating respectively to the Cretaceous and Jurassic periods.[48] 'Millions of years in the making' though in its present state relatively young, the Reef forms its own deposits of limestone.[49] Mts Tabor, Hermon and Sinai each have associations with the sacred, beyond and possibly preceding Hebrew and Christian traditions.[50] There is no certainty about the location of Mt Sinai or concerning whether Mts Tabor, Hermon or another particular place, if any, was intended by the Lukan author or the earlier traditions on which the author drew. Nonetheless, the material liveliness of mountains, their

---

47. Amy-Jill Levine and Ben Witherington III, *The Gospel of Luke* (New Cambridge Bible Commentary; Cambridge: Cambridge University Press, 2018), p. 259; Michael Avi-Yonah and Abraham J. Brawer, 'Tabor, Mount', in *Encyclopaedia Judaica* (ed. Michael Berenbaum and Fred Skolnik; 2nd edn; vol. 19, Detroit, MI: Macmillan Reference USA, 2007), pp. 426–7, *Gale eBooks*, link.gale.com/apps/doc/CX2587519500/GVRL?u=monash&sid=bookmark-GVRL&xid=905a311e (accessed 20 July 2021).

48. Avi-Yonah and Brawer, 'Tabor, Mount', p. 427; Michael Avi-Yonah and Efraim Orni, 'Hermon, Mount', in *Encyclopaedia Judaica* (ed. Michael Berenbaum and Fred Skolnik; 2nd edn; vol. 9: Detroit, MI: Macmillan Reference USA, 2007), pp. 30–1, *Gale eBooks*, link.gale.com/apps/doc/CX2587508811/GVRL?u=monash&sid=bookmark-GVRL&xid=00c74182 (accessed 20 July 2021).

49. 'How to Build a "Great" Barrier Reef', Australian Academy of Science (website), available online: https://www.science.org.au/curious/earth-environment/how-build-great-barrier-reef (accessed 21 July 2021).

50. Avi-Yonah and Brawer, 'Tabor, Mount', p. 427; Avi-Yonah and Orni, 'Hermon, Mount', p. 31; Ora Lipschitz, S. David Sperling and Shimon Gibson, 'Sinai, Mount', *Encyclopaedia Judaica* (ed. Michael Berenbaum and Fred Skolnik; 2nd edn; vol. 18; Detroit, MI: Macmillan Reference USA, 2007), pp. 627–9. *Gale eBooks*, link.gale.com/apps/doc/CX2587518631/GVRL?u=monash&sid=bookmark-GVRL&xid=330b2ff9 (accessed 20 July 2021).

rocky solidities and porosities, their soils and plants, their capacities to channel rain and snowmelt underscore their appearance in texts such as Lk. 9.28, as does the tradition of mountains as sacred places of encounter with the divine. Can I understand mountains as more-than-human forebears and progenitors of biblical texts and traditions, alongside the atmosphere that carries the voices of oral communication, the plants that provide matter for the production of written texts, and the many human communities whose songs and stories inform a text?

As noted in the previous chapter, a kind of biblical animism enlivens metaphors of mountains. In biblical traditions, mountains are described as holy; they are places of refuge and lifegiving; they also suffer destruction. But they are not passive. Mountains respond actively to Yhwh (e.g. Judg. 5.5; Pss. 97.5, 114.4-6). Psalmists and prophets call to mountains, and call on mountains to answer with song and praise (Pss. 68.15-16; 148; Isa. 44.23; 49.13). Ezekiel must 'prophesy to the mountains of Israel, and say: O mountains of Israel, hear the word of Yhwh' (Ezek. 36.1). Mountains will be active in responding to the returning exiles (Isa. 55.12; Ezek. 36.8). Mountains are not simply settings for divine-human relationship but part of more-than-human meetings that include but are not limited to human and divine characters.

As he does in Lk. 6.12, in 9.28 Jesus goes into the sacred space of a mountain to pray. The mountain is significant as an Earth place, grounded but touching sky, the cosmic home of the divine. While the text tends to use the mountain as symbolic setting, the liveliness of the mountain in its interplay with atmospheric conditions draws the cloud towards itself (9.34) and makes this scene of shifting human perception and divine-human encounter one of more-than-human relatedness. An unspecified mountain receives a visit of four climbers, the Lukan Jesus and his companions, Peter, John and James (9.28). Why is the mountain not named? Where are women?

I recall that in Judg. 11.38 an unnamed young woman/a girl, known by her association with her father Jephthah, goes onto the mountains with her female companions to mourn the life-giving she will yield when her father sacrifices her to honour his foolhardy vow to Yhwh. In a first-century CE Jewish text, Pseudo-Philo's *Biblical Antiquities*, the author names her Seila, 'the one asked for'. Of her mourning, Seila says she will 'go into the mountains' and 'stay in the hills and walk among the rocks' (*L.A.B.* 40.3).[51] Not only does she plan to share her mourning with her human companions, but she expects her more-than-human associates to respond:

> I will pour out my tears there and tell of the sadness of my youth. And the trees of the field will weep for me, and the beast of the field will lament over me. (*L.A.B.* 40.3)

51. D. J. Harrington, 'Pseudo-Philo: A New Translation and Introduction', in *The Old Testament Pseudepigrapha* (ed. James H. Charlesworth; vol. 2: Expansions of the 'Old Testament' and Legends, Wisdom and Philosophical Literature, Prayers, Psalms, and Odes, Fragments of Lost Judeo-Hellenistic Works; Garden City, NY: Doubleday, 1985), pp. 297–377 (353).

In the mountains, she then calls:

> Hear, you mountains, my lamentations;
> and pay attention, you hills, to the tears of my eyes;
> and be witnesses, you rocks, of the weeping of my soul ...
>
> You trees, bow down your branches and weep over my youth,
> You beasts of the forests, come and bewail... (*L.A.B.* 40.5, 7).

It is as if from the mountains, her lamentation will be heard by the plants and animals in the fields and forests below and, as they join in, her mourning is more-than-human. The mountains moreover witness her declaration – 'I will tell the mountains' – not only of her grief but also of her decision to accept her death willingly (*L.A.B.* 40.3). The narrator has explicitly placed Seila alongside Isaac as a willing sacrifice in the Akedah tradition (*L.A.B.* 40.2).[52] In the narrative, the divine voice announces that Seila will 'fall into the bosom of her mothers' (*L.A.B.* 40.4). Against the patriarchal violence of a father's attachment to his vow and divine critique of, but nonetheless assent to, this violence, Seila's more-than-human outpouring of grief is focused around female embodiment and the kinship of women (*L.A.B.* 40.3-7). For an ecological feminist hermeneutics, this interplay of more-than-human grief and patriarchal violence against women, answered by a more-than-human relatedness entwined with the kinship of women, is not incidental. Nor is its apparent absence from the gospel Transfiguration accounts.

In introducing Pseudo-Philo's Seila and her going into the mountains, I am not suggesting any direct link with the Lukan text. Rather, I want to let her visit to mountains and the more-than-human prayer of lamentation which she initiates stand in conversation with the mountain visit of the Lukan Jesus in Lk. 9.28-36. I will consider below the extent to which the Akedah tradition can also be a conversation partner to this Lukan text.

Preceding the Transfiguration account, after praying alone the Lukan Jesus asks the disciples near him 'who do the crowds say I am?' (9.18). This question of identity and perception carries into a series of sayings: the promise-warning of suffering and loss (9.22-25) and the warning about being ashamed of Jesus' teaching (9.26). Immediately before the Transfiguration episode, the Lukan Jesus says, 'some standing here ... will not taste death before they *see* the reign (βασιλεία) of G-d' (9.27, my emphasis). For Dorothy Lee, 'the way of the cross

---

52. See the discussion in Cheryl Anne Brown, *No Longer Be Silent: First Century Jewish Portraits of Biblical Women* (Gender and the Biblical Tradition; Louisville: Westminster John Knox, 1992), pp. 95-9; see also, Tavis A. Bohlinger, 'The Akedah in Pseudo-Philo: A Paradigm of Divine-Human Reciprocity', *JSP* 25, no. 3 (2016), pp. 189-227 (193-4, 214-25). See, too, Phyllis Trible, *Texts of Terror: Literary-Feminist Readings of Biblical Narratives* (London: SCM, 1992), pp. 92-116. While Pseudo-Philo gives a greater role to Seila, the text is still terrible, in that the sacrifice proceeds, as it does in Judges 11.

and the transfiguration... are joined by the saying about G-d's reign or kingdom (*basileia*, 9.27)'.⁵³ The sense of sight is a further link.

After the Lukan Jesus and his companions ascend the mountain, an immediacy to the sense of seeing shifts the flow of Luke's story. 'And while he was praying, the appearance of his face changed, and his clothes became dazzling white' (9.29). Where Mark uses the term 'he was transfigured/transformed' (μετεμορφώθη, Mk. 9.2), Luke describes the perceived change to the appearance (τὸ εἶδος) of Jesus' face (τοῦ προσώπου αὐτοῦ), when it becomes other/different (ἕτερον). Perception is critical here; in the narrative, the three disciples (and perhaps the narrator, and by extension the writer and readers) perceive Jesus differently.⁵⁴ They recognize an alterity in him, but more particularly in their relationship with him. Second Temple Jewish traditions suggest that the description 'the appearance of his face' (τὸ εἶδος τοῦ προσώπου αὐτοῦ) can be understood as evoking the 'image of G-d'.⁵⁵ Jesus' clothing, too, alters, becoming dazzling white. The passive suggests divine action. The material change in the colour of Jesus' garments echoes biblical vision accounts and apocalyptic texts.⁵⁶ At this mountain place of more-than-human (including divine-human) meeting, human perception encounters – in the sights of Jesus' body (signified by his face) and his clothing – a material alterity, at an intersection of Earth and skies/heaven.

The Great Barrier Reef

I think of Queensland and the Reef, the references to Paradise, the advertisements 'Beautiful one day, perfect the next' and the shift of perception as climate change and extractivist interests such as Adani's coal mining infrastructure and transport impact the Reef.⁵⁷ In 2018, *Reef 2050*, an Australian Government long-term sustainability plan for the reef, was signed by then Minister for the Environment and Energy, The Honourable Josh Frydenberg MP, currently Treasurer, and The Honourable Leeanne Enoch MP, Minister for the Environment and the Great Barrier Reef, Minister for Science and Minister for the Arts.⁵⁸ The

53. Dorothy Lee, *Transfiguration* (London: Continuum, 2004), p. 67.

54. François Bovon, *Luke 1: A Commentary on the Gospel of Luke 1:1–9:50* (trans. Christine M. Thomas; Hermeneia, 63A; ed. Helmut Koester; Accordance electronic edn; Minneapolis: Fortress, 2002), p. 375.

55. Andrei A. Orlov, *Demons of Change: Antagonism and Apotheosis in Jewish and Christian Apocalypticism* (eBook; Albany: SUNY, 2020), ch. 1.

56. Bovon, *Luke 1*, p. 375.

57. Annastacia, Palaszczuk, Hon., and Kate Jones, Hon., 'Queensland STILL "Beautiful One Day, Perfect The Next"', Joint Statement (Sunday, 1 April 2018), Queensland Government website, available online: http://statements.qld.gov.au/Statement/2018/4/1/queensland-still-beautiful-one-day-perfect-the-next (accessed 12 November 2019).

58. Australian Government, *Reef 2050 Long Term Sustainability Plan – July 2018*, available online: http://www.environment.gov.au/system/files/resources/35e55187-b76e-4aaf-a2fa-376a65c89810/files/reef-2050-long-term-sustainability-plan-2018.pdf (accessed 12 November 2019).

report comments that despite the Reef's resilience, 'the overall outlook for the Reef is poor, has worsened since 2009 and is expected to further deteriorate unless actions to build its resilience, and reduce pressures, are expanded and accelerated'.[59] The report then nominates the effects of climate change as the gravest and heightening 'threat' to the health of the Reef.[60] As ocean temperatures rise as a result of global heating, so will there be 'more frequent mass coral bleaching'; moreover, 'increasing ocean acidification will restrict coral growth and survival'.[61] Referencing loss of coral colour in mass bleaching events, Kristin Hannaford makes a political protest cry in her villanelle, 'Coral not Coal', with the repeated lines

> coral polyps, like ashen fingers raised,
> whiten as our politicians betray.[62]

Caitlin Maling engages with the visible, linking colonization and the seen in her poem, 'Recommendations for a Western Australian Coastal Pastoral':

> 12. From space, two things about Australia are visible: the clearing line–a yellow chevron through the wheat belt, and the Barrier Reef–dark green in lighter green.
> A. The Reef is slowly lightening.[63]

In nineteen parts, the prose poem is a list linking ocean and imported agriculture, through scientific and historical information, and reflections on how colours are seen through the colonial eye. Scientific and poetic perceptions of the Great Barrier Reef register changes in health signalled by whitening that stands in contrast to representations of the Reef as organically lively, beautifully colourful, a tourist paradise and natural wonder, 'a sight to see'.

---

59. Australian Government, *Reef 2050*, p. 3.
60. Australian Government, *Reef 2050*, p. 3.
61. Australian Government, *Reef 2050*, p. 3.
62. Kristin Hannaford, 'Coral not Coal', in *Hope for Whole: Poets Speak Up to Adani* (ed. Anne Elvey; eBook; Seaford, Vic.: Rosslyn Avenue Productions, 2018), p. 39; available online: https://plumwoodmountain.com/hope-for-whole-ebook/ (accessed 9 July 2021). Reproduced by permission of the author.
63. Caitlin Maling, 'Recommendations for a Western Australian Coastal Pastoral', in *Hope for Whole*, ed. Elvey, pp. 102–3; previously published in *Cordite* 54: No Theme V (May 2016), available online: http://cordite.org.au/poetry/notheme5/recommendations-for-a-western-australian-coastal-pastoral/ (accessed 13 July 2021). Reproduced with permission of the author. Maling's latest book of poetry is focused on the Great Barrier Reef and emerges from field work with marine scientists. Caitlin Maling, *Fish Work* (Crawley, WA: UWAP, 2021).

The call of the visible

In Lk. 9.30, the alteration of perception that occurred in 9.29 shifts. Beginning with 'and behold or look' (καὶ ἰδοὺ), suggesting an interruption or advent, the text tells that two men appear beside the Lukan Jesus. The narrator (and by implication Peter and his companions) identifies them as Moses and Elijah, linking Jesus with his Jewish ancestry through the Law and Prophets, the traditions of their corpses not being found, and their sacred mountain encounters.[64] They appear here in glory and they speak of Jesus' departure or exodus (ἔξοδος) which will be accomplished or fulfilled in Jerusalem (9.31). This echo of the liberation through the Exodus event is here joined to Jesus' suffering and execution in Jerusalem. In 9.51 he embraces this path when he sets his face (τὸ πρόσωπον) to go towards Jerusalem.

Despite their sleepiness, perhaps a response to the overwhelming affective impact of the experience, Peter and his companions see the glory, and the beauty (signalled by the adjective καλός) of this place-based encounter ('it is good for us to be *here*', 9.33, my emphasis). There is an apophatic aspect to Peter's response to this alterity: 'not knowing what he said' (9.33). A different kind of unknowing is at work in the face of climate-related damage to the Reef. In his 'A Sonnet at the Edge of the Reef', Craig Santos Perez tells of a visit to the Waikiki Aquarium with his young daughter; together they see and touch the exhibits and hear the story of coral spawning annually, registering the beauty of the process.[65] The poem conveys the goodness of their being there. Afterwards, at home the parents read a book, titled *The Great Barrier Reef*, to their child. The poet says that they don't mention the bleaching of corals and asks if their silence is 'a kind of shelter'.[66]

The scene shifts again

Drawn to the mountain, a cloud overshadows (ἐπεσκίαζεν) them, namely Jesus, and presumably Moses and Elijah, as well as Peter, John and James (9.34). The use of the verb to overshadow (ἐπισκιάζω) recalls Gabriel's announcement to the Lukan Mary in 1.35, 'the power of the Most High will overshadow (ἐπισκιάσει) you'. Later, in Acts 5.15, people bring the sick to be overshadowed (ἐπισκιάσῃ) by Peter's own shadow (ἡ σκιά). Divine power in Luke is life-giving, inter-relational and potentially shared. In the inter-relational moment of the cloud's arrival, the focus on sight (the seeing of the disciples and also the reader/hearer) shifts to voice – as invitation or imperative – from the overshadowing cloud: 'Listen to him' (9.35). As Michael Trainor comments, 'Communion with Earth's features [the cloud over the mountain] becomes the means by which God's voice speaks to the human community represented in Peter and his companions.'[67] As I have argued

---

64. Levine and Witherington, *Gospel of Luke*, p. 260.

65. Craig Santos Perez, *Habitat Threshold* (Oakland, CA: Omnidawn, 2020), p. 21.

66. Santos Perez, *Habitat Threshold*, p. 21.

67. Michael Trainor, *About Earth's Child: An Ecological Listening to the Gospel of Luke* (Earth Bible Commentary, 2; Sheffield: Sheffield Phoenix, 2012), p. 162.

elsewhere, this is a visible voice; in Luke's 'glorified Jesus, the face calls'.[68] With the reference to Jesus' execution in Jerusalem, glory and suffering meet in 9.28-36. This interplay of beauty and suffering, transfiguration and disfiguration, is alive in the call of the visible, requiring response.[69]

Transfigurations and disfigurations

In discussing the theology of the Transfiguration, Lee makes a distinction between transfiguration and disfiguration; the Transfiguration and Crucifixion are connected, and not only by contrast.[70] The coincidence since 1945 of the Feast of Transfiguration (fixed by Pope Calixtus III in 1457) and Hiroshima Day (6 August) has set up a poignant parallel that has resonance in addressing the biblical narratives of transfiguration themselves.[71] In the Lukan Transfiguration account there is forewarning of disfiguration, but the reference to departure or exodus (ἔξοδος) suggests that Jesus' anticipated execution is also a moment of freedom. For the more-than-human communities of the Great Barrier Reef, what transfigurations might emerge from the disfigurations related to climate change?

The *Reef 2050* report mentioned above posits that the survival of coral reefs is possible, but depends on 'whether the rising levels of greenhouse gases, in particular carbon dioxide, can be halted and reversed fast enough'; this means 'holding the global temperature increase to 1.5°C or less'.[72] The scientists on whose advice the report is based are likewise a voice that with the Reef calls. It is not the first time that activists have listened. Australian poet Judith Wright was at the forefront of the 1967 struggle to protect the reef when its complex ecology was threatened by oil drilling, a campaign that was catalyst for the formation of the Great Barrier Reef Marine Park.[73] Over the past several years, the Wangan and Jagalingou Family Council and a network of activists opposed to the proposed Adani (Bravus) coal mine in the Galilee Basin, North Queensland, and its related infrastructure at Abbott Point on the North Queensland coast, have been highlighting the threat to

---

68. Anne Elvey, *The Matter of the Text: Material Engagements between Luke and the Five Senses* (Sheffield: Sheffield Phoenix, 2011), p. 149; Chrétien, *Call and the Response*, p. 33.

69. Chrétien, *Call and the Response*, p. 43.

70. Lee, *Transfiguration*, p. 132.

71. Melbourne poet Peter Steele SJ makes this connection in a poem titled 'August 6th'. Cited in Colette Rayment, '"A Comet Streamed in Language Far Down Time": Poetry of Earth', *Spirit of Place: Source of the Sacred? 1998 Australian International Religion, Literature and the Arts Conference Proceedings* (Sydney Studies in Religion, 1998), pp. 187–95 (188–9), available online: https://openjournals.library.sydney.edu.au/index.php/SSR/article/view/12101 (accessed 6 August 2021).

72. Australian Government, *Reef 2050*, p. 3.

73. Judith Wright, *The Coral Battleground* (New edn; North Melbourne: Spinifex, 2014 [1977]).

the Great Barrier Reef, not only through the exacerbation of climate change that proposed mega coal mines represent, but also through sea traffic across the Reef as coal is shipped overseas.[74] Taking inspiration from Wright, a number of poets have spoken out against the Adani mine and its impact on the Reef.[75] Traditional owners, other activists and poets link colonial attitudes with the fate of the Reef and its capacity to serve its many creatures.

The Reef has been disfigured and with high probability will suffer further disfiguration in coming decades and centuries. This disfiguration repeats into a future, where damage may outstrip the Reef's resilience. It is a cry, much as the Wangan and Jagalingou Family Council's call for support for their campaign against mega coal mines in the Galilee Basin is a cry. I evoke in this reference to 'cry', the cry of the oppressed as an imperative turning the divine towards the suffering of the people, an imperative that calls forth the kind of response heard in Lk. 4.18-19.[76] Citing Isaiah, Luke envisions a kind of material freedom (ἄφεσις) from oppression (debt and slavery), that is also forgiveness characteristic of divine visitation.[77]

The visual dimension of disfiguration, for example, of mountain, reef or body can also be understood in relation to Levinasian ethics and its emphasis on the priority of the face. The face of the other is an epiphany precluding murder, because the encounter with the other makes murder an 'ethical impossibility'.[78] The face cries out.[79] Not only the glorified face, but also the disfigured face, calls – the face disfigured-transfigured, perhaps at the same time. This call presents challenges to biblical interpreters.

---

74. Wangan and Jagalingou Family Council, https://wanganjagalingou.com.au/ (accessed 26 July 2021); Stop Adani, available online: https://www.stopadani.com/ (accessed 27 May 2021); Ben Smee, 'Adani Coal Port Faces Possible "stop order" after Traditional Owners Object', *The Guardian* (5 July 2018), available online: https://www.theguardian.com/environment/2018/jul/05/adani-coal-port-faces-possible-stop-order-after-traditional-owners-object (accessed 12 November 2019).

75. Anne Elvey (ed.), *Hope for Whole: Poets Speak Up to Adani* (eBook; Seaford, Vic.: Rosslyn Avenue Productions, 2018), available online: https://plumwoodmountain.com/hope-for-whole-ebook/ (accessed 9 July 2021).

76. Walter Brueggemann, *The Prophetic Imagination* (2nd edn; Minneapolis: Augsburg Fortress, 2001); Jan Morgan, *Earth's Cry: Prophetic Ministry in a More-than-human World* (Preston, Vic.: Uniting Academic Press, 2013); Rigby, *Reclaiming Romanticism*, pp. 118, 124–5.

77. Anne Elvey, 'Can There Be a Forgiveness That Makes a Difference Ecologically? An Eco-materialist Account of Forgiveness as Freedom (ἄφεσις) in the Gospel of Luke', *Pacifica* 22, no. 2 (2009), pp. 148–70.

78. Emmanuel Lévinas, *Totality and Infinity: An Essay on Exteriority* (trans. Alphonso Lingis; Dordrecht: Kluwer Academic, 1991), p. 171; idem, *Of God Who Comes to Mind* (trans. Bettina Bergo; Stanford: Stanford University Press, 1998), pp. 162–3.

79. Lévinas, *Totality and Infinity*, p. 66.

In Gen. 22.2, the divine (Elohim) directs Abraham to take his beloved son, Isaac, into the land of Moriah and sacrifice him on a mountain there which Elohim will tell him. Abraham takes Isaac and the requirements for the sacrifice, and proceeds to the place Elohim has told him (Gen. 22.3); that Abraham must then look up to see the place emphasizes its elevation (Gen. 22.4). This familiar story is the basis of the Akedah tradition, the binding of Isaac, a story of horror; in saying 'Here I am' to Elohim's call (Gen. 22.1), a father consents to kill his son in sacrifice. The story echoes in Pseudo-Philo's telling of the sacrifice of Seila, the daughter of Jephthah (*L.A.B.* 40.2), and in Christian traditions of the death of Jesus of Nazareth. For Emmanuel Lévinas the critical ethical moment in this scene is when a messenger from Yhwh stays Abraham's hand (Gen. 22.11-12), shifting his perception of what is required for relationship with divinity.[80] For Jeffrey Stolle, it is Isaac himself who stops Abraham from killing him; in the face of Isaac, Abraham hears the imperative 'do not kill'.[81] The mountain is witness.

The sparing of Isaac is not the end of the story. Abraham finds a ram, and sacrifices it instead (Gen. 22.13). This sacrifice of a sheep echoes in the Lukan passion account. For Luke, the suffering and death of Jesus are part of a situational necessity (signalled by the terms δεῖ, ἔδει) found in the passion predictions throughout the narrative (9.22; 17.25; 24.5-7, 25-26) and in the requirement to sacrifice the Passover lamb in 22.7, a sacrifice with which the Lukan Jesus becomes both metaphorically and metonymically linked. The first of these passion predictions (9.22) occurs shortly before the Lukan Transfiguration account.

The voice from the cloud in Luke's Transfiguration account (9.35) parallels and contrasts with the voice from the sky (heaven) accompanied by a bird in the baptism account (3.22). In both accounts the voice announces the Lukan Jesus as 'my son'; in the Transfiguration account, the son is described as 'chosen' (ἐκλελεγμένος), while in the baptism narrative, he is 'the beloved' (ὁ ἀγαπητός). There is an aural reminder of the Akedah; in the Septuagint 'beloved' (ἀγαπητός) is used to modify 'son' (υἱός) three times, describing Isaac in relation to Abraham, in Gen. 22 (vv. 2, 12, 16 LXX).[82] Where both the Matthean and Markan transfiguration accounts describe Jesus as 'beloved', Luke has used 'chosen' (Mt. 17.5; Mk 9.7; Lk. 9.35). The description 'chosen' places the Lukan Jesus in the tradition of other chosen ones

---

80. Jeffrey Stolle, 'Levinas and the Akedah: An Alternative to Kiekegaard', *Philosophy Today* 45, no. 2 (Summer 2001), pp. 132–43 (138); Eric S. Nelson, 'Levinas and Kierkegaard: The Akedah, the Dao, and Aporetic Ethics', *Journal of Chinese Philosophy* 40, no. 1 (March 2013), pp. 164–84 (172). Note, too, the shift in the name for the divine from Elohim to Yhwh, suggesting the interweaving of two or more ancient traditions.

81. Stolle, 'Levinas and the Akedah', p. 138.

82. Bovon, *Luke 1,* p. 130. Here, Bovon, however, reads this echo as less significant that other possible associations, highlighting what he sees as a 'Christian intensification of the father-son relationship'.

whose divine election entailed suffering (see, esp. Pss 89.19, 106.23; Isa. 42.1).[83] Like Pseudo-Philo's Seila, Luke's Jesus assents to this suffering. But what of the sheep?

Drawing on Rabbinic traditions, Yvonne Sherwood suggests that the boy, Isaac, and the sheep are co-identified, and through their sacrificial death life multiplies grandly in the descendants of Abraham.[84] Pseudo-Philo's Seila stands in contrast, calling forth a more-than-human mourning of her life shortened before she can produce descendants. Sherwood identifies Isaac and Jesus in this logic of sacrifice, not only at the point of the Eucharistic transformation of matter, but more particularly at the nexus of human-animal distinction.[85] In the Lukan transfiguration, other animals seem absent, although the mountain of meeting is likely habitat for more than humans.

When she considers Lévinas's understanding of the face of the other as calling forth an ethical response, Deborah Bird Rose highlights the human focus of his approach.[86] Poignantly she asks if other creatures, companions and familiars, those whose extinction is imminent, those sacrificed to extractivist interests, also address us with a face. In the Lukan Transfiguration account, the face of Jesus is the focus of a shift of perception on the part of the disciples (and by extension communities of readers). The appearance of the face is other. With this alterity, a deeper attention is called forth. In the Lukan Transfiguration, the face, altered – its wonder and beauty, its anticipated disfiguration in suffering – calls.

The face of the Reef

Does the Reef have a face? The Reef has a multiplicity of faces: the complex, often beautiful, colourful visage of living coral formations and their other-than-human inhabitants; the human custodians of the Reef and their customary epistemologies in its behalf; scientists and policy makers. There is also the bleached face of the Reef's death, provisional or permanent. Through all of these, the Reef invites an identification, in respect of which I need to be conscious of a western incapacity to identify with an organism so vast and with Indigenous knowledges so longstanding, and yet to try. The experience of the disciples, their sleepiness at the too-much-ness of the glory of the transfiguration scene, comes to mind (9.32).

---

83. Barbara E. Reid, OP, and Shelly Matthews, *Luke 1–9* (Wisdom Commentary; Collegeville: Liturgical Press, 2021), p. 288; see also, Bovon, *Luke 1*, p. 380.

84. Yvonne Sherwood, 'Cutting Up Life: Sacrifice as a Device for Clarifying – and Tormenting – Fundamental Distinctions between Human, Animal, and Divine', in *The Bible and Posthumanism* (ed. Jennifer L. Koosed; SemeiaSt; Atlanta: SBL, 2014), pp. 247–97 (287).

85. Sherwood, 'Cutting up Life', pp. 286–91.

86. Deborah Bird Rose, *Wild Dog Dreaming: Love and Extinction* (Under the Sign of Nature: Explorations in Ecocriticism; Charlottesville: University of Virginia Press, 2011), ch. 1.

Vibrant materiality: Reef and mountain

As Luke's Peter recognizes, the experience of the mountain epiphany is beautiful (καλός). So, too, is the vibrant materiality of the Great Barrier Reef. They call forth awe. In such moments, how can a reader employ an ecological hermeneutics of identification with such excess: the unnamed mountain (9.28, 37); the cloud (9.34-35); the air through which the characters see and hear; the plant matter on the mountainside from which Peter proposes to construct booths (9.33)? The mountain is more than setting; it is a mountain-selfness that is contagious to the spirit, actively gifting to human actors: material space; a lightness perhaps of breath; the scope for long-seeing across distance; a place apart from the everyday. Like the Reef the mountain is already engaged, perhaps more slowly, in its own transformations through weathering, soil formation and plant growth, as conduit for rains, a place to gather clouds, a place to hold a narrative. In the Lukan story, a cloud signals the overshadowing of divine creator; it is a visible voice: listen (9.35). But before the disciples and readers see-hear that word 'listen', they have already heard the narrator speak of departure or exodus (ἔξοδος, 9.31).

Sacred/Divine listening

A whole history of divine listening to a people's cry attends this word of Jesus' departure through his coming death. In the moment of transfiguration, let me again retrieve this word exodus (ἔξοδος) in conjunction with the cloud's directive 'listen', as time out from the horrors of what is to come and as imperative speaking back from those material disfigurations. It is also recollection of what is for Luke a divine purpose (that as I have argued elsewhere has its problems), a purpose that finds expression in the divine visitation of hospitality, forgiveness, compassion, the envisioned jubilee of a deep freedom (ἄφεσις) to go ahead actively.[87] The reference to the exodus (ἔξοδος) in Jerusalem (9.31) is a moment of profound compassion in response to the suffering ahead, that is transformative. Not only the Lukan Jesus but the disciples, albeit pretty shabbily at times, are sent out to complex, responsive and difficult, sometimes silence-inducing, action (9.36). Drawing on Audre Lorde, Seforosa Carroll calls for 'a transformation of silence into language and action' in the face of contemporary violence against women, First Nations and Earth.[88] Might the Reef itself be calling forth such a transformation?

---

87. Anne Elvey, *An Ecological Feminist Reading of the Gospel of Luke: A Gestational Paradigm* (Lewiston, NY: Mellen, 2005); Brendan Byrne, *The Hospitality of God: A Reading of Luke's Gospel* (Strathfield, NSW: St Paul's, 2000).

88. Seforosa Carroll, 'Speaking Up! Speaking Out! Naming the Silences', in *Contemporary Feminist Theologies: Power, Authority, Love* (ed. Kerrie Handasyde, Cathryn McKinney and Rebekah Pryor; London: Routledge, 2021), pp. 9–20 (17); Audre Lorde, 'The Transformation of Silence into Language and Action', in *Sister Outsider: Essays and Speeches* (Freedom, CA: The Crossing Press, 1984), pp. 40–4.

Conclusion

While I am cautious about this crossing from biblical text to contemporary context in a braided reading, this is the best way I feel I can engage with biblical texts today. Rather than transfiguration, the echo of transformation of the disciples, partial and awkward, their altered perception that intersects with the alterity arriving in the face of the other, has resonances for activism now. That means listening to the multiple facets of the Reef and its First Nations custodians.[89] Beyond the commercialization of aesthetic value occurring in more tendentious forms of tourism, beyond capitalist extractivist agendas that fuel a politics of denial of harm, the more-than-human community of the Reef persists, remaking itself as far as it can and calling forth love from local custodians, scientists, poets and many others.

---

89. David Chen, 'Indigenous Rangers to Be the Eyes and Ears for Great Barrier Reef Protection', ABC News, ABC North Qld (19 May 2018), available online: https://www.abc.net.au/news/2018-05-19/indigenous-rangers-to-be-the-eyes-and-ears-of-great-barrier-reef/9777328 (accessed 12 November 2019); Allan Dale, Melissa George, Rosemary Hill and Duane Fraser, *Traditional Owners and Sea Country in the Southern Great Barrier Reef – Which Way Forward?* (Report to the National Environmental Science Programme; Cairns: Reef and Rainforest Research Centre Limited, 2016), available online: https://nesptropical.edu.au/wp-content/uploads/2016/05/NESP-TWQ-3.9-FINAL-REPORT.pdf (accessed 12 November 2019); Madelaine Dickie and Hannah Cross, 'Traditional Owner Knowledge Pivotal to Protecting Great Barrier Reef', *National Indigenous Times* (17 July 2019), available online: https://nit.com.au/traditional-owner-knowledge-pivotal-to-protecting-great-barrier-reef/ (accessed 12 November 2019); Glenda Kwek, 'Great Barrier Reef Survival Key to Indigenous Identity' (2 October 2014), Phys.org, available online: https://phys.org/news/2014-10-great-barrier-reef-survival-key.html (accessed 6 November 2019).

Chapter 11

CONCLUDING REFLECTION

Prophetically, Judith Wright wrote in 1977, 'The Reef's fate is a microcosm of the fate of the planet.'[1] The fate of the planet, for me, calls forth an ecological feminist engagement with biblical literature that is dedicated to the here and now. In this moment, where the face of Earth calls in all its vibrant materiality, I attend to and address biblical literature as part of wider conversations with artists, poets and philosophers. I recognize that to avoid biblical texts altogether is to allow both the life-giving and life-denying aspects of texts, and their traditions of interpretation, to eddy unremarked in the flows of culture that remain indebted to them. I put to the fore my impetus towards a shift in western culture *from* a logic of mastery, of hyper-separation, of the violence of consumer capital and its partner extractivism, *towards* a logic of material entanglement. I affirm Earth's deep history in which the Bible is a relative latecomer.

From this perspective, I do not take the Bible as normative, but I respect its layers, its communities of writing, hearing and reading, and its careful interpreters, as part of the interconnectedness of more-than-human communities. Love L. Sechrest writes of the 'associative reasoning' that Martin Luther King Jr used when he appealed to biblical literature in his speeches.[2] I resonate with this approach, the affirmation of 'analogy as a hermeneutic resource' and by implication, the homiletic impulse in biblical interpretation undertaken in an ecological feminist modality.[3]

---

1. Judith Wright, *The Coral Battleground* (New edn; North Melbourne: Spinifex, 2014 [1977]), p. 186.
2. Love L. Sechrest, 'Double Vision for Revolutionary Religion: Race Relations, Moral Analogies, and African-American Biblical Interpretation', in *Ethnicity, Race, Religion: Identities and Ideologies in Early Jewish and Christian Texts, and in Modern Biblical Interpretation* (ed. Katherine M. Hockey and David G. Horrell; paperback edn; London: T&T Clark, 2020), pp. 202–18 (203).
3. Sechrest, 'Double Vision', p. 203.

Exhortation, encouragement and consolation

In the complex and disturbing contemporary contexts for ecological feminist hermeneutics in which biblical readers are situated, I propose that critical and creative biblical interpretation can be a form of *paraclesis* from the Greek, παράκλησις, that is at once exhortation, encouragement and consolation.[4] In koine Greek, the word παράκλησις is related to the word παράκλητος, meaning comforter, advocate, paraclete, used in both the Gospel of John and 1 John to describe the Sacred Breath (Holy Spirit, τὸ πνεῦμα τὸ ἅγιον, Jn 14.26). Catherine Keller writes that the materiality of breath, air, wind, atmosphere, spirit 'breezes through the tightest texts'.[5] This sense of inhabiting and unsettling even those texts that are most problematic (from ecological, feminist and related perspectives) underscores the way I think of paraclesis: not so much as an affirmation of a kind of divine inspiration that makes texts normative for theology and ethics, but as a material feature of texts and readings that opens to the breath of 'otherwise possibilities'.[6]

In Lk. 2.25, the narrator depicts Simeon as anticipating the consolation (παράκλησις) of Israel. Given the situation of Judea under Roman occupation, is not consolation a material response (both as sensory comfort and material hope) to the political and social stress of the time? The socio-political content of paraclesis is borne out in 6.24, the Lukan beatitudes and woes: 'But woe to you who are rich, for you have received your consolation'. This warning echoes in 16.19-31, the parable of the rich man and Lazarus (esp. 16.25). Paraclesis has economic, social and political registers, and marks the longed-for divine reign that stands in contrast with empire. Juxtaposed with the narrator's description of Simeon's anticipation of consolation for a people, is the comment: 'and the spirit/breath was holy on him, or the sacred breath was on Simeon' (2.25, my translation). In Acts 9.31 the connection between paraclesis and the sacred breath occurs in parallel with 'fear of the Lord'. While the usage of the language of lordship retains problematic echoes of kyriarchal and imperial power, it occurs here in the context of the enmeshment of relationship with the divine and the association of paraclesis with the sacred breath.

---

4. The NRSV translates the word παράκλησις variously as comfort (e.g. Acts 9.31), consolation (e.g. Lk. 2.25, 6.24), encouragement (Rom. 15.4) and exhortation (e.g. Acts 13.15, 15.31), according to context. In Luke-Acts the related verb παρακαλέω can be translated beg, urge, exhort, encourage, plead, even apologize or invite, as well as console or comfort (Lk. 3.18; 7.4; 8.31-32, 41; 15.28; 16.25; Acts 2.40; 8.31; 9.38; 11.23; 13.42; 14.22; 15.32; 16.9, 15, 39-40; 19.31; 20.1-2, 12; 21.12; 24.4; 25.2; 27.33-34; 28.14, 20).

5. Catherine Keller, *Apocalypse Now and Then: A Feminist Guide to the End of the World* (Boston: Beacon, 1996), p. 37.

6. Ashon T. Crawley, *Blackpentecostal Breath: The Aesthetics of Possibility* (New York: Fordham University Press, 2017), pp. 2, 85.

In the material situation of Roman empire, paraclesis conveys a range of possibilities, including comfort, consolation, encouragement and exhortation. The notion of exhortation includes the sense of a call to behavioural change, not only or even primarily as individual moral response but also as response to oppression (θλῖψις, 2 Cor. 1.4). With an ear to and extrapolating from both Isaiah 40 and Luke, I am proposing that the context for reading as paraclesis is the entanglement of the socio-political circumstances of biblical readers' experience of eco-social oppression and their relationship with the material sacred.[7] Both texts, as I discussed in Chapter 9 in relationship to Mountaintop Removal Mining, are at best ambiguous from an ecological perspective. This ambiguity forms part of the material situation which the notion of paraclesis – as consolation-exhortation – addresses not as a Band-Aid. Rather paraclesis signals an impetus to understand (however partially), and respond from inside, the tangle of situational materialities – socio-political, corporeal, cultural and ecological – in which biblical hearers and readers are enmeshed in wonder and grief. This is a hermeneutic practice of 'staying with the trouble'.[8]

The notion of reading as paraclesis picks up on multiple meanings, recognizing the ambiguity of the ancient text from ecological and feminist perspectives.[9] It recognizes, too, the challenge of contemporary reading situations, and the need both for consolation and ongoing transformation through personal and cultural change, and through activism in relation to eco-social justice across multiple

---

7. Connections exist between Luke and Isaiah 40, not only in Lk. 3.5. For example, the Lukan Mary's self-description in her song of protest and praise (Lk. 1.46-55) echoes the description of Jerusalem in the Septuagint version of Isaiah 40. In Isa. 40.1-2 (LXX), three times the prophet/priest is called to comfort, console or exhort (παρακαλεῖτε) the people of Jerusalem. The context of humiliation (ταπείνωσις) of the people and its aftermath (Isa. 40.2 LXX) finds an echo when Mary describes herself under the divine gaze in her humiliation (ἐπέβλεψεν ἐπὶ τὴν ταπείωωσιν, Lk. 1.48). Her humiliation needs to be read not only in relation to her personal status, but also in her status as both member and type of a particular social group under Roman occupation with the gendered as well as class violence her position entails. Barbara E. Reid, 'Women Prophets of God's Alternative Reign', in *Luke-Acts and Empire: Essays in Honor of Robert L. Brawley* (ed. D. Rhoads, D. Esterline and Jae Won Lee; Princeton Theological Monograph Series, 151; Eugene, OR: Pickwick, 2011), pp. 44-59 (54-5); Jane Schaberg, *The Illegitimacy of Jesus: A Feminist Theological Interpretation of the Infancy Narratives* (New York: Crossroad, 1990), pp. 95, 100; Sharon H. Ringe, *Luke* (Westminster Bible Companion; Louisville, KY: Westminster John Knox, 1995), p. 34. See also Michael Pope, 'Gabriel's Entrance and Biblical Violence in Luke's Annunciation Narrative', *JBL* 137 (2018), pp. 701-10.

8. I adopt this term from Donna Haraway, *Staying with the Trouble: Making Kin in the Chthulucene* (Durham: Duke University Press, 2016), p. 1.

9. Heather Eaton, 'Ecofeminist Contributions to an Ecojustice Hermeneutics', in *Readings from the Perspective of Earth* (ed. Norman C. Habel; Earth Bible, 1; Sheffield: Sheffield Academic, 2000), pp. 54-71 (70).

dimensions. Consolation is not a mode of re-accommodation to a destructive status quo but a strengthening to act and an exhortation to change.

An ecological materialism informs my ecological feminist hermeneutics and reminds me that this exhortation to change is mediated by more-than-human actants, even those left half-dead beside the road. The vulnerable materiality in which humans share predates the composition of the texts that come to me as biblical literature. Biblical texts themselves are mediated through material artefacts. Mountains and reefs, seas and skies, the air itself, are both ancestral and contemporary companions to texts and their readers. Earth's atmosphere breathes with spirit through texts and their readers. The text itself is embedded in this vibrant materiality that calls. An ecological aesthetics of reading invites connections that enable shifts in perception that I hope may empower my and our action in cooperation with those more than humans whose faces continue to call us forth.

BIBLIOGRAPHY

Abram, David, 'Afterword: The Commonwealth of Breath', in *Material Ecocriticism* (ed. Serenella Iovino and Serpil Oppermann; Bloomington: Indiana University Press, 2014), pp. 301–14.

Abram, David, *The Spell of the Sensuous* (New York: Vintage Books, 1997).

Adams, Carol J., 'The War on Compassion', in *The Animal Catalyst: Towards Ahuman Theory* (ed. Patricia MacCormack; London: Bloomsbury, 2014), pp. 15–25.

Alaimo, Stacy, 'Trans-Corporeal Feminism and the Ethical Space of Nature', in *Material Feminisms* (ed. Stacy Alaimo and Susan Hekman; Bloomington: Indiana University Press, 2008), pp. 237–64.

Alaimo, Stacy and Susan Hekman (eds), *Material Feminisms* (Bloomington: Indiana University Press, 2008).

Albrecht, Glenn, 'Exiting the Anthropocene and Entering the Symbiocene', Psychoterratica blog (17 December 2015), available online: https://glennaalbrecht.wordpress.com/2015/12/17/exiting-the-anthropocene-and-entering-the-symbiocene/ (accessed 15 March 2021).

Allam, Lorena, '"Deaths in Our Backyard": 432 Indigenous Australians Have Died in Custody since 1991', *The Guardian* (1 June 2020), available online: https://www.theguardian.com/australia-news/2020/jun/01/deaths-in-our-backyard-432-indigenous-australians-have-died-in-custody-since-2008 (accessed 17 November 2020).

Allam, Lorena, and Calla Wahlquist, 'More Than 100 Aboriginal Sacred Sites – Some Dating before the Ice Age – Could Be Destroyed by Mining Companies', *The Guardian* (28 August 2020), available online: https://www.theguardian.com/australia-news/2020/aug/28/more-than-100-aboriginal-sacred-sites-some-dating-before-the-ice-age-could-be-destroyed-by-mining-companies (accessed 1 October 2020).

Alston, Onleilove, 'Faultlines in Coal Country: An Interview with Allen Jones, Cofounder of Christians for the Mountains', *Sojourners Magazine* 39, no. 6 (June 2010), p. 21.

American Public Health Association, 'Climate Change Decreases the Quality of the Air We Breathe', Fact Sheet, available online: https://apha.org/-/media/files/pdf/factsheets/climate/air_quality.ashx (accessed 26 November 2020).

Appalachian Voices, 'End Mountaintop Removal Coal Mining', available online: http://appvoices.org/end-mountaintop-removal/ (accessed 28 May 2021).

de Araujo, Romana Coêho, Jorge Madeira Nogueira and Paul Martin, 'Biodiversity Risk Management in Mining', in *Achieving Biodiversity Protection in Megadiverse Countries: A Comparative Assessment of Australia and Brazil* (ed. Paul Martin, Márcia Dieguez Leuzinger, Solange Teles da Silva and Gabriel Leuzinger Coutinho; Abingdon: Routledge, 2020), pp. 47–66.

Argyrou, Aikaterini, and Harry Hummels, 'Legal Personality and Economic Livelihood of the Whanganui River: A Call for Community Entrepreneurship', *Water International* 44, no. 6–7 (2019), pp. 752–68, doi: 10.1080/02508060.2019.1643525.

Austin, Kelly, and Brett Clark, 'Tearing Down Mountains: Using Spatial and Metabolic Analysis to Investigate the Socio-Ecological Contradictions of Coal Extraction in Appalachia', *Critical Sociology* 38, no. 3 (2011), pp. 437–57.

Australian Earth Laws Alliance, 'Interview with Gudju Gudju about the Great Barrier Reef', YouTube, available online: https://youtu.be/ntKI2bLKRvY (accessed 13 August 2021).
Australian Government, Great Barrier Reef Marine Park Authority (GBRMPA) website, available online: http://www.gbrmpa.gov.au/ (accessed 12 November 2019).
Australian Government, 'Indigenous Rangers Protecting the Great Barrier Reef', National Indigenous Australians Agency (27 April 2016), available online: https://www.indigenous.gov.au/news-and-media/stories/indigenous-rangers-protecting-great-barrier-reef-0 (accessed 15 July 2021).
Australian Government, *Reef 2050 Long Term Sustainability Plan – July 2018*, available online: http://www.environment.gov.au/system/files/resources/35e55187-b76e-4aaf-a2fa-376a65c89810/files/reef-2050-long-term-sustainability-plan-2018.pdf (accessed 12 November 2019).
Australian Marine Conservation Society (AMCS), 'Fact Check: Reef World Heritage in Danger?' (event listing for 7 July 2021), available online: https://www.marineconservation.org.au/events/fact-check-reef-world-heritage-in-danger/ (accessed 15 July 2021).
Australian Religious Response to Climate Change (ARRCC), available online: https://www.arrcc.org.au/ (accessed 27 May 2021).
Australia Remastered: Wild Treasures – Great Barrier Reef (presented by Aaron Pedersen; produced by Wild Bear Entertainment in Association with the Australian Broadcasting Corporation, 2020), ABC iView, available online: https://iview.abc.net.au/video/DO1841H001S00 (accessed 13 July 2021).
Avi-Yonah, Michael, and Abraham J. Brawer, 'Tabor, Mount', in *Encyclopaedia Judaica* (ed. Michael Berenbaum and Fred Skolnik; 2nd edn; vol. 19, Detroit, MI: Macmillan Reference USA, 2007), pp. 426–7, *Gale eBooks*, link.gale.com/apps/doc/CX2587519500/GVRL?u=monash&sid=bookmark-GVRL&xid=905a311e (accessed 20 July 2021).
Avi-Yonah, Michael, and Efraim Orni, 'Hermon, Mount', in *Encyclopaedia Judaica* (ed. Michael Berenbaum and Fred Skolnik; 2nd edn; vol. 9; Detroit, MI: Macmillan Reference USA, 2007), pp. 30–1, *Gale eBooks*, link.gale.com/apps/doc/CX2587508811/GVRL?u=monash&sid=bookmark-GVRL&xid=00c74182 (accessed 20 July 2021).
Bakht, Natasha and Lynda Collins, '"The Earth Is Our Mother": Freedom of Religion and the Preservation of Indigenous Sacred Sites in Canada', *McGill Law Journal* 62, no. 3 (2017), pp. 777–812.
Balabanski, Vicky, 'The Step of "Identification" in Norman Habel's Ecological Hermeneutics: Hermeneutical Reflections on "Ecological Conversion"', in *Where the Wild Ox Roams: Biblical Essays in Honour of Norman C. Habel* (ed. Alan H. Cadwallader with Peter L. Trudinger; HBM, 59; Sheffield: Sheffield Phoenix, 2013), pp. 20–31.
Banjeree, Neela, 'Taking On a Coal Mining Practice as a Matter of Faith', *The New York Times* (28 October 2006), available online: https://www.nytimes.com/2006/10/28/us/28mountains.html (accessed 3 August 2021).
Barad, Karen, 'What Flashes Up: Theological-Political-Scientific Fragments', in *Entangled Worlds: Religion, Science, and New Materialism* (ed. Catherine Keller and Mary-Jane Rubenstein; New York: Fordham University Press, 2017), pp. 21–88.
Barker, Ash, *Risky Compassion* (Kindle eBook; Bournville, Birmingham: Urban Life Together Publishing, 2014).
Barr, James, *Biblical Words for Time* (2nd revised edn; Naperville, IL: A. R. Allenson, 1969).

Barr, James, 'Man and Nature: The Ecological Controversy and the Old Testament', in *Ecology and Religion in History* (ed. David Spring and Eileen Spring; New York: Harper and Row, 1974), pp. 48–75.
Barry, Joyce M., *Standing Our Ground: Women, Environmental Justice, and the Fight to End Mountaintop Removal* (Athens: Ohio University Press, 2012).
Bauer, Walter, *A Greek–English Lexicon of the New Testament and Other Early Christian Literature* (trans., rev. and augmented William F. Arndt, F. Wilbur Gingrich and Frederick W. Danker; Chicago: University of Chicago Press, 1979).
Bawaka Country, Sarah Wright, Sandie Suchet-Pearson, Kate Lloyd, Laklak Burarrwanga, Ritjilili Ganambarr, Merrkiyaway Ganambarr-Stubbs, Banbapuy Ganambarr, and Djawundil Maymuru, 'Working with and Learning from Country: Decentring Human Author-ity', *Cultural Geographies* 22, no. 2 (2015), pp. 269–83, available online: https://doi.org/10.1177%2F1474474014539248.
de Beauvoir, Simone, *The Coming of Age* (trans. Patrick O'Brian; New York: Norton, 1996).
de Beauvoir, Simone, *The Second Sex* (ed. and trans. H. M. Parshley; London: Random House, 1953).
Bennett, Jane, *Vibrant Matter: A Political Ecology of Things* (Durham, NC: Duke University Press, 2010).
Beresford, Quentin, *Adani and the War over Coal* (Sydney: NewSouth Publishing, 2018).
Bergmann, Sigurd, 'Climate Change Changes Religion: Space, Spirit, Ritual, Technology – through a Theological Lens', *ST* 63 (2009), pp. 98–118.
Bergmann, Sigurd, *Creation Set Free: The Spirit as Liberator of Nature* (trans. Douglas Stott; Grand Rapids: Eerdmans, 2005).
Berry, Thomas, *The Sacred Universe: Earth, Spirituality, and Religion in the Twenty-First Century* (ed. Mary Evelyn Tucker; New York: Columbia University Press, 2009).
Berry, Thomas, *The Great Work: Our Way into the Future* (New York: Bell Tower, 1999).
Berry, Thomas, 'The Wild and the Sacred', in *Religions and Environments: A Reader in Religion, Nature and Ecology* (ed. Richard Bohannon; London: Bloomsbury, 2014), pp. 73–8.
Bigell, Werner, 'Beauty as Ideological and Material Transcendence', in *Ecocritical Aesthetics: Language, Beauty, and the Environment* (ed. Peter Quigley and Scott Slovic; Proquest Ebook Central; Bloomington: Indiana University Press, 2018), pp. 187–200.
Billings, Dwight B., and Will Samson, 'Evangelical Christians and the Environment: "Christians for the Mountaintops" and the Appalachian Movement against Mountaintop Removal Coal Mining', *Worldviews* 16, no. 1 (2012), pp. 1–29.
Birch, Tony, 'Climate Change, Mining and Traditional Knowledge in Australia', *Social Inclusion* 4, no. 1 (2016), pp. 92–101.
Birch, Tony, '"We've Seen the End of the World and We Don't Accept It": Protection of Indigenous Country and Climate Justice', in *Places of Privilege: Interdisciplinary Perspectives on Identities, Change and Resistance* (ed. Nicole Oke, Christopher Sonn and Alison Baker; Leiden: Brill, 2018), pp. 139–52.
Bohlinger, Tavis A., 'The Akedah in Pseudo-Philo: A Paradigm of Divine-Human Reciprocity', *JSP* 25, no. 3 (2016), pp. 189–227.
Böhme, Gernot, *The Aesthetics of Atmospheres* (ed. Jean-Paul Thibaud; Abingdon: Routledge, 2017).
Boisseau, Michelle, 'Parchment', in *Trembling Air* (Fayetteville: University of Arkansas Press, 2003), p. 21.
Boochani, Behrouz, 'A Letter from Manus Island', *The Saturday Paper* 186 (9–15 December 2017), pp. 1, 4.

Bovon, François, *Luke 1: A Commentary on the Gospel of Luke 1: 1–9:50* (trans. Christine M. Thomas; Hermeneia, 63A; ed. Helmut Koester; Accordance electronic edn; Minneapolis: Fortress, 2002).

Boyles, Abee L. et al., 'Systematic Review of Community Health Impacts of Mountaintop Removal Mining', *Environment International* 107 (2017), pp. 163–72, available online: https://doi.org/10.1016/j.envint.2017.07.002.

Braidotti, Rosi, 'The Politics of "life itself" and New Ways of Dying', in *New Materialisms: Ontology, Agency, and Politics* (ed. Diane Coole and Samatha Frost; Durham: Duke University Press, 2010), pp. 201–18.

Braidotti, Rosi, '"We" May Be in This Together, but We Are Not All Human and We Are Not One and the Same', *Ecocene* 1, no. 2 (June 2020), pp. 24–31.

Bratton, Susan Power, 'Christian Ecotheology in the Old Testament', *Environmental Ethics* 6 (1984), pp. 195–209.

Brazal, Agnes M., 'Ethics of Care in Laudato Si': A Postcolonial Feminist Critique', *Feminist Theology* 29, no. 3 (2021), pp. 220–33.

The Breathe Project, available online: https://breatheproject.org/ (accessed 26 November 2020).

Brennan, Teresa, *Exhausting Modernity: Grounds for a New Economy* (London: Routledge, 2000).

Brett, Mark G., *Political Trauma and Healing: Biblical Ethics for a Postcolonial World* (Grand Rapids: Eerdmans, 2016).

Brooten, Bernadette, *Women Leaders in the Ancient Synagogue: Inscriptional Evidence and Background Issues* (Chico: Scholars Press, 1982).

Brown, Cheryl Anne, *No Longer Be Silent: First Century Jewish Portraits of Biblical Women* (Gender and the Biblical Tradition; Louisville: Westminster John Knox, 1992).

Brown, Francis, S. R. Driver and Charles A. Briggs (eds.), *A Hebrew and English Lexicon of the Old Testament: With an Appendix Containing the Biblical Aramaic* (based on the Lexicon of William Genesius; trans. Edward Robinson; Oxford: Clarendon Press, 1951).

Brown, Raymond E., *The Birth of the Messiah: A Commentary on the Infancy Narratives of Matthew and Luke* (New York: Image Books, 1979).

Brueggemann, Walter, *The Prophetic Imagination* (2nd edn; Minneapolis: Augsburg Fortress, 2001).

Bruehler, Bart B., *A Public and Political Christ: The Social-Spatial Characteristics of Luke 18:35-19:43 and the Gospel as a Whole in Its Ancient Context* (Princeton Theological Monograph Series, 157; Eugene: Pickwick, 2011).

Burns, Shirley Stewart, *Bringing Down the Mountains: The Impact of Mountaintop Removal Surface Coal Mining on Southern West Virginia Communities, 1970–2004* (Morgantown, WV: West Virginia University Press, 2007).

Burrus, Virginia, 'The Gospel of Luke and the Acts of the Apostles', in *A Postcolonial Commentary on the New Testament Writings* (ed. Fernando F. Segovia and R. S. Sugitharajah; London: T&T Clark, 2009), pp. 133–55.

Burt, J. A., E. F. Camp, I. C. Enochs, J. L. Johansen, K. M. Morgan, B. Riegl and A. S. Hoey, 'Insights from Extreme Coral Reefs in a Changing World', *Coral Reefs* 39 (2020), pp. 495–507, available online: https://doi.org/10.1007/s00338-020-01966-y.

Buth, Randall, 'Hebrew Poetic Tenses and the Magnificat', *JSNT* 21 (1984), pp. 67–83.

Byrne, Brendan, *The Hospitality of God: A Reading of Luke's Gospel* (Strathfield, NSW: St Pauls, 2000).

Byrne, Brendan, *Inheriting the Earth: The Pauline Basis of a Spirituality for Our Time* (Homebush, NSW: St Paul Publications, 1990).

Byron, John, *Slavery Metaphors in Early Judaism and Pauline Christianity* (Tübingen: Mohr Siebeck, 2003).
Cadwallader, Alan H., 'The Fall, the Samaritan and the Wounded Man: An Example of Multiple Readings of Scripture (Lk. 10:25-37)', in *Lost in Translation?: Anglicans, Controversy and the Bible* (ed. Scott Cowdell and Muriel Porter; Thornbury, Vic.: Desbooks, 2004), pp. 155-84.
Cadwallader, Alan H., 'The Roman Army as a Total Institution and the Implications for Gospel Interpretation', paper given at the Bible and Critical Theory Seminar, Brisbane, 5-6 November 2011.
Caldicott, Helen, 'Maude Barlow', in *Loving This Planet: Leading Thinkers Talk about How to Make a Better World* (ed. Helen Caldicott; New York: The New Press. Proquest Ebook Central, 2011), pp. 1-13.
Callahan, Allen Dwight, Richard A. Horsley and Abraham Smith, 'Introduction: The Slavery of New Testament Studies', *Semeia* 83/84 (1998), pp. 1-15.
Camilleri, Joseph and Jim Falk, *Worlds in Transition: Evolving Governance across a Stressed Planet* (Cheltenham, UK: Edward Elgar, 2009).
Campbell, J. Elliott, James F. Fox and Peter M. Acton, 'Terrestrial Carbon Losses from Mountaintop Coal Mining Offset Regional Forest Carbon Sequestration in the 21st Century', *Environmental Research Letters* 7, no. 4 (2012), pp. 1-6, available online: http://iopscience.iop.org/1748-9326/7/4/045701 (accessed 3 August 2021).
Cancer Weekly News Reporter-Staff News Editor, 'Asthma, Heart Disease, Cancer and General Illness Found in Kentucky Mountain Top Removal Community', *Cancer Weekly* (2 April 2013), p. 173.
Carroll, Seforosa, 'Reimagining Home: Migration and Identity in a Changing Climate', in *Theological and Hermeneutical Explorations from Australia: Horizons of Contextuality* (ed. Jione Havea; Lanham: Lexington Books, 2021), pp. 167-79.
Carroll, Seforosa, 'Speaking Up! Speaking Out! Naming the Silences', in *Contemporary Feminist Theologies: Power, Authority, Love* (ed. Kerrie Handasyde, Cathryn McKinney and Rebekah Pryor; London: Routledge, 2021), pp. 9-20.
Carter, Warren, *The Roman Empire and the New Testament: An Essential Guide* (Nashville: Abingdon, 2006).
Carter, Warren, 'Singing in the Reign: Performing Luke's Songs and Negotiating the Roman Empire (Luke 1-2)', in *Luke-Acts and Empire: Essays in Honor of Robert L. Brawley* (ed. David Rhoads, David Esterline and Jae Won Lee; Princeton Theological Monograph Series, 151; Eugene, OR: Pickwick, 2011), pp. 23-43.
Cassidy, Bonny, *Final Theory* (Artarmon, NSW: Giramondo, 2014).
Cassidy, Richard J., *Jesus, Politics and Society: A Study of Luke's Gospel* (Maryknoll: Orbis, 1978).
Cavanaugh, William T., *Being Consumed: Economics and Christian Desire* (Grand Rapids: Eerdmans, 2008).
Ceccarelli, Daniela M., Richard D. Evans, Murray Logan, Philippa Mantel, Marji Puotinen, Caroline Petus, Garry R. Russ and David H. Williamson, 'Long-Term Dynamics and Drivers of Coral and Macroalgal Cover on Inshore Reef of the Great Barrier Reef Marine Park', *Ecological Applications* 20, no. 1 (2020), pp. 1-20 (15), available online: https://doi.org/10.1002/eap.2008.
Celan, Paul, 'The Meridian' (trans. Rosemarie Waldrop), in *Selections* (ed. and with an introduction by Pierre Joris; Berkeley: University of California Press, 2005), pp. 154-69.
Chakrabarty, Dipesh, 'The Climate of History: Four Theses', *Critical Inquiry* 35, no. 2 (2009), pp. 197-222.

Chalmers, Matthew, 'Rethinking Luke 10: The Parable of the Good Samaritan Israelite', *JBL* 139 (2020), pp. 543–66.
Chen, David, 'Indigenous Rangers to Be the Eyes and Ears for Great Barrier Reef Protection', ABC News, ABC North Qld (19 May 2018), available online: https://www.abc.net.au/news/2018-05-19/indigenous-rangers-to-be-the-eyes-and-ears-of-great-barrier-reef/9777328 (accessed 12 November 2019).
Cherokee Nation, 'Remember the Removal', Cherokee Nation, available online: https://rtr.cherokee.org/ (accessed 7 June 2021).
Chrétien, Jean-Louis, *The Call and the Response* (trans. Anne A. Davenport; New York: Fordham University Press, 2004 [Fre. 1992]).
Christensen, Erik, 'Sermon: Sunday September 23, 2012: Season of Creation – Mountain Sunday', *By Proclamation* (23 September 2012), available online: http://byproclamation.wordpress.com/tag/mountaintop-removal-mining/ (accessed 1 June 2021).
Christians for the Mountains (CFTM), 'Our Mission' (2012), available online: http://www.christiansforthemountains.org/site/Topics/About/ourMission.html.
Clark, Timothy, *Ecocriticism on the Edge: The Anthropocene as a Threshold Concept* (London: Bloomsbury, 2015).
Clarke, Kevin, 'And Every Mountain Brought Low', *US Catholic* 64, no. 9 (September 1999), p. 23.
Cobb, Christy, *Slavery, Gender, Truth, and Power in Luke-Acts and Other Ancient Narratives* (Cham, Switzerland: Palgrave Macmillan, 2019).
Code, Lorraine L., *Ecological Thinking: The Politics of Epistemic Location* (New York: Oxford University Press, 2006).
Collins, John J., 'The Zeal of Phineas: The Bible and the Legitimation of Violence', *JBL* 122 (2003), pp. 3–21.
Collins, Patricia Hill, *Black Feminist Thought: Knowledge, Consciousness, and the Politics of Empowerment* (Perspectives on Gender, 2; New York: Routledge, 1991).
Collins, Patricia Hill and Sirma Bilge, *Intersectionality* (ProQuest Ebook Central; Cambridge, UK: Polity, 2016).
Cooke, Stuart, *Departure into Cloud* (Sydney: Vagabond Press, 2013).
Copeland, Claudia, *Mountaintop Mining: Background on Current Controversies*, Congressional Research Services, CRS Report for Congress 7.5700 (2 December 2013; updated 13 December 2016), p. 1, available online: https://crsreports.congress.gov/product/pdf/RS/RS21421 (accessed 28 May 2021).
Cosgrove, Charles H., 'The Divine Δεῖ in Luke-Acts', *NovT* 26 (1984), pp. 168–90.
Costa, Jedda, 'Wellington Shire Council Votes to Keep Angus McMillan Monuments, Despite Explorer's Link to Murders', ABC Gippsland (17 June 2020), available online: https://www.abc.net.au/news/2020-06-17/wellington-council-votes-down-mcmillan-cairn-removal/12361546 (accessed 21 July 2020).
Crabbe, Kylie, *Luke/Acts and the End of History* (BZAW, 238; Berlin: De Gruyter, 2019).
Crawley, Ashon T., *Blackpentecostal Breath: The Aesthetics of Possibility* (New York: Fordham University Press, 2017).
Crossan, John Dominic, 'Roman Imperial Theology', in *In the Shadow of Empire: Reclaiming the Bible as a History of Faithful Resistance* (ed. Richard A. Horsley; Louisville: Westminster John Knox, 2008), pp. 59–73.
Crowder, Stephanie Buckhanon, 'Another View of Community Mothering', in *Luke 1–9* (ed. Barbara E. Reid, OP and Shelly Matthews; Wisdom Commentary; Collegeville: Liturgical Press, 2021), pp. 39–41.

Cuomo, Chris J., *Feminism and Ecological Communities: An Ethic of Flourishing* (London: Routledge, 1998).
Dale, Allan, Melissa George, Rosemary Hill and Duane Fraser, *Traditional Owners and Sea Country in the Southern Great Barrier Reef – Which Way Forward?* (Report to the National Environmental Science Programme; Cairns: Reef and Rainforest Research Centre Limited, 2016), available online: https://nesptropical.edu.au/wp-content/uploads/2016/05/NESP-TWQ-3.9-FINAL-REPORT.pdf (accessed 12 November 2019).
Dalton, Anne Marie, 'The Great Work in a Sacred Universe: The Role of Science in Berry's Visionary Proposal', in *The Intellectual Journey of Thomas Berry: Imagining the Earth Community* (ed. Heather Eaton; Lanham, NY: Lexington Books, 2014), pp. 173–93.
D'Angelo, Mary Rose, 'Women in Luke-Acts: A Redactional View', *JBL* 109 (1990), pp. 441–61.
Das, Patitapaban, 'Hearing the Unheard: Voices of the Silent', *Tattva Journal of Philosophy* 12, no. 2 (2020), pp. 59–70.
David Attenborough's Reef: An Interactive Journey (interactive online; Atlantic Productions, 2018), available online: https://attenboroughsreef.com/ (accessed 13 July 2021).
Davis, Ellen F., 'Land as Kin: Renewing the Imagination', in *Rooted and Grounded: Essays on Land and Christian Discipleship* (ed. Ryan D. Harker and Janeen Bertsche Johnson; Eugene: Pickwick, 2016), pp. 3–12.
Davis, Ellen F., *Opening Israel's Scriptures* (Oxford: Oxford University Press, 2019).
Daw, Sarah, '"If He Chooses to Speak from These Roots": Entanglement and Uncertainty in Charles Olson's Quantum Ecopoetics', *Green Letters* 23, no. 4 (2019), pp. 350–66.
Deane-Drummond, Celia, *Eco-Theology* (London: Darton, Longman and Todd, 2008).
Deane-Drummond, Celia, *Wonder and Wisdom: Conversations in Science, Spirituality, and Theology* (Philadelphia: Templeton Foundation Press, 2006).
'Deaths Inside', *The Guardian* (Saturday 24 August 2019), available online: https://www.theguardian.com/australia-news/ng-interactive/2018/aug/28/deaths-inside-indigenous-australian-deaths-in-custody (accessed 17 November 2020).
Deloria, Vine Jr, 'The Sacred and the Modern World', in *Encyclopedia of Religion and Nature* (ed. Bron R. Taylor; London: Thoemmes Continuum, 2005), pp. 1446–8.
Derrida, Jacques, *Given Time: 1. Counterfeit Money* (trans. Peggy Kamuf; Chicago: University of Chicago Press, 1992).
Deverell, Garry Worete, *Gondwana Theology: A Trawloolway Man Reflects on Christian Faith* (Reservoir, Vic.: Morning Star Publishing, 2018).
Diangelo, Robin, *White Fragility: Why It's So Hard for White People to Talk about Racism* (Boston: Beacon, 2018).
Dickie, Madelaine, and Hannah Cross, 'Traditional Owner Knowledge Pivotal to Protecting Great Barrier Reef', *National Indigenous Times* (17 July 2019), available online: https://nit.com.au/traditional-owner-knowledge-pivotal-to-protecting-great-barrier-reef/ (accessed 12 November 2019).
Diehl, Judy, 'Anti-Imperial Rhetoric in the New Testament', *CurBR* 10, no. 1 (2011), pp. 9–52.
Dietzel, Andreas, Michael Bode, Sean R. Connolly and Terry P. Hughes, 'Long-term Shifts in the Colony Size Structure of Coral Populations along the Great Barrier Reef', *Proceedings of the Royal Society B: Biological Sciences* 287, no. 1936 (14 October 2020), pp. 1–9, available online: https://royalsocietypublishing.org/doi/10.1098/rspb.2020.1432 (accessed 19 July 2021).
Dillard, Annie, 'Teaching a Stone to Talk', in *This Sacred Earth: Religion, Nature, Environment* (ed. Roger S. Gottlieb; New York: Routledge, 1996), pp. 32–6.

Dixon, Edward P., 'Descending Spirit and Descending Gods: A "Greek" Interpretation of the Spirit's "Descent as a Dove" in Mark 1:10', *JBL* 128 (2009), pp. 759–80.

Dowling, Elizabeth V., 'Luke-Acts: Good News for Slaves?', *Pacifica* 24 (June 2011), pp. 123–40.

Dowling, Elizabeth V., 'Slave Parables in the Gospel of Luke', *AusBR* 56 (2008), pp. 61–8.

Dowling, Elizabeth V., *Taking Away the Pound: Women, Theology and the Parable of the Pounds in the Gospel of Luke* (London: T&T Clark International, 2007).

Earth Bible Team, 'Conversations with Gene Tucker and Other Writers', in *The Earth Story in Genesis* (ed. Norman C. Habel and Shirley Wurst; Earth Bible, 2; Sheffield: Sheffield Academic, 2000), pp. 21–33.

Earth Bible Team, 'Guiding Ecojustice Principles', in *Readings from the Perspective of Earth* (ed. Norman C. Habel; Earth Bible, 1; Sheffield: Sheffield Academic, 2000), pp. 38–53.

Earth Bible Team, 'The Voice of the Earth: More Than Metaphor?', in *The Earth Story in the Psalms and the Prophets* (ed. Norman C. Habel; Earth Bible, 4; Sheffield: Sheffield Academic, 2001), pp. 23–8.

Eaton, Heather, 'Ecofeminist Contributions to an Ecojustice Hermeneutics', in *Readings from the Perspective of Earth* (ed. Norman C. Habel; Earth Bible, 1; Sheffield: Sheffield Academic, 2000), pp. 54–71.

Eaton, Heather, 'Ecofeminist Theologies in the Age of Climate Crisis', *Feminist Theology* 29, no. 3 (2021), pp. 209–19.

Eaton, Heather, and Lois Ann Lorentzen, *Ecofeminism and Globalization: Exploring Culture, Context, and Religion* (Lanham, MD: Rowman & Littlefield, 2003).

Eckard, Paula Gallant, 'Queerness, Opioids, and Mountaintop Removal: The Politics of Destruction in *The Evening Hour*', *South Atlantic Review* 83, no. 3 (2018), pp. 24–43.

Edwards, Denis, *Breath of Life: A Theology of the Creator Spirit* (Maryknoll: Orbis, 2004).

Edwards, Denis, *Deep Incarnation: God's Redemptive Suffering with Creatures* (Maryknoll: Orbis, 2019).

Edwards, Denis, *Ecology at the Heart of Faith: The Change of Heart That Leads to a New Way of Living on Earth* (Maryknoll: Orbis, 2006).

Edwards, Denis, '"Everything Is Interconnected": The Trinity and the Natural World in *Laudato Si*", *ACR* 94, no. 1 (2017), pp. 81–92.

Elsworthy, Emma, 'NSW Bushfires Lead to Deaths of over a Billion Animals and "hundreds of billions" of Insects, Experts Say', ABC News (January 9, 2020), available online: https://www.abc.net.au/news/2020-01-09/nsw-bushfires-kill-over-a-billion-animals-experts-say/11854836 (accessed 13 May 2020).

Elvey, Anne, 'Ashes and Dust: On (Not) Speaking About God Ecologically', in *Eco-Theology* (ed. Elaine Wainwright, Luiz Carlos Susin and Felix Wilfred; *Concilium* 2009, no. 3; London: SCM Press, 2009), pp. 33–42.

Elvey, Anne, 'Beyond Culture? Nature/Culture Dualism and the Christian Otherworldly', *Ethics & the Environment* 1, no. 2 (2006), pp. 63–84.

Elvey, Anne, 'Can There Be a Forgiveness That Makes a Difference Ecologically? An Eco-materialist Account of Forgiveness as Freedom (ἄφεσις) in the Gospel of Luke', *Pacifica* 22, no. 2 (2009), pp. 148–70.

Elvey, Anne, 'Climate Embodied: Exploring a Poetics of Strained Breath', *Axon* 10, no. 1 (May 2020), available online: https://www.axonjournal.com.au/issue-vol-10-no-1-may-2020/climate-embodied (accessed 12 November 2020).

Elvey, Anne, 'Desiring the "Peaceable Kingdom"? Use/Respect Dualism, the Enigma of Predation and Human Relationships to Other Animals', *PAN* 3 (2005), pp. 31–40.

Elvey, Anne, 'Ecological Feminist Hermeneutics', in *The Oxford Handbook for Bible and Ecology* (ed. Hilary Marlow and Mark Harris; Oxford: Oxford University Press, 2022), pp. 35–48.

Elvey, Anne, *An Ecological Feminist Reading of the Gospel of Luke: A Gestational Paradigm* (Studies in Women and Religion, 45; Lewiston, NY: Edwin Mellen, 2005).

Elvey, Anne, 'Feminist Ecologies in Religious Interpretation: Australian Influences', in *Feminist Ecologies: Changing Environments in the Anthropocene* (ed. Lara Stevens, Peta Tait and Denise Varney; Cham, Switzerland: Palgrave Macmillan, 2018), pp. 209–29.

Elvey, Anne, 'The Fertility of God: A Study of the Characterizations of Pseudo-Philo's Hannah and Luke's Mary' (unpublished TheolM Dissertation, Melbourne College of Divinity, Biblical Studies, 1994).

Elvey, Anne, 'From Cultures of Violence to Ways of Peace: Reading the Benedictus in the Context of Australia's Treatment of Asylum Seekers in Offshore Detention', in *Things That Make for Peace: Traversing Text and Tradition in Christianity and Islam* (ed. Anthony Rees; Lanham: Lexington Books, 2020), pp. 41–57.

Elvey, Anne, 'A Hermeneutics of Retrieval: Breath and Earth Voice in Luke's Magnificat – Does Earth Care for the Poor?', *AusBR* 63 (2015), pp. 68–84.

Elvey, Anne, 'Homogenizing Violence, Isa 40:4 (and Luke 3:5) and MTR (Mountaintop Removal Mining)', *Worldviews* 19, no. 3 (2015), pp. 226–44.

Elvey, Anne, 'Interpreting the Time: Climate Change and the Climate in/of the Gospel of Luke', in *Climate Change – Cultural Change: Religious Responses and Responsibilities* (ed. Anne Elvey and David Gormley O'Brien; Preston, Vic.: Mosaic Press, 2013), pp. 78–91.

Elvey, Anne, 'Legacies of Violence toward the Other: Toward a Consideration of the Outsider within the Lukan Narrative', *Colloquium* 34, no. 1 (2002), pp. 21–34.

Elvey, Anne, 'Living One for the Other: Eucharistic Hospitality as Ecological Hospitality', in *Reinterpreting the Eucharist: Explorations in Feminist Theology and Ethics* (ed. Anne Elvey, Carol Hogan, Kim Power and Claire Renkin; Sheffield: Equinox, 2013), pp. 186–205.

Elvey, Anne, 'Love and Justice in the Gospel of Luke: Ecology, the Neighbour and Hope', *AusBR* 60 (2012), pp. 1–17.

Elvey, Anne, 'Material Elements: The Matter of Women, the Matter of Earth, the Matter of God', in *Post-Christian Feminisms: A Critical Approach* (ed. Lisa Isherwood and Kathleen McPhillips; Aldershot: Ashgate, 2008), pp. 53–69.

Elvey, Anne, 'The Material Given: Bodies, Pregnant Bodies and Earth', *Australian Feminist Studies* 18, no. 4 (2003), pp. 199–209.

Elvey, Anne, 'Matter, Freedom and the Future: Re-framing Feminist Theologies through an Ecological Materialist Lens', *Feminist Theology* 23, no. 2 (2015), pp. 186–204.

Elvey, Anne, *The Matter of the Text: Material Engagements between Luke and the Five Senses* (BMW, 37; Sheffield: Sheffield Phoenix, 2011).

Elvey, Anne, 'A Multidimensional Approach in Feminist Ecological Biblical Studies', in *The Oxford Handbook of Feminist Approaches to the Hebrew Bible* (ed. Susanne Scholz; Oxford: Oxford University Press, 2021), pp. 555–73.

Elvey, Anne, *Reading the Magnificat in Australia: Unsettling Engagements* (Sheffield: Sheffield Phoenix, 2020).

Elvey, Anne, 'Reimagining Decolonising Praxis for a Just and Ecologically Sustainable Peace in an Australian Context', in *Towards a Just and Ecologically Sustainable Peace: Navigating the Great Transition* (ed. Joseph Camilleri and Deborah Guess; Singapore: Palgrave Macmillan, 2020), pp. 275–95.

Elvey, Anne, 'Rethinking Neighbour Love: A Conversation between Political Theology and Ecological Ethics', in *Where the Wild Ox Roams: Biblical Essays in Honour of Norman C. Habel* (ed. Alan H. Cadwallader with Peter L. Trudinger; HBM, 59; Sheffield: Sheffield Phoenix, 2013), pp. 58–75.

Elvey, Anne, 'Retrieving an Earth Voice: Ecological Hermeneutics, the Matter of the Text and Reading "as if it's holy" (Jennifer Harrison, "Book Sculptor")', *AeJT* 22, no. 2 (August 2015), pp. 81–94.

Elvey, Anne, 'Roadsides: Toward an Ecological Feminist Theology of Cross-Species Compassion', in *Contemporary Feminist Theologies: Power, Authority, Love* (ed. Kerrie Handasyde, Cathryn McKinney and Rebekah Pryor; London: Routledge, 2021), pp. 133–44.

Elvey, Anne, 'Storing Up Death, Story Up Life: An Earth Story in Luke 12:13-34', in *The Earth Story in the New Testament* (ed. Norman C. Habel and Vicky Balabanski; Earth Bible, 5; London: Sheffield Academic, 2002), pp. 95–107.

Elvey, Anne, 'Strained Breath and Open Text: Exploring the Materiality of Breath in Relation to Reading Luke 4:16-30', *BCT* 16, no. 1–2 (2020), pp. 1–14.

Elvey, Anne, 'To Bear the Other: Toward a Passionate Compassion (an ecological feminist reading of Luke 10:25–37)', *Sea Changes* 1 (2001), available online: https://www.wsrt.asn.au/seachanges (accessed 22 October 2020).

Elvey, Anne (ed.), *Hope for Whole: Poets Speak Up to Adani* (eBook; Seaford, Vic.: Rosslyn Avenue Productions, 2018), available online: https://plumwoodmountain.com/hope-for-whole-ebook/ (accessed 9 July 2021).

Engberg-Pedersen, Troels, 'The Material Spirit: Cosmology and Ethics in Paul', *NTS* 55 (2009), pp. 179–97.

'Environment Minister Says Government Will Challenge UNESCO Move to List Great Barrier Reef as "in Danger"', ABC News (22 June 2021), available online: https://www.abc.net.au/news/2021-06-22/environment-minister-great-barrier-reef-listed-in-danger/100233088 (accessed 12 July 2021).

Eriksson, Kenneth A. and W. Lee Daniels, 'Environmental Implications of Regional Geology and Coal Mining in the Appalachians', in *Appalachia's Coal-Mined Landscapes* (ed. Carl E. Zipper and Jeff Skousen; Cham, Switzerland: Springer Nature, 2021), pp. 27–53.

Farris, Stephen, *The Hymns of Luke's Infancy Narratives* (JSNTSup, 9; Sheffield: JSOT Press, 1985).

Felstiner, John, *Can Poetry Save the Earth? A Field Guide to Nature Poems* (New Haven, CT: Yale University Press, 2009).

Fijn, Natasha, 'Impacts on the Kings Highway: A Photo Essay', *Plumwood Mountain* 1, no. 2 (August 2014), available online: http://plumwoodmountain.com/photo-essay-by-natasha-fijn/ (accessed 14 May 2020).

Fincher, Megan, 'Christian Stewardship Group Seeks to Blow Top Off Mountaintop Removal', *National Catholic Reporter* (4 February 2014), available online: http://ncronline.org/blogs/eco-catholic/christian-stewardship-group-seeks-blow-top-mountaintop-removal (accessed 22 April 2022).

Fitzmyer, Joseph A., *The Gospel According to Luke I–IX: Introduction, Translation, and Notes* (New York: Doubleday, 1981).

Fitzmyer, Joseph A., *The Gospel According to Luke X–XIV: Introduction, Translation, and Notes* (The Anchor Bible; New York: Doubleday, 1985).

Ford, J. Massyngbaerde, *My Enemy Is My Guest: Jesus and Violence in Luke* (Maryknoll, NY: Orbis Books, 1984).

Ford, Thomas H., 'Aura in the Anthropocene', *symplokē* 21, no. 1–2 (2013), pp. 65–82.
Foster, Emma, 'Ecofeminism Revisited: Critical Insights on Contemporary Environmental Governance', *Feminist Theory* 22, no. 2 (2021), pp. 190–205.
Foster, John Bellamy, *Marx's Ecology: Materialism and Nature* (New York: Monthly Review Press, 2000).
Foster, John Bellamy, Brett Clark and Richard York, *The Ecological Rift: Capitalism's War on the Earth* (New York: Monthly Review Press, 2010).
Francis (Pope), *Encyclical Letter Laudato Si' of the Holy Father Francis on Care for Our Common Home* (Australian edn; Strathfield, NSW: St Pauls, 2015).
Gaard, Greta, 'Rejecting Essentialism and Re-Placing Species in a Material Feminist Environmentalism', *Feminist Formations* 23, no. 2 (Summer 2011), pp. 26–53.
Gaard, Greta, 'Toward an Ecofeminist Aesthetic of Reconnection', in *Ecocritical Aesthetics: Language, Beauty, and the Environment* (ed. Peter Quigley and Scott Slovic; Bloomington: Indiana University Press, 2018), pp. 97–113.
Gaard, Greta, 'Towards a Queer Ecofeminism', *Hypatia* 12, no. 1 (1997), pp. 114–37.
Galinsky, Karl, 'The Cult of the Roman Emperor: Uniter or Divider?' in *Rome and Religion: A Cross-Disciplinary Dialogue on the Imperial Cult* (ed. Jeffrey Brodd and Jonathan L. Reed; WGRWSup, 5; Atlanta: SBL, 2011), pp. 1–22.
Gander, Forrest, 'The Future of the Past', in *Redstart: An Ecological Poetics* (Forrest Gander and John Kinsella; Iowa City: University of Iowa Press, 2012), pp. 1–3.
Gardiner, Beth, 'Pollution Made COVID-19 Worse. Now Lockdowns Are Clearing the Air', *National Geographic* (8 April 2020), available online: https://www.nationalgeographic.com/science/2020/04/pollution-made-the-pandemic-worse-but-lockdowns-clean-the-sky/ (accessed 12 November 2020).
Gebara, Ivone, *Longing for Running Water: Ecofeminism and Liberation* (Minneapolis: Fortress Press, 1999).
Ghosh, Amitav, *The Great Derangement: Climate Change and the Unthinkable* (Berlin Family Lectures; Kindle eBook; Chicago: The University of Chicago Press, 2016).
Gilbert, Gary, 'Luke-Acts and the Negotiation of Authority and Identity in the Roman World', in *The Multivalence of Biblical Texts and Theological Meanings* (ed. Christine Helmer and Charlene Higbe; Atlanta: SBL, 2006), pp. 83–104.
Ginsberg, Allen, *Howl, Kaddish and Other Poems* (Melbourne: Penguin, 2010 [1956]).
Goff, Philip, William Seager and Sean Allen-Hermanson, 'Panpsychism', *The Stanford Encyclopedia of Philosophy* (ed. Edward N. Zalta; Summer 2020 edn), available online: https://plato.stanford.edu/archives/sum2020/entries/panpsychism/ (accessed 9 March 2021).
Goldingay, John, *Isaiah* (Understanding the Bible Commentary Series; Grand Rapids: Baker Books, 2012).
Goldingay, John, *The Message of Isaiah 40–55: A Literary-Theological Commentary* (London: T&T Clark International, 2005).
Goldingay, John, and David Payne, *Isaiah 40–55* (Vol. 1; ICC; London: T&T Clark International, 2006).
Good, Crystal, 'Valley Girl', available online: https://crystalgood.squarespace.com/valley-girl (accessed 5 June 2021).
Goodman, Martin, 'The First Jewish Revolt: Social Conflict and the Problem of Debt', *JJS* 33, no. 1–2 (Spring–Autumn 1992), pp. 417–27.
Gottardi, Francesca, 'Sacred Sites Protection and Indigenous Women's Activism: Empowering Grassroots Social Movements to Influence Public Policy. A Look into the "Women of Standing Rock" and "Idle No More" Indigenous Movements', *Religions* 11, no. 380 (2020), pp. 1–13.

Gottlieb, Roger S. (ed.), *This Sacred Earth: Religion, Nature, Environment* (New York: Routledge, 1996).
Great Barrier Reef Foundation, 'Traditional Owner Reef Protection', available online: https://www.barrierreef.org/what-we-do/reef-trust-partnership/traditional-owner-reef-protection (accessed 15 July 2021).
Grassi, Joseph, *Peace on Earth: Roots and Practices from Luke's Gospel* (Collegeville: Liturgical Press, 2004).
Green, Joel B., *The Gospel of Luke* (NICNT; Grand Rapids, MI: Eerdmans, 1997).
Gregersen, Niels, 'The Cross of Christ in an Evolutionary World', *Dialog* 40, no. 3 (2001), pp. 192–207.
Gregersen, Niels (ed.), *Incarnation: On the Scope and Depth of Christology* (Minneapolis: Fortress, 2015).
Griffin, Susan, *The Eros of Everyday Life: Essays on Ecology, Gender and Society* (New York: Anchor Books, 1995).
Grosz, Elizabeth, 'Feminism, Materialism, and Freedom', in *New Materialisms: Ontology, Agency, and Politics* (ed. Diana Coole and Samantha Frost; Durham: Duke University Press, 2010), pp. 139–57.
Guess, Deborah, 'Deep Incarnation: A Resource for Ecological Christology', in *Climate Change – Cultural Change: Religious Responses and Responsibilities* (ed. Anne Elvey and David Gormley-O'Brien; Preston, Vic.: Mosaic Books, 2013), pp. 107–17.
Guess, Deborah, 'Oil beyond War and Peace: Rethinking the Meaning of Matter', in *Ecological Aspects of War: Religious and Theological Perspectives* (ed. Anne Elvey, Deborah Guess and Keith Dyer, *A Forum for Theology in the World* 3, no. 2; Adelaide: ATF Theology, 2016), pp. 73–93.
Habel, Norman C., *An Inconvenient Text: Is a Green Reading of the Bible Possible?* (Adelaide: ATF Press, 2009).
Habel, Norman C., 'Introducing Ecological Hermeneutics', in *Exploring Ecological Hermeneutics* (ed. Norman C. Habel and Peter L. Trudinger; Atlanta: SBL, 2008), pp. 1–8.
Habel, Norman C., 'Introducing the Earth Bible', in *Readings from the Perspective of Earth* (ed. Norman C. Habel; Earth Bible, 1; Sheffield: Sheffield Academic, 2000), pp. 25–37.
Habel, Norman C., *The Land Is Mine: Six Biblical Land Ideologies* (Overtures to Biblical Theology; Minneapolis: Fortress, 1995).
Habel, Norman C., *Rainbow of Mysteries: Meeting the Sacred in Nature* (eBook; Kelowna, BC: CopperHouse, 2012).
Habel, Norman C. (ed.), *The Earth Story in the Psalms and the Prophets* (Earth Bible, 4; Sheffield: Sheffield Academic, 2001).
Habel, Norman C. (ed.), *Readings from the Perspective of Earth* (Earth Bible, 1; Sheffield: Sheffield Academic, 2000).
Habel, Norman C. and Vicky Balabanski (eds), *The Earth Story in the New Testament* (Earth Bible, 5; London: Sheffield Academic, 2002).
Habel, Norman C. and Peter Trudinger (eds), *Exploring Ecological Hermeneutics* (SBL Symposium Series, 46; Atlanta: SBL, 2008).
Habel, Norman C. and Shirley Wurst (eds), *The Earth Story in Genesis* (Earth Bible, 2; Sheffield: Sheffield Academic, 2000).
Habel, Norman C. and Shirley Wurst (eds), *The Earth Story in Wisdom Traditions* (Earth Bible, 3; Sheffield: Sheffield Academic, 2001).
Hamburger, Michael, *The Truth of Poetry: Tensions in Modernist Poetry since Baudelaire* (London: Anvil Press Poetry, 1996).

Hamilton, Chris R., 'Testimony of Chris R. Hamilton, Senior Vice President, West Virginia Coal Association and Chairman, West Virginia Business and Industry Council before the Subcommittee on Energy and Mineral Resources of the Natural Resources Committee Oversight Hearing: "EPA V. American Mining Jobs: The Obama Administration's Regulatory Assault on the Economy"', *West Virginia Coal Association* (11 October 2013), available online: https://wvcoalassociation.wordpress.com/current-events/page/16/ (accessed 1 June 2021).

Hamilton, Clive, *Defiant Earth: The Fate of Humans in the Anthropocene* (Sydney: Allen & Unwin, 2017).

Hamylton, Sarah, Leah Gibbs, Kim Williams and Lucas Ihlein, 'Can Interdisciplinary Insights Encourage Meaningful Response to the Climate Crisis? Narratives from the Great Barrier Reef, Australia', *GeoHumanities* 6, no. 2 (2020), pp. 394–412, available online: https://doi.org/10.1080/2373566X.2020.1819167.

Hannaford, Kristin, 'Coral Not Coal', in *Hope for Whole: Poets Speak Up to Adani* (ed. Anne Elvey; eBook; Seaford, Vic.: Rosslyn Avenue Productions, 2018), p. 39; available online: https://plumwoodmountain.com/hope-for-whole-ebook/ (accessed 9 July 2021).

Hanson, Paul D., *Isaiah 40–66* (IBC; Louisville: John Knox, 1995).

Haraway, Donna, 'Otherworldly Conversations; Terran Topics; Local Terms', *Science as Culture* 3, no. 1 (1992), pp. 64–98.

Haraway, Donna, *Staying with the Trouble: Making Kin in the Chthulucene* (Durham: Duke University Press, 2016).

Harrill, J. Albert, *Slaves in the New Testament: Literary, Social, and Moral Dimensions* (Minneapolis: Fortress, 2006).

Harrington, D. J., 'Pseudo-Philo: A New Translation and Introduction', in *The Old Testament Pseudepigrapha* (ed. James H. Charlesworth; vol. 2: Expansions of the 'Old Testament' and Legends, Wisdom and Philosophical Literature, Prayers, Psalms, and Odes, Fragments of Lost Judeo-Hellenistic Works; Garden City, NY: Doubleday, 1985), pp. 297–377.

Harrison, Jennifer, 'Book Sculptor', in *Colombine: New and Selected Poems* (North Fitzroy, Vic.: Black Pepper, 2010), p. 223.

Harrison, Jennifer, 'Book Sculptor', *Salt Lick Quarterly* (Autumn 2003), p. 9.

Harrison, Robert Pogue, *Forests: The Shadow of Civilization* (Chicago: The University of Chicago Press, 1992).

Hart, Kevin, 'Horizons and Folds: Elizabeth Presa', *Contretemps* no. 2 (May 2001), pp. 171–5.

Hart, Kevin, *Poetry and Revelation: For a Phenomenology of Religious Poetry* (London: Bloomsbury Academic, 2017).

Hart, Kevin, *Young Rain: New Poems* (Artamon, NSW: Giramondo, 2008).

Hawkins, Ronnie Zoe, 'Ecofeminism and Nonhumans: Continuity, Difference, Dualism and Domination', *Hypatia* 13, no. 1 (1998), pp. 158–97.

Hawthorne, Susan, *Wild Politics* (North Melbourne: Spinifex Press, 2002).

Hays, Christopher M., *Luke's Wealth Ethics: A Study in Their Coherence and Character* (WUNT 2, 275; Tübingen: Mohr Siebeck, 2010).

Heaney, Seamus, 'Feeling into Words', in *Preoccupations: Selected Prose 1968–1978* (London: Faber and Faber, 1980), pp. 41–60.

Heaney, Seamus, *Opened Ground: Poems 1966–1996* (London: Faber and Faber, 1998).

Heidegger, Martin, *The Fundamental Concept of Metaphysics* (trans. William McNeill and Nicholas Walker; Bloomington: Indiana University Press, 1995).

Heidegger, Martin, 'The Question Concerning Technology' (trans. William Lovitt), in *Martin Heidegger: Basic Writings: From Being and Time (1927) to The Task of Thinking (1964)* (ed. David Farrell Krell; revised and expanded edition; London: Routledge, 1993), pp. 307–41.

Heinämäki, Leena and Thora Martina Herrmann (eds), *Experiencing and Protecting Sacred Natural Sites of Sámi and Other Indigenous Peoples: The Sacred Arctic* (1st edn; Springer Polar Sciences; Cham, Switzerland: Springer Nature, 2017).

Hekman, Susan, *The Material of Knowledge: Feminist Disclosures* (Bloomington: Indiana University Press, 2010).

Hermann, Kenn, 'Isaiah's Vision and Mountaintop Mining', Radix Perspectives blog (28 February 2006), available online: https://khermann.wordpress.com/2006/02/28/isaiahs-vision-of-mountaintop-mining/ (accessed 1 June 2021).

Hiebert, Theodore, 'Air, the First Sacred Thing: The Conception of רוח in the Hebrew Scriptures', in *Exploring Ecological Hermeneutics* (ed. Norman C. Habel and Peter Trudinger; Atlanta: SBL, 2008), pp. 9–19.

Hiebert, Theodore, 'The Human Vocation: Origins and Transformations in Christian Traditions', in *Christianity and Ecology: Seeking the Well-Being of Earth and Humans* (ed. Dieter T. Hessel and Rosemary Radford Ruether; Cambridge, MA: Harvard University Press, 2000), pp. 135–54.

Hiers, Richard H., 'Ecology, Biblical Theology, and Methodology: Biblical Perspectives on the Environment', *Zygon* 19, no. 1 (1984), pp. 43–59.

Hogan, Linda, 'We Call It Tradition', in *The Handbook of Contemporary Animism* (ed. Graham Harvey; Milton Park, Abingdon: Routledge, 2014), pp. 17–26.

Holzman, David C., 'Mountaintop Removal Mining: Digging into Community Health Concerns', *Environmental Health Perspectives* 119, no. 11 (November 2011), pp. 476–83.

hooks, bell, 'Appalachian Elegy (Sections 1–6)', from *Appalachian Elegy* (Lexington: University of Kentucky Press, 2012), reproduced at Poetry Foundation, available online: https://www.poetryfoundation.org/poems/148751/appalachian-elegy-1-6 (accessed 7 June 2021).

hooks, bell, *Talking Back: Thinking Feminist, Thinking Black* (Boston: South End Press, 1989).

Hopkins, Gerard Manley, *Poems and Prose* (selected and edited by W. H. Gardner; Middlesex: Penguin, 1953).

Horrell, David G., *The Bible and the Environment: Towards a Critical Ecological Biblical Theology* (eBook, Abingdon: Routledge, 2014).

Horrell, David G., 'Ecological Hermeneutics: Reflections on Method and Prospects for the Future', *Colloquium* 46, no. 2 (November 2014), pp. 139–65.

Horrell, David G., 'Introduction', in *Ecological Hermeneutics: Biblical, Historical and Theological Perspectives* (ed. David G. Horrell, Cherryl Hunt, Christopher Southgate and Francesca Stavrakopoulou; London: T&T Clark, 2010), pp. 1–12.

Horrell, David G., Cherryl Hunt and Christopher Southgate, 'Appeals to the Bible in Ecotheology and Environmental Ethics: A Typology of Hermeneutical Stances', *Studies in Christian Ethics* 21, no. 2 (2008), pp. 219–38.

Horrell, David G., Cherryl Hunt, Christopher Southgate and Francesca Stavrakopoulou (eds), *Ecological Hermeneutics: Biblical, Historical and Theological Perspectives* (London: T&T Clark, 2010).

Horsley, Richard A., 'Jesus and Empire', in *In the Shadow of Empire: Reclaiming the Bible as a History of Faithful Resistance* (ed. Richard A. Horsley; Louisville: Westminster John Knox, 2008), pp. 75–96.

Horsley, Richard A., 'Jesus-in-Movement and the Roman Imperial (Dis)order', in *An Introduction to Empire in the New Testament* (ed. Adam Winn; Atlanta: SBL, 2016), pp. 47–69.

Horsley, Richard A., 'Oral Communication, Oral Performance, and New Testament Interpretation', in *Method and Meaning: Essays on New Testament Interpretation in Honor of Harold W. Attridge* (ed. Andrew B. McGowan and Kent Harold Richards; Atlanta: SBL, 2011), pp. 125-55.

Horsley, Richard A., Jonathan A. Draper, John Miles Foley and Werner H. Kelber, *Performing the Gospel: Orality, Memory, and Mark* (Minneapolis: Fortress, 2006).

House, Silas, and Jason Howard, *Something's Rising: Appalachians Fighting Mountaintop Removal* (Lexington: University of Kentucky Press, 2009).

'How to Build a "Great" Barrier Reef', Australian Academy of Science (website), available online: https://www.science.org.au/curious/earth-environment/how-build-great-barrier-reef (accessed 21 July 2021).

Howie, Gillian, *Between Feminism and Materialism: A Question of Method* (New York: Palgrave Macmillan, 2010).

Hughes, Terry, Jon C. Day and Ove Hoegh-Guldberg, 'Is Australia Really Doing Enough for the Great Barrier Reef? Why Criticisms of UNESCO's "in Danger" Recommendation Don't Stack Up', *The Conversation* (30 June 2021), available online: https://theconversation.com/is-australia-really-doing-enough-for-the-great-barrier-reef-why-criticisms-of-unescos-in-danger-recommendation-dont-stack-up-163641 (accessed 12 July 2021).

Hull, Crispin, 'I Saw the Great Barrier Reef Die Last Weekend and I Wept', *The Age* (11 March 2017), available online: http://www.theage.com.au/comment/i-saw-the-great-barrier-reef-die-last-weekend-and-i-wept-20170310-guu0r0.html (accessed 12 November 2019).

Hundloe, Tor, *Adani versus the Black-Throated Finch* (Pampleteer Series, 6; North Melbourne: Australian Scholarly Publishing, 2018).

Hunt, Peter, 'Insurance Claims for Kangaroo Damage Down, Says RACV', *The Weekly Times* (6 May 2020), available online: https://www.weeklytimesnow.com.au/news/victoria/insurance-claims-for-kangaroo-damage-down-says-racv/news-story/de93df81cb7a099b5fd06e7737ed7019 (accessed 13 May 2020).

ilovemountains.org, 'Successful Rally at the White House Council on Environmental Quality', News (12 September 2014), available online: http://ilovemountains.org/news/5012 (accessed 2 August 2021).

Iovino, Serenella and Serpil Oppermann (eds), *Material Ecocriticism* (Bloomington: Indiana University Press, 2014).

IPCC, 'Chapter 7 Energy Systems', *Fifth Assessment Report (AR5), Working Group III, Mitigation* (2014), available online: http://report.mitigation2014.org/drafts/final-draft-fgd/ipcc_wg3_ar5_final-draft_fgd_chapter7.pdf (accessed 31 May 2021).

Irigaray, Luce, 'The Age of the Breath' (trans. Katja van de Rakt, Staci Boeckman and Luce Irigaray), in *Key Writings* (ed. Luce Irigaray; London: Continuum, 2004), pp. 165–70.

Irigaray, Luce, *Divine Women* (trans. Stephen Muecke; Local Consumption Paper 8; Sydney: Local Consumption, 1986).

Irigaray, Luce, 'Equal to Whom?', trans. Robert L. Mazzola, *Differences* 1 (1989), pp. 59–76.

Irigaray, Luce, *An Ethics of Sexual Difference* (trans. Carolyn Burke and Gillian C. Gill; Ithaca, NY: Cornell University Press, 1993 [Fre. 1984]).

Irigaray, Luce, *The Forgetting of Air in Martin Heidegger* (trans. Mary Beth Mader; Austin, TX: University of Texas Press, 1999).

Irigaray, Luce, 'The Redemption of Women' (trans. Jennifer Wong, Jennifer Zillich with Luce Irigaray), in *Key Writings* (ed. Luce Irigaray; London: Continuum, 2004), pp. 150–64.

Irigaray, Luce, *Sexes and Genealogies* (trans. Gillian C. Gill; New York: Columbia University Press, 1993).

IWDA, 'What Does Intersectional Feminism Actually Mean?', International Women's Development Agency (11 May 2018), available online: https://iwda.org.au/what-does-intersectional-feminism-actually-mean/ (accessed 2 February 2021).

Jackson, Zakiyyah Iman, *Becoming Human: Matter and Meaning in an Antiblack World* (New York: New York University Press, 2020).

Jacobs, Harrison, 'Here's Why the Opioid Epidemic Is So Bad in West Virginia – the State with the Highest Overdose Rate in the US', *Business Insider* (2 May 2016), available online: https://www.businessinsider.com.au/why-the-opioid-epidemic-is-so-bad-in-west-virginia-2016-4?r=US&IR=T (accessed 31 May 2021).

John Paul II (Pope), 'General Audience', (17 January 2001), available online: http://www.vatican.va/holy_father/john_paul_ii/audiences/2001/documents/hf_jp-ii_aud_20010117_en.html (accessed 29 August 2014).

Johnson, Allen, 'The Kentucky Coal Association Weighs in on Mountaintop Mining', Go Tell It on the Mountains blog (4 January 2010), available online: https://gotell.wordpress.com/2010/01/04/ (accessed 1 June 2021).

Johnson, Elizabeth A., *Ask the Beasts: Darwin and the God of Love* (Kindle eBook; London: Bloomsbury, 2014).

Johnson, Luke Timothy, *The Gospel of Luke* (SP; Collegeville: Liturgical Press, 1991).

Jones, Owain and Paul Cloke, 'Non-Human Agencies: Trees in Place and Time', in *Material Agency: Toward a Non-Anthropocentric Approach* (ed. Carl Knappett and Lambros Malafouris; New York: Springer, 2008), pp. 79–96.

Kahl, Brigitte, 'Acts of the Apostles: Pro(to)-Imperial Script and Hidden Transcript', in *In the Shadow of Empire: Reclaiming the Bible as a History of Faithful Resistance* (ed. Richard A. Horsley; Louisville: Westminster John Knox, 2008), pp. 137–56.

Kahl, Brigitte, 'Reading Luke against Luke: Non-Uniformity of Text, Hermeneutics of Conspiracy and the "Scriptural Principle"', in *A Feminist Companion to Luke* (ed. Amy-Jill Levine, with Marianne Blickenstaff; FCNTECW, 3; London: Sheffield Academic, 2002), pp. 70–88.

Kearns, Laurel, 'Cooking the Truth: Faith, Science, the Market, and Global Warming', in *Ecospirit: Religions and Philosophies for the Earth* (ed. Laurel Kearns and Catherine Keller; New York: Fordham University Press, 2007), pp. 99–124.

Keats, John, 'Letter to George and Thomas Keats', Hampstead, 22 December 1817, in *Letters of John Keats to His Family and Friends* (ed. Sidney Colvin; The Project Gutenberg eBook), available online: http://www.gutenberg.org/files/35698/35698-h/35698-h.htm#XXIV (accessed 22 October 2020).

Keith930, '40 Years Later: The Buffalo Creek Disaster and Its Aftermath', *Daily Kos* (February 7, 2012), available online: https://www.dailykos.com/stories/2012/2/7/1062372/-40-Years-Later-The-Buffalo-Creek-Disaster-Its-Aftermath (accessed 3 August 2021).

Keller, Catherine, *Apocalypse Now and Then: A Feminist Guide to the End of the World* (Boston: Beacon, 1996).

Keller, Catherine, *Face of the Deep: A Theology of Becoming* (London: Routledge, 2003).

Keller, Catherine, *Facing Apocalypse: Climate, Democracy, and Other Last Chances* (Kindle eBook; Maryknoll, NY: Orbis Books, 2021).

Keller, Catherine, 'Talk about the Weather: The Greening of Eschatology', in *Ecofeminism and the Sacred* (ed. Carol J. Adams; New York: Continuum, 1993), pp. 30–49.

Keller, Catherine, and Mary-Jane Rubenstein, 'Introduction: Tangled Matters', in *Entangled Worlds: Religion, Science, and New Materialism* (ed. Catherine Keller and Mary-Jane Rubenstein; New York: Fordham University Press, 2017), pp. 1–18.

Keller, Evelyn Fox, *A Feeling for the Organism: The Life and Work of Barbara McClintock* (New York: Freeman, 1983).

Kelso, Julie, 'Irigaray's Madonna', *Feminist Theology* 23, no. 2 (2015), pp. 171–85.

Kentucky Coal Association, 'Mountaintop Mining Issues and Responses', *KCA: Kentucky Coal Association*, available online: http://www.kentuckycoal.org/index.cfm?pageToken=mtmIssues (accessed 15 October 2013).

Kim, Seyoon, *Christ and Caesar: The Gospel and the Roman Empire in the Writings of Paul and Luke* (Grand Rapids: Eerdmans, 2008).

Kirk, Alan, '"Love Your Enemies," The Golden Rule, and Ancient Reciprocity (Luke 6.27-35)', *JBL* 122 (2003), pp. 667–86.

Knappett, Carl, 'The Neglected Networks of Material Agency: Artefacts, Pictures and Texts', in *Material Agency: Toward a Non-Anthropocentric Approach* (ed. Carl Knappett and Lambros Malafouris; New York: Springer, 2008), pp. 139–56.

Koster, Hilda P., 'Trafficked Lands: Sexual Violence, Oil, and Structural Evil in the Dakotas', in *Planetary Solidarity: Global Women's Voices on Christian Doctrine and Climate Justice* (ed. Grace Ji-Sun Kim and Hilda P. Koster; Minneapolis: Ausburg Fortress, 2017), pp. 155–75.

Kovarik, Bill, 'Does the Bible Justify Mountaintop Removal Coal Mining?' *The Appalachian Voice* (1 December 2006), available online: https://appvoices.org/2006/12/01/2626/ (accessed 1 June 2021).

Krieg, C. Parker, 'Coal Optimism: Carbon Ideologies and the Good Lives of Extraction', *Textual Practice* 35, no. 3 (2021), pp. 431–48.

Kristeva, Julia, *Revolution in Poetic Language* (trans. Margaret Waller; New York: Columbia University Press, 1984).

Kruks, Sonia, 'Simone de Beauvoir: Engaging Discrepant Materialisms', in *New Materialisms: Ontology, Agency, and Politics* (ed. Diane Coole and Samatha Frost; Durham: Duke University Press, 2010), pp. 258–80.

Kwaymullina, Ambelin, *Living on Stolen Land* (Broome, WA: Magabala Books, 2020).

Kwek, Glenda, 'Great Barrier Reef Survival Key to Indigenous Identity' (2 October 2014), Phys.org, available online: https://phys.org/news/2014-10-great-barrier-reef-survival-key.html (accessed 6 November 2019).

LaCapra, Dominic, *History, Literature, Critical Theory* (Ithaca: Cornell University Press, 2013).

Lamar, William H. IV, 'It's Not Just the Coronavirus – Bad Theology Is Killing Us', Faith & Leadership (26 May 2020), available online: https://faithandleadership.com/william-h-lamar-iv-its-not-just-coronavirus-bad-theology-killing-us (accessed 26 November 2020).

Law, John, and Annemarie Mol, 'The Actor-Enacted: Cumbrian Sheep in 2001', in *Material Agency: Toward a Non-Anthropocentric Approach* (ed. Carl Knappett and Lambros Malafouris; New York: Springer, 2008), pp. 57–77.

Lazzaro, Kellie, 'Angus McMillan Monument Removal Considered by Council over His Links to Indigenous Murders', ABC Gippsland (16 June 2020), available online: https://www.abc.net.au/news/2020-06-16/victorian-council-to-vote-on-removal-of-angus-mcmillan-monuments/12355930 (accessed 21 July 2020).

Leane, Jeanine, 'Voicing the Unsettled Space: Rewriting the Colonial Mythscape', paper given at Unsettling Ecological Poetics Conference, University of Sydney, Thursday 24 October 2019.

Lee, Dorothy, *Transfiguration* (London: Continuum, 2004).

Lee, Jae Won, 'Pilate and the Crucifixion of Jesus in Luke-Acts', in *Luke-Acts and Empire: Essays in Honor of Robert L. Brawley* (ed. David Rhoads, David Esterline and Jae Won Lee; Princeton Theological Monograph Series, 151; Eugene: Pickwick, 2011), pp. 84–106.

Lee-Park, Sun Ai, 'The Forbidden Tree and the Year of the Lord', in *Women Healing Earth: Third World Women on Ecology, Feminism, and Religion* (ed. Rosemary Radford Ruether; Maryknoll: Orbis Books, 1996), pp. 107–16.

Levertov, Denise, *Poems 1960–1967* (New York: New Directions, 1983).

Levertov, Denise, *Sands of the Well* (New York: New Directions, 1996).

Lévinas, Emmanuel, 'Is Ontology Fundamental?' (1951) (trans. Peter Atterton, Simon Critchley and Graham Noctor), in *Basic Philosophical Writings* (ed. Adriaan T. Peperzak, Simon Critchley and Robert Bernasconi; Bloomington: Indiana University Press, 1996), pp. 1–10.

Lévinas, Emmanuel, *Of God Who Comes to Mind* (trans. Bettina Bergo; Stanford: Stanford University Press, 1998).

Lévinas, Emmanuel, *Totality and Infinity: An Essay on Exteriority* (trans. Alphonso Lingis; Dordrecht: Kluwer Academic, 1991).

Levine, Amy-Jill, and Ben Witherington III, *The Gospel of Luke* (New Cambridge Bible Commentary; Cambridge: Cambridge University Press, 2018).

Lieu, Judith, *The Gospel of Luke* (Epworth Commentaries; Peterborough: Epworth, 1997).

Lingis, Alphonso, 'The Voices of Things', *Senses and Society* 4, no. 3 (2009), pp. 273–81.

Lipschitz, Ora, S. David Sperling and Shimon Gibson, 'Sinai, Mount', in *Encyclopaedia Judaica* (ed. Michael Berenbaum and Fred Skolnik; 2nd edn; vol. 18; Detroit, MI: Macmillan Reference USA, 2007), pp. 627–9. *Gale eBooks*, link.gale.com/apps/doc/CX2587518631/GVRL?u=monash&sid=bookmark-GVRL&xid=330b2ff9 (accessed 20 July 2021).

Lloyd, Rohan, '"Wealth of the Reef": The Entanglement of Economic and Environmental Values in Early Twentieth Century Representations of the Great Barrier Reef', *Melbourne Historical Journal* 43, no. 1 (January 2015), pp. 40–62.

Loeb, Penny, *Moving Mountains: How One Woman and Her Community Won Justice from Big Coal* (Lexington: The University Press of Kentucky, 2007).

Logan, William Bryant, *Air: The Restless Shaper of the World* (New York: Norton, 2012).

Longenecker, Bruce W., 'Peace, Prosperity, and Propaganda: Advertisement and Reality in the Early Roman Empire', in *An Introduction to Empire in the New Testament* (ed. Adam Winn; Atlanta: SBL, 2016), pp. 15–45.

Lorde, Audre, 'The Transformation of Silence into Language and Action', in *Sister Outsider: Essays and Speeches* (Freedom, CA: The Crossing Press, 1984), pp. 40–4.

Lowe, J. R., D. H. Williamson, D. M. Ceccarelli, R. D Evans and G. R. Russ, 'Environmental Disturbance Events Drive Declines in Juvenile Wrasse Biomass on Inshore Coral Reef of the Great Barrier Reef', *Environmental Biology of Fishes* 103 (2020), pp. 1279–93, available online: https://doi.org/10.1007/s10641-020-01022-2.

Luz, Ulrich, *Matthew 1–7: A Commentary on Matthew 1–7* (trans. James E. Crouch; Hermeneia, 61A; ed. Helmut Koester; Accordance electronic edn; Minneapolis: Fortress, 2007).

Lysaght, Gary-Jon, 'Indigenous Sacred Site Lake Torrens Faces Exploratory Drilling for Resources', ABC News, ABC North and West SA, available online: https://www.abc.net.au/news/2020-09-28/lake-torrens-sacred-site-faces-exploratory-mining/12696750 (accessed 1 October 2020).

Mackinlay, Shane, *Interpreting Excess: Jean-Luc Marion, Saturated Phenomena, and Hermeneutics* (New York: Fordham University Press, 2009).

Maher, Jane-Maree, 'The Promiscuous Placenta: Crossing Over', in *Contagion: Historical and Social Studies* (ed. Alison Bashford and Claire Hooker; London: Routledge, 2001), pp. 201–16.

Maiden, Jennifer, *Appalachian Fall: Poems about Poverty in Power: New Poems* (Penrith, NSW: Quemar Press, 2018).

Maigret, Thomas A., John J. Cox, and Jian Yang, 'Persistent Geophysical Effects of Mining Threaten Ridgetop Biota of Appalachian Forests', *Frontiers in Ecology and the Environment* 17, no. 2 (March 2019), pp. 85–91, doi:10.1002/fee.1992.

Malafouris, Lambros, 'At the Potter's Wheel: An Argument for Material Agency', in *Material Agency: Toward a Non-Anthropocentric Approach* (ed. Carl Knappett and Lambros Malafouris; New York: Springer, 2008), pp. 19–36.

Maling, Caitlin, *Fish Work* (Crawley, WA: UWAP, 2021).

Maling, Caitlin, 'Recommendations for a Western Australian Coastal Pastoral', in *Hope for Whole: Poets Speak Up to Adani* (ed. Anne Elvey; eBook; Seaford, Vic.: Rosslyn Avenue Productions, 2018), pp. 102–3; available online: https://plumwoodmountain.com/hope-for-whole-ebook/ (accessed 9 July 2021).

Marberry, M. Katie and Danilea Werner, 'The Role of Mountaintop Removal Mining in the Opioid Crisis', *Journal of Social Work Practice in the Addictions* 20, no. 4 (2020), pp. 302–10, available online: https://doi.org/10.1080/1533256X.2020.1821539.

Marion, Jean-Luc, 'The Banality of Saturation', in *Counter-Experiences: Reading Jean-Luc Marion* (ed. Kevin Hart; Notre Dame: University of Notre Dame Press, 2007), pp. 383–418.

Marion, Jean-Luc, *Being Given: Toward a Phenomenology of Givenness* (trans. Jeffrey L. Kosky; Stanford: Stanford University Press, 2002).

Marion, Jean-Luc, 'The Saturated Phenomenon', *Philosophy Today* 40, no. 1 (1996), pp. 103–24.

Marshall, I. Howard, *The Gospel of Luke* (The New International Greek Testament Commentary; Grand Rapids, MI: Eerdmans, 1978).

Marx, Karl, *Economic and Philosophical Manuscripts of 1844* (trans. M. Milligan; Moscow: Progress Publishers, 1959).

Mathews, Freya, *The Ecological Self* (London: Routledge, 1991).

Mathews, Freya, *For Love of Matter: A Contemporary Panpsychism* (Albany: SUNY, 2003).

McCann, Andrew, 'The Obstinacy of the Sacred', *Antipodes* 19, no. 2 (December 2005), pp. 152–8.

McCredden, Lyn, 'Contemporary Poetry and the Sacred: Vincent Buckley, Les Murray and Samuel Wagan Watson', *Australian Literary Studies* 23, no. 2 (October 2007), pp. 153–67.

McDonagh, Sean, *Climate Change: The Challenge to All of Us* (Blackrock, Dublin: The Columba Press, 2006).

McFague, Sallie, *Blessed Are the Consumers: Practicing Restraint in a Culture of Consumption* (Minneapolis: Fortress, 2013).

McKibben, Bill, *The End of Nature* (New York: Random House, 1989).

McNeil, Bryan T., *Combating Mountaintop Removal: New Directions in the Fight against Big Coal* (Urbana: University of Illinois Press, 2011).

McQuaid, John, 'Mining the Mountains', *Smithsonian Magazine* 39, no. 10 (January 2009), pp. 74–85, available online: https://www.proquest.com/magazines/mining-mountains/docview/236861789/se-2?accountid=12528 (accessed 28 May 2021).

McWeeny, Jennifer, 'Topographies of Flesh: Women, Nonhuman Animals, and the Embodiment of Connection and Difference', *Hypatia* 29, no. 2 (Spring 2014), pp. 269–86.

Mellor, Mary, *Feminism and Ecology* (Cambridge: Polity, 1997).

Merovich, George T. Jr., Nathaniel P. Hitt, Eric R. Merriam and Jess W. Jones, 'Response of Aquatic Life to Coal Mining in Appalachia', in *Appalachia's Coal-Mined Landscapes* (ed. Carl E. Zipper and Jeff Skousen; Cham, Switzerland: Springer Nature, 2021), pp. 245–85.

Mies, Maria and Vandana Shiva, *Ecofeminism* (North Melbourne: Spinifex Press, 1993).

Miller, Amanda C., 'Good Sinners and Exemplary Heretics: The Sociopolitical Implications of Love and Acceptance in the Gospel of Luke', *RevExp* 112, no. 3 (2015), pp. 461–9.

Miller, Andrew J. and Nicolas Zégre, 'Landscape-Scale Disturbance: Insights into the Complexity of Catchment Hydrology in the Mountaintop Removal Region of the Eastern United States', *Land* 5, no. 3 (2016), pp. 1–23, available online: https://doi.org/10.3390/land5030022.

Miller, Richard W., 'Deep Responsibility for the Deep Future', *TS* 77, no. 2 (2016), pp. 436–65.

Mitchell, Chantelle, 'Airy Matters: Turning toward a Contemporary Breath Poetics', lecture, Free Association and Bus Projects, 1 August 2019.

Monro, Anita J., 'A Kaleidoscopic Vessel Sailing a Kyriarchal Ocean: The Third Wave Feminist Theologies of Women-Church (1987–2007)', in *Theological and Hermeneutical Explorations from Australia: Horizons of Contextuality* (ed. Jione Havea; Lanham: Lexington Books, 2021), pp. 25–42.

Moore, Niamh, 'Eco/feminist Genealogies: Renewing Promises and New Possibilities', in *Contemporary Perspectives on Ecofeminism* (ed. Mary Phillips and Nick Rumens; Routledge Explorations in Environmental Studies; Milton Park, Abingdon: Routledge, 2016), pp. 19–37.

Moreton-Robinson, Aileen, *Talkin' Up to the White Woman: Indigenous Women and Feminism* (St Lucia, Qld: University of Queensland Press, 2000).

Morford, Stacy, 'Religion's View from Appalachia: Only God Should Move Mountains', *Inside Climate News* (26 March 2009), available online: https://insideclimatenews.org/news/26032009/religions-view-appalachia-only-god-should-move-mountains/ (accessed 3 August 2021).

Morgan, Jan, *Earth's Cry: Prophetic Ministry in a More-than-human World* (Preston, Vic.: Uniting Academic Press, 2013).

Morton, Timothy, 'Ecological Awareness as Blindness' (Keynote address presented at Regarding the Earth: ASLEC-ANZ Conference, 1 September 2012, Monash University, Caulfield), available online: http://ecologywithoutnature.blogspot.com.au/2012/09/ecological-awareness-as-blindness-mp3.html (accessed 3 February 2021).

Morton, Timothy, *The Ecological Thought* (Cambridge, MA: Harvard University Press 2010).

Nancy, Jean-Luc, *Listening* (trans. Charlotte Mandell; New York: Fordham University Press, 2007).

Nancy, Jean-Luc, *The Sense of the World* (trans. Jeffrey S. Librett; Minneapolis: University of Minnesota Press, 1997).

Nash, James A., 'Toward the Ecological Reformation of Christianity', *Int* 50, no. 1 (1996), pp. 5–15.
National Archives of Australia, 'Royal Commission into Aboriginal Deaths in Custody', available online: https://www.naa.gov.au/explore-collection/first-australians/royal-commission-aboriginal-deaths-custody (accessed 17 November 2020).
Nelson, Eric S., 'Levinas and Kierkegaard: The Akedah, the Dao, and Aporetic Ethics', *Journal of Chinese Philosophy* 40, no. 1 (March 2013), pp. 164–84.
Neville, David J., *A Peaceable Hope: Contesting Violent Eschatology in New Testament Narratives* (Grand Rapids: Baker Academic, 2013).
Newberry, Beth, 'Mountain Defender', *Sojourners Magazine* 34, no. 3 (March 2005), pp. 26–30.
Nippgen, Fabian, Matthew R. V. Ross, Emily S. Bernhardt and Brian L. McGlynn, 'Creating a More Perennial Problem? Mountaintop Removal Coal Mining Enhances and Sustains Saline Baseflows of Appalachian Watersheds', *Environmental Science & Technology* 51 (2017), pp. 8324–34, available online: http://dx.doi.org/10.1021/acs.est.7b02288.
O'Connell, Maureen H., *Compassion: Loving Our Neighbor in an Age of Globalization* (Kindle eBook; Maryknoll: Orbis Books, 2009).
O'Day, Gail, 'Singing Woman's Song: A Hermeneutic of Liberation', *CurTM* 12, no. 4 (August 1985), pp. 203–10.
O'Gorman, Francis, 'Coleridge, Keats, and the Science of Breathing', *Essays in Criticism* 61, no. 4 (2011), pp. 365–81.
Oh, Jea Sophia, *A Postcolonial Theology of Life: Planetarity East and West* (Upland, CA: Sopher Press, 2011).
Orlov, Andrei A., *Demons of Change: Antagonism and Apotheosis in Jewish and Christian Apocalypticism* (eBook; Albany: SUNY, 2020).
Oliver, Mary, *A Poetry Handbook: A Prose Guide to Understanding and Writing Poetry* (Orlando: Harcourt, 1994).
Olson, Charles, 'Projective Verse', Poetry Foundation ([1950] first published online 13 October 2009), available online: https://www.poetryfoundation.org/articles/69406/projective-verse (accessed 7 May 2020).
Ong, Walter J., *Orality and Literacy* (Milton Park, Abingdon: Methuen, 1982).
Oppermann, Serpil. 'Nature's Colors: A Prismatic Materiality in the Natural/Cultural Realms', in *Ecocritical Aesthetics: Language, Beauty, and the Environment* (ed. Peter Quigley and Scott Slovic; Proquest Ebook Central; Bloomington: Indiana University Press, 2018), pp. 157–71.
Palaszczuk, Annastacia, Hon., and Hon Kate Jones, 'Queensland STILL "Beautiful One Day, Perfect The Next"', Joint Statement (1 April 2018), Queensland Government website, available online: http://statements.qld.gov.au/Statement/2018/4/1/queensland-still-beautiful-one-day-perfect-the-next (accessed 12 November 2019).
Pancake, Ann, *Strange as This Weather Has Been: A Novel* (Berkeley: Counterpoint, 2007).
Paredes-Castellanos, Angelina, and Ricardo Rozzi, 'Biocultural Exoticism in the Feminine Landscape of Latin America', in *From Biocultural Homogenization to Biocultural Conservation* (ed. Ricardo Rozzi et al.; Ecology and Ethics, 3; Cham, Switzerland: Springer Nature, 2018), pp. 167–83, available online: https://doi.org/10.1007/978-3-319-99513-7_10.
Pattel-Gray, Anne, 'Dreaming: An Aboriginal Interpretation of the Bible', in *Text and Experience: Toward a Cultural Exegesis of the Bible* (ed. Daniel L. Smith-Christopher; Sheffield: Sheffield Academic, 1995), pp. 247–59.
Pattel-Gray, Anne, *The Great White Flood: Racism in Australia: Critically Appraised from an Aboriginal Historico-Theological Viewpoint* (AAR Cultural Criticism Series 2; Atlanta: Scholars Press, 1998).

Pattel-Gray, Anne, 'Not Yet Tiddas: An Aboriginal Womanist Critique of Australian Church Feminism', in *Freedom and Entrapment: Women Thinking Theology* (ed. Maryanne Confoy, Dorothy A. Lee and Joan Nowotny; North Blackburn: Dove, 1995), pp. 165–92.

Paul, Shalom M., *Isaiah 40–66: Translation and Commentary* (Eerdmans Critical Commentary; Grand Rapids: Eerdmans, 2012).

Paulson, Graham, and Mark Brett, 'Five Smooth Stones: Reading the Bible through Aboriginal Eyes', *Colloquium* 45, no. 2 (November 2013), pp. 199–214.

Perdue, Leo G., and Warren Carter, *Israel and Empire: A Postcolonial History of Israel and Early Judaism* (London: Bloomsbury T&T Clark, 2015).

Phillips, Mary and Nick Rumens (eds), *Contemporary Perspectives on Ecofeminism* (Routledge Explorations in Environmental Studies; Milton Park, Abingdon: Routledge, 2016).

Pickett, Raymond, 'Luke and Empire: An Introduction', in *Luke-Acts and Empire: Essays in Honor of Robert L. Brawley* (ed. David Rhoads, David Esterline and Jae Won Lee; Princeton Theological Monograph Series, 151; Eugene: Pickwick, 2011), pp. 1–22.

Pinsky, Robert, *The Sounds of Poetry: A Brief Guide* (New York: Farrar, Straus and Giroux, 1998).

Plummer, Robert L., *40 Questions about Interpreting the Bible* (Grand Rapids: Kregel, 2010).

Plumwood, Val, 'Decolonizing Relationships with Nature', in *Decolonizing Nature: Strategies for Conservation in a Post-colonial Era* (ed. William M. Adams and Martin Mulligan; London: Earthscan, 2003), pp. 51–78.

Plumwood, Val, *Environmental Culture: The Ecological Crisis of Reason* (Environmental Philosophies; London: Routledge, 2002).

Plumwood, Val, *Feminism and the Mastery of Nature* (Feminism for Today; London: Routledge, 1993).

Plumwood, Val, 'Shadow Places and the Politics of Dwelling', *Australian Humanities Review* 44, Ecological Humanities (March 2008), available online: http://australianhumanitiesreview.org/2008/03/01/shadow-places-and-the-politics-of-dwelling/ (accessed 3 February 2021).

Pope, Michael, 'Gabriel's Entrance and Biblical Violence in Luke's Annunciation Narrative', *JBL* 137 (2018), pp. 701–10.

Poppick, Laura, 'The Ocean Is Running Out of Breath Scientists Warn', *Scientific American* (25 February 2019), available online: https://www.scientificamerican.com/article/the-ocean-is-running-out-of-breath-scientists-warn/ (accessed 26 November 2020).

Primavesi, Anne, *Gaia and Climate Change: A Theology of Gift Events* (London: Routledge, 2009).

Pryor, Robin, and Cath James, 'Addressing Change through the Two Books of God: Education for Cultural Change in Religious Communities', in *Climate Change – Cultural Change: Religious Responses and Responsibilities* (ed. Anne Elvey and David Gormley-O'Brien; Preston, Vic.: Mosaic Press, 2013), pp. 176–90.

Ramp, Daniel, 'Roads as Drivers of Change for Macropods', in *Macropods: The Biology of Kangaroos, Wallabies and Rat-Kangaroos* (ed. Graeme Coulson and Mark Eldridge; Collingwood: CSIRO Publishing, 2010), pp. 279–91.

Rausch, John S., 'The Cross in the Mountains: Mountaintop Removal in Appalachia', in *Sacred Acts: How Churches Are Working to Protect Earth's Climate* (ed. Mallory McDuff; Gabriola Island, BC: New Society Publishers, 2012), pp. 149–62.

Rayment, Colette, '"A Comet Streamed in Language Far Down Time": Poetry of Earth', *Spirit of Place: Source of the Sacred? 1998 Australian International Religion, Literature* and the Arts Conference Proceedings (Sydney Studies in Religion, 1998), pp. 187–95, available online: https://openjournals.library.sydney.edu.au/index.php/SSR/article/view/12101 (accessed 6 August 2021).

Rayner, Peter. 'On the Science and Ethics of Climate Change: Why Utilitarian Responses Are Not Enough', in *Climate Change – Cultural Change: Religious Responses and Responsibilities* (ed. Anne Elvey and David Gormley-O'Brien; Preston, Vic.: Mosaic Press, 2013), pp. 21–34.

Readfearn, Graham, 'After Adani: Whatever Happened to Queensland's Galilee Basin Coal Boom?', *The Guardian* (9 January 2022), available online: https://www.theguardian.com/australia-news/2022/jan/09/after-adani-whatever-happened-to-queenslands-galilee-basin-coal-boom (accessed 14 January 2022).

Readfearn, Graham, 'World Heritage Committee Agrees Not to Place Great Barrier Reef on "in danger" List', *The Guardian* (24 July 2021), available online: https://www.theguardian.com/environment/2021/jul/23/world-heritage-committee-agrees-not-to-place-great-barrier-reef-on-in-danger-list (accessed 26 July 2021).

Reasoner, Mark, 'The Theme of Acts: Institutional History or Divine Necessity in History?', *JBL* 118 (1999), pp. 635–59.

Reid, Barbara E., *Choosing the Better Part? Women in the Gospel of Luke* (Collegeville: Liturgical Press, 1996).

Reid, Barbara E., 'An Overture to the Gospel of Luke', *CurTM* 39, no. 6 (December 2012), pp. 428–34.

Reid, Barbara E., *Taking Up the Cross: New Testament Interpretations through Latina and Feminist Eyes* (Minneapolis: Fortress, 2007).

Reid, Barbara E., 'Women Prophets of God's Alternative Reign', in *Luke-Acts and Empire: Essays in Honor of Robert L. Brawley* (ed. D. Rhoads, D. Esterline and Jae Won Lee; Princeton Theological Monograph Series, 151; Eugene, OR: Pickwick, 2011), pp. 44–59.

Reid, John, 'Spotlight: Road Kill', *Plumwood Mountain* 1, no. 1 (February 2014), available online: https://plumwoodmountain.com/spotlight-road-kill/ (accessed 12 May 2020).

Rhoads, David, 'Reading the New Testament in the Environmental Age', *CurTM* 24, no. 3 (1997), pp. 259–66.

Rhoads, David, David Esterline and Jae Won Lee (eds), *Luke-Acts and Empire: Essays in Honor of Robert L. Brawley* (Princeton Theological Monograph Series, 151; Eugene: Pickwick, 2011).

Ricoeur, Paul, *The Rule of Metaphor: The Creation of Meaning in Language* (trans. Robert Czerny, Kathleen McLaughlin and John Costello, SJ; Routledge Classics; London: Routledge, 2003).

Rigby, Kate, *Dancing with Disaster: Environmental Histories, Narratives, and Ethics for Perilous Times* (Charlottesville: University of Virginia Press, 2015).

Rigby, Kate, 'Earth, World, Text: On the (Im)possibility of Ecopoiesis', *New Literary History* 35 (2004), pp. 427–42.

Rigby, Kate, 'Ecocriticism', in *Introducing Criticism at the Twenty-first Century* (ed. Julian Wolfreys; Edinburgh: Edinburgh University Press, 2002), pp. 151–78.

Rigby, Kate, 'Introduction', *Religion and Literature* 40, no. 1 (Spring 2008), pp. 1–8.

Rigby, Kate, *Reclaiming Romanticism: Towards an Ecopoetics of Decolonization* (Environmental Culture Series; London: Bloomsbury, 2020).

Rigby, Kate, 'Women and Nature Revisited: Ecofeminist Reconfigurations of an Old Association', in *Feminist Ecologies: Changing Environments in the Anthropocene* (ed. Lara Stevens, Peta Tait and Denise Varney; Cham, Switzerland: Palgrave Macmillan, 2018), pp. 57–81.

Ringe, Sharon H., *Luke* (Westminster Bible Companion; Louisville, KY: Westminster John Knox, 1995).
Roberts, Samuel K., 'Becoming the Neighbor: Virtue Theory and the Problem of Neighbor Identity', *Int* 62, no. 2 (April 2008), pp. 146-55.
Rose, Deborah Bird, 'Country and the Gift', in *Humanities for the Environment: Integrating Knowledge, Forging New Constellations of Practice* (ed. Joni Adamson and Michael Davis; London: Routledge, 2017), pp. 33-44.
Rose, Deborah Bird, 'Double Death', Love at the Edge of Extinction, available online: https://deborahbirdrose.com/144-2/ (accessed 3 July 2019).
Rose, Deborah Bird, 'The Goodness of Creation and the Darkening World of Extinctions', paper presented at the Climate Change – Cultural Change: Religious Responses and Responsibilities Symposium, 29 October 2011, Centre for Theology and Ministry, Parkville, Victoria, Australia.
Rose, Deborah Bird, *Nourishing Terrains: Australian Aboriginal Views of Landscape and Wilderness* (Canberra: Australian Heritage Commission, 1996).
Rose, Deborah Bird, *Reports from a Wild Country: Ethics for Decolonisation* (Sydney: UNSW Press, 2004).
Rose, Deborah Bird, *Wild Dog Dreaming: Love and Extinction* (Under the Sign of Nature: Explorations in Ecocriticism; Charlottesville: University of Virginia Press, 2011).
Rose, Deborah Bird, Thom van Dooren, Mathew Chrulew, Stuart Cooke, Matthew Kearnes and Emily O'Gorman, 'Thinking through the Environment: Unsettling the Humanities', *Environmental Humanities* 1, no. 1 (2012), pp. 1-5, available online: https://doi.org/10.1215/22011919-3609940 (accessed 9 March 2021).
Rosenblatt, M. E., 'Ecology and the Gospels', *TBT* 33, no. 1 (1995), pp. 28-32.
Rosenzweig, Franz, *The Star of Redemption* (trans. Barbara E. Galli; Madison, WI: The University of Wisconsin Press, 2005).
Ross, Matthew R. V., Brian L. McGlynn and Emily S. Bernhardt, 'Deep Impact: Effects of Mountaintop Mining on Surface Topography, Bedrock Structure, and Downstream Waters', *Environmental Science & Technology* 50 (2016), pp. 2064-74, available online: http://dx.doi.org/10.1021/acs.est.5b04532.
Rossing, Barbara, 'God Laments with Us: Climate Change, Apocalypse and the Urgent *Kairos* Moment', *The Ecumenical Review* 62 (2010), pp. 119-30.
Rozzi, Ricardo, 'Biocultural Homogenization: A Wicked Problem in the Anthropocene', in *From Biocultural Homogenization to Biocultural Conservation* (ed. Ricardo Rozzi et al.; Ecology and Ethics, 3; Cham, Switzerland: Springer Nature, 2018), pp. 21-48, available online: https://doi.org/10.1007/978-3-319-99513-7_2.
Ruether, Rosemary Radford, 'The Biblical Vision of the Ecological Crisis', in *Readings in Ecology and Feminist Theology* (ed. Mary Heather MacKinnon and Moni McIntyre; Kansas City: Sheed and Ward, 1995), pp. 75-81.
Ruether, Rosemary Radford, *Gaia and God: An Ecofeminist Theology of Earth Healing* (San Francisco: HarperCollins, 1992).
Ruether, Rosemary Radford (ed.), *Women Healing Earth: Third World Women on Ecology, Feminism, and Religion* (Maryknoll: Orbis Books, 1996).
Rushton, Kathleen P., 'The Cosmology of John 1:1-14 and Its Implications for Ethical Action in this Ecological Age', *Colloquium* 45, no. 2 (November 2013), pp. 137-53.
Sadler, Rodney S., Jr., 'Guest Editorial: Who Is My Neighbor? Introductory Explorations', *Int* 62, no. 2 (April 2008), pp. 115-21.
Salleh, Ariel, *Ecofeminism as Politics: Nature, Marx and the Postmodern* (London: Zed Books, 1997).

Salleh, Ariel (ed.), *Eco-sufficiency and Global Justice: Women Write Political Ecology* (North Melbourne: Spinifex Press, 2009).

Santner, Eric L., 'Miracles Happen: Benjamin, Rosenzweig, Freud, and the Matter of the Neighbor', in *The Neighbor: Three Inquiries in Political Theology* (ed. Slavoj Žižek, Eric L. Santner and Kenneth Reinhard; Chicago: The University of Chicago Press, 2005), pp. 76–133.

Santner, Eric L., *On Creaturely Life: Rilke, Benjamin, Sebald* (Chicago: The University of Chicago Press, 2006).

Santos Perez, Craig, *Habitat Threshold* (Oakland, CA: Omnidawn, 2020).

Satha-Anand, Chaiwat, 'Breathing the Others, Seeing the Lives: A Reflection on Twenty-First-Century Nonviolence', in *Towards a Just and Ecologically Sustainable Peace: Navigating the Great Transition* (ed. Joseph Camilleri and Deborah Guess; Singapore: Palgrave Macmillan, 2020), pp. 229–48.

Schaberg, Jane, *The Illegitimacy of Jesus: A Feminist Theological Interpretation of the Infancy Narratives* (New York: Crossroad, 1990).

Scheuer, Blaženka, *The Return of YHWH: The Tension between Deliverance and Repentance in Isaiah 40–55* (Berlin: De Gruyter, 2008).

Schottroff, Luise, 'The Creation Narrative: Genesis 1:1–2:4a', in *A Feminist Companion to Genesis* (ed. Athalya Brenner; Sheffield: Sheffield Academic, 1993), pp. 24–38.

Schroer, Silvia, and Thomas Staubli, *Body Symbolism in the Bible* (trans. Linda M. Maloney; Collegeville: Liturgical Press, 2001).

Schüssler Fiorenza, Elisabeth, *But She Said: Feminist Practices of Biblical Interpretation* (Boston: Beacon, 1992).

Schüssler Fiorenza, Elisabeth, *Congress of Wo/men: Religion, Gender, and Kyriarchal Power* (Cambridge, MA: Feminist Studies in Religion Books, 2016).

Schüssler Fiorenza, Elisabeth, *The Power of the Word: Scripture and the Rhetoric of Empire* (Minneapolis: Fortress, 2007).

'Scott Morrison Brings a Chunk of Coal into Parliament' (video), *The Guardian* (9 February 2017), available online: https://www.theguardian.com/global/video/2017/feb/09/scott-morrison-brings-a-chunk-of-coal-into-parliament-video (accessed 27 May 2021).

Scott, Rebecca R., 'Dependent Masculinity and Political Culture in Pro-Mountaintop Removal Discourse: Or, How I Learned to Stop Worrying and Love the Dragline', *Feminist Studies* 33, no. 3 (Fall 2007), pp. 484–509.

Sebald, W. G., *Austerlitz* (trans. A. Bell; reissued with a new introduction by J. Wood; eBook; London: Penguin, 2011 [2001]).

Sechrest, Love L., 'Double Vision for Revolutionary Religion: Race Relations, Moral Analogies, and African-American Biblical Interpretation', in *Ethnicity, Race, Religion: Identities and Ideologies in Early Jewish and Christian Texts, and in Modern Biblical Interpretation* (ed. Katherine M. Hockey and David G. Horrell; paperback edn; London: T&T Clark, 2020), pp. 202–18.

Seed Indigenous Youth Climate Network, 'Our Stories Are Connected to the Reef', YouTube, available online: https://youtu.be/lr1Zx2ZQ_WA (accessed 13 August 2021).

Serres, Michel, *The Five Senses: A Philosophy of Mingled Bodies (I)* (trans. Margaret Sankey and Peter Cowley; London: Continuum, 2008 [Fre. 1985]).

Sharp, Nonie, 'Being True to the Earth – in Peril: Finding a Voice to Touch the Heart', *PAN*, no. 5 (2008), pp. 47–58.

Sheldrake, Merlin, *Entangled Life: How Fungi Make Our Worlds, Change Our Minds, and Shape Our Futures* (London: The Bodley Head, 2020).

Sherwood, Yvonne, 'Cutting Up Life: Sacrifice as a Device for Clarifying – and Tormenting – Fundamental Distinctions between Human, Animal, and Divine', in *The Bible and Posthumanism* (ed. Jennifer L. Koosed; SemeiaSt; Atlanta: SBL, 2014), pp. 247–97.

Sider, Ron, *Rich Christians in an Age of Hunger: Moving from Affluence to Generosity* (5th edn; Nashville: Thomas Nelson, 2005 [1977]).

Simkins, Ronald A., *Creator and Creation: Nature in the Worldview of Ancient Israel* (Peabody, MA: Hendricksons, 1994).

Simpson, Lindsay, *Adani, Following Its Dirty Footsteps: A Personal Story* (North Geelong: Spinifex, 2018).

Sittler, Joseph, *The Care of the Earth* (Facets edn; Minneapolis: Fortress, 2004 [1964]).

Skinner, Jonathan, 'Thoughts on Things: Poetics of the Third Landscape', in *)((ECO(LANG) (UAGE(READER)): The Eco Language Reader* (ed. Brenda Iijima; New York: Portable Press at Yo-Yo Labs and Nightboat Books, 2010), pp. 9–51.

Skousen, Jeff, and Carl E. Zipper, 'Coal Mining and Reclamation in Appalachia', in *Appalachia's Coal-Mined Landscapes* (ed. Carl E. Zipper and Jeff Skousen; Cham, Switzerland: Springer Nature, 2021), pp. 55–83.

Skye, Lee Miena, *Kerygmatics of the New Millennium: A Study of Australian Aboriginal Women's Christology* (Delhi: ISPCK, 2007).

Slezak, Michael, 'Australia Avoids Great Barrier Reef Global Embarrassment, but the Dangers of Climate Change Remain for the Reef', ABC News (24 July 2021), available online: https://www.abc.net.au/news/2021-07-24/australia-avoids-great-barrier-reef-global-embarrassment/100319950 (accessed 26 July 2021).

Smaill, Belinda, 'Historicising David Attenborough's Nature: Nation, Continent, Country and Environment', *Celebrity Studies* (2020), pp. 1–22, doi:10.1080/19392397.2020.18 55995.

Smee, Ben, 'Adani Coal Port Faces Possible "stop order" after Traditional Owners Object', *The Guardian* (5 July 2018), available online: https://www.theguardian.com/environment/2018/jul/05/adani-coal-port-faces-possible-stop-order-after-traditional-owners-object (accessed 12 November 2019).

Smith, Mitzi J., 'Review of J. Albert Harrill, *Slaves in the New Testament: Literary, Social, and Moral Dimensions* (Minneapolis: Fortress, 2006)', *JAAR* 75, no. 1 (2007), pp. 219–23.

Snodgrass, Klyne R., 'Streams of Tradition Emerging from Isaiah 40:1-5 and Their Adaptation in the New Testament', *JSNT* 8 (1980), pp. 24–45.

Song, C. S., *Jesus and the Reign of God* (eBook; Minneapolis: Fortress, 1993).

Spivak, Gayatri Chakravorty, *Outside in the Teaching Machine* (London: Routledge 1993).

Spring, Úrsula Oswald, Hans Günter Brauch and Keith G. Tidball, 'Expanding Peace Ecology: Peace, Security, Sustainability, Equity, and Gender', in *Expanding Peace Ecology: Peace, Security, Sustainability, Equity and Gender. Perspectives of IPRA's Ecology and Peace Commission* (ed. Úrsula Oswald Spring, Hans Günter Brauch and Keith G. Tidball; Springer Briefs in Environment, Security, Development and Peace, Peace and Security Studies, 12; Cham, Switzerland: Springer, 2014), pp. 1–30.

Squires, John T., *The Plan of God in Luke-Acts* (Cambridge: Cambridge University Press, 1993).

Steffensen, Victor, *Fire Country: How Indigenous Fire Management Could Help Save Australia* (Richmond, Vic.: Hardie Grant Travel, 2020).

Stevens, Lara, Peta Tait and Denise Varney (eds), *Feminist Ecologies: Changing Environments in the Anthropocene* (Cham, Switzerland: Palgrave Macmillan, 2018).

Stewart, Susan, *Poetry and the Fate of the Senses* (Chicago: The University of Chicago Press, 2002).
Stolle, Jeffrey, 'Levinas and the Akedah: An Alternative to Kiekegaard', *Philosophy Today* 45, no. 2 (Summer 2001), pp. 132–43.
Stop Adani, available online: https://www.stopadani.com/ (accessed 27 May 2021).
Stowers, Stanley, 'Matter and Spirit, or What Is Pauline Participation in Christ?', in *The Holy Spirit: Classic and Contemporary Readings* (ed. Eugene F. Rogers, Jr; Chichester: Wiley-Blackwell, 2009), pp. 91–105.
Sturgeon, Noël, *Ecofeminist Natures: Race Gender Feminist Theory and Political Action* (London: Routledge, 1997).
Styan, Andrew, *Catch Your Breath*, available online: https://catch-your-breath.com/ (accessed 2 July 2019).
Tannehill, Robert C., *Luke* (Abingdon New Testament Commentaries; Nashville: Abingdon, 1996).
Taubman, Aliza, 'Protecting Aboriginal Sacred Sites: The Aftermath of the Hindmarsh Island Dispute', *Environmental and Planning Law Journal* 19, no. 2 (2002), pp. 140–58.
Taylor, Dorceta E., 'Women of Color, Environmental Justice, and Ecofeminism', in *Ecofeminism: Women, Culture, Nature* (ed. Karen J. Warren; Bloomington: Indiana University Press, 1997).
Thompson, Andrew R. H., *Sacred Mountains: A Christian Ethical Approach to Mountaintop Removal* (Lexington: The University of Kentucky Press, 2015).
Thompson, Michael, *Isaiah 40–66* (Epworth Commentaries; Peterborough: Epworth, 2001).
Thoracic Society of Australia and New Zealand, 'Declaration on Climate Change' (10 December 2019), available online: https://www.thoracic.org.au/documents/item/1800 (accessed 26 November 2020).
Tilford, Nicole L., *Sensing World, Sensing Wisdom: The Cognitive Foundation of Biblical Metaphors* (Atlanta: SBL, 2017).
Trainor, Michael, *About Earth's Child: An Ecological Listening to the Gospel of Luke* (Earth Bible Commentary, 2; Sheffield: Sheffield Phoenix, 2012).
Trible, Phyllis, *Texts of Terror: Literary-Feminist Readings of Biblical Narratives* (London: SCM, 1992).
Tucker, Gene, 'Rain on a Land Where No One Lives: The Hebrew Bible on the Environment', *JBL* 116 (1997), pp. 3–17.
UNESCO, Great Barrier Reef, World Heritage List, available online: https://whc.unesco.org/en/list/154/ (accessed 12 July 2021).
UNESCO, 'State of Conservation of Properties Inscribed on the World Heritage List', World Heritage Committee, extended forty-fourth session, Fuzhou (China), online meeting, 16–31 July 2021, Item 7B of the Provisional Agenda, WHC/21/44.COM/7B.Add (Paris, 21 June 2021), pp. 83–7, available online: https://whc.unesco.org/archive/2021/whc21-44com-7B.Add-en.pdf (accessed 12 July 2021).
United Nations, Sustainable Development Knowledge Platform, available online: https://sustainabledevelopment.un.org/ (accessed 3 July 2019).
Vásquez, Manuel A., 'Vascularizing the Study of Religion: Multi-Agent Figurations and Cosmopolitics', in *Entangled Worlds: Religion, Science, and New Materialism* (ed. Catherine Keller and Mary-Jane Rubenstein; New York: Fordham University Press, 2017), pp. 228–47.
Vatican II, *Gaudium et Spes* (7 December 1965), in *Vatican Council II: The Conciliar and Post Conciliar Documents* (ed. Austin Flannery, O.P.; Collegeville: Liturgical Press, 1975).

Vizenor, Gerald, *Manifest Manners: Narratives on Postindian Survivance* (Lincoln: University of Nebraska Press, 1994).
Wainwright, Elaine M., *Habitat, Human, and Holy: An Eco-Rhetorical Reading of the Gospel of Matthew* (Earth Bible Commentary, 6; Sheffield: Sheffield Phoenix, 2016).
Wainwright, Elaine M., 'Images, Words, Stories: Exploring Their Transformative Power in Reading Biblical Texts Ecologically', *BibInt* 20 (2012), pp. 280–304.
Wainwright, Elaine M., 'A Metaphorical Walk through Scripture in an Ecological Age', *Pacifica* 4, no. 3 (1991), pp. 273–94.
Wainwright, Elaine M., 'Response to Horrell', *Colloquium* 4, no. 2 (November 2014), pp. 166–9.
Wainwright, Elaine M., 'Unbound Hair and *Ointmented* Feet: An Ecofeminist Reading of Luke 7.36-50', in *Exchanges of Grace: Festschrift for Ann Loades* (ed. Natalie K. Watson and Stephen Burns; London: SCM, 2008), pp. 178–89.
Wainwright, Elaine M., *Women Healing/Healing Women: The Genderization of Healing in Early Christianity* (London: Equinox, 2006).
Wallace, Mark I., *Finding God in the Singing River: Christianity, Spirit, Nature* (Minneapolis: Fortress, 2005).
Wallace, Mark I., *When God Was a Bird: Christianity, Animism, and the Re-Enchantment of the World* (New York: Fordham University Press, 2019).
Walsh, Brian J., Marianne B. Karsh and Nik Ansell, 'Trees, Forestry, and the Responsiveness of Creation', in *This Sacred Earth: Religion, Nature, Environment* (ed. Roger S. Gottlieb; New York: Routledge, 1996), pp. 423–35.
Wangan and Jagalinguou Family Council, 'Traditional Owners Continue to Resist Adani's "Invasion"', Latest News (25 January 2019), available online: https://wanganjagalingou.com.au/traditional-owners-continue-to-resist-adanis-invasion/ (accessed 15 March 2021).
Wangan and Jagalingou Family Council, available online: https://wanganjagalingou.com.au/ (accessed 26 July 2021).
Wasson, Matt, 'Study Shows Steep Decline in Fish Populations near Mountaintop Removal', *The Appalachian Voice* (10 August 2014), available online: http://appvoices.org/2014/08/10/study-shows-steep-decline-in-fish-populations-near-mountaintop-removal/ (accessed 31 May 2021).
Weil, Simone, *Gravity and Grace* (trans. Emma Crawford; Routledge Classics; London: Routledge, 2002 [French 1947]).
Wenell, Karen J., *Jesus and Land: Sacred and Social Space in Second Temple Judaism* (London: T&T Clark, 2007).
West Virginia Coal Association, *Coal Facts: West Virginia Coal: Building a Future for Our People* (Charleston, WV: West Virginia Coal Association, 2012), available online: http://www.wvcoal.com (accessed 1 June 2021).
White, Carol Wayne, 'Stubborn Materiality: African American Religious Naturalism and Becoming Our Humanity', in *Entangled Worlds: Religion, Science, and New Materialism* (ed. Catherine Keller and Mary-Jane Rubenstein; New York: Fordham University Press, 2017), pp. 251–73.
White, Lynn, 'The Historical Roots of Our Ecological Crisis' [1967], in *This Sacred Earth: Religion, Nature, Environment* (ed. Roger S. Gottlieb; New York: Routledge, 1996), pp. 184–93.
White, R. S., *John Keats: A Literary Life* (Basingstoke: Palgrave Macmillan, 2010).
Whittaker, Alison, 'So White. So What', *Meanjin* 79, no. 1 (Autumn 2020), pp. 50–61.
Whyte, Kyle Powys, 'Is It Colonial *Déjà vu*? Indigenous Peoples and Climate Injustice', in *Humanities for the Environment: Integrating Knowledge, Forging New Constellations of Practice* (ed. Joni Adamson and Michael Davis; London: Routledge, 2017), pp. 88–105.

Wickham, James et al., 'The Overlooked Terrestrial Impacts of Mountaintop Mining', *BioScience* 63, no. 5 (2013), pp. 335–48.
Williams, William Carlos, *The Collected Poems of William Carlos Williams Volume II: 1939–1962* (ed. Christopher MacGowan; New York: New Directions, 1991).
Winn, Adam, 'Striking Back at the Empire: Empire Theory and Responses to Empire in the New Testament', in *An Introduction to Empire in the New Testament* (ed. Adam Winn; Atlanta: SBL, 2016), pp. 1–14.
WIRES: Wildlife Rescue, available online: https://www.wires.org.au/ (accessed 13 May 2020).
Wirzba, Norman, 'Throwaway People, Throwaway Land', *Books and Culture: A Christian Review* (December 2007), pp. 44–5.
Wishart, William Ryan, 'Underdeveloping Appalachia: Toward an Environmental Sociology of Extractive Economies' (PhD thesis, Department of Sociology and the Graduate School, University of Oregon, 2014).
Witherington, Ben III, *Isaiah Old and New: Exegesis, Intertextuality, and Hermeneutics* (Minneapolis: 1517 Media and Fortress Press, 2017), doi:10.2307/j.ctt1ggjhbz.
Witt, Joseph D., *Religion and Resistance in Appalachia: Faith and the Fight against Mountaintop Removal Coal Mining* (Lexington: The University of Kentucky Press, 2016).
Wohlleben, Peter, *The Hidden Life of Trees: What They Feel, How They Communicate* (trans. Jane Billinghurst; Carlton, Vic.: Black Inc., 2016).
Wooden, Thomas, 'The "1954 Hague Convention": Aboriginal and Torres Strait Islander Sacred Sites as Cultural Property', *Australian Year Book of International Law* 34 (2017), pp. 127–48.
Woods, Brad R., and Jason S. Gordon, 'Mountaintop Removal and Job Creation: Exploring the Relationship Using Spatial Regression', *Annals of the Association of American Geographers* 101, no. 4 (2011), pp. 806–15.
Wordsworth, William, *Selected Poems* (ed. with an introduction and notes by Stephen Gill and Duncan Wu; Oxford World's Classics; Oxford: Oxford University Press, 1997).
Wright, Judith, *The Coral Battleground* (New edn; North Melbourne: Spinifex, 2014 [1977]).
Youngblood, Patricia, 'Two West Virginia Poems', *Vox Populi*, available online: https://voxpopulisphere.com/2017/08/08/patricia-youngblood-two-west-virginia-poems/ (accessed 5 June 2021).
Yunkaporta, Tyson, *Sand Talk: How Indigenous Thinking Can Save the World* (Melbourne: Text Publishing, 2019).
Zalasiewicz, Jan, Paul Crutzen and Will Steffen, 'The Anthropocene', in *The Geological Time Scale 2012* (ed. Felix M. Gradstein, James G. Ogg, Mark D. Schmitz and Gabi M. Ogg; Boston: Elsevier, 2012), pp. 1033–40, available online: https://doi.org/10.1016/B978-0-444-59425-9.00032-9.
Zalasiewicz, Jan, Will Steffen, Reinhold Leinfeld, Mark Williams and Colin Waters, 'Petrifying Earth Process: The Stratigraphic Imprint of Key Earth System Parameters in the Anthropocene', *Theory, Culture & Society* 34, no. 2–3 (2017), pp. 83–104.
Zipper, Carl E., Mary Beth Adams, and Jeff Skousen, 'The Appalachian Coalfield in Historical Context', in *Appalachia's Coal-Mined Landscapes* (ed. Carl E. Zipper and Jeff Skousen; Cham, Switzerland: Springer Nature, 2021), pp. 1–26.

INDEX OF REFERENCES

Hebrew Bible/Old Testament

Genesis
1.2	71–2, 74
2.7	35
9.9–17	171
22.1–4	195
22.11–13	195
22.16	195
30.13	37–8

Exodus
15.19–21	33
24.15–18	187
34.2, 29–35	187

Leviticus
19.15–19	130

Deuteronomy
6.4–5	130
30.19	131

Judges
5.5	188
11.38	188

1 Samuel
1.11	37
2.1–10	33

Job
12.10–11	72
27.3–4	72
28.9, 12	164

Psalms
24.1	165, 168
34	57
68.15–16	188
72.3	168
89.19	196
97.5	188
98.7–9	32
106.23	196
114.4–6	188
135.7	114
148	188

Isaiah
11.6–9	162
11.9	164
40	171, 173, 201
40–55	169–72
40.1	170, 174
40.1–11	170, 172
40.3–5	172–3
40.4	21, 108, 153, 155–6, 160, 162–3, 165–9, 172–5
40.4–5	167, 169
41.17–19	172
42.1	196
42.7	75
44.23	188
45.1–8	170
49.13	188
55.12	188
58.3–6	76
58.6	75, 148
58.11	77
61.1	72
61.1–2	75, 148
61.11	76
65.25	162

Jeremiah
4.18, 22, 28	171

Ezekiel
36.1	188
36.8	188

Index of References

NEW TESTAMENT

Matthew
16.2–3	109
17.5	195
17.20	168

Mark
9.2	190
9.7	195

Luke
1.15	73
1.17	73
1.20	113
1.35	73, 192
1.38	41 n. 74
1.39–56	33
1.41	73
1.45	37–8
1.46–47	73, 76
1.46–55	20, 36, 73, 131, 201 n. 7
1.47	39
1.48	37–8, 41–2, 201 n. 7
1.50	37, 42
1.51	41
1.51–53	173
1.52	36, 42
1.54	76
1.54–55	37–8
1.55	38, 42
1.67	73
1.76–79	128
1.77	114
1.78	134
1.79	114
1.80	73
2.1–5	127
2.1–14	113
2.14	110, 114, 130
2.25	200
2.25–27	73
2.34–35	110
2.35	39
3.1–2	127
3.3–6	173
3.5	21, 155, 160, 163, 169, 173, 201 n. 7
3.9	110
3.10–14	173
3.16	73
3.22	73, 195
4.1	73
4.14	73
4.16	74
4.16–30	21, 62, 63–4, 74–9
4.18	43
4.18–19	110–11, 114, 128, 131, 148, 173, 194
4.19	77
4.21	113
6.9	39
6.12	188
6.17–49	131
6.20–26	131, 173
6.24	200
6.27	131–2
6.27–29	133
6.28	131
6.31	132
6.35	131
7.1–10	132
7.11–17	147
7.13	134, 148
7.22	131
7.23	147
7.30	110
7.40–48	111, 131
9.18	189
9.22	112, 128, 195
9.22–25	189
9.24	39
9.26	189
9.27	189–90
9.28	188, 197
9.28–36	153, 177, 181, 186–7, 189, 193
9.29	190, 192
9.30	192
9.31	21, 192, 197
9.32	196
9.33	192, 197
9.34	188, 192
9.34–35	197
9.35	192, 195, 197
9.36	197
9.37	197
10.1–11	128–9

10.2	113	17.33	39
10.9	113	19.9	113
10.11	113, 129	19.40	32
10.12–24	130	19.41–44	110, 112–13, 116, 128–9
10.25	130	19.42	114
10.25–37	21, 54, 119, 121, 147	19.43–44	127
10.26	130	20.10	113
10.27	130	21.20–24	127
10.28	131	22.7	195
10.29	133–4, 148–9	22.36–37	128
10.30	133, 147	23.4, 15, 25	127
10.30–35	130	23.6–25	127
10.30–37	21, 141–3	24.5–7	112, 128, 195
10.31	134	24.25–26	112, 128, 195
10.31–32	148	24.39	74
10.32	134		
10.33	134, 147–8	John	
10.34	150	14.26	200
10.34–35	133, 135		
10.36	134, 148	Acts	
10.37	134–5, 149	1.2, 5, 8, 16	74
11.27	38	2.2, 4	74
11.27–28	74	2.44–47	114
11.28	38	4.27	127
12	5, 103	4.32–37	114
12.1	109	5.15	192
12.19	39	9.31	200
12.20	39	14.17	113
12.22–23	40		
12.24–28	42	2 Corinthians	
12.24–30	112	1.4	201
12.42	113		
12.49–53	110	1 Timothy	
12.54–56	21, 102, 104, 108–10, 114, 117	5.8	167
12.56	21, 110–13, 115	PSEUDEPIGRAPHA	
12.57	110		
12.58–59	110	Pseudo-Philo's *Biblical Antiquities* (*L.A.B.*)	
13.9	114	40.2	189, 195
13.31–35	112, 116, 128	40.3	188–9
14.19	113	40.3–7	189
15.11–32	147		
15.20	147–8	CLASSICAL AND ANCIENT CHRISTIAN LITERATURE	
15.28	200 n. 4		
16.16	110	Virgil	
16.19–31	131, 200	*Aeneid*	
16.25	200	6.851–53	41 n. 75
17	115		
17.22–25	128	Gospel of Thomas	
17.25	112, 195	91	109

INDEX OF NAMES

Abram, D. 3 n. 7, 26 n. 9, 65
Adams, C. J. 146–7
Attenborough, D. 182–3

Balabanski, V. 29–30, 51, 69
Barker, A. 144–6
Bawaka Country 186
Bennett, J. 14, 90–2, 95
Berry, T. 45–7, 49, 53
Bigell, W. 185–6
Birch, T. 106 nn. 19–20, 107
Bonds, J. 164–5
Bovon, F. 37 n. 58, 195 n. 82

Cadwallader, A. 132 n. 40, 148–9
Carroll, S. 197
Carter, W. 34, 41
Celan, P. 31 n. 31, 70
Chakrabarty, D. 96–7
Chalmers, M. 135 n. 57
Chrétien, J.-L. 53, 99–100, 134 n. 54, 186 n. 44
Christensen, E. 165
Code, L. 5 n. 11, 11, 122
Collins, J. J. 163
Collins, P. H. 83
Crabbe, K. 111–12, 114
Crawley, A. T. 22 n. 78, 28, 69–70
Crossan, J. D. 129 n. 32

de Beauvoir, S. 88
Deloria, V. 49
Derrida, J. 12, 59 n. 80, 62, 66, 132 n. 42
Deverell, G. W. 3 n. 5, 29–30, 46

Eaton, H. 32, 143 n. 9, 177
Engberg-Pedersen, T. 73

Fitzmyer, J. A. 37 n. 58, 109, 133
Ford, T. H. 71

Foster, J. B. 86–7, 159
Francis (Pope) 43, 117–18, 152

Gaard, G. 11 n. 28, 19
Gander, F. 55–6
Gebara, I. 19, 143–4
Ghosh, A. 108, 118–19
Gottlieb, R. S. 45, 47
Grassi, J. 129 n. 32
Grosz, E. 93–5, 101

Habel, N. 6–8, 27, 31, 34, 46–7, 50–1, 53–4, 171 n. 91, 172–3
Hamburger, M. 61
Hamilton, C. 104–5, 118
Haraway, D. 105–6, 151–2, 201 n. 8
Heaney, S. 55, 59
Hiebert, T. 26, 39, 71–2
Hogan, L. 91
hooks, b. 85, 176
Horrell, D. G. 8, 28 n. 18, 51–2, 107 n. 26, 171 n. 88
Horsley, R. A. 35–6, 68, 131
House, S. 176
Howie, G. 87–8

Irigaray, L. 26, 48, 64–5, 68, 93

Jackson, Z. I. 16–18, 150–1
John Paul II (Pope) 117–18, 152
Jones, A. 162

Keats, J. 55, 66
Keller, C. 6 n. 11, 71–2, 115–16, 200
Kirk, A. 132–3
Kristeva, J. 14, 99

Lamar, W. 74 n. 76, 78
Lee, D. 189–90, 193
Lévinas, E. 194–6
Lingis, A. 52

Loeb, P. 166 n. 58, 168
Logan, W. B. 25–6, 65, 68 n. 34
Lorde, A. 16, 197

McCann, A. 60
McCredden, L. 48
McQuaid, J. 159–60
Marion, J.-L. 12 n. 35, 49–50
Marx, K. 87, 159
Mathews, F. 91, 147 n. 30
Moreton-Robinson, A. 17–18, 83–4, 90, 161
Morgan, J. 53

Neville, D. 129 n. 32
Newberry, B. 165

O'Connell, M. 146
Oppermann, S. 184–5

Pattel-Gray, A. 17–18
Paul, S. M. 170 nn. 81–2, 172 n. 103
Plummer, R. L. 168
Plumwood, V. 15 n. 55, 17, 88–90, 95, 160–1, 166 n. 57

Reid, B. E. 33–4, 39, 41–2, 73
Reid, J. 145–6, 149
Rigby, K. 19, 65, 182, 185–6
Ringe, S. H. 109–11, 114, 131 n. 37, 133 n. 51
Rose, D. B. 3 n. 5, 29, 39, 97, 100 n. 92, 106, 141 n. 2, 196
Ruether, R. R. 89, 149, 171

Santner, E. 22 n. 78, 119, 121 n. 1, 123–4
Satha-Anand, C. 84
Sechrest, L. L. 135 n. 57, 199
Schüssler Fiorenza, E. 5 n. 10, 11, 31, 52 n. 43, 53–4, 89 n. 32
Scott, R. 162
Serres, M. 38, 48 n. 18
Shelby, A. 167–8
Sherwood, Y. 196
Sittler, J. 62
Smaill, B. 182
Spivak, G. C. 12
Stewart, S. 55
Stowers, S. 73
Styan, A. 25–6

Thompson, A. R. H. 164
Thompson, M. 171 n. 95, 172 n. 103
Trainor, M. 32 n. 40, 40 n. 71, 43–4, 74 n. 75, 192
Tucker, G. 28 n. 18, 52

Vizenor, G. 70

Wainwright, E. M. 5 n. 11, 14, 18, 28 n. 18, 30, 125–6
Wallace, M. I. 91
Weil, S. 59
Wirzba, N. 169
Witt, J. D. 168–9
Wordsworth, W. 49, 57
Wright, J. 193–4, 199

INDEX OF SUBJECTS

Aboriginal Deaths in Custody 2, 69
activism 9, 11, 159, 164–5, 168–9, 176, 181–3, 193–4, 198, 201
Adani (Bravus) 106 n.19, 107, 158, 190–1, 193–4
aesthetics, ecological feminist 20, 176–7, 181–4, 202
agency; *see also* material agency
  Earth 8, 32, 76–7, 138
  more-than-human 5, 11, 17, 53, 71, 86, 90, 93, 119, 124, 183
air 25–8, 31, 39, 54, 63–78, 141–2, 166, 176, 197, 200, 202
Akedah 189, 195
ancestors, ancestry 29, 34, 37–8, 42–3, 84, 90, 92, 171, 202
androcentrism 52 n. 43, 84, 152, 161, 171, 175
animal (as category) 15–17, 30, 32, 67–8, 146, 150–1, 196
animism 32, 91, 106, 119, 175, 188
Anthropocene 6, 96, 104–6, 108, 118, 151
anthropocentrism 5, 8, 16, 27–8, 31, 51–2, 104–5, 117, 161, 170–2, 175
anthropogenic impacts 14, 69, 96, 103–5, 108, 118, 138, 185
aphesis (ἄφεσις) 76, 79, 100, 114, 148, 194, 197
apocalyptic imaginary 78, 106, 115–16
Appalachians 21, 155–60, 164–9, 174–6, 180
atmosphere (Earth's) 25, 27–8, 39–40, 65–6, 69, 71–2, 74, 96, 108, 112, 202
auratic citation 71, 75, 77

basileia (βασιλεία, reign) of G-d 41–2, 106, 113–14, 123, 128–9
beauty 19, 56, 59, 134 n. 54, 177, 181, 183–6, 192–3, 196
Bible, uses and impacts of 3–4, 6–9, 14–15, 57, 107, 160, 164–9, 175, 199

Black Lives Matter 2, 18, 69–70
Black women 16–17, 83
body 27, 34, 38–40, 73–4, 77, 88, 94, 147; *see also* corporeality; pregnant body
braided reading 1, 4–6, 18–20, 22, 108, 153, 177, 181–2, 186, 198
breath 25–8, 33–6, 38–40, 63–79, 83–4, 200

call-response 33, 49, 52–4, 83, 99–102, 105, 134, 138, 141, 186 n. 44, 188, 192–8
capitalism 12–13, 30, 46, 66, 87, 90–1, 96, 107, 158–9, 179
Capitolocene 106
Christians for the Mountains 162, 164–5, 174
Christology, Pauline 73
Chthulucene 105–6
climate change 15, 27, 30, 38, 63–5, 69–75, 95–7, 101, 103–8, 115–19, 138, 142–3, 157–9, 180–3, 190–1
colonization 1–4, 16–18, 106–7; *see also* invasion
  Bible as agent of 9, 15
  logic of 17, 30, 88–90, 97 n. 78, 160–1, 179
colour, as phenomenon 181, 184–5, 190–1, 196
compassion 21–2, 54, 124, 128, 134–8, 141–50, 153, 197
commodification 87, 90, 123–4, 136–7, 159
consumerism 4, 14, 66, 87 n. 22, 90, 104, 182, 199
coral bleaching 4, 138, 179–84, 191–3, 196
corporeality 13–15, 19, 48, 52–4, 64, 66–7, 69, 73–4, 123, 149; *see also* body
cosmology, Pauline 73

Country (Aboriginal English) 3, 12–13, 29–30, 84, 106–7, 179, 183, 186–7
covenant 38, 131, 165, 170–2, 174–5
Covid-19 3, 63, 78, 142–3
creation 27 n. 13, 32 n. 40, 38, 40, 43, 116–18, 123, 136 n. 61, 144, 164–5, 168, 175
creaturely life 119, 123–4, 136
cringe, the 119, 123, 138
cry
   of Earth 4–5, 53, 55, 194
   sacred 53, 57, 60, 197

debt (in Luke) 33 n. 42, 42, 76–7, 110–11, 114, 116–17, 122, 128, 131, 133 n. 49, 137, 148, 194
decolonization (ethic and praxis of) 9, 20, 107
deep incarnation 48, 175
deep time 84, 176–7
disciples (in Luke) 40, 42, 109–10, 112, 127 n. 25, 129–30, 189–90, 192, 196–8
disfiguration/s 21, 177, 193–4, 196–7
dualism 3 n. 7, 15, 17, 88–90, 93, 95, 98, 144, 160

Earth Bible 6–9, 20, 28 n. 18, 29, 50–5, 59, 63, 68, 84, 108, 125
ecojustice principles 7–8, 20, 28, 32, 50, 52–4, 59, 63, 68, 122–3, 125
ecological conversion 21, 29–30, 51, 69, 117–19, 150, 152
ecological feminism/s 4–6, 9–13, 17, 20, 83–5, 98, 100–1, 103, 141, 153, 155, 160–2, 166 n. 57, 175, 181, 183
ecological feminist hermeneutics 3–5, 11, 18–22, 67, 84, 102, 106–7, 122, 177, 182, 186, 189, 199–201
ecological feminist theology 10, 100–1, 103, 143–4, 149
ecological hermeneutics 5–9, 20, 45, 52–4, 63–4, 108, 122, 125
   of identification 9, 28–30, 51, 69, 197
   of retrieval 9, 20, 27–32, 45, 51, 62, 68–9
   of suspicion 9, 28–9, 51, 68
ecological materialism 5, 9, 21, 86–8, 90, 95, 100, 102, 119, 121, 124–5, 135–6, 138, 164 n. 49, 181, 186, 202

ecotheology 8, 27 n. 13, 116–18, 124
empire 9, 78–9, 122, 125, 173
   Babylonia 169–70
   European imperialism 91, 97 n. 78
   Persian 170
   Roman 33–4, 40–3, 76, 116, 126–9, 131, 137, 148, 150, 200–1
entanglement 13, 30, 40, 69, 105–6, 117, 143–4, 150–3, 161–2
eschatology 106, 114–15, 118, 129 n. 32, 145
Eucharist 42, 137, 196
exile, Babylonian 170–1, 173–4, 188
extinction 3, 13, 30, 39, 96, 151, 196
extractivism 5, 156, 158, 160, 176, 179, 186, 190, 196, 198–9

face, the 141, 193–6, 198–9, 202
feminist
   theology 17, 84–6, 100–2, 116, 141
   theory 6, 11 n. 28
   white 17–18, 84
First Nations 2–3, 7, 9, 16, 18, 84–5, 164, 198
   epistemologies/knowledges 15, 17, 29, 46–7, 90–1, 106, 119, 151–2, 161, 176, 179, 182–3, 186–7
   resistance 2, 158, 197
   theologians 46, 91, 116
   women 83, 90
flourishing, more-than-human 4, 43, 88, 100–1, 104–6, 112, 151, 171, 182
forgiveness 100, 111, 117, 128, 131, 137, 148, 173, 194, 197
fossil fuels 14–15, 21, 39–40, 108, 137
freedom 21, 40, 68, 70, 76, 79, 86–7, 93–8, 100–1, 103, 117, 193–4, 197
   necessity/freedom dualism 89, 95, 98
future
   deep future 38, 69, 79, 86, 104, 117–18, 183
   future generations 38, 84, 95
   imagined/hoped-for 21, 79, 95–7, 100–1, 114–15, 128, 163, 186

Gaudium et Spes 103 n. 2, 104
gender, *see* multidimensional and intersectionality
gift 12, 33, 40, 42, 64, 66, 98, 132, 171
globalization 16, 20, 96, 146, 182

Great Barrier Reef 4–5, 19–21, 153, 177, 179–84, 186–7, 190–4, 197–9
grief 4, 57–8, 112, 116–17, 128, 181–4, 189, 201

habitat 5 n. 11, 11, 30, 38, 99–101, 125–6, 157–8, 161–2, 185
Holoreflexive Epoch 105
homogenization 89, 155, 160–3, 165 n. 52, 174–5
hospitality, divine 128–9, 135, 137–8, 142, 148, 197
human, the (constructions of) 15–16, 91, 100, 146, 150, 153
hyper-separation 15, 47, 95, 101, 199

Indigenous, *see* First Nations
intersectionality 18, 68, 85
intertextuality 9, 19, 79
    material intertextuality 14, 64, 70–2
invasion, colonial 2–3, 9–10, 15, 17, 46, 61, 90, 106–7, 155

Jerusalem, destruction of 112, 116, 127–9, 131 n. 37
Jesus, death of (in Luke) 22, 112, 128, 192–3, 195–7
judgement (in Luke) 109–10, 113–14, 128–30, 137

kairos (καιρός) 21, 103–4, 109–16
kyriarchy 5, 11, 21, 41 n. 74, 89 n. 32, 129, 144, 152, 175

labour 66, 87, 95, 159
    indentured 18, 90
    more-than-human 17, 31, 42, 56–7, 86, 100–1, 136, 150
    reproductive 13, 90, 98
land, *see* Country
    in the Bible 32–4, 42–3, 111, 131, 137, 171–2
Laudato Si' 43, 117–18, 152
listening, creative/ecological 44, 55, 122, 134 n. 54, 176, 197–8
love
    love of enemies 131–3
    neighbour love 21, 79, 119, 121–4, 130, 134–8

Magnificat
    as song of protest 20, 27–8, 32–4, 40–3
Marxism 87, 124
material agency 3, 14, 54, 56, 90–5, 97–101, 106, 119, 125, 136–7, 160, 176
material artefact, text as 9, 15, 56–7, 59–61, 125, 202
material given 6, 10, 12–14, 16–17, 21, 33, 42, 65–7, 69–71, 74, 95, 98–9, 112, 141, 147, 149
materialism
    historical/practical 87, 94–5, 100
    see also ecological materialism; new materialism
material sacred 45–9, 61, 138, 175–6, 201
material transcendence 48, 99, 185
material turn, *see* new materialism
maternal, the 13–14, 16–17, 22, 33, 38, 64, 70, 74, 99, 141, 143, 147
matter 14–17, 38–9, 48–9, 52–3, 72–3, 86, 94–5, 98–9, 137, 141
metabolic rift 158–9
mining 46, 107, 155, 158–60, 173, 176, 180, 190; *see also* Mountaintop Removal Mining
moral force (of more than humans) 19–20, 182–4
Mountaintop Removal Mining 21, 108, 155–60, 162–9, 174–6
multidimensional approach/ multidimensionality 5 n. 11, 11, 18, 20, 84–5, 125

nature
    alienation of 87, 159
    as construct 30, 86, 89, 115, 161, 185
new materialism 5–6, 9–10, 14, 20–1, 83–6, 90–1, 104–5, 118, 175

orality 68
    studies 35–6

panpsychism 91, 119
paraclesis (as reading practice) 200–1
patriarchy 5, 11–12, 17–18, 37–8, 64–5, 68, 78, 93–4, 189
peace (in Luke) 110–11, 114, 129–30
peaceable kingdom 162–3
pneuma (πνεῦμα) 26–7, 39, 71–4, 76, 200

poetics
  ecological poetics 55–6, 67, 182
  poetic craft and technique 55, 59, 61–2
  projective verse 67
poetry
  'Appalachian Elegy' (bell hooks) 176
  'Binsley Poplars' (Gerard Manley Hopkins) 57
  'Book Sculptor' (Jennifer Harrison) 59–61
  'Coral not Coal' (Kristin Hannaford) 191
  Final Theory (Bonny Cassidy) 182–3
  'Lines Written a Few Miles Above Tintern Abbey' (William Wordsworth) 49
  'To Live in the Mercy of God' (Denise Levertov) 58–9
  'Mud' (Kevin Hart) 50
  'O Taste and See' (Denise Levertov) 57–8
  'Parchment' (Michelle Boisseau) 56–7
  'Recommendations for a Western Australian Coastal Pastoral' (Caitlin Maling) 191
  'A Sonnet at the Edge of the Reef' (Craig Santos Perez) 192
  'A Sort of a Song' (William Carlos Williams) 61–2
political theology 121–4, 126
poverty 5, 34, 40–1, 43, 127, 145–6
pregnant body 12–14, 33, 98, 147
psyche (ψυχή) 38–40, 73
purpose, divine (in Luke) 41 n. 75, 110, 112–13, 128, 197

race 11, 18, 20, 69, 84–5, 135 n. 57, 149
  racialization 16–17, 141, 150, 153
  racism 2–3, 13, 16, 18, 70–1, 78
reading, performative 21, 70–1, 74–8
reciprocity (in Luke) 132–3
relatedness 18–19, 21, 141–4, 147–9, 151–2, 183, 188–9
road kill 5, 141–7, 149

semiotic, the 13–14, 16, 22, 70, 99
senses 4–5, 14, 19–20, 27, 32, 34, 38, 48, 76–7, 99, 125, 184
signs of the time 103–4, 116
situational/situated materialities 15–19, 22, 67, 83, 88, 94, 112, 114, 125–6, 158, 161–2, 169, 182, 186, 201

slavery 2–3, 90, 123 *see also*, labour, indentured
  in Roman empire 41, 76, 111, 122, 131, 150
social justice 3, 7, 11, 42, 95, 98, 116, 124, 171
sovereignty 21, 121
  Earth 21, 138
  First Nations, Indigenous 9, 11, 107, 179 n. 3, 187
  Lukan 126–9, 137–8
  skewed 123
species
  cross-species 100, 142–3, 151–3
  humans as 94, 96–7, 101, 105 n. 9, 115, 117, 152
spirituality/ies
  Earth-based 11, 47, 53, 89–90, 164, 185
  First Nations' perspectives 46, 83–4, 90
Symbiocene 105
sympoiesis 151–2

theocentric ethic 168–9, 175–6
Transfiguration 21, 181, 189–90, 193, 195–8
trauma, intersecting ecological and social 1, 11, 13, 30, 138, 149, 157–8

UNESCO World Heritage List 180–1
Urban Neighbourhoods of Hope 144
Uses of the Bible in Environmental Ethics Project 6, 8–9, 108

visitation, divine (in Luke) 110–14, 116–17, 128–30, 134–5, 137–8
voice
  of Earth 4, 8, 14, 27–8, 31–2, 34–5, 38, 43–5, 50–6, 68–9, 71, 172
  of Lukan Mary 28, 34, 38, 42–3
  materiality of 54–5, 59, 67, 99
  visible 4–5, 134, 186 n. 44, 192–3, 197
  of women 33, 68
vulnerability, shared 21, 141–2, 147, 149, 153, 155, 158

Wangan and Jagalingou People and Country 107, 158, 193–4
whiteness 11, 17–18, 22, 83–4, 90, 146, 151
wonder 176–7, 181–4, 196

www.ingramcontent.com/pod-product-compliance
Lightning Source LLC
Chambersburg PA
CBHW062135300426
44115CB00012BA/1925